ADVANCED PRAISE FOR
THE DECLINE OF AMERICA

This extremely perceptive scholarly work is relevant, historical, and easy to read. In this provocative volume, Schein provides a seamless pathway across the history and achievement of presidents—explaining their strengths and weaknesses; how their actions shaped our country. The respected references and balanced set of qualitative and quantitative opinions make this book a must-read experience.

—Mirta M. Martin, Ph.D. Senior Scholar, American Association
of State Colleges and Universities;
President, Fairmont State University, Fairmont, WV

This is a book for all ages. It covers a breathtaking swath of American history in a way that should interest young adults and mature readers. In today's hyper-partisan environment, it was wonderful to read an objective, fact-based narrative of American presidential history. It is destined to become a veritable "go to" source to learn about U.S. Presidents.

—Vikas Mittal, Ph.D., J. Hugh Liedtke Professor of Marketing,
Jones Graduate School of Business, Rice University,
Houston, TX

David Schein has articulated the concerns that many Americans have been thinking for many years, especially since the 2016 Presidential election. That is the United States has been in a sharp and grave decline from its world leadership role for the better part of 50 to 100 years. This book offers an in-depth evaluation of every American president for the last 100 years and gives them each a grade, most of which are barely passing. In doing so, he uncovers underlying themes that have contributed to the decline we are now experiencing. He also provides a prescription for returning the country to its rightful world leadership role, which includes asking Americans to better educate themselves on the issues, not as the pundits, political consultants, and candidates spin them, but based on their own objective and non-partisan research and experience. Reading Dr. Schein's book is a huge first step in that process.

—James D. Phillips Ph.D. J.D. Associate Dean, School of
Management, Marist College, New York

While *The Decline of America* offers a historical perspective of the presidency and the men who have occupied it for the last century, it also serves as a precursor to what we might expect from Oval Office inhabitants in years and generations to come. His look backward can shed light on what we, our children, and our grandchildren might have in store.

—Ed Barks, President, Barks Communications

I thoroughly enjoyed reading *The Decline of America: 100 Years of Leadership Failures*. Based on performance and not popularity polls, Dr. Schein has assigned a grade for each president which represents an overall evaluation on their ethics and leadership. The recommendations for correcting the problems in the U.S. are clear and insightful. This remarkable book will help the reader with a new view of the last 100 years of U.S. presidents.

—Wei Song, Ph.D. Professor of Marketing, School of Business,
Black Hills State University, Spearfish, SD

The book gives a vivid picture of US presidents during the last 100 years and examines two important aspects of the presidents—their leadership decisions and their ethical orientation. The author is contributing to the field of research of the social, political and economic systems around the world. Socially, the author has brought up the responsibility of presidency from the perspective of ethics and leadership. Politically, the author has brought out the failure of presidents from the angle of the US political system. Economically, the author has showed the municipal bankruptcies as a warning signal. I recommend that my students in China read this book to broaden their vision of US society.

—Crystal Feng, Ph.D. Associate Professor, International College of Business and Technology, Tianjin University of Technology, Tianjin, China

A POST HILL PRESS BOOK

ISBN: 978-1-68261-503-4
ISBN (eBook): 978-1-68261-504-1

The Decline of America
100 Years of Leadership Failures

© 2018 by David D. Schein
All Rights Reserved

Cover Design by Tricia Principe, principedesign.com

Post Hill Press
New York • Nashville
posthillpress.com

Published in the United States of America

THE DECLINE OF
AMERICA

100 YEARS OF
LEADERSHIP FAILURES

DAVID D. SCHEIN

Post Hill
PRESS

For Isla, Alara, Gideon, and Leo,
may they grow up in a better world

TABLE OF CONTENTS

PREFACE

From as long as I can recall, I have been interested in the American presidents. My life experiences and education have helped form my unique viewpoint. I grew up in a military family, which caused me to be more aware of domestic and national affairs. I remember the concern in America during the failed Bay of Pigs Invasion and the Cuban Missile Crisis. On a chilly day in November, the Kennedy assassination changed how America looked at itself. While in high school, the news was dominated by the war in Vietnam. My classmates who did not attend college were drafted. Most of them went to Vietnam and some died there.

I was fortunate to earn a scholarship to the University of Pennsylvania. Penn was home to many Vietnam War protests. Coming from a military family, I felt isolated from the university community. I moved out of the dorms and into the West Philadelphia community. While continuing to attend classes, I hosted a weekly radio program on public radio and started a small business. My education on the streets taught me a great deal more about business, life, and society than I learned in the classroom. My neighborhood was one of the first to have a "neighborhood watch" program and I participated in that. I met some of the local Democrat party leaders in the neighborhood and learned how grassroots politics worked.

Next, I pursued my MBA at the Darden Graduate School of Business at the University of Virginia. Spiro Agnew and then Richard Nixon resigned from office. America's leadership, already questionable, would never be the same. I attended law school at the University of Houston. Like many in Houston, I worked for oil companies during and after law school. I remember Jimmy Carter passing through a parade route in downtown Houston while running for the presidency. During my corporate employment, I lived in three states and worked throughout the United States. The uncertainty of the Carter presidency dominated by the Iran Hostage Crisis transitioned into the Reagan administration.

As I left corporate life and began private law practice in 1987, I became involved in local and national politics. This led to my candidacy in two elections. By the end of the second unsuccessful campaign, I had learned a great deal about the political process from the ground up. My interest in being a candidate waned. I then had an opportunity to move to the Washington, D.C., area. During my several years there, I attended many political functions, closely observing the political process, including lobbying efforts and many industry groups. This was during the Clinton era in Washington, a troubled time for the U.S. presidency.

While in the D.C. area, I saw the flames rise from the Pentagon on the morning of 9/11. That day was a defining moment for Americans of my generation just as Pearl Harbor was for my parents' generation. It was a vivid reminder of how important the leadership of the United States is to the future of our country and to the world. I watched George W. Bush's popularity soar, only to crash a few years later. I taught at several universities in the D.C. area. I then made a major life decision and went to work on a PhD at UVA. I began teaching in collegiate business schools with a focus on business ethics and business law.

The idea for this book came together about a decade ago; it was seriously researched over the last three years. During that time, the economy collapsed and Obama was elected. The development of the ideas for this book, however, dates to my childhood under Eisenhower and Kennedy.

The author takes sole responsibility for the contents of this book, including the potentially controversial nature of the assigned grades and conclusions reached. The acknowledgment section at the end gives credit to the people who provided assistance with research and editing. Many others provided less critical assistance and their help is appreciated, but not cited here.

This book is aimed at readers interested in the presidents of the United States, from baby boomers to younger readers who have little knowledge of any presidents who served before the 21st century. For readers who lean toward Democrat or Republican politics, this book will provide a platform full of detailed research to stimulate debate and discussion. Collegiate business ethics and leadership classes may find this a useful book to reach beyond traditional textbooks. Anyone who is concerned that America is on the brink of failure will be able to trace the path of its leadership over the last century and consider the recommended solutions at the end of this book. Finally, this book may provide answers as to how the path of presidential leadership led to the surprising results of the 2016 election.

David D. Schein, Houston, Texas

INTRODUCTION

Numerous autobiographies by the presidents as well as biographies provide insights into presidential lives and accomplishments. Wading through even a fraction of these books is daunting. My focus is on what the reader would need to know in order to evaluate the ethics and leadership decisions of recent presidents. Consequently, part of the objective of this book is to distill some of these other volumes into a manageable number of words.

Generally speaking, biographers of the presidents were in most cases fans, or more correctly, sycophants of these leaders. While biographies have been consulted on specific points, they are not considered dispositive since they are often written with a distinctly favorable bias. Such biographies are usually written specifically about the time period of the presidency while this book focuses on the outcomes of their terms in office. Outcomes are not always evident during a presidential term.

The core of this book is on two specific characteristics. The first is whether each president is someone Americans and the rest of the world would actually admire and want to both respect and follow. For that purpose, I use the term "ethical" and view each president from the view of the individual, private ethics, and then as a public person, or public ethics.

The leadership of the most powerful country on earth must be defined differently than if someone were discussing the CEO of a major corporation or even a governor of a U.S. state. A concise evaluation can be based on what happened while that person was the leader of the U.S. and the impact of the president's decisions on subsequent generations of Americans.

The focus of this book on presidential leadership is about the short-term and long-term results of their time in office. Expressed another way, if America were a corporation, and each voter were a member of the board of directors, would the board vote to keep this person as president based on the decisions he or she made? Leadership decisions have led to the decline of America. Drawing from those decisions, this book warns of the inevitable consequences if this decline continues. The American presidents are not solely to blame. They must share the blame with the voters who elected them and the sorry state of governance in the United States, from the Capitol in Washington, D.C., to almost every city hall and county seat. The recent municipal bankruptcies have as yet not served as a wake-up call for America. Nor has nearly a 20 trillion-dollar national debt set off alarms with either the politicians or the electorate.

A special effort has been made to create a book that is as nonpartisan as possible. There is plenty of blame to share with both major political parties around the United States. In addition to my own diverse background, the contents have been assembled using a variety of sources. In some cases, there is more objective material today than there was in the past. Documents that were classified as confidential have been declassified. Deathbed memoirs shed new light on past presidents. I tried to use the most authoritative studies and statistical data. I utilized well-established publications and outlets over sources that are generally regarded as being "far left" or "far right."

In the vein of a college teacher, I have assigned each American president a letter grade. No president from either party earns even an "A-." The one hundred years represents eight Democrat and nine Republican presidents. Every president, alive or deceased, has his advocates. As this edition goes to press, five former presidents are alive. Teachers do not change grades because students or parents of students are unhappy with the grades. Likewise, advocates for any of the presidents, or even the politicians themselves, will not succeed in changing the grades assigned here. So, read on and see if the grade you would assign differs from mine.

PART I

WORLD LEADERSHIP

CHAPTER 1
WORLD LEADERSHIP IN PERSPECTIVE

The title of this book may be viewed as an homage to English historian Edward Gibbon's masterwork, *The Decline and Fall of the Roman Empire*. While Gibbon traced a period of fifteen hundred years, this book only covers about one hundred years. But, what a century it has been! Two official world wars have been fought. Multiple other wars have taken place that have not earned the moniker of world wars, but were still important. Man has traveled to the moon. As this edition is going to press, NASA is planning a manned flight to Mercury.

Beginning in 1912 with the election of the 28th president of the United States, Woodrow Wilson, this book traces the leadership of this country through the end of the term of the 44th president, Barack Obama. The period is slightly longer than one hundred years, but the reader may consider that as a bit of artistic license. During this period, "America," as most know the United States, has unquestionably been the most powerful country on earth.

While Gibbon examined a myriad of factors and attempted to explain the many opportunities that were lost and the ultimate end of the Roman Empire, this book has a more modest, but still ambitious task. A failure of ethical leadership over the last one hundred years helped lead America to a point where its decline in world dominance has already begun. Just as the fall of the Roman Empire led to approximately one thousand years of trouble and chaos following *Pax Romana*, America's decline may lead to a similar "fall," with equally catastrophic results for the civilizations of the world.

The progressive threats from terrorist attacks in the U.S. with the first World Trade Center bombing in 1993, the second attack on September 11, 2001, through the current wave of violent terrorist attacks throughout the world do not yet seem to have awakened a resolve to govern better. Many observers predict another attack like 9/11 is likely. It is unclear whether another such attack will finally spur more consistent as well as decisive action.

MYTH BUSTING

It's particularly important in examining the leadership of America to consider the persistent myths, many of which are untrue, about presidential leadership. Just one example of serial responsibility is the American involvement in Vietnam. That involvement spans five presidents. Eisenhower first sent in advisors. Kennedy increased involvement slightly. Johnson turned it into a full-scale war. Nixon planned to exit the U.S. from the war, but actually increased U.S. military involvement before essentially surrendering. Ford was in office when Saigon and South Vietnam fell to North Vietnamese insurgents. As this is a nonpartisan analysis, it is fair to share the blame since both Democrat and Republican presidents were engaged in this tragic exercise in futility.

Looking at America's involvement in Vietnam in more depth, it becomes apparent that the U.S. must have stronger objectives than simply "fighting the spread of Communism." The reason to spend one dollar or to risk the loss of one American life must be clear. A persistent problem is that American forces have been sent into countries without having a clear objective. Simple analysis would dictate that having a local government that deserves American support would be an early indicator of a worthy partner. Even if the residents are deserving of that support, without solid local leadership, it is unlikely that U.S. efforts will actually be successful.

There are many examples of the U.S. failure to develop and cultivate good leadership in the countries the U.S. has attempted to help. Just two examples are Cuba in the 1950s and Vietnam in the 1950s and '60s. Just as America has suffered with presidents who lack a moral compass, the U.S. has backed leaders in other countries who lack fundamental ethical qualities. Under the blanket justification of opposing the U.S.S.R. during the Cold War and various forces around the world today, the U.S. has damaged its reputation. Fixing the U.S. brand will require much more thoughtful analysis before entering future conflicts.

Engagement in military matters around the world is not simply a matter of standing back and waiting for the crisis. A good world leader understands the overall circumstances and enters at the right time. In some cases, entering before there is a crisis would be the mark of good world leadership. The U.S. disgraced itself in both world wars by coming late to the fight. Shamefully, Woodrow Wilson delayed America's involvement in WWI since he was concerned that it would hurt his election chances in 1916. While U.S. involvement in 1917 brought about a fairly quick end to that war, there were untold losses by U.S. allies while the U.S. stood by from 1915 to 1917 and then lost more soldiers and had to expend greater assets to overcome a more entrenched enemy.

In WWII, Franklin Roosevelt should have taken action at a much earlier time to head off the aggression by both Japan and Germany. Instead, he waited while Japan invaded China, at that time a U.S. ally.

Japan positioned itself to control all of the South Pacific while the U.S. did nothing. The culmination, of course, was the attack on Pearl Harbor. The U.S. fleet was unwittingly moved to Hawaii just in time to be attacked by the insurgent Japanese. In Europe, Roosevelt had as much to do with the appeasement of Germany as did the British prime minister at the time, Neville Chamberlain. However, while Chamberlain's name is synonymous with the failure of appeasement with Germany, Roosevelt has continued to receive undeserved praise as president.

AMERICA'S STANDING IN THE WORLD

A special challenge of the American presidency is that one person is the leader of both a huge economy with millions of persons impacted by those decisions at home and protecting the U.S. brand around the world. The American dollar has become the standard around the world, including the benchmark for oil as well as other traded goods. At the same time, the U.S. economy has battled bouts of inflation, slow economic growth, unemployment, and a national debt that is spiraling out of control as it approaches an official figure of 20 trillion dollars.

At home, the obligation of a U.S. president is to lead the economy in such a way as to meet the sometimes-competing objectives of encouraging the economy to grow so that businesses can expand and employment will be strong while at the same time controlling inflation and making sure all the bills get paid. The president is expected to lead social welfare programs like medical care for the impoverished and disabled and various publicly funded education and other assistance programs. Providing for the domestic economy is often in conflict with providing military assistance abroad and economic assistance to countries around the globe.

In the period covered by this book, tax policies have focused on the personal income tax. The income tax came in permanently with the Wilson administration; the enabling constitutional amendment was passed prior to his taking office. It has become the infamous "one-trick pony," as both political parties over the last one hundred years have raised taxes, changed deductions, and lowered taxes, all in an effort to achieve a variety of goals that appear to be moving even further away from achieving consistent economic growth without deficit financing.

While the presidential candidates of both Democrat and Republican parties have made a variety of promises about income taxes over the years, the fact is that little progress has been made. The U.S. has witnessed near annual tax "reforms," some designed to bring in more revenue and some designed to stimulate commerce. Whatever the reason, the economy has either been in recession or nearly flat for a decade. Clearly, recent U.S. tax policy did not improve the U.S. economy. Over the last forty years, several unsuccessful presidential candidates of both major parties and some third-party candidates have suggested real reforms like a "flat tax" or a value-added tax (VAT) instead of the current complex income tax rules. However, both political parties in control of Washington, D.C., gain part of their political patronage by manipulating the current system. Change may only come with significant changes in the electoral system, as discussed in Chapter 21.

Parallel to the personal income tax is the corporate income tax. A number of U.S. corporations have moved their headquarters out of the U.S. to avoid the U.S. corporate tax that, when combined with state corporate tax rates, makes the tax among the very highest in the world. Some of the biggest that have moved their headquarters out of the U.S. include consulting firm Accenture, insurance giant Aon, and numerous firms in the oil and gas industry, including Halliburton, Noble Drilling, and Nabors Industries. A second phenomenon is billions of dollars held overseas to avoid repatriating the profits and being required to pay the corporate taxes here at home. The U.S. cannot maintain its world leadership as an economic power while these forces are at work.

Presidents discussed in this book have indeed made efforts to improve life in America. Franklin Roosevelt's "New Deal" produced little than more dependence on government; Lyndon Johnson's "Great Society's" war on poverty has clearly been lost; and the "Reaganomics" of Ronald Reagan produced what was up to that time a record increase in the national debt in just one administration. Many of the natural advantages that the U.S. has enjoyed in the past have faded. The surpluses of the past are gone. In their place, the U.S. has a huge national debt, and many states and municipalities have substantial and growing unfunded pension liabilities. Reports of a pending financial crisis both in Social Security and Medicare are consistent and, if anything, appear to be understated. America cannot be a world leader without fixing the structural problems that caused the current crisis.

AROUND THE WORLD

Immediately following WWII, it seemed that the U.S. was enjoying the pinnacle of success. Smart actions in Europe and Japan demonstrated that the U.S. and its allies had learned from the punishing reparations imposed on Germany after WWI. Those reparations were used as an excuse by Hitler to rally the German people to his side. The U.S. then embarked on a path which was attributed to the "Cold War." The U.S. sent money to various governments and factions around the globe without fully vetting them in order to supposedly fight communist aggression. The results are a series of failures as the world appears far more dangerous today than it did at any time since WWII.

The U.S. has entangled itself in military actions around the globe that, if anything, have hurt the U.S. brand. The Iran-Contra Affair (see Chapter 14) illustrated just how complex and unrewarding playing the new game of international diplomacy can be. Losses in Korea, Lebanon, Vietnam, and the Middle East, discussed in the chapters to follow, have badly damaged the U.S. brand. The U.S. has now established itself as a random actor that may or may not support its allies and may or may not fight to win when engaged in a conflict. There have been exceptions. The U.S. military won a successful engagement in Kuwait after its invasion by Iraq under the leadership of George H.W. Bush. Operation Desert Storm in 1990-1991 successfully pushed Iraq back to its capital. However, reviewing the long-term results in Iraq indicates that America again made a mistake and should have required the removal of Saddam Hussein as part of the peace process. This mistake parallels the "draw" obtained in Korea forty years earlier.

It is clear that America fails to protect its citizens and its allies when it fails to use its military might in an effective and decisive manner around the world. Shortly after he became president, Barack Obama gave speeches in numerous countries appearing to apologize for America. What was labeled by some as his "Apology Tour" is precisely the wrong message in a dangerous world. The surge in terrorism attacks around the world is a sad reflection of what happens when the U.S. fails to stand strong.

Many of the flaws in the international picture for the U.S. have resulted from the fear of being viewed as imperialists. Colonizing key locations for the overall safety and long-term interests of the U.S. simply makes sense. The most immediate example is Cuba, which could be a successful territory or state, but instead is a country that represented a threat to the U.S. while the Cold War wore on and is now another failed communist economy.

THE CHAPTERS THAT FOLLOW

Any work of this nature will produce a spate of criticism regarding opinion versus facts. No author, including a great historian like Gibbon, can claim to be free of bias. This author does not make that claim. This book has been constructed with a focus on facts. The author has the advantage of "20-20 hindsight" with regard to many of the facts that form the core of this book. Great leaders have a vision for the place of their country in the world and history. Some, like Wilson, exhibited a sense of vision, but failed miserably in the execution. More recent American presidents have exhibited a stunning lack of vision and the resulting decline of America's influence and leadership is evident. Most recent presidents have struggled to create a legacy in either domestic or foreign affairs. America should return to the positive visionary leaders of the past, like Washington, Jefferson, and Lincoln, or it is doomed to fall like the Roman Empire.

PART II

ONE HUNDRED YEARS OF AMERICAN PRESIDENTS

PART II

ONE HUNDRED YEARS OF AMERICAN PRESIDENTS

CHAPTER 2
WOODROW WILSON

(Harris & Ewing, 1913)

Born Thomas Woodrow Wilson (1856–1924), he served as the twenty-eighth president of the United States, from 1913 to 1921. Thomas R. Marshall served as vice president for Wilson's entire time in office. Wilson swept to victory as a Democrat in the 1912 election with only 42 percent of the popular vote. Theodore Roosevelt's Bull Moose party won 27 percent, Taft for the Republican Party got 22 percent, and Debs, the Socialist, 6 percent. The split vote resulted in Wilson's 82 percent massive electoral college win. His electoral win declined to 52 percent of the vote in his reelection in 1916 (Office of the Federal Register, n.d.).

Wilson had one of the more unusual marital situations with his marriage to Ellen Louise Axson in 1885 and continuing through her death

13

in 1914, while Wilson was in his first term as president. He married Edith Bolling Galt in 1915, and remained married to her until his death in 1924. It is reported that Wilson had a long-standing relationship with Mrs. Mary Hubert Peck beginning around 1907 and continuing during his time in office (Ross, 1988). Wilson's quick remarriage to a woman other than his reported mistress adds to the mystery surrounding his private life and moral compass.

OCCUPATIONAL ACCOMPLISHMENTS

His ties to academia were strong, with a Princeton degree, then law study at the University of Virginia. He later earned a PhD at Johns Hopkins. He is the only American president to earn a PhD although a good handful earned law degrees. The record indicates that Wilson did not graduate from law school. His early career was the practice of law, so it is likely that he "read for the law," which was the on-the-job approach to law practice. He taught at several universities over a thirty-year period, ending with three years as president of Princeton University. While often reported that he went from Princeton to the White House, he actually was relieved of his position at Princeton in 1910 and then served as the governor of New Jersey until his election as president (Linky, n.d.).

SIGNIFICANT EVENTS DURING WILSON'S TIME IN OFFICE

1913
- The Sixteenth Amendment to the U.S. Constitution, which authorized the income tax
- The Seventeenth Amendment to the U.S. Constitution, which authorized direct election of U.S. Senators

1914

- Federal Trade Commission, "FTC," is formed.
- Clayton Antitrust Act passed
- Archduke Ferdinand is assassinated, leading to the beginning of World War I.
- First U.S. income tax
- Panama Canal opens.
- Wilson supports Pancho Villa in Mexico.

1915

- World War I: The Dardanelles campaign begins, Zeppelin raids of England begin, poison gas used in the trench warfare, passenger liner *Lusitania* sunk by torpedo, British warship *Formidable* sunk by German submarine
- Wilson withdraws his support of Pancho Villa.

1916

- Pancho Villa attacks Americans on a train in Columbus, New Mexico.
- Mexico allows the United States Army under the leadership of General Pershing to search for Pancho Villa.
- World War I: Battle of the Somme begins, Battle of Jutland

1917

- Beginning of the Russian Revolution
- Puerto Rican nationals given U.S. citizenship
- America enters World War I after German submarine attacks on American ships. America sends General Pershing and troops to

Europe. The British forces capture Jerusalem, dealing a blow to the Ottoman forces aligned with Germany.

1918

- The Bolsheviks end Russian involvement in World War I and later execute Czar Nicholas II and his family.
- World War I: First use of aircraft by U.S. in war, "The Red Baron" German fighter ace killed, Germany surrenders

1919

- Treaty of Versailles formally ends World War I.
- Wilson suffers a stroke. His wife reportedly then ran the White House.

1920

- Prohibition comes into effect after the Eighteenth Amendment was ratified in 1919.
- Nineteenth Amendment to the U.S. Constitution provides women's suffrage.
- Radical anarchists bomb Wall Street, killing 38. The Palmer Raid follows with the deportation of six thousand foreign aliens who were suspected radical leftists.
- The League of Nations comes into being in Paris and the U.S. Senate votes against joining.

THE DOMESTIC FRONT AND RACE RELATIONS

Wilson faced a mixed picture with Congress, which was under Democratic control during his early years, but became Republican by his final two years in office. With the loss of a Democratic majority, Wilson had significant difficulty passing his agenda during his latter years in office. It is suggested that this may have hastened the stroke that he suffered in 1919 (Sisung, 2000).

Despite Wilson's fame as a father of the "progressive political movement in America," he was not a progressive on most scales. Most notably, African-Americans consistently lost ground during Wilson's administration (Wolgemuth, K.L.,1958). To curry southern support in Congress, Wilson, like several other presidents covered later, allowed discriminatory practices to continue. In his cabinet, William McAdoo and Albert Burleson instituted segregated working conditions in their departments (Sisung, 2000). Burleson served as Postmaster General and was known for reinstituting segregated conditions in the U.S. Postal Service. McAdoo served as Wilson's Treasury Secretary and was married to Wilson's daughter. He is associated with both segregation and racism and was reported to have been endorsed by the Ku Klux Klan when he later ran for office in California. Attributed to Wilson: "Segregation is not humiliating, but a benefit, and ought to be so regarded by you gentlemen (Barnett, 2015)."

Balancing only somewhat his racial record, among Wilson's three U.S. Supreme Court appointments was the noted jurist Louis D. Brandeis in 1916. Brandeis was the first Jewish person to sit on the Supreme Court and was noted for defending civil liberties (Sisung, 2000). Other than racism, Wilson's administration, despite its somewhat positive image today, suffered from various problems. "Wilsonianism," the idea of attaching moral principles and idealism to foreign policy, came to be seen as a mistake. A

17

1935 Gallup poll revealed that 70 percent of those polled believed that intervention in WWI had been a mistake (Sisung, 2000).

THE WILSON INTERNATIONAL RECORD

As WWI began in the second year of his term, 1914, Wilson cannot be held responsible for the war itself. The United States could have done little to avoid the war in Europe and the Mediterranean. While some Americans criticized the entry into the war at all, it is obvious today that at the latest, the United States should have entered the war after the sinking of the *Lusitania* in 1915. This unarmed passenger liner had nearly two thousand passengers and more than half died in the attack, including 127 Americans. While it is reported that public opinion was against involvement in the war, support for Britain was strong and with continued loss of life and American shipping assets, the public did support entry into WWI. The politically motivated Wilson used the reelection campaign slogan, "He Kept Us Out of War," in 1916 (National Trust for Historic Preservation, n.d.). Wilson negotiated with the German aggressors by agreeing to keep America out of WWI if Germany would not attack American ships. The German version of the same deal was that they would allow the passengers of unarmed ships to abandon the ships before they sunk them ("Germans unleash U-Boats," n.d..).

In early 1917, Germany announced that it would no longer honor its deal with Wilson. However, it took more American ships sinking and discovery of the Zimmermann telegram before America would enter the war. The telegram was a bold offer from Germany to give Mexico part of the land it had lost to the United States in the Mexican-American War, in exchange for its support for Germany. On April 2, 1917, Wilson asked Congress to approve a declaration of war, which was granted by overwhelming majorities in both houses of Congress ("PBS American Experience," n.d.)

Millions of lives were lost throughout the world and the cost of the war was much greater with America's late entry. The involvement of the United State almost immediately turned the course of the war. In the Battle of Somme, the two sides had been only about two American "football fields" apart for two years. With American involvement, the allied forces began an uninterrupted march into Germany. This progress came despite Russia's withdrawal from the war following the Russian Revolution.

LEAGUE OF NATIONS

Following the war, Wilson failed to create any type of stability in Europe. The League of Nations, or at least the idea of such an organization, was one of Wilson's "14 Points." He tried on the world stage to craft a path toward a lasting peace. "The War to End All Wars" introduced people of the world to mass destruction and loss of life not previously seen. The use of heavy armaments, air power and submarines in addition to large warships meant that few in the world would be safe in the future from such losses. Any systems in place previously for negotiating disputes failed miserably (Ober, 2014).

Wilson succeeded in presenting his proposals in France in 1918. But he failed to gain the support of the United States Senate, and America never joined the League of Nations (Ober, 2014). Without the most powerful country in the world, such an organization was doomed to failure. Clearly, it did not prevent WWII. From the current perspective, it is unclear if the then Republican-controlled Senate voted against it to vote against Wilson, or flaws in its design.

MEXICO AND PANCHO VILLA

Wilson failed to deal with the terrorist attacks from Pancho Villa in the southwestern U.S. Wilson initially supported him, but then a year later withdrew his support. Mexico gave the U.S. permission for U.S. Army General Pershing to pursue Villa in Mexican territory. This supposedly bred resentment in Mexico that still exists today.

BY THE NUMBERS

The economy under Wilson closely tracked the impact of WWI. The average inflation rate for his administration went from nominal to as high as 18 percent per year by 1918 (Coin News Media Group, LLC, 2017):

Year	Inflation Rate
1913	Not Calculated
1914	1.0%
1915	1.0%
1916	7.9%
1917	17.4%
1918	18.0%
1919	14.6%
1920	15.6%

Typical of the cyclical economy, following the inflationary cycle as the economy adjusted to the post-war economy, the economy crashed in 1921 with significant deflation. This recession was caused by the Wilson administration's failure to plan for the post-war economy or to take action to absorb the sudden drop in production demand from America's European allies.

The national debt skyrocketed in a predictable fashion as wartime expenditures increased (U.S. Department of the Treasury, Bureau of the Fiscal Service, 2013):

Year	National Debt
1913	$2,916,204,913
1914	$2,912,499,269
1915	$3,058,136,873
1916	$3,609,244,262
1917	$5,717,770,279
1918	$14,592,161,414
1919	$27,390,970,113
1920	$25,952,456,406
1921	$23,977,450,552

MAKING THE GRADE

Wilson's legacy remains fairly strong. Arthur Schlesinger, a "presidential historian," cites a 1996 poll rating American presidents from Great, 4.0; Near Great, 3.0; Average, 2.0; Below Average, 1.0; and Failure. Using this myth and popularity system, Wilson garners an amazingly high 3.21 (Schlesinger, 2004).

In the cold light of history, Wilson's myth cannot stand. Social progress appears to have been made with the Clayton Antitrust Act, direct election of senators, and the right for women to vote (which he opposed). It now appears unquestioned that Wilson was either a racist at heart, or openly tolerated racism by those who surrounded him. His extramarital relationship does not suggest a person of high moral character. On the domestic front, other than the few accomplishments mentioned above, the country was burdened with debt at the end of the war and Wilson's administration did not successfully convert the economy back to peacetime. In hindsight, the implementation of the income tax must be hung on the Wilson administration and it is unquestionably a failed system of special interests and ineffective enforcement.

On the world stage, the U.S.'s decisive victory in WWI would seem to have given Wilson the lead role in the post-WWI world. However, his impact was quite limited. Wilson's rhetoric was nice, but he failed to get results. The League of Nations, or at least the idea of such an organization, was one of Wilson's "14 Points." He acted on the world stage to try to craft a path toward a lasting peace. The deliberate delay in entering WWI for purely political reasons speaks volumes in itself. Wilson sustained a stroke very near the end of his second term. The stroke itself may create sympathy for Wilson, but does not excuse his personal and performance failures. It remains a mystery as to why Wilson supported the Marxist Bolsheviks in Russia. The Bolsheviks did not support American capitalist or democratic principles. Wilson's position on Russia was at odds with his concept of "Wilsonianism."

Wilson Grade: D

CHAPTER 3
WARREN G. HARDING

(Harris & Ewing, circa 1920)

Warren Gamaliel Harding (1865–1923), a Republican, served as the twenty-ninth president of the United States, from 1921 until he died in office in 1923. His vice president was Calvin Coolidge, who succeeded to the presidency upon Harding's death. Harding served only 882 days in office (Trani & Wilson, 1977).

Parallel to Woodrow Wilson, Harding had an active social life. He married divorcée Florence Kling De Wolfe in 1891 (Black, n.d.). He was involved in an affair from 1905 through 1921 with Carrie Fulton Phillips (Library of Congress, 2014). Other affairs were alleged to have occurred. His death while on a tour of the West Coast on August 2, 1923, was attributed to the multiple stresses, from the "Teapot Dome Scandal" (discussed in the following pages), his affairs, and the long trip. No autopsy was performed because Mrs. Harding refused to allow it, although it was requested by his doctors. This led to the rumor that she might have poisoned the president (Benjamin Harrison Presidential Site, n.d.).

Carrie Phillips was reportedly paid off by the GOP prior to the 1920 Republican convention to buy her silence (Dean, 2004). In the book, *The President's Daughter*, released after Harding's death, Nan Britton described her six-year affair with Harding, including sex with Harding in a White House closet. She was harshly criticized during her lifetime for writing about her affair. However, very recent DNA testing indicates that he indeed fathered a child with her.

OCCUPATIONAL ACCOMPLISHMENTS

Starting with studies at Ohio Central College and a brief study of law, Harding was an active businessman prior to his political career (Malone, 1932). He worked for a newspaper and shortly thereafter, bought the newspaper in 1884. His political career began in 1898 and he rose to the U.S. Senate in 1915. He won a sweeping victory with his "return to normalcy" campaign, garnering 60 percent of the popular vote in the 1920 election over Democrat James Cox (Freidel & Sidey, n.d.). While Cox's name is not well-known, his VP running mate, Franklin Roosevelt, went on to become president. Some pundits attribute Harding's election to his reported handsomeness, as the 1920 election was the first where women were allowed to vote (Warren, 2008). Without the extensive detailed polling done now it is difficult to know if this was the case.

SIGNIFICANT EVENTS DURING HARDING'S TIME IN OFFICE

1921

- The Emergency Quota Act becomes law on May 19.
- The Tulsa Race Riot on May 31-June 1
- Harding transfers supervision of the Naval oil reserves lands to the Department of the Interior.
- Charles R. Forbes is appointed head of the Veterans' Administration.

1922

- Secretary of the Interior Albert Bacon Fall grants Harry F. Sinclair of Mammoth Oil Company exclusive rights to the Teapot Dome reserves in Wyoming.
- Adolf Hitler rises to Chairman of the Nazi Party in Germany.
- Mussolini comes to power in Italy.

1923

- The Ku Klux Klan begins a show of force throughout the southern states.
- Rosewood, Florida, massacre takes place in January.

THE DOMESTIC FRONT AND RACE RELATIONS

During his time in office, Harding enjoyed a significant Republican majority in both houses of Congress. This helped him pass legislation. He appointed four U.S. Supreme Court justices. A former president, William Howard Taft, was the most notable of his appointments. Harding also appointed numerous federal judges, most of whom were Republican.

Considered an accomplishment of his administration was the enactment of the Budget and Accountancy Act of 1921, which created a Bureau of the Budget in the Treasury Department and created the General Accounting Office (Dean, 2004). At the same time, Harding's administration adopted the Fordney-McCumber Tariff Act in 1922. This law raised tariffs on manufactured and farm goods from other countries. While this supported domestic business, in the long run, "protective" tariffs tend to do more harm than good. Of course, the downside of this law was not fully realized until the Great Depression.

Most students of U.S. history know of the Teapot Dome Scandal and associate that with the Harding administration. While no person is completely responsible for the acts of another, a mark of good leadership is the appointment of quality people to the positions that report to the leader. Under this benchmark, Harding scores very poorly. Harding appointed Albert Bacon Fall as Secretary of the Interior. From this position, Fall was able to collect bribes for selling U.S. petroleum reserves in Teapot Dome, Wyoming, for less than market value. Harding's Secretary of the Navy, Edwin Denby, signed the leases involved, but was not charged with a crime (Miller Center of Public Affairs, University of Virginia, n.d.a). A lesser known scandal was Harding's appointment of Charles R. Forbes as the first head of the Veterans' Bureau, later to become the Veterans Administration. Forbes, in less than two years in the position, reportedly looted up to 2 million dollars from his agency. When the scandal came to light, he became a federal fugitive and fled the country. He was later returned and did remarkably little jail time (Library of Congress, n.d.).

Harding appointed Harry M. Daugherty, a political supporter, as U.S. Attorney General. While there is no direct proof of scandal in his actions, others around him were steeped in scandal. Daugherty resigned in 1924 after Coolidge became president. The circle around and supporting

Harding became known as the "Ohio Gang," after Harding's home state. Colorful figures, in addition to Daugherty, included Jesse W. Smith, who held no official title but had an office in Daugherty's Justice Department. Smith reportedly committed suicide to avoid prosecution for some of his criminal acts (Baker, 2015). Harding participated in weekly poker parties with the Ohio Gang at a house known as the "Little Green House on K Street" (Benjamin Harrison Presidential Site, n.d.). To his credit, Harding also appointed department heads Andrew Mellon, Treasury; Herbert Hoover, Commerce; and Charles Evan Hughes, State Department. Hoover went on to become president. Mellon, a successful banker, served as Treasury Secretary under three presidents. Hughes, already with a record of professional success, went on to serve as Chief Justice of the Supreme Court.

There is no direct evidence that Harding was a racist in the sense of his predecessor, Wilson. He supported an anti-lynching law, although he also opposed interracial marriage (Berman, 2015). During his presidency, the Tulsa Race Riot took place on June 1, 1921. Based on a single incident between a black man and a white woman, white men attacked the predominantly black area of Tulsa, resulting in the destruction of thirty-five city blocks, eight hundred reported injured, and as many as three hundred persons killed (Tulsa Historical Society and Museum, n.d.). Later, in January 1923, the Rosewood, Florida, massacre resulted in the total destruction of the small, African-American-only town. While early loss of life was put at eight, some suggest the number was closer to 150 dead. There was no intervention by state or federal authorities (Jones, 1993).

THE HARDING INTERNATIONAL RECORD

America retreated from the world stage during Harding's brief administration. The official policy of isolation seemed to satisfy the U.S. population following the horrors of WWI. Hitler and Mussolini began their march to power, sowing the seeds for WWII during this time. There is little to credit Harding.

BY THE NUMBERS

The economy under Harding continued to show the impact of World War I. The national debt decreased slightly as wartime expenditures decreased, but the economy was poorly positioned after the war (U.S. Department of the Treasury, Bureau of the Fiscal Service, 2013):

Year	National Debt
1921	$23,977,450,552
1922	$22,963,381,708
1923	$22,349,707,365

Many economists decry deflation as worse than inflation. Persons with debt essentially pay their debts back with dollars that are worth more than the lender and borrower anticipated. The average inflation rate for his administration was largely negative (Coin News Media Group, LLC, 2017):

Year	Inflation Rate
1921	-10.5%
1922	-6.1%
1923	1.8%

MAKING THE GRADE

Harding often ranks at or near the bottom in polls of American presidents. Some historians have recently attempted to "rehabilitate" Harding's reputation based on his short tenure and a handful of modest accomplishments (Dean, 2004; Trani & Wilson, 1977).

Harding served long enough to pass major legislation, appoint numerous Supreme Court and federal judges, and preside over a good handful of scandals. Both his personal morals and his public morals fell well below any reasonable standard for a world leader. While not directly implicated as a racist, his administration did not move minorities forward or intervene after major racial incidents.

The scandals that are attributed to his administration are significant because they not only happened in his period of leadership, but he appointed the perpetrators. If his administration was evaluated on its best known event, that event would be the Teapot Dome Scandal. His personal life was anything but exemplary.

Harding Grade: D-

CHAPTER 4
CALVIN COOLIDGE

(Notman Photo Co., circa 1919).

Calvin Coolidge (1872–1933) served as vice president to Harding and became the thirtieth president of the United States upon Harding's death. The Republican was president from 1923 to 1929. He had no vice president until he stood for reelection in 1924; Charles G. Dawes became his vice president for the remainder of his time in office. Despite the scandals of the Harding administration that surfaced, or were becoming known, as Coolidge ran for president in his own right, he managed to win over Democratic and Progressive candidates (Meyers, 2014).

In contrast to his predecessors Wilson and Harding, Coolidge was married to the same woman, Grace Anna Goodhue Coolidge, from 1905 until his death, and there were no reported affairs.

OCCUPATIONAL ACCOMPLISHMENTS

Coolidge attended Amherst College. He then held a series of elected positions in his home state of Massachusetts, beginning as member of a city council in 1898 through governor of the state in 1918 (Calvin Coolidge Presidential Foundation, Inc., n.d.).

Coolidge, also known as "Silent Cal" (Mallon, 2013), enjoyed the benefit of a Republican Congress during his entire term in office. He inherited the scandals of the Harding administration. But despite being Harding's VP, the public and historians do not hold Coolidge responsible for Harding. He appointed one Supreme Court justice during his presidency (U.S. Senate, n.d.).

SIGNIFICANT EVENTS DURING COOLIDGE'S TIME IN OFFICE

1923

- Adolf Hitler leads the Nazi Party in failed coup d'état attempt in Germany.

1924

- World War Adjusted Compensation Act of May 19
- J. Edgar Hoover is appointed as the head of the Bureau of Investigation.
- The Indian Citizenship Act
- Lenin dies and Stalin competes to replace him.

1925

- Mussolini declares himself dictator of Italy.

1926

- Air Commerce Act
- Public Buildings Act creates modern Washington, D.C.
- Gangster turf wars in Chicago
- Hirohito is crowned Emperor of Japan.

1927

- Lindbergh's solo flight across the Atlantic
- In April, the Great Mississippi Flood affects 700,000 people in the largest national disaster in U.S. history.
- Leon Trotsky is expelled from the Communist Party and Josef Stalin takes control.

1928

- Japan breaks off relations with China.

THE DOMESTIC FRONT AND RACE RELATIONS

During his administration, the government acted to further control business interests in support of growth:

Amid an economic boom, the 69th Congress (1925-1927) reduced a variety of taxes. President Calvin Coolidge vetoed the McNary-Haugen Act which would have established federal price supports for agriculture, but the Air Commerce Act, the Railway Labor Act, and the Radio Control Act promoted long-term growth in those industries. The Public Buildings Act transformed a substantial part of Pennsylvania Avenue in the heart of Washington, D.C. (Office of the Historian, n.d.).

The World War Adjusted Compensation Act was passed in 1924. This act was originally proposed under Harding, who opposed it. It provided very modest benefits for WWI vets. Unless certain circumstances were met, these modest benefits were not to be paid for twenty years. The vets were allowed to borrow against the insurance policies and many did. The main support for the bill was from the American Legion. Part of the push for helping vets was that other federal employees received bonuses, but not the military. Despite the obvious appeal and rationale for such a bill, Coolidge vetoed the bill, but the Republican Congress overrode his veto a few days later (Miller Center of Public Affairs, University of Virginia, n.d.b).

The National Origins Act of 1924 provided for immigration quotas designed to keep the composition of the United States in the same proportions as in 1890. This was a xenophobic bill designed to keep the U.S. predominantly populated by the northern Europeans who had originally settled the country. This would exclude persons from Eastern Europe, which had a larger percentage of Jewish persons. Asians were specifically excluded (IAC Publishing, LLC., n.d.).

The Great Mississippi Flood of 1927 was a negative mark in race relations during Coolidge's presidency. This massive flood in the middle of the country impacted more than seven hundred thousand people. Predominantly black areas were helped after the predominantly white areas. Further, black laborers were used to do much of the work, even helping white Americans move out of the impacted areas while they were left behind. This event, rarely mentioned in American history, is credited with helping to cause black Americans to move to northern cities and to move toward voting for Democrats, since the GOP was in charge at the time ("Mississippi River Flood of 1927," n.d.).

Coolidge is probably best known for fiscal conservatism. Ironically, the main vehicle for reducing the national debt was to stimulate the economy by lowering taxes. The Revenue Acts of 1924 and 1926, also known as the "Coolidge/Mellon Tax Cuts," lowered tax rates a great deal. With high income limits, the vast majority of Americans paid no income tax. Other federal excise taxes were eliminated and the federal budget itself was significantly reduced (Calvin Coolidge Presidential Foundation, Inc., n.d.).

THE COOLIDGE INTERNATIONAL RECORD

America continued its official policy of isolation during the Coolidge administration, while Hitler and Mussolini continued to consolidate and expand their power. Hirohito was crowned Emperor of Japan; Japan and China then broke off diplomatic relations. The foundations of WWII were fully in place during Coolidge's administration with no effective response from the U.S.

BY THE NUMBERS

The national debt was reduced during Coolidge's time in office, despite the tax cuts referenced above (U.S. Department of the Treasury, Bureau of the Fiscal Service, 2013):

Year	National Debt
1923	$22,349,707,365
1924	$21,250,812,989
1925	$20,516,193,887
1926	$19,643,216,315
1927	$18,511,906,931
1928	$17,604,293,201
1929	$16,931,088,484

It should be emphasized that part of the reduction in the national debt at a time of tax reductions was the shrinking expenditures in the federal budget.

The economy under Coolidge closely tracked the impact of a post-World War economy. The average inflation rate for his administration was rather low, despite the generally good and expanding economy of the 1920s (Coin News Media Group, LLC, 2017):

Year	Inflation Rate
1923	1.8%
1924	0%
1925	2.3%
1926	1.1%
1927	1.7%
1928	1.7%
1929	0%

MAKING THE GRADE

Coolidge gets low marks as President, with his average ranking around thirtieth (Meyers, 2014). Part of the challenge is that a person who does not toot his own horn often is overlooked. After all, he was known as "Silent Cal." As the United States has moved further and further into a big government approach with large deficits, there is less appreciation for Coolidge's focus on cutting taxes and reducing the size of government (Johnson, 2013).

Coolidge appears to meet the high moral standards that a world leader should possess. While there were scandals during his administration, it appears that these were left over from the Harding administration.

Public morality is a harder case to make for Coolidge. His lack of response and handling of racial disharmony and immigration law are black marks on his presidency. The Mob took over numerous American cities with bootlegging operations and used their cash flow to expand into gambling, drugs, and prostitution. They gained enough power to buy off or kill law enforcement officials. While the famed early head of the FBI, J. Edgar Hoover, was appointed by Coolidge, the power of the FBI took quite some time to catch up to the gangsters.

There were some positive legislative developments during Coolidge's presidency. His term witnessed strong economic growth while limiting taxes. The laws made it easier for small businesses to compete with larger businesses. The national debt declined steadily during his term in the White House. On the other hand, the Great Depression happened roughly ten months after his presidency ended. While Herbert Hoover, his successor, bore the brunt of the public and international shame for this sad end to the "Roaring Twenties," the Coolidge administration's failure to monitor banking and investing activity clearly laid the groundwork for the Great Depression.

On the international scene, America was asleep at the wheel. As Japan bullied its neighbors and Germany and Italy moved into aggressive dictatorships, America did next to nothing. There does not appear to be any appreciation for what the world would be like in less than ten years from the end of Coolidge's term.

Coolidge Grade: C-

CHAPTER 5

HERBERT HOOVER

(National Archives & Records Administration, 1928)

Herbert Clark Hoover (1874–1964) was the thirty-first president of the United States. The Republican was president from 1929 to 1933. Charles Curtis served as his vice president. Hoover won election in a landslide of 58 percent to 40 percent over Democrat Al Smith, reflecting the positive tones of the dying days of the "Roaring Twenties" (Miller Center of Public Affairs, University of Virginia, n.d.a).

Similar to his predecessor, Coolidge, Hoover was married to the same woman, Lou Henry Hoover, from 1899 until her death in 1944. He did not remarry. There were no reported affairs (Warters, 2006). Lou Hoover, after receiving her degree in teaching, met her future husband while attending Stanford University, its first female geology graduate. She was active in her husband's business and charitable activities. As first lady, she got considerably better media coverage than her husband, the president, making regular appearances on radio to encourage national relief programs. Both Herbert and Lou were fluent in Chinese and would converse in the language to avoid eavesdropping in the White House.

OCCUPATIONAL ACCOMPLISHMENTS

Hoover graduated from Stanford University in 1895 with a geology degree. His occupational pursuits took him to Australia in 1897 and China in 1899, working as a mining engineer (Mouat & Phimister, 2008). He continued to consult around the world and opened his own consulting firm in 1908. He was an entrepreneur and gained wealth from ownership of silver mines in Asia and even earned royalties for writing a top textbook on mining engineering (Hoxie, 1977). During WWI, Herbert and Lou raised millions of dollars for food and medicine for the Belgian people. He was appointed by President Wilson to run the U.S. Food Administration. Hoover was Secretary of Commerce for the U.S. from 1921 to 1928 (Hoover & Lohof, 1970). After Hitler invaded Poland in 1939, he established the Commission for Polish Relief (CPR), providing food and clothing to the impoverished people until the U.S. entered the war. Truman appointed him in 1946 to run the United Nations Relief and Rehabilitation Administration (UNRRA). After this he helped to establish two other parts of the UN–UNICEF and CARE. Truman and Eisenhower appointed him to commissions to improve government efficiency. He did not believe in advertising his private philanthropy so we will never know exactly how much he gave–but estimates are as much as half of his fortune. He did not accept his salary as president–donating it instead. A vocal critic of Roosevelt's "New Deal," he wrote several books during the 1930s laying out his position.

SIGNIFICANT EVENTS DURING HOOVER'S TIME IN OFFICE

1929

- St. Valentine's Day Massacre on February 14 in Chicago attributed to Al Capone's gang.
- The Wall Street Crash–Black Thursday, Black Monday and Black Tuesday, October 24-28, 1929–considered start of the Great Depression

1930

- Smoot-Hawley Tariff Act signed
- Bank panic begins. Thirteen hundred banks close, including the largest, The Bank of the United States, in New York City.

1931

- Nine black youths are convicted of raping a white woman in Scottsboro, Alabama. Convictions are later overturned by the U.S. Supreme Court.
- Japanese military stages an incident in the Manchurian town of Mukden.
- Britain goes off the gold standard and the U.S. has another run on banks.

1932

- "Stimson Doctrine" is used to condemn Japanese action in Manchuria.
- Reconstruction Finance Corp established

1933

- Hitler is appointed Chancellor of Germany.

THE DOMESTIC FRONT AND RACE RELATIONS

Perhaps one of the bitter ironies of all U.S. presidents in this book is that the biography of Hoover makes it appear on paper that he would have been one of the great business leaders in the White House (Hirschman, 1983). And yet, the Great Depression marked his administration as one of the biggest failures in U.S. history. After twelve years of Republican control from 1920 through 1932, the Great Depression helped to drive voters to Democrat presidential candidates for the next twenty years (Campbell, 1966).

Hoover had a Republican-controlled Congress during his first two years, and an evenly divided Congress during his second two years. The dramatic shift in party representation in the 1930 election helped to telegraph the unhappiness of the voters with the long-term Republican control (Lee, 1984). Perhaps his most significant accomplishment came from two of his three U.S. Supreme Court appointments. In 1930, he appointed Charles Evan Hughes as Chief Justice, and Hughes served until 1941. Hoover also appointed Owen Josephus Roberts and Benjamin Nathan Cardozo to the high court (Taylor, 2004). Cardozo was one of the best-known jurists of his day and is still cited in court briefs and legal analysis. The composition of the Supreme Court, largely appointed by a dozen years of Republican administrations, helped to constrain a number of the more extreme moves by Hoover's successor, Franklin Roosevelt.

The impact of a major economic depression on the average American is hard to comprehend since fear of inflation dominated economic policy in the '70s and '80s. During the 1930s, unemployment is often reported at 25 percent to 30 percent. These numbers often fail to account for minority and female unemployment. By modern reporting standards, the unemployment rate was much higher during this time frame (Hamilton, 1982).

During the Great Depression, home values declined by approximately 50 percent. The refinancing of loans was not possible since so many homeowners were "underwater," meaning the value of the home was less than the amount of the mortgage (Green & Wachter, 2005). The high number of foreclosures during the Depression was one hallmark of the economic impact on the average American.

Hoover, contrary to lingering popular impression, did not sit idly by and watch the majority of Americans suffer. Nor, were his actions intended to help the rich at the expense of the poor. America's Great Depression became a world depression and this deepened the depression for most of the world economies. Prior to the stock market crash, Hoover had signed the Agricultural Marketing Act, a bill Coolidge had opposed. The act was designed to provide relief for farmers by implementing federal programs to support agricultural cooperatives and to purchase surplus farm production (US History.org, n.d.). Hoover recognized that farmers in general did not benefit from the boom of the 1920s. The economy continued its downward slide and it is still difficult to determine if the federal government could have done more to avert the October 1929 stock market crash.

Late in his term, Hoover supported establishment of the Reconstruction Finance Corporation (often misattributed to Roosevelt), which was funded with two billion dollars to help businesses and financial institutions in the U.S. (Stabile, 1986). The World War Adjusted Compensation Act established under Coolidge became a continuing thorn in Hoover's side. Veterans tried to get Congress to allow them early access to the money, which was not due to be paid until 1945. This led to large protests in Washington, D.C., including the Bonus March of 1932 (Ortiz, 2010).

At the same time, Hoover revamped the struggling Veterans Bureau and renamed it the Veterans Administration to better provide healthcare and other benefits to vets (Baker, 2012).

Hoover was the last president to strongly support state/local versus national actions when it came to the welfare of the individual citizens. He established a pattern which was continued by Roosevelt and others to expand public works projects during low economic times. Hoover proposed an old age support system that evolved into the Social Security system that Roosevelt is credited with creating a few years later (Hoover, 1952).

The largest economic miscue of the Hoover administration was the enactment of the Smoot-Hawley Tariff Act in 1930. As the U.S. economy continued its downward track, Congress passed this act, which increased tariffs on some imported goods. This had the predictable effect of similar retaliatory tariff increases by America's trading partners. Many economists attribute the length and depth of the Depression to this act (Freidel & Sidey, 2006). On the heels of this mistake, America experienced a series of bank failures that wiped out the finances of many Americans (Glant, 2002). The colloquial reference to "hiding money under the mattress" was certainly in order when banks could not be trusted.

Gang violence, which had become an American phenomenon during the 1920s, continued into the 1930s. One of the most publicized events was the "St. Valentine's Day Massacre" in Chicago in 1929. The killings were attributed to Al Capone, although he made a point to be in another state when the murders took place (Carcasson, 1998). This and other acts set in motion a movement to end Prohibition, although Hoover supported Prohibition while Roosevelt supported its repeal. The FBI under Hoover rose to prominence while attempting to contain the gang activities. Capone himself was eventually jailed, not for murders, but for tax evasion (Zieger, 1975).

The trauma of the Great Depression dominates the literature, with little said of the plight of minorities in America. Race relations were not good. In California, an often overlooked case, *Roberto Alvarez v. the Board of Trustees of the Lemon Grove School District*, 1931, is considered the first case to rule against school segregation. The issue was whether Mexican-Americans could be excluded from white schools in a suburb of San Diego (Alverez, 1986). Also in 1931, in Alabama, nine young black men were convicted by an all white jury in what many considered a bogus trial. Multiple retrials of the "Scottsboro Nine" ultimately lead to reversal of their convictions by the U.S. Supreme Court.

THE HOOVER INTERNATIONAL RECORD

While struggling on the economic front, the U.S. was also consistently ineffectual on the international front. The Kellog-Briand Pact of 1929, the London Naval Treaty of 1930, and the Second Geneva Naval Conference of 1932 were all agreements that involved the world's leading economies disarming and favoring peace. The participating countries would not use submarines and other warships to attack each other (Arnold, 1980). No enforcement mechanism was put in place in these treaties. The "Stimson Doctrine," named for the U.S. Secretary of State, was ineffectual in getting powers like Japan, which was engaging in aggression in Manchuria, to behave (Shideler, 1956). Hitler continued his rise to power in Germany with virtually no opposition from the U.S. (Engerman, 1997).

BY THE NUMBERS

Not surprisingly, the national debt, which had declined steadily under Coolidge, increased under Hoover as the Great Depression required more government deficit spending (U.S. Department of the Treasury, Bureau of the Fiscal Service, 2015):

Year	National Debt
1929:	$16,931,088,484
1930:	$16,185,309,831
1931:	$16,801,281,491
1932:	$19,487,002,444

The inflation rates for Hoover's single term in office detail the impact of the Great Depression (Coin News Media Group LLC, n.d.):

Year	Inflation Rate
1929	-1.2%
1930	0%
1931	-7%
1932	-10.1%

MAKING THE GRADE

Hoover is unfairly treated by history. He did not cause the Great Depression, as the factors were in motion prior to his taking office only eight months earlier. Some other major countries were already in recession before the crash in October 1929. Hoover, as Commerce Secretary, encouraged Coolidge to enact some banking regulations to prevent speculation and control fraud. Coolidge refused to act. Hoover's personal morality appears as clean as his predecessor, Coolidge. We know from his writings that Hoover was open to helping all people regardless of color or religion but race relations were not necessarily better under Hoover.

The gang violence during Hoover's term in office was a black mark against him as he opposed the repeal of one of its major causes–Prohibition. The jailing of Capone, although only one gangster, at least began the process which has continued into the 21st century of eliminating the Mob.

Many of the essentially ineffectual economic moves by the Hoover administration were actually attributed to the Roosevelt administration. In international relations, parallel to Coolidge, America failed to assert leadership in key situations. Hoover's administration signed abjectly silly agreements like one that mandated that peace would be the world standard. Of course, as there was no enforcement mechanism of any kind, Japan and Germany took advantage of the ignorance and lack of attention by America, England, France, and their allies.

Hoover Grade: D

CHAPTER 6
FRANKLIN DELANO ROOSEVELT

"Franklin Delano Roosevelt Portrait" (n.d.)

Franklin Delano Roosevelt (1882–1945) swept to a landslide victory with his "New Deal" platform as the thirty-second president of the U.S. in 1932. A Democrat, he served until his death in 1945 . He was the only president to violate George Washington's tradition of serving only two terms in office. As a consequence, the Constitution was later amended to prevent another president from serving more than two terms (Dye, 2000). His first vice president was John Garner, from 1933 to 1941. His next VP was Henry Wallace, from 1941 to 1945. Harry Truman, who was to become president on Roosevelt's death, only served as VP briefly before Roosevelt died on April 12, 1945 (Rosenfeld, & Harrison, 2010).

Roosevelt, despite mobility problems from polio, was rather famous as a womanizer (Shields, 1995). Little was reported of his affairs during his lifetime, but reports of his exploits leaked for many years after similar reports came out about John F. Kennedy. Roosevelt was married to Eleanor Roosevelt, his fifth cousin once removed, from 1905 until his death (History.com staff, 2009). Roosevelt was a distant cousin of former Republican President Theodore Roosevelt ("Franklin D. Roosevelt: Life," 2017).

In 1918, Eleanor discovered that Roosevelt was having an affair with her secretary, Lucy Mercer. At that time, a divorce or scandal might have ruined the future for the politically ambitious Roosevelt, so the couple reached an accommodation. Depending on various reports, Roosevelt promised either to be faithful to Eleanor, or they promised to have a marriage in name only. Roosevelt was not faithful to Eleanor. Another documented affair was with his secretary, Missy LeHand. Roosevelt's son, Elliott, was a witness to some of their interactions (History.com staff, 2009). Lucy Mercer was with Roosevelt at his death in Warm Springs, Georgia (Stewart, 2015).

OCCUPATIONAL ACCOMPLISHMENTS

From a wealthy family, Roosevelt was home-schooled and then attended the Groton School prior to Harvard College. He graduated with a history degree in 1903. He attended law school at Columbia University, but did not graduate, and passed the New York bar exam in 1907. He practiced law briefly, but then ran for the state senate in 1910. He supported the Woodrow Wilson campaign in 1912 and when Wilson was elected, Roosevelt was rewarded with the position of Assistant Secretary of the Navy. Unlike Wilson, Roosevelt advocated for a stronger Navy during the early years of WWI. Following America's entry into the war, Roosevelt was heavily involved in the administration of the naval war effort. He capped his early political life as the vice presidential candidate in 1920 for James Cox, who was soundly defeated by Harding. Roosevelt then briefly served as an executive of a finance company (Miller Center of Public Affairs, University of Virginia, n.d.a).

For Roosevelt, a life-changing event happened in 1921 when he contracted polio. While never to walk normally again, he was able to have reasonable mobility with canes and a wheelchair following an aggressive rehabilitation program (Miller Center of Public Affairs, University of Virginia, n.d.a). He then turned his attention to Democrat Al Smith, who ran for governor of New York in 1922. Smith ran an unsuccessful campaign for President in 1928 against Hoover. Roosevelt rebounded by winning the New York governor's race. The consummate politician, Roosevelt used his connections with candidates like Smith and his base in populous New York to advance his political visibility (Breitman & Lichtman, 2013).

SIGNIFICANT EVENTS DURING ROOSEVELT'S TIME IN OFFICE

1933
- Roosevelt's first "Fireside Chat" radio address
- Roosevelt takes the United States off the gold standard.
- The Federal Securities Act of 1933 passes.
- The Banking Act of 1933
- Roosevelt agrees to establish diplomatic relations with the U.S.S.R.
- Constitutional Amendment passes to end Prohibition.

1934

- Cuba is released from restrictions of the Spanish-American War.
- Hitler becomes Führer of Germany.
- The Securities Exchange Act of 1934 is enacted, creating the Securities Exchange Commission (SEC).

1935

- The Supreme Court rules in *Schechter Poultry Corp. v. United States* that the National Industrial Recovery Act of 1933 is unconstitutional.
- The National Labor Relations Act, creating the National Labor Relations Board (NLRB), is enacted.
- Social Security Act passes.

1936

- In *U.S. v. Butler*, the Supreme Court rules the Agricultural Adjustment Act to be unconstitutional.
- Ethiopia falls to the aggression of Mussolini of Italy.
- Spanish Civil War begins.
- Japan withdraws from treaties reducing the size of its Navy and military.

1937

- Roosevelt unsuccessfully attempts to "pack" the U.S. Supreme Court.
- Third Neutrality Act passed (known as the "Cash and Carry" Law).
- Japanese Air Force attack the gunboat USS *Panay* in China's Yangtze River.

1938

- German troops move into Austria.
- Mexico nationalizes all oil properties of the United States and other foreign-owned companies.
- Germany is allowed to annex the Sudetenland part of Czechoslovakia.

1939

- The German Army invades and conquers the remainder of Czechoslovakia.
- Roosevelt recognizes the Fascist government of Francisco Franco in Spain.
- Italy invades Albania.
- Germany and U.S.S.R. sign a nonaggression pact.
- Germany invades Poland, regarded as the "official start" of WWII.
- France and Britain declare war on Germany and Roosevelt announces neutrality.
- Germany and U.S.S.R. divide Poland.
- The U.S.S.R. invades Finland.

1940

- German army invades northern Europe.
- Winston Churchill becomes the Prime Minister of Britain and requests that America assist Britain.
- Germany sweeps through France.
- The Selective Training and Service Act is passed to begin a "peacetime" draft.

1941

- Lend-Lease Act is enacted to help Britain continue its war efforts.
- Germany defeats Greece and Yugoslavia.
- Germany invades U.S.S.R. and Roosevelt pledges aid to U.S.S.R.
- Pearl Harbor is attacked by Japanese bombers and attack planes.
- Japan invades the Philippines and Hong Kong.
- Germany and Italy declare war on the United States.

1942

- 122,000 Japanese-Americans living on the West Coast are relocated to camps.
- MacArthur abandons the Bataan peninsula, leaving seventy-five thousand troops who later surrender to the Japanese, followed by the "Bataan Death March."
- The Battle of the Coral Sea is won by the U.S. Navy.
- The Battle of Midway
- First nuclear chain reaction is demonstrated at the University of Chicago.

1943

- The Battle of the Bismarck Sea in the Pacific
- Victory in North Africa for the Allies, including securing control of the Suez Canal
- Roosevelt, Churchill, and Generalissimo Chiang Kai-shek of China meet to plan their approach to peace in the Pacific after defeat of Japan.
- Roosevelt meets with U.S.S.R. leader Joseph Stalin and British Prime Minister Winston Churchill, later known as the "Big Three."

1944

- D-Day and "Operation Overlord" result in victory, but with heavy losses.
- War in the Pacific imposes heavy losses for both sides
- The Battle of the Philippine Sea results in another U.S. victory.
- Servicemen's Readjustment Act, also known as the "G. I. Bill of Rights," is enacted.
- Bretton Woods Conference takes place in New Hampshire.
- Dumbarton Oaks Conference begins in Washington, D.C.
- Battle of the Bulge results in additional losses for American and Allied troops.

1945

- The Yalta Conference takes place with Roosevelt, Churchill, and Stalin.
- U.S. Marines capture islands in the South Pacific.
- Roosevelt dies from cerebral hemorrhage in Warm Springs, Georgia.
- Vice President Harry S. Truman becomes the thirty-fourth President.

THE GREAT DEPRESSION

The United States had previously encountered severe recessions, including in Roosevelt's lifetime: 1893, 1907, and 1920–21 (Hughes, 2011). Following each such recession, there was a period of recovery, and America was used to this cycle of difficulties and then economic growth. The Great Depression was a perfect storm of factors that were exacerbated by miscues like the Smoot-Hawley Tariff Act of 1930, which triggered a series of retaliatory tariff-raising by America's trading partners around the world. This deepened the U.S. economic depression and expanded it to a world depression (Meltzer, 1976). A major drought hit the midwestern United States and this added to the woes of American farmers. (Blankfield, 2016).

By the time he became president, Roosevelt had political experience at the federal and state level, but no significant experience with private sector business operations or financing. Despite the negligible recovery from the Depression during his first term, he actually received a slightly higher percentage of votes during his reelection in 1936. In 1940 and 1944, he won by still high, but decreasing, margins (Office of the Federal Register, n.d.). Roosevelt enjoyed significant Democrat voting margins in both houses of Congress for his entire time in office, although the lead narrowed in the later years of his administration (U.S. Senate, n.d.; U.S. House of Representatives, n.d.).

Roosevelt used the economic crisis and control of Congress to advance an agenda that was aggressive and expansive. It expanded the role of the federal government into nearly every aspect of American life. Opponents branded it as an offense to states' rights, but that was not an effective argument in light of the Great Depression. Known as Roosevelt's "One Hundred Days," a flood of laws was passed as Roosevelt began to implement his "New Deal" (Bolt, 1985). This included the Emergency Banking Act, which allowed solvent banks to reopen. About one thousand banks reopened at this time (Caldwell, M. C., & Titsworth, 1996). The Reforestation Relief Act was passed, creating the Civilian Conservation Corps (CCC). This was one of the most popular New Deal programs, as three million to four million young men were given the opportunity to work on rural lands to create national parks and other facilities. This program ended in 1942 with the U.S. entry into WWII. This was followed with the Federal Emergency Relief Act, which provided grants to states to create projects to put people to work (Digital Public Library of America, n.d.b).

The Agricultural Adjustment Administration was created, which provided relief for farmers (Agricultural Adjustment Administration, 2016). Some of this relief was counterintuitive, as during a period of food shortages, farmers were paid not to plant crops in order to raise farm prices. Roosevelt created the Civil Works Administration (CWA) by executive order, which provided short-term employment on public works projects. This program is often cited as another public works success since as many as four million people were put to work on projects that improved the nation's infrastructure and may have averted starvation for some of the workers (Digital Public Library of America, n.d.a).

Perhaps the worst piece of legislation from the flurry of activity in 1933 was the National Industrial Recovery Act, which created the Public Works Administration and National Recovery Administration (NRA). The NRA was designed to set fair codes of business dealing for a variety of industries (Clemens, 1949). It tried to establish prices and required businesses in the same industries to work together, clearly deviating from America's antitrust policies of the prior forty years. This ran parallel to the disastrous planned economy of the Marxist U.S.S.R. during the same period. The U.S. Supreme Court ruled against it in 1935, preventing full implementation. *Schechter Poultry Corp. v. United States* (2nd Cir., 1935) is discussed later in this chapter. The high court held that the program exceeded the authority of the federal government by attempting to set prices for private industries. This was the first of a series of losses for the Roosevelt administration in the then conservative-dominated U.S. Supreme Court.

Despite the patchwork of short-term assistance funded by the federal government, there were some true accomplishments. The Securities Act of

1933 provided guidance on how to issue stocks and subjected interstate security offerings to fairly strict rules to attempt to avoid another stock market crash (Security and Exchange Commission, 2013). The Tennessee Valley Authority (TVA) provided work for many during construction, but more importantly, it provided low-cost electrical service to the impoverished areas of Appalachia once it was completed. This provided both family and business advancement in a historically low-income part of America (Tennessee Valley Authority, n.d.). The Banking Act of 1933, also known as the Glass-Steagall Act, required banks to separate investments from traditional banking services. It also established the Federal Deposit Insurance Corporation, giving U.S. citizens confidence in their banks (Maues, 1933).

Prohibition ended in 1933 by a constitutional amendment (Gage, 2009). Unfortunately, the dozen years of Prohibition had given organized crime the start it needed to be a menace to America for decades to come.

Another flurry of activity came in 1934 as most of what was done the prior year had not served to revive the economy. Some humanitarian relief was provided and various public works projects, including the construction of the National Park System, was progressing. The Gold Reserve Act removed gold from the monetary system of the United States and restricted Americans' personal gold ownership for the next forty years (Richardson et al., 1934). This was part of Roosevelt's approach to devaluing the U.S. dollar (Rosen, 2005).

The Farm Mortgage Refinancing Act was designed to help American farmers burdened by mortgage debt to avoid foreclosures. The Federal Farm Bankruptcy Act was also enacted in 1934 (Doss, 2009). Both acts were part of a variety of steps taken during the mid-1930s to help American farmers. Unfortunately, foreclosures still continued. Compounding the farm crisis was the "Dust Bowl" in the Midwest and Southwest. Explained in graphic detail in the award-winning John Steinbeck novel *The Grapes of Wrath*, farmers using new mechanized plows were able to plow long stretches, and they did just that. In some cases, they even connected their furrows to the farms surrounding their own. When the severe drought hit, there was no barrier to the winds stripping millions of pounds of topsoil away and causing dust storms (Isaac, 1989).

Roosevelt established the Export-Import Bank by executive order to stimulate trade with South America. The idea of the program, despite its name, was to encourage sales of U.S.-made goods to other countries by providing financing for exports by U.S. producers. The program has been expanded in numerous ways over the years (Patterson, 1943). The Reciprocal Trade Agreements Act was also designed to encourage international trade. The act delegated to the president the authority to negotiate tariffs with U.S. trading partners without seeking prior approval from Congress (Office of the Historian, 1934).

Concluding its regulation of the securities industry in response to the stock market crash, Congress also passed the Securities Act of 1934. This legislation created the Securities and Exchange Commission (SEC) and was designed to regulate the trading of securities once issued pursuant to the 1933 Act rules (Security and Exchange Commission, 2013).

The first two years of the New Deal failed to make much headway in reversing unemployment and stimulating the economy. Another cluster of acts designed to end the Great Depression were passed in 1935. The Emergency Relief Appropriations Act, (Calabresi & Yoo, 2008), the Soil Conservation Service, the Works Progress Administration (WPA), and the Rural Electrification Administration were established ("Rural Electrification," n.d.; Shaheen, 2016). This latter administration was heavily criticized for putting the federal government in competition with private utilities in providing power to underserved areas of the US. On the other hand, the WPA, repeatedly referred to as the most "famous" of the New Deal programs, put millions to work on public works projects. This was another program that fizzled as the U.S. entered WWII and approached full employment for the war effort. The construction projects helped usher America into the industrial age by adapting its transportation system for autos and trucks shortly after both became readily available in the 1920s. One of the more colorful of the WPA projects was its support for artists and authors. The support for authors may have assisted Roosevelt's public image in America as they were thankful for the work and attributed their support to Roosevelt personally.

Still surviving today, the National Labor Relations Act was passed in 1935 and created the National Labor Relations Board (NLRB) ("National Labor Relations Act," 2016). This act provided unfettered support for formation of unions with little or no control over the unions, but significant punishment for employers who opposed them. The NLRB was established as an agency separate from the U.S. Department of Labor (DOL), although there was no rationale for this agency to be outside the USDOL then or now. A year earlier, a "General Strike" was held in San Francisco. Originally started as a maritime workers strike, it spread throughout the area. The local government officially opposed the strike and police used weapons and billy clubs to punish the strikers. Roosevelt stayed out of this conflict (Carlsson, n.d.).

Failing to learn from Coolidge's example that lower taxes and less government stimulated the economy, Roosevelt raised tax rates substantially with the Revenue Act of 1935 (Internal Revenue Service, n.d.). Marginal tax rates were as high as 75 percent under this act. Not surprisingly, Roosevelt's reliance on government action and even competition with the private sector extended the Great Depression, now fully owned by the Roosevelt administration.

The creation of the Social Security Administration in 1935 is one of the handful of well-known outcomes of the New Deal. A supposedly self-funded program, this required most wage earners to participate (Social Security Administration, 1935). Social commentators often mention that it originally excluded agricultural and household workers, who were more likely to be minorities. Among the many economic mistakes made by the Roosevelt administration, this act caused employees and employers to pay into the SSA at the same time that wages were at record lows and unemployment continued at record levels. By requiring employers to pay into the SSA at the same rate as employees, this created a disincentive for employers to hire more workers (Social Security Administration, 1935). The program was essentially a hoax in promising retirement benefits at age 65. In 1935, male life expectancy was only 59.9 years and female life expectancy was only 63.9 years (Noymer, 1998). Other parts of the program provided benefits for the disabled and dependent survivors of wage earners.

During the fourth and fifth years of the Roosevelt administration, 1936 and 1937, the frantic pace of federal legislation and agencies slowed. The U.S. Supreme Court dealt another blow to the New Deal by ruling in *U.S. v. Butler* (1936) that the Agricultural Adjustment Act of 1933 was unconstitutional. Congress passed the Adjusted Compensation Act over Roosevelt's veto (U-S-history.com, n.d.). This act provided immediate benefits to WWI veterans instead of forcing them to wait until 1945 for those meager benefits.

A second flurry of legislative activity took place in 1938. In another rebuke to the president by his own party, Congress passed the Revenue Act of 1938 over Roosevelt's veto, reducing corporate income tax as part of a continuing effort to find anything that would stimulate private sector expansion and hiring (Blumenthal & Morone, 2008). There was some progress in that persons reported to be on welfare shrank from 3.2

million to 2.1 million (Harry & Strickland, 1995). Congress also created the Civil Aeronautics Act in recognition of the growing importance of civil aviation (Gribble, 2002). The Food, Drug and Cosmetic Act was designed to strengthen controls already in place (Gulick, 1965). Perhaps the best-known legislation from this year was the Fair Labor Standards Act of 1938 (FLSA). This act established a national minimum wage, overtime rules, and child labor limitations (Johnson, 1965).

RACE RELATIONS

The Indian Reorganization Act of 1934, also known as the Wheeler-Howard Act (48 Stat. 984 - 25 U.S.C. § 461 et seq), is sometimes referred to as the "New Deal for American Indians." From the time of the first British settlements, Native Americans have been relocated away from their original tribal lands. Numerous treaties with them were made and often broken. A survey of conditions on reservations commissioned in the late 1920s revealed very poor conditions. The 1934 act was intended to right some of those wrongs by providing for more self-governance by the tribes and to restrict further taking of lands designated for reservations.

Some aspects of the conditions for black Americans were improving during the 1930s. Roosevelt appointed the first black federal district judge, William H. Hastie, in 1937. He later became the first black appellate judge (Wynn, 1995).

In several states, the battle was beginning for an end to "separate, but equal" school systems for blacks and whites in the U.S. Parallel to this was a battle to end disparate pay for black and white teachers. Thurgood Marshall, later to be the first black justice of the U.S. Supreme Court, joined the NAACP and began to work toward both goals. Incorrectly reported in numerous sources as a U.S. Supreme Court case, *Gibbs v.*

Montgomery County Maryland Board of Education is actually *Gibbs v. Broome*, a Maryland state case from 1936. This case was settled out of court with Gibbs's salary nearly doubling to match his white peers (Middleton, 1993). While professional sports in the U.S. were still segregated, the four gold medals won by Jesse Owens in the 1936 Summer Olympics helped to lay the groundwork for future gains by black athletes throughout the sports world (Ray, 2004). The Olympics were held in Berlin and Owens succeeded under the nose of Hitler, dealing a blow to his "Aryan race theory."

As the buildup for WWII began to accelerate in 1941, Roosevelt was faced with a threat of a major march on Washington, D.C., by black union activists and the NAACP to compel more employment opportunities for black Americans in the federal war effort. They were specifically going to march for an end to segregation in the military and for equal opportunity in federal defense jobs. Roosevelt designated Eleanor Roosevelt and New York City Mayor Fiorello LaGuardia to negotiate for him. To the protestors, the goal of desegregating the military was the more important of the two goals. Roosevelt resisted this and instead created the Fair Employment Practices Board (FEPC) by Executive Order 8802 (Brick & Regenhardt, n.d.).

Sadly, the war effort did not end decades of segregation. Discrimination was well established in the South, but in reality, discrimination existed in more subtle ways throughout the United States. Race relations were frayed, rather than improved, during much of the war effort. Historically, all white craft jobs were facing integration and there was much resistance and some violence. Discrimination was not reserved for blacks as other racial, ethnic, and religious minorities faced a variety of challenges. For black Americans, the war effort meant opportunities in menial jobs, but not in craft or supervisory positions (Wright, 2010; Burns & Novick, 2017). Race riots took place around the U.S. despite the focus on the war effort. The worst reported riot was in Detroit in 1942 (Roosevelt, F. D., 1984).

In 1943, Executive Order 9347 created the Office of War Mobilization, a super-agency to coordinate a large number of war effort activities into one agency for better coordination. Roosevelt required that all federal defense contractors provide equal employment opportunity across the board with this order. While this was largely unenforced, and many blacks and other minorities were not afforded access to the better positions, there was a significant increase in minority employment (NARA, 2015). The Summer of 1943 marked the "Zoot Suit Riots" in the Los Angeles area. Young Mexican and Mexican-American men were targeted, often by white members of the military (Coroian, 2016).

In one of the more infamous chapters in modern race relations, a reported 122,000 Japanese-Americans were forced to move into camps inland from the West Coast of the U.S. during WWII. Close to seventy thousand of those relocated were American citizens (Burns & Novick, 2007; OurDocuments.gov, n.d.).

Voting rights for black Americans was a legal issue during Roosevelt's administration. In *Smith v. Allwright* (321 U.S. 649, 1944), the U.S. Supreme Court ruled that blacks could not be excluded from voting in a primary election in Texas on the basis of race.

ROOSEVELT AND THE U.S. SUPREME COURT

In the early years of his long administration, Roosevelt had a tough time with the high court. This was the only branch of government that was not giving him a green light. The National Industrial Recovery Act (NIRA) required businesses to coordinate on codes, standards, and prices. Argued in 1934, the U.S. Supreme Court ruled in early 1935 in *Panama Refining Co. v. Ryan* (293 U.S. 388) that part of NIRA, an attempt by Roosevelt to limit trade in American oil internationally, was unconstitutional. The basis for the ruling, known as the "Hot Oil" case, was that Congress lacked the constitutional authority to give the president this type of power. As mentioned earlier in this chapter, another part of NIRA was slapped down later in 1935 in *Schechter Poultry Corp. v. United States*. Also known as the "Sick Chicken" case, the high court held that the program exceeded the authority of the federal government with vague language and attempting to set prices for private industries in intrastate commerce situations. The federal government did not have authority to intervene in matters that did not involve interstate commerce (Gely & Spiller, 1992).

Another loss for Roosevelt in the Supreme Court in 1935 was in *Railroad Retirement Board v. Alton Railroad Co.* (295 U.S. 330). The Railroad Retirement Act of 1934 was a sweeping piece of legislation that gave pension benefits to a large number of present and former railroad employees. The key target of the legal attack was the allocation of pension funds. The high court ruled with the railroads that this amounted to an unauthorized taking of private assets by the federal government.

The Supreme Court continued its 1935 anti-New Deal rulings with *Louisville Joint Stock Land Bank v. Radford* (295 U.S. 555), and *Humphrey's Executor v. United States* (295 U.S. 602). In *Louisville*, the court ruled that a law preventing mortgage foreclosures of farms was unconstitutional as an unauthorized taking by the federal government. In *Humphrey's*, the court ruled that Roosevelt's removal of a Federal Trade Commissioner for a reason not outlined in the Federal Trade Commission Act violated that act.

The Supreme Court ruled against Roosevelt's administration in *United States v. Butler* (297 U.S. 1, 1935), invalidating provisions of the Agricultural Adjustment Act. In *Carter v. Carter Coal Company* (298 U.S. 238, 1936), the high court declared most of the Guffey Bituminous Coal Conservation Act of 1935 (49 Stat. 991) unconstitutional (Gely & Spiller, 1992). The Supreme Court ruled against a New York state minimum wage bill in *Morehead v. New York ex rel. Tipaldo* (298 U.S. 587,1936) as unconstitutional for interfering in the private contractual relationship between an employer and its employees.

In frustration, Roosevelt proposed the Judicial Procedures Reform Bill of 1937 to Congress. The bill is quite famous as Roosevelt's effort to "pack the Supreme Court," even though Congress never voted on the proposed bill (Shipman, 1945). The Supreme Court had a core of four conservative justices sometimes called the "Four Horsemen." All four of them were over the age of seventy and they consistently voted against the New Deal legislation brought before the court. The fifth vote against the New Deal was generally Justice Owen Roberts. The reason is unclear today, but later Roberts began voting for the New Deal. In a clear reversal of *Morehead*, above, the Supreme Court upheld a Washington state law establishing a minimum wage for women (*West Coast Hotel Co. v. Parrish*, 300 U.S. 379, 1937) (Chambers, 1969). Several subsequent cases also supported major New Deal legislation.

During Roosevelt's many terms as president, he was able to put his imprint on the Supreme Court for more than twenty-five years after his death. Some of his better-known appointments were liberal-leaning and included Hugo Black, 1937; William Douglas, 1939; and Harlan Stone, 1941. In all, he appointed nine justices to the U.S. Supreme Court. (U.S. Senate, n.d.) He appointed Felix Frankfurter in 1939, whose approach was known as "judicial restraint." Frankfurter was viewed as a conservative in most matters. This gave some balance to the liberalism of Black and Douglas (Urofsky, 1988).

ELEANOR ROOSEVELT

Since the focus of this book is on the ethical leadership of the presidents, space does not permit additional discussions of the first ladies beyond a brief mention in each chapter. Eleanor Roosevelt was a major force by helping Roosevelt get back on track after he contracted polio and in getting Roosevelt elected president. She had a life of her own as a civic champion. After Roosevelt's death, she became a delegate to the United Nations and was involved in drafting the UN's Universal Declaration of Human Rights. She is remembered as a champion for civil rights in the U.S. (History.com staff, 2009). Eleanor Roosevelt was America's exemplary first lady in every sense of the word.

THE ROOSEVELT INTERNATIONAL RECORD

On the international scene, the early years of the Roosevelt administration were marked by a failure to understand the enormous risks to America and its allies building around the world. Still a mystery, Roosevelt recognized the government of the U.S.S.R. despite its Marxist basis and the way the government seized power by murder and force. In 1934, Hitler became Führer in Germany. There was no obvious reaction by Roosevelt. The Platt Amendment was passed, which returned local control to Cuba, which terminated the terms of the treaty that ended the Spanish-American War in 1900 (US Department of State, n.d.). Given the proximity of Cuba to the U.S, this move was indeed puzzling and substantially increased the risk to the U.S. Japan telegraphed its intent to move away from peace and any type of a relationship with America and its allies, with no apparent response by Roosevelt.

The world continued to become a more dangerous place as Roosevelt did little or nothing to assert America's influence. Ethiopia fell to Italy in aggression by Mussolini. The Spanish Civil War began with General Francisco Franco leading a faction against the government. Japan withdrew from treaties that required it to reduce the size of its navy and military. The U.S. and other countries did not intervene.

Congress enacted what is known as the "First" Neutrality Act in 1935. This act was passed in recognition that another world war was on the horizon, and this was a markedly unsuccessful attempt to stay out of the war. It required U.S. arms manufacturers doing business with countries at war, even allies of the U.S, to obtain export licenses in order to sell to these countries. The act was then extended in 1936, now requiring that U.S. companies not loan money to countries engaged in war. The 1937 act, in recognition of the rapidly more dangerous world and with a focus on the Spanish Civil War, expanded the act's restrictions and introduced a "cash and carry" provision that allowed solvent countries at war to purchase goods for cash if they could also transport them in their own ships. This was allegedly set up to allow arms sales to continue to England and France since these allies had the resources to utilize the law's provision (Office of the Historian, n.d.).

The relative quiet on the domestic front in 1936 and 1937 afforded Roosevelt an opportunity to move forward internationally. Unfortunately, he did nothing. In what should have been interpreted as a prelude to war in the Pacific, Japan attacked the USS *Panay*, a gunboat, in the Yangtze River of China (Craig & Radchenko, 2008). At that time, China was an ally of the U.S. An excuse often made for Roosevelt's failure to protect allies and discourage aggression by Germany, Japan, and Italy was that the average American was against such involvement. However, given Roosevelt's enormous popularity and political advantage, this argument does not hold water. Many more Americans were killed due to the late entry into WWI, by allowing the aggressors a head start. The popular Roosevelt could have explained that historical reality in one of his many "fireside chats."

The international scene became more dangerous in 1938. Germany occupied Austria and later annexed the Sudetenland area of Czechoslovakia. A conference in Munich approved the annexation, despite the fact that the country whose land was taken, Czechoslovakia, was not at the conference. Germany, Italy, Britain, and France agreed to this deal. This act of "appeasement," as it was later known, was soon to be the downfall of Neville Chamberlain, the British Prime Minister (Cavendish, 2016; Bilger et al., 1999). In North America, Mexico nationalized all oil holdings in its country, including holdings belonging to U.S. companies.

The year 1939 is almost totally dominated by international considerations and the advent of WWII. The German army took the rest of Czechoslovakia. This is the "official start" of WWII (Kenny, 2008), although Germany's conquest of Poland with the assistance of the U.S.S.R. a short time later is often cited as the start of war (Hunnicutt, 2013). The U.S.S.R. and Germany then divided Poland (Eves, 2011). Roosevelt recognized the fascist government of Francisco Franco in Spain, despite Franco's rise to power after a brutal civil war (Jordan, 2011). After Italy invaded Albania, Roosevelt sent a proposal to Germany and Italy requesting a ten-year peace deal if they would not conquer any more countries (Meschutt, 1986). France and Britain declared war on Germany while Roosevelt declared neutrality despite U.S. support for the French and English (Milam, 1941). The emboldened U.S.S.R. then invaded Finland.

In 1940, Roosevelt violated the tradition set by Washington of limiting a president to two terms in office (Page et al., 1974). He maintained a substantial margin in the polls, although not as great as in 1936. Despite his continued strong support, he failed to use that support to properly position the U.S. for war. France and Britain, allies of the U.S., took heavy losses and yet, Roosevelt still maintained neutrality (McGarity, 2013). Despite the fall of France and the request of new British Prime Minister Winston Churchill, Roosevelt held the U.S. out of the war (Calabresi & Yoo, 2008). The U.S. did implement a "peacetime" draft (Pederson, 2016), through lend/lease began to sell arms to the Allies and established an Office of Emergency Management (Swanson, 1975).

There are many books and movies that depict WWII from Pearl Harbor on December 7, 1941, through the surrender of Japan in 1945. The purpose of this book is not to retell the story of WWII, but to focus on presidential leadership and key decisions that were made by those presidents. The extended explanation of the buildup to WWII establishes that the U.S. had ample opportunity to cooperate with its historical allies to defeat the Axis powers and avoid terrible losses following its late entry into the war. The U.S. began to openly support Britain and its allies with the Lend-Lease Act of 1941 (Rapoport, 1945). It is unclear how Roosevelt thought such open support of Britain's war effort would somehow not involve the U.S. in WWII.

One of the more bizarre moves by Roosevelt early in WWII was his response to the invasion of the U.S.S.R. by Germany. The U.S.S.R. had been an ally of Germany as well as an aggressor in Northern and Eastern Europe. Stalin and Hitler had carved up Poland, as noted above. Roosevelt's offer of aid to Stalin when the U.S. was not providing significant help to its true allies at that point was an example of the poor handling of international relations that marked Roosevelt's entire time in office. Throughout WWII, the U.S. ignored the aggression by Stalin in the late 1930s into the early 1940s and treated him like an equal with Churchill and Roosevelt. In the modern era, this would be equivalent to treating Saddam Hussein as an equal to the U.S. president.

Even prior to Pearl Harbor, Japan attacked U.S. shipping interests and U.S. Navy ships, and the U.S. did nothing. Roosevelt, in an extraordinary display of naiveté, failed to recognize the threat Japan posed to the U.S. On the eve of the bombing of Pearl Harbor, Japan had representatives in Washington asking America to ignore Japan's expansion plans into China. In response, Roosevelt sent the U.S. Pacific fleet to Pearl Harbor in a mock show of force (Michaels, 2016). These soldiers and sailors were sent there to die without proper support and reconnaissance required to protect them. Roosevelt failed to appreciate the incredible risk he took in not taking action earlier. Thousands of men and U.S. Navy assets were destroyed in just a few hours at Pearl Harbor (Mueller, 1991). America finally joined the war officially. Roosevelt was now involved in a multifront world war against well-prepared and equipped enemies instead of having intervened earlier and neutralized some of the threats the U.S. now faced (Bilger et al., 1999; Sudman, 1982; Henderson, 1998; Micallef, n.d.). In sports parlance, the U.S. was playing a football game in the fourth quarter, having ceded the first three quarters of the game to its opponents.

BY THE NUMBERS

The national debt increased steadily during Roosevelt's time in office despite numerous tax increases (U.S. Department of the Treasury, Bureau of the Fiscal Service, 2013):

Year	National Debt
1933	$22,538,672,560
1934	$27,053,141,414
1935	$28,700,892,624
1936	$33,778,543,493

1937	$36,424,613,732
1938	$37,164,740,315
1939	$40,439,532,411
1940	$42,967,531,037
1941	$48,961,443,535
1942	$72,422,445,116
1943	$136,696,090,329
1944	$201,003,387,221

The national debt increased steadily after 1941 with war expenses. Roosevelt doubled the national debt from 1933 through 1940 with his multiple programs to solve the Great Depression. It is notable that had Roosevelt acted in the interest of the U.S. when the international affairs were going off the track from the beginning of his administration, the U.S. might have avoided not only a huge loss of life, but also avoided the tremendous expense involved.

Using the average inflation rate from 1933 through 1941 as a proxy for economic performance, it is absolutely clear that the Great Depression was ended only by WWII and not by the actions of the Roosevelt administration. The well-documented negative or low inflation rates from 1937 through 1940 demonstrate the contrary. The economy was still in trouble when the U.S. entered WWII (Coin News Media Group LLC, n.d.):

Year	Inflation Rate
1933	-9.8%
1934	2.3%
1935	3.19%
1936	1.5%
1937	0.7%

1938	-1.7%
1939	-1.4%
1940	-0.7%
1941	1.4%
1942	11.3%
1943	7.6%
1944	3.0%

MAKING THE GRADE

A key element of this book is to debunk the myths that have been created around and about American presidents. The greatest disparity between accomplishments and reputation unquestionably belongs to Roosevelt. The two great myths are first, Roosevelt ended the Great Depression, and second, Roosevelt won WWII. These myths are so enduring that Roosevelt is often at the top of more recent presidential performance polls. A classic example is the Schlesinger Poll, which incredibly ranked him even at 3.97 with George Washington. Only Lincoln scored higher at 4.0 (1996). Like many polls of this nature, they are politically driven as Roosevelt is a hero to the liberal and pro-government ranks.

First is an evaluation of the man as a private person. There is not a lot to recommend him given the documented facts of his personal life. While going from polio to the White House is an extraordinary accomplishment, it is doubtful this would have happened without his personal wealth and support of Eleanor Roosevelt. It is an accomplishment, but a personal one and not on behalf of others. To use one word to sum up Roosevelt as a person, it is "arrogant." He was the only president so arrogant as not to surrender the White House or even groom his successor. His womanizing reportedly continued during his time in the White House. It is hard to argue with the anecdotal reports of his activities that include a woman other than his wife with him at his death.

He earns mixed grades for his public ethics. While he appointed both the first woman cabinet member, Frances Perkins, and the first black federal judge, William H. Hastie, he did not desegregate the American military. He did not enforce his executive orders that required equal opportunity for government work regardless of race. America fought WWII with a segregated military. Racial relations declined during WWII rather than improved. He failed to help Jewish refugees, ignoring their plight even with knowledge of Hitler's "final solution."

On the domestic front, his early initiatives to get food and shelter to millions in exchange for help with public works projects is admirable. Were one to evaluate his administration for the first half of his first term, he might have escaped with a higher grade. Evaluating results and not a flurry of activity, his efforts were counterproductive and only WWII saved him from being discovered as a failure in the domestic economy.

Second is his major failure in international relations. To stand by and watch allies from China to France to England suffer terrible losses devastated the perception of America throughout the world. Millions were gassed by Germany while America negotiated a nonexistent peace. Neville Chamberlain deservedly sits at the bottom of most historians' lists as the "appeaser" in Europe. It is unclear why Roosevelt is not dealt with in the same way in the U.S. Roosevelt tried to cut deals with Hitler and Mussolini while they savaged much of Eastern Europe, parts of the Middle East, and northern Africa.

His toleration of dictators, Franco in Spain and Stalin in the U.S.S.R., speaks poorly for his decision-making. Consolidating most of the U.S.

Pacific Fleet in harm's way in Pearl Harbor should not be forgotten or forgiven. The ultimate ignominy was having Japan's representatives in Washington, D.C., on the eve of Pearl Harbor, courting Roosevelt to afford them the freedom to conquer more of China without interference from the U.S.

Others may argue, yes, he failed to prepare America for war or support our historic allies. He still mobilized the war effort and "won" WWII. The facts are that the U.S. was never going to lose WWII. Examining the Pacific theater, the U.S. won virtually every major naval encounter with the Japanese starting only six months after Pearl Harbor. With Japan's enormous head start, hundreds of thousands of American servicemen and civilians suffered death and inhuman treatment. The U.S. spent hundreds of billions of dollars in the war effort.

In Europe, Italy and Germany had expanded their influence to North Africa by the time the U.S. entered the war. The heavily entrenched Axis armies provided substantial resistance as the Allied forces were equipped and then fully supported by the U.S. The advance of the Axis powers was stopped and the tide turned quickly. However, it took three and a half years before the coordinated Allied effort destroyed the Italian army and most of the German air force and then destroyed virtually all of the German manufacturing capacity. Despite the German war effort, Hitler actually increased the murder of Jews and others in concentration camps while resisting the Allied offensive. Turning to the D-Day invasion, Germany was afforded four-plus years to fortify the Atlantic coast of France. The devastating losses suffered on D-Day, especially by American troops, was largely caused by poor leadership from Eisenhower compounded by the long delay between France's fall and the U.S. and British arrival on the Normandy beaches. Germany defended itself from heavily fortified concrete bunkers that were built over a long period of time. In both the south and the north, the time for Germany and Italy to prepare for the Allied counteroffensive was afforded them by Roosevelt's delay.

On the political front, Roosevelt brought Stalin in as an equal with Winston Churchill and himself. Stalin was never an equal to any British or American leader. The price the world and America paid for Stalin's "support" was giving the U.S.S.R. most of Eastern Europe after the war ended. Stalin reportedly murdered more during his reign of terror behind the "Iron Curtain" after WWII than Hitler murdered (Stein, 2004). Further, the entire "Cold War" was the result of Roosevelt's incompetence. There never would have been a Cold War had Stalin been treated as the two-faced dictator that he was. While the war with Germany might have lasted a few months longer without the U.S.S.R.'s support on the Eastern Front, the price paid by America and the citizens of Europe was far too great—both during the war and for forty years after the war.

We judge a great leader by the results obtained, both short-term and long-term. Roosevelt failed both tests in his domestic and international policies. Perhaps as history has time to reevaluate his presidency, a more accurate picture will emerge. When that happens, the embarrassing two-block monument to this failed leader in Washington, D.C., will be removed.

Roosevelt Grade: D-

CHAPTER 7
HARRY S. TRUMAN

(Gatteri, 1945 ca.)

Harry S. Truman (1884–1972) became the thirty-third president of the U.S. upon the sudden death of Franklin Roosevelt in April 1945. The "S." does not stand for a name. He has only an S for his middle name (Giglio, 2016). A Democrat, he completed Roosevelt's term and then won a surprise victory for a second term in 1948 promoting his "Fair Deal" as a continuation of Roosevelt's "New Deal." His VP was Alben Barkley from 1949 to 1953. Truman did not go to college. He attended high school in Independence, Missouri (Helicher, 1984).

Truman's wife from 1919 to his death was Elizabeth Virginia "Bess" Truman. Truman, similar to Coolidge and Hoover, had no reported affairs (Maddox, 1990). Mrs. Truman was well-liked during her time as First Lady, although overshadowed by her high-profile predecessor, Eleanor Roosevelt. The most colorful aspect of Truman's personal life was the couple's only daughter, Margaret Truman, a singer, pianist, and later a novelist and historian. Given the exposure through the White House, she had a number of opportunities to perform on radio, television, and live (House, 1955). Her biographies of each of her parents received strong reviews.

OCCUPATIONAL ACCOMPLISHMENTS

Truman worked on the family farm, but also attempted a number of unsuccessful businesses. He received positive reports on his performance as a soldier during WWI.

He came to the attention of Thomas J. Pendergast, the Democratic boss of Kansas City, who asked Truman to become involved in local politics. Despite his low-key approach, he was later elected to the U.S. Senate in 1934 (Geselbracht, 2006). In most ways, Truman was the opposite of Roosevelt, coming from modest beginnings and a person who exemplified humility and established a connection to the "common man."

Truman was poorly positioned to assume the presidency (Morrissey, 1964). As a Senator, he had limited exposure to foreign affairs. He was put on the 1944 ballot as the political bosses thought they would be able to manipulate him. He did not know of the Manhattan Project, the secret project that led to the development of the atomic bomb, at the time he became president. Truman had a Democrat majority in Congress to start, then a Republican majority from 1947–1949, with Democrats in the majority again for his last four years (Bernstein, 1988). He appointed four members of the U.S. Supreme Court, with perhaps the best-known being Truman's Attorney General, Tom Clark. Clark, who generally leaned toward the liberal view, served for the next eighteen years (U.S. Senate, n.d.).

SIGNIFICANT EVENTS DURING TRUMAN'S TIME IN OFFICE

1945

- Roosevelt dies and Truman becomes president.
- Germany's unconditional surrender
- The Potsdam Conference
- Atomic bombs dropped on Hiroshima and Nagasaki, Japan
- Japan's unconditional surrender
- U.S. joins the newly formed United Nations.

1946

- Wave of strike activity cripples the American economy.

1947

- The Labor-Management Relations Act, also known as Taft-Hartley Act, passed
- "Truman Doctrine" to provide resources to American allies to fight Communism
- National Security Act passed, creating the CIA and Department of Defense

1948

- Cold war begins in earnest with the U.S.S.R.
- Truman elected in a surprise victory promoting the "Fair Deal."
- Truman orders U.S. Armed Forces to desegregate through Executive Order 9981.

1949

- NATO formed
- Germany divided into East and West
- Mao declares creation of the Marxist People's Republic of China.

1950

- China and U.S.S.R. agree to Sino-Soviet Alliance.
- Korean Conflict begins.
- Assassination attempt on Truman by Puerto Rican nationalists

1951

- Truman removes Gen. MacArthur from Korean battlefront.
- Seoul falls to Chinese and then retaken by Allied forces

1952

- Truman seizes control of the steel industry.
- The Immigration and Nationality Act of 1952 (The McCarran-Walter Act) passed

THE DOMESTIC FRONT AND RACE RELATIONS

The domestic front was not kind to Truman. Following the end of WWII, the American economy was hobbled by a record level of strike activity. Truman was heavily indebted to the unions for their support of the Democratic party. He needed their support for his campaign in 1948. He also needed a strong economy to adjust the U.S. to peacetime (Richter & Montgomery, 1994). The labor strife and the relationship between the unions and the Democratic party may have led to the major reversal between Democrat and Republican control of Congress in the 1946 midterm elections. Following those elections, Congress pushed through the Taft-Hartley Act, 29 U.S.C. 186 (1947), which balanced the very pro-union National Labor Relations Act of 1935. The new act limited some union actions, allowed states to pass "Right to Work" laws, and banned "closed shops," where employees could be forced to join unions in order to work (Fenton, 1959). While Truman reportedly was upset with the unions for their actions during WWII and following the war, he vetoed the act. The GOP-controlled Congress quickly overrode his veto.

Truman compounded his labor issues following the 1948 election. Viewing his victory as an endorsement of his Fair Deal campaign, he continued to follow a pro-labor agenda. Truman introduced new price and labor controls in 1950. The steel industry faced a tough challenge where the heavily unionized steel workers wanted raises and the steel industry was only willing to grant the raises if they could in turn raise the price of steel. Truman, in a surprise action reminiscent of Roosevelt, seized control of the steel industry rather than risk a strike. The issue was quickly taken to a U.S. District Court, which ruled his action unconstitutional. This court ruling was affirmed by the U.S. Supreme Court. With the government seizure released, a long strike ensued (Miller Center of Public Affairs, University of Virginia, n.d.a).

RACE RELATIONS

Truman may justifiably be regarded as the first true advocate for civil rights in the White House. He proposed a civil rights act in 1948. This followed on the heels of his Executive Order 9981, which ordered desegregation of the U.S. military and U.S. civil service employment ("Executive Order 9981," n.d.). He faced opposition from his own party as Southern Democrats, also known as "Dixiecrats," fought any effort to provide equal employment and housing opportunities for blacks (Bartley, 1995). Major League Baseball, not without controversy, broke the color barrier when Jackie Robinson joined the Brooklyn Dodgers, the first black to play a major pro sport (Miller Center of Public Affairs, University of Virginia, n.d.a).

Despite the fact that the GI Bill was enacted in 1944 while Roosevelt was still in office, it is often tied to Truman since the bulk of returning vets used their education and housing benefits after the end of WWII. The GI Bill is rarely presented as a racial issue. A little told story was that the bill was unevenly administered between black and white veterans. White vets were referred to colleges, while black vets were usually referred for good, but still lower-paid, craft or vocational training (Humes, 2006).

The Immigration and Nationality Act of 1952 (The McCarran-Walter Act), 8 U.S.C. §§ 1101-1537, generally extended the racial quotas established by the 1924 Immigration Act. There was an interest in supporting family unity and a new focus on admission by immigrants possessing certain skills. The Cold War brought about a concern over national security in immigration policy. The new balancing act included concern that by limiting immigration to certain Western and Northern European countries, the U.S. was alienating persons in the rest of the world, including Eastern Europe and Asia. There were very low quotas for Asians and a bias toward the current ethnic composition of the U.S. Truman opposed the law, though it was proposed by Democrat leaders, because it continued the current bias toward European Americans. His veto was overturned by a bipartisan vote in Congress ("The Immigration and Nationality Act of 1952," n.d.).

THE TRUMAN INTERNATIONAL RECORD

The Potsdam Conference in July 1945 was Truman's first exposure to world politics. Truman met with Churchill, who was replaced by new British Prime Minister Clement Attlee during the conference, and Stalin. The latter was treated as an equal to the leaders of Britain and the U.S. The purpose of the conference was to determine the borders of Europe following the fall of Germany. The conference was unsuccessful in resolving a variety of issues, including Stalin's desire to extract reparations from Germany and ultimately, the seizing of Eastern Europe by the U.S.S.R (Xidis, 1992).

Perhaps the most significant acts by Truman during his nearly eight years in office were the atomic bombs dropped on Hiroshima and Nagasaki. This was a difficult choice, balancing the estimated 200,000 deaths of Allied soldiers by continuing battles through the South Pacific, ultimately leading to taking the Japanese home islands. In turn, the atomic weapons killed approximately 200,000 Japanese within a few days, but brought an immediate and unconditional surrender by Japan. (Albert, 1987). The majority of Americans supported that decision, especially in light of the sneak attack on Pearl Harbor and then the Bataan Death March that illustrated the cruelty of the Japanese military to the captured Allied troops (Lee, 1987).

Dealing with a dangerous post-WWII world was a concern of Truman. He proposed the "Truman Doctrine" in 1947. The policy allowed the U.S. to provide financial support to allies that were fighting against Communism. The first objective was to provide financial support to Turkey and Greece to keep them independent from the U.S.S.R. (Jackson, 2003). The Marshall Plan was adopted to help Europe recover from the ravages of war. This incredibly successful plan was based on avoiding the excessive "reparations" demanded of Germany following WWI. Hitler campaigned against those punishing financial penalties, aiding in his rise to power (Bernstein, 1998).

Roosevelt's failure to appreciate Stalin's imperialist objectives positioned Stalin to claim numerous countries for the U.S.S.R. As a participant in the Potsdam Conference, an inexperienced Truman lent tacit approval to Stalin's continued aggression toward Eastern Europe, and divided control of Germany among the Allied powers, including Stalin. In 1948, the U.S.S.R. closed the roadways to the capital city of Berlin, which was located in East Germany. The objective was to get Britain, France, and the U.S. to cede the other half of Berlin to the U.S.S.R. The famed Berlin Airlift continued for over a year until the U.S.S.R. relented and opened the roadways supplying the city (Calabresi & Yoo, 2008). In 1961, the U.S.S.R. constructed a wall, further separating the two parts of the city of Berlin.

In China, the truce declared between the Nationalist and Communist parties during the Japanese invasion dissolved with Japan's defeat by the Allies. With the victory of Mao's Communist Party in 1948, Chiang Kai-shek retreated to the island of Taiwan, surrendering the vast mainland of China to Mao (Office of the Historian, n.d.). Mao's victory was to very quickly cost lives and resources as North Korea, supported by Mao's government, invaded South Korea in 1950 (Daugherty & Bowden, 2004). This shortly followed the Sino-Soviet Agreement where the two Marxist powers agreed to mutual defense and cooperation (Kaple, 2015).

Often referred to as the "Korean Conflict," there was never a formal declaration of war. Nor was there ever a formal treaty ending the conflict (Helicher, 1984). General Douglas MacArthur, famed for his leadership in reclaiming the South Pacific during WWII, took control of the U.S. and UN forces defending South Korea from the aggression from the North. MacArthur advocated a full conquest of North Korea, as had been the case with Japan, Germany, and Italy. Truman decided to seek a truce rather than continue the battle. When MacArthur resisted the direction from Truman and publicly expressed his disagreement, he was removed by Truman. The American public supported MacArthur. The two factions fought to a stalemate around the historic border between North and South Korea and there was never a satisfactory final resolution (Miller Center of Public Affairs, n.d.a). The Korean Conflict and the internal dispute with MacArthur may have been a key consideration in Truman's decision to not seek a second full term in 1952. Truman's failure in Korea looms large in the present day with North Korea developing nuclear weapons and the missiles to deliver them.

BY THE NUMBERS

The national debt held fairly steady during the Truman years (U.S. Department of the Treasury, Bureau of the Fiscal Service, 2013):

Year	National Debt
1945	$258,682,187,409
1946	$269,422,099,173
1947	$258,286,383,108
1948	$252,292,246,512
1949	$252,770,359,860
1950	$257,357,352,351
1951	$255,221,976,814
1952	$259,105,178,785

The failure to reduce the national debt during the late 1940s when the U.S. had a surging economy and was not at war reflected Truman's Fair Deal agenda to expand expenditures rather than pay down the debt.

Reviewing the annual inflation rates from 1945 through 1953 indicates a "roller coaster" economy going from low to high to low inflation rates.

The union activism in 1945–1946 can be credited with the surge in inflation in 1947 and 1948. The surge in 1951 was due to spending for the Korean Conflict (Coin News Media Group LLC, n.d.):

Year	Inflation Rate
1945	2.3%
1946	2.2%
1947	18.1%
1948	10.2%
1949	1.3%
1950	-2.1%
1951	8.1%
1952	4.3%
1953	0.4%

MAKING THE GRADE

Truman, perhaps more than any president discussed in this book, represents the cliché, "What you see is what you get." While many may disagree with some of his decisions, he stood steadfast in his positions. As a private person, he had many admirable traits. He exhibited an unusual humility for someone serving as president. He appeared to be consistently truthful in his actions and statements.

His public ethics were consistent and showed a concern both for the poor and minorities. Truman's push for civil rights and his desegregation of the military and civil service by executive order was the most significant individual effort at improving racial equality by any American president up to that time.

His loyalty to the unions was part of his undoing. The unions pushed to take advantage of his support and to extract a sad "quid pro quo" for their political support. Truman's economy was marked by extreme union strife despite his consistent public support for unions.

On the international scene, Truman's bold decision to use the atomic bomb to quickly end the war in the Pacific was without equal. The Marshall Plan and the restoration of rights to Japan and Germany marked true diplomacy of the first order. On the other hand, Truman's failures in international relations closely tracked his predecessor. He continued Roosevelt's unwarranted trust in the U.S.S.R., which led to the near enslavement of much of Eastern Europe for approximately forty years. It is unclear if, at the time he took over from Roosevelt, whether a serious effort to help Chiang Kai-shek might have changed the course of history in China. An argument could be made that the better approach when the U.S.S.R. closed the roadway to Berlin would have been decisive military action that might have avoided the Cold War.

The Korean Conflict was another black eye for Truman. Unfortunately for America, this began a series of significant losses of American lives, lost respect for America across the world, and billions of dollars of resources fought in losing battles. No matter how this is viewed, MacArthur's approach of defeating the North Koreans and the Chinese was the correct approach. North Korea's testing of nuclear weapons and missiles in the 21st century is an example of the outcome when an enemy is not defeated. At the same time, when MacArthur refused to follow the direction of the President, his Commander in Chief, Truman's decision to remove him was unquestionably the right decision. MacArthur was right about the war, but wrong in not obeying the chain of command.

The various presidential popularity surveys continue to move Truman up the ratings, although the surveys consistently show an extreme liberal bias. One recent poll puts him at the No. 6 position of all American presidents (Rottinghaus, B. & Vaughn, 2015). Losing the Korean Conflict and not taking on communist aggression in a more effective manner is rarely addressed in such surveys and pandering to unions despite their misbehavior is also not addressed.

Truman Grade: B-

CHAPTER 8

DWIGHT D. EISENHOWER

(Bachrach, 1952)

Dwight David Eisenhower (1890–1969), popularly known as "Ike," was elected the thirty-fourth president of the U.S. He was widely promoted as a "hero" of WWII, as the "Supreme Commander of the Allied Forces in Europe" (U.S. Army Center for Military History, 2006). Eisenhower was considered apolitical. He ran as a Republican and won a solid victory in 1952 and then won in 1956 with an even larger margin, despite only modest progress during his first term. His VP for his entire term was Richard M. Nixon, who himself was elected president in 1968. A career military man, Eisenhower graduated from the Military Academy at West Point (Miller Center of Public Affairs, University of Virginia, n.d.a; Kelly, 2016)

Eisenhower's wife from 1916 to his death was Mary Geneva Doud Eisenhower, known to the public as "Mamie" (Miller Center of Public Affairs, University of Virginia, n.d.a). Mamie was well-liked during and following Eisenhower's time in office and enjoyed a popularity similar to Bess Truman, who preceded her as First Lady. Eisenhower reportedly had a long-running affair with his WWII chauffeur, Kay Summersby (Kifner, 1991). The pair were extremely close during the war, although there is some dispute about the secrecy of the relationship. One report was that Eisenhower was ready to divorce Mamie and marry Summersby, but he was stopped by the head of the Army in Washington, D.C., General George Marshall (Kifner). The latter became well-known after the war as the architect of the European recovery, "The Marshall Plan." Consistent with the news coverage of several presidents reviewed in this book, the affair was not extensively reported until Summersby released a deathbed confession in 1975: *Past Forgetting: My Love Affair with Dwight D. Eisenhower* (Morgan & Wyden, 1977).

OCCUPATIONAL ACCOMPLISHMENTS

An evaluation of Eisenhower's accomplishments as president must start with why he was elected. The great myth about Eisenhower that helped propel him into the White House was that he was America's great military leader who won the war in Europe. While it is unquestionable that America won the war with the help of its beleaguered allies, especially Britain and the rest of the United Kingdom, Eisenhower's role was blown out of proportion by misguided historians and the media. It is understandable that during WWII the media and public wanted to show consistent momentum and support for its military leaders. The failure to tell the whole story for at least two generations is not easy to overlook.

Quotes from the field generals of WWII tell the real story:

○ Field Marshal Lord Montgomery said of Eisenhower: "Nice chap, no general."

○ Field Marshal Lord Alanbrooke wrote in his diary on December 28, 1942, that Eisenhower as a general was "hopeless. He submerges himself in politics and neglects his military duties, partly...because he knows little if anything about military matters."

○ General George Patton once lamented that it was too bad that Eisenhower had no personal knowledge of war.

○ General Omar Bradley would write that Eisenhower "had little grasp of sound battlefield tactics."

○ American Admiral John Hall, the commander of Amphibious Force "O," which landed the 1st Division at Omaha Beach, wrote that Eisenhower "was one of the most overrated men in military history." (Edwards, 2016)

Aside from the quotes above, objective information supports such opinions. Eisenhower was widely credited as the mastermind of Operation Overlord, which included the D-Day Invasion. The appeasement policy of Neville Chamberlain and Franklin Roosevelt gave Germany a huge head start in defending its conquered territory in Europe. The extensive concrete batteries installed for miles along the Atlantic coast, many of which can still be seen today, document the failure of America to enter the war at an earlier point. That delay was not Eisenhower's fault. However, the poorly designed invasion of the beaches of Normandy that led to the death of several thousand American soldiers on Omaha Beach speaks poorly of Eisenhower's tactics and strategy (Warren, 2014).

The Allies had an enormous lead by D-Day in almost complete air superiority, manpower, and armaments. Despite this advantage, poor planning under Eisenhower led to far too many deaths and wasted resources (Ednie, 1944). The failure of planning is further documented by the Battle of the Bulge ("The Bloodiest Battle," 2014). Poorly-supported Allied troops were overrun in a last-ditch German counterattack that should never have happened (Wheeler, 2015).

Eisenhower was a career military man, which meant he was employed by the military, not that he was a battlefield commander. He was credited even by his critics as understanding the Washington, D.C. political realities. He might have used that political savvy to good use. An objective evaluation of Eisenhower's two terms does not suggest an effective use of those talents.

SIGNIFICANT EVENTS DURING EISENHOWER'S TIME IN OFFICE

1953
- Eisenhower signs the Armistice ending Korean Conflict.
- CIA coup installs Shah of Iran.

1954
- Geneva Convention leads to divided Vietnam.
- CIA leads coup in Guatemala.

1955
- *Brown v. Board of Education* ends "separate, but equal" education.

1956
- Federal Aid Highway Act creates the Interstate Highway System.

- The Suez Crisis
- *Browder v. Gayle*: U.S. Supreme Court ends Bus Segregation.

1957

- Eisenhower sends troops to Little Rock, Arkansas, to enforce integration.
- "Eisenhower Doctrine" announced
- U.S.S.R. launches *Sputnik,* starting the "Space Race."

1958

- Alaska becomes the 49th state.
- U.S. forces enter Lebanon.
- NASA created to move U.S. into space.

1959

- Castro ousts U.S.-backed Batista in Cuba.
- Hawaii becomes 50th state.

1960

- Francis Gary Powers, as the pilot of the U-2 spy plane, is shot down over Soviet airspace.
- The Kennedy-Nixon televised presidential debates

THE DOMESTIC FRONT AND RACE RELATIONS

America in the 1950s was an interesting place. Senator Joe McCarthy (R-WI) kept the attention of many Americans by supposedly exposing significant communist infiltration of the Department of Defense, military contractors, and the entertainment industry. Frequently referred to as a "witch hunt," an environment of fear pervaded the U.S. (History.com staff, 2009.c). The internal fear was being accused of being a Communist, or of America becoming infested with communist spies.

This fear was expanded into an external threat later in the 1950s as the U.S. became home to black and yellow metal signs marking "Bomb Shelters," and school children engaged in drills to hide under their desks in the event of a nuclear attack (Wuthnow, 2010). The fact that a "war hero" was in the White House did not seem to make much of a difference.

(Civil Defense Museum, n.d.)

On the domestic front, the economy struggled to recover from the expense of the Korean Conflict and the defense spending triggered by the Cold War. The U.S. was making significant gains in civil rights. Eisenhower deserves credit for continuing Truman's efforts in desegregating the military, despite his failure to do so during WWII. The U.S. Supreme Court ruled in *Brown v. Board of Education* (1954) that separate was not equal in education regarding the schools in Topeka, Kansas (Administrative Office of the U.S. Courts, n.d.; Bledsoe, 1951). The high court also ruled that segregation in transportation was unconstitutional in *Browder v. Gayle*, (352 U.S. 903, 1956; Huston, 1956). Eisenhower sent troops into Little Rock, Arkansas, to enforce the desegregation ruling (Eisenhower, 1957.a).

The first boost to post-WWII America was the GI Bill. It helped launch an educated American population that surged ahead of the rest of the world during the mid-1940s through the 1950s (Smith, 2016). The second boost was the Eisenhower administration's Interstate Highway System. This system was presented as part of the preparation of the U.S. to defend itself in the event of a hostile invasion (Cox & Love, 1996; Eisenhower, 1955). While that invasion did not come to pass, the construction of the highway system made American economic expansion possible. The third boost to the American economy grew out of a surprise source. The U.S.S.R. launched Sputnik in 1957, the first satellite in outer space (Pearson, n.d.b). The "Space Race" was on! A year later, Eisenhower created an agency that grew into NASA (History.com staff, 2010). The U.S. provided an additional education boost with the National Defense Education Act of 1958, which created a direct federal loan program for college students (New America.org, n.d.). The underlying rationale for the Act was that America needed more scientists to help win the Space Race. This enabled millions more Americans who were not veterans to go to college. Some attribute the federal involvement in making student loans readily available to the incredible increase in higher education costs. Excessive federal and state regulations and standards are more likely the cause.

THE EISENHOWER INTERNATIONAL RECORD

Entering office at the height of the Cold War, Eisenhower compounded Truman's error by signing off on the Korean Truce. In fairness to Eisenhower, he may have felt that Truman situated the deal in such a way that he did not have a choice but to agree. The truce, strongly criticized by MacArthur, enhanced the position of China. China, through its puppet, North Korea, had fought the most powerful country on earth essentially to a draw. The boost externally and internally to China from the outcome of the Korean Conflict is still being felt by the U.S. and the world today.

During much of his time in office, Eisenhower tried to thwart the spread of Communism in the world. The Refugee Act of 1953 was designed to provide a safe destination for political escapees and others fleeing communist oppression (Eisenhower, 1953). Eisenhower espoused the "Eisenhower Doctrine," which stood for a three-part plan of action:

Support any country in the Middle East trying to fight Communism;

Help other countries around the world fight Communism; and

Assistance may include direct military intervention as well as economic assistance (Eisenhower, 1957.b).

Eisenhower explained: "Unless we can put things in the hands of people who are starving to death we can never lick Communism" (Ryan, 1993).

Eisenhower's diplomatic efforts during his administration were less than stellar. Representatives of the U.S., Britain, France, U.S.S.R., and People's Republic of China (PRC), referred to during this time as "Red China," met in 1954 to discuss various issues. The French brought in the issue of Vietnam ("The Geneva Conference, Final Declaration" 1954). At Geneva, the French were attempting to maintain Vietnam as a French colony, but were facing stiff opposition from Communist forces under the leadership of Ho Chi Minh. The French were ready to abandon Vietnam, but the U.S. was concerned that this would merely hand over the country to the Communists to use as a foothold in Southeast Asia. An agreement to divide the country into North and South at the 17th Parallel was reached. National elections were supposed to be held, but the U.S. feared that this would still result in a Communist takeover. The U.S. then entered Vietnam and helped install a provisional government in the South. The U.S. entry into the "Vietnam War," as it was later called, actually began under Eisenhower, not under Kennedy or Johnson (Eisenhower, 1954; History.com staff, 2009.a).

By this time, France could hardly be regarded as a world power, having just lost Vietnam and overrun by Germany in both world wars. This was to be the only meeting between Eisenhower and the U.S.S.R's Nikita Khrushchev. The stated purpose of the meeting was to reduce the tensions of the Cold War. Issues like reunification of Germany and disarmament were on the agenda ("Summit Conferences - Dwight D. Eisenhower," 2016; "Geneva Summit," 2016). Eisenhower's personal popularity soared to 79 percent, as the American public was told he was tough with the U.S.S.R. in the meetings (Pew Research Center, 2016). The reality is that nothing was accomplished but the elevation in status of the U.S.S.R. as an equal world power.

During the second half of the Eisenhower administration, the world rocked from crisis to crisis. In the Suez Crisis in 1956, Israel, backed by Britain and France, engaged in a ground war with Egypt. A critical waterway, the Suez Canal had been controlled by Britain since 1936. Egyptian President Nasser nationalized the canal, triggering the military engagement. Nasser was upset that the U.S. had refused to help finance a major capital project, the Aswan Dam. Ultimately the U.S.S.R. financed the dam. In an odd alignment of powers, the U.S. and the U.S.S.R. were united against the invading forces of Britain and France and forced them to withdraw.

During this brief time, Khrushchev threatened to use nuclear weapons, but was rebuffed by Eisenhower. While it was widely believed that by 1956 the U.S.S.R. had the atomic bomb, it is unlikely that it had the ability to use tactical nuclear weapons as Khrushchev had threatened. The Aswan Dam project marked an important aspect of the Cold War. The "war" was not just about guns. There was the financial aspect of "buying friends." Many reviewers of the Cold War period have opined that the U.S.S.R. actually did a better job of buying friends than the U.S. (History.com staff, 2009.e).

In 1958, the PRC attacked islands controlled by Taiwan, challenging a U.S. ally. In what nearly turned into a nuclear war, the Taiwan air force went head to head, in planes supplied by the U.S., with Chinese pilots and were successful. The U.S. sent naval forces to the area and despite the U.S.S.R.'s backing of the PRC, the PRC eventually realized that they could not win against a U.S. ally supported by the might of the U.S. ("Second Taiwan Strait Crisis," 2011; The Cold War Museum, n.d.). This is a classic example of the need for the U.S. to provide timely and unequivocal support for its allies, and the result was a rare positive international outcome for Eisenhower.

In 1958, Eisenhower authorized a brief military intervention in Lebanon. The country was controlled by Christians, but the Muslim majority felt that they should have control. This position was driven by the anti-Western Egyptian President Nasser, emboldened by an apparent "win" in the Suez Crisis (Sibilla, n.d.). The U.S. eventually removed its land forces, further damaging its reputation in the Middle East. The anti-U.S. movement across much of the Middle East can be traced to the post-WWII time period and particularly Eisenhower's administration.

Cuba, an island fewer than 90 miles from the U.S. mainland, was taken over by the Communist forces of Fidel Castro during the late 1950s.

Castro overthrew the incompetent and corrupt dictator Fulgencio Batista. Batista was nominally supported by the U.S. (History.com staff, 2009.b) but allowed the Mob to run casinos, prostitution, and drugs on the island. Castro provided the U.S.S.R. a convenient base both to attack and to spy on the U.S. Among a host of international failures during the Eisenhower administration, this was perhaps the most costly. The loss underscores another failure of American diplomacy during the one hundred-year focus of this book: support for corrupt leaders like Batista.

In a rare bit of levity, in 1959, VP Nixon met in the model kitchen display with Khrushchev when both were attending the American National Exhibition in Moscow. The exhibit was part of an attempt to reduce the tensions of the Cold War by exchanging lifestyle exhibits. The two supposedly met by accident and engaged in what is reported to have been a very heated exchange about the relative merits of the two countries and their political systems (History.com staff, 2009.d). The outcome of this meeting may have propelled Nixon into the GOP presidential candidacy in 1960.

On Capitol Hill, despite Eisenhower's personal popularity, Democrats continually gained ground politically. The pattern of a supposedly popular president paired by the voters with a Congress of the opposite party is repeated many times in recent U.S. history.

BY THE NUMBERS

Eisenhower added to the national debt level, largely after the Korean Conflict, so he could not use war spending as an excuse (U.S. Department of the Treasury, Bureau of the Fiscal Service, 2013):

Year	National Debt
1953	$266,071,061,638
1954	$271,259,599,108
1955	$274,374,222,802
1956	$272,750,813,649
1957	$270,527,171,896
1958	$276,343,217,745
1959	$284,705,907,078
1960	$286,330,760,848

Given that economists recommend an inflation rate of at least 2.0 percent to show an expanding economy, the 1950s were clearly not a time of rapid growth with only two years in eight over 2 percent (Coin News Media Group LLC, 2017):

Year	Inflation Rate
1953	0.8%
1954	0.7%
1955	-0.4%
1956	1.5%
1957	3.3%
1958	2.8%
1959	0.7%
1960	1.7%

MAKING THE GRADE

Various recent opinion surveys referred to our next president, John Kennedy, as one of the "most overrated" presidents in U.S. history.

Interestingly, Eisenhower usually ends up in the middle: not bad, not good. Reviewing the hard facts and outcomes discussed above, Eisenhower seems to have been given a "pass" from the media and many historians. He was neither a war hero, nor a success in world affairs during his presidency. His economic record is not remarkable. His reputation is established with a handful of domestic accomplishments, including progress in race relations driven by U.S. Supreme Court decisions and two voting rights acts, the U.S. Interstate Highway System, and starting the U.S. space program.

Eisenhower can hardly earn good ratings for internal ethics because of his relationship with Kay Summersby. His public ethics are buoyed by his support for the voting rights acts and supporting with action the major Supreme Court decisions regarding the illegality of segregation. This is countered by his leadership of a segregated armed forces during WWII.

In international affairs, his administration continued the generally disastrous record of his predecessors. Rolling from confirming the loss of the Korean Conflict, through failed efforts in Vietnam, Lebanon, and the Suez Crisis, he ended his administration with an inexplicable loss in Cuba.

The 1950s was a time of financial hardship for many with a slow economy for most of Eisenhower's administration. Fear dominated much of the decade, ranging from fear of being accused of being a Communist to being a victim of a communist nuclear attack. "Troubled Times" and not "Happy Days," might have been a better title for the Eisenhower administration.

Eisenhower Grade: D

CHAPTER 9
JOHN F. KENNEDY

(Stoughton, 1963)

John Fitzgerald Kennedy (1917–1963), popularly known as "JFK," was elected the thirty-fifth president of the U.S. in 1960. A Democrat, he won a narrow victory over Richard Nixon, Eisenhower's VP (Office of the Federal Register, n.d.). He was the first Catholic to be elected president (Freidel & Sidey, 2006). Kennedy famously was at odds with his VP, Lyndon Johnson, and rumors were that he would not be Kennedy's VP for a second term. Kennedy's assassination in November 1963, in Dallas, ended that speculation and elevated Johnson to the presidency (Caro, 2012).

Kennedy's wife from 1953 to his death was Jacqueline Bouvier, also known to the public as "Jackie" (Fenn, 1979). Their brief period in the White House was labeled by the media as "Camelot," implying that

America had a couple who matched with the legendary royal couple in the romantic Lerner and Loewe musical (Cosgrove, 2013). Unlike the musical, as the real story unfolded over the subsequent decades, there was nothing especially romantic about Kennedy's time in the White House. Kennedy was a reported "womanizer" associated with a number of paramours (Stevenson, 2013).

OCCUPATIONAL ACCOMPLISHMENTS

Kennedy's father, Joseph Kennedy, was a major business success and had close connections throughout the country. Kennedy attended the Choate School in Connecticut, an exclusive boarding school (The History Place™, 2015). While many associate the Kennedys with Harvard, Kennedy actually started college at Princeton. He left during his freshman year with chronic medical issues (The Trustees of Princeton University, 2011). After extensive medical treatment, he enrolled in Harvard, where he graduated in 1940 (Freidel & Sidey, 2006).

Kennedy served as a lieutenant in the Navy during WWII. His exploits were recounted in the 1962 movie *PT 109*, starring Cliff Robertson as Kennedy (Johnson, 2013). Kennedy's father used his Hollywood contacts to push to get the movie made as a publicity push for his son's reelection campaign. He was actively involved, making JFK appear more heroic. This was not a documentary and it was not a commercial success, despite its association with the popular president.

Injuries sustained during the PT 109 episode further complicated Kennedy's earlier chronic illness, which was later diagnosed as Addison's disease, a serious hormonal illness (Maugh, 2009; Mayo Clinic Staff, 2015). Kennedy claimed to be in good health while running for office. This is despite the fact that Kennedy had trouble standing upright and had to wear a special support garment similar to a woman's girdle to support his back and torso (Caro, 2012). Later in his life, it was discovered that cortisone injections could alleviate some of the symptoms of the disease and he began to receive secret injections in an attempt to hide his disability from the public (Caro).

Returning from WWII service, Kennedy entered politics in his home state of Massachusetts, serving six years as a congressman and then elected twice to the U.S. Senate before he was elected president. One of his more interesting accomplishments during this time was winning the Pulitzer Prize for his 1957 book, *Profiles in Courage* (Miller Center of Public Affairs, University of Virginia, 2015). His congressional attendance was poor due to surgeries and illness. In addition, he was working to raise his national recognition, always focused on achieving the presidency

Other than the American tragedy of his assassination, Kennedy was well-known for his inauguration. The day was marked by a major snowstorm that blanketed Washington, D.C., and much of the Northeast. Kennedy famously said during his inaugural address: "Ask not what your country can do for you -ask what you can do for your country" (Kennedy, 1961). Kennedy enjoyed a Democratic majority in Congress (Office of the Historian, n.d.). Congress under his leadership established the Peace Corps, designed to send young American volunteers overseas to help people in undeveloped countries. This helped to balance the U.S.S.R.'s success in "buying friends."

SIGNIFICANT EVENTS DURING KENNEDY'S TIME IN OFFICE

1961

- Bay of Pigs invasion
- Kennedy commits to landing a man on the Moon within the decade.
- U.S.S.R. begins construction of the Berlin Wall.
- Kennedy commits to an "independent" Vietnam
- U.S.S.R. puts first man in space.

1962

- Court orders University of Mississippi to admit black student, James Meredith.
- "Cuban Missile Crisis"
- U.S. lands rocket on Moon.
- John Glenn becomes first American to orbit Earth.

1963

- U.S.S.R. and U.S. agree on nuclear test ban treaty.
- Kennedy is assassinated during campaign stop in Dallas.

THE DOMESTIC FRONT AND RACE RELATIONS

Kennedy's administration appears to have been truly interested in achieving better race relations in the U.S. While Johnson received credit for maneuvering the 1964 Civil Rights Act through Congress, in fact, Kennedy pioneered the law that Johnson eventually passed. Kennedy's time in office was marked by the first black man to attend the University of Mississippi, James Meredith, following a court order to the school to admit him. His attendance spurred riots during 1962, which were only quelled when federal troops went to the campus to provide security for Meredith (Evans, 1965). Kennedy's time in office was also marred by the 1963 tragedy of four girls murdered in a bomb attack on a black church in Alabama. The attack was attributed to a Klu Klux Klan member and three thugs associated with him. Initially not prosecuted, allegedly due to the intervention of J. Edgar Hoover of the FBI, three of the four conspirators eventually were sent to prison (History.com staff, 2010).

Although the Space Race began under Eisenhower, Kennedy is associated with unequivocal leadership in setting the standard of a man on the Moon within a decade. In just a short period of time, the U.S. surpassed the U.S.S.R., which had launched first. The key early moment was when John Glenn successfully orbited Earth in 1962. Each space-bound liftoff at that time was broadcast live on television as Americans became familiar with the "5-4-3-2-1" countdown.

Kennedy's initiative for the poor was the "New Frontier" program. The idea was to provide basic services for the poor and increase provision of medical care for the poor and elderly (Dove, 2008). He was an early advocate of welfare reform. Kennedy pushed for a change in depreciation rules to allow businesses to recover capital expenditures more quickly and thereby encourage businesses to invest. Kennedy also reduced tax rates in an effort to stimulate the economy. Such ideas were subsequently associated with Republican lawmakers, so it is notable that this was prompted by a Democrat.

During his short time in office, he made two U.S. Supreme Court appointments: Arthur Goldberg and Byron White. Neither had a particularly remarkable record on the high court.

KENNEDY'S SCANDALS

As referenced previously, Kennedy was famous as a womanizer. While a more recent president is accused of a White House scandal with an intern, Kennedy reportedly had an affair with an intern 30 years earlier. Mimi Beardsley, then a freshman at Wheaton College in Massachusetts, reportedly had multiple sexual liaisons with Kennedy (Kiger, 2013). There are also persistent reports about two other aides or interns only identified as "Fiddle and Faddle" who reportedly entertained Kennedy frequently (Sabato, 2013).

A darker allegation of sexual misconduct involved Judith Campbell Exner. She claimed to have had an affair with Kennedy while he was in the White House while at the same time having trysts with reported Mafioso Sam Giancana. Both confidants of Kennedy and Giancana deny the relationship, but certain dates and facts may support some of her claims (Pace, 1999).

Even stranger was an alleged Kennedy affair with Mary Pinchot Meyer, who was a D.C. artist and the ex-wife of a C.I.A. operative. She was killed about a year after Kennedy's death. Her murder was never solved and reports are that her diary and other papers were deliberately destroyed (Morrow, 2008).

The most persistent and colorful tale about Kennedy's mistresses involved actress and femme fatale Marilyn Monroe. Their meeting came about since well-known British actor Peter Lawford, a brother-in-law of Kennedy, arranged a fundraising birthday party where Kennedy and the crowd on hand were treated to a special rendition of "Happy Birthday" by Monroe (Cosgrove, 2014). Lawford also was Kennedy's connection to singer-actor Frank Sinatra. While Sinatra consistently denied it, he was rumored to have some connection to the Mob (Fessier & Sun, 2015), potentially linking Kennedy to Mob connections. As of this writing, there is no proof of an actual sexual liaison between Monroe and Kennedy. In fact, both parties might have exploited the potential relationship for its publicity value.

THE KENNEDY INTERNATIONAL RECORD

It is often said that Kennedy possessed a special "charisma." In addition to his good looks and smooth upper-class Bostonian accent, he had a wit and polish about him that helped to make friends and to command attention (HealthResearchFunding.org, 2014). All the charisma in the world would not help cover his successive failures in Cuba. In the disastrous "Bay of Pigs" invasion, approximately fourteen hundred Cuban refugees were trained by the CIA, first under Eisenhower, and then Kennedy. They launched an attack on Cuba from the U.S. The expectation was that the U.S. would provide extensive military support to this force to oust Castro. In perhaps the biggest single military failure by any American president, the "invasion" did not last a day as the U.S. failed to support the attempted invasion. It was later reported that the attack never had a chance as the Cuban army had advance notice of the location of the attack and were braced for it (History.com staff, 2009). With regard to the withdrawal of support, the explanation was that Kennedy feared retaliation from the U.S.S.R. if the U.S. supported the invading force. This resulted in over a half century of communist rule just ninety miles from Florida. The U.S. withdrew any political contact with Cuba and ordered an end to imports of Cuban sugar and other goods to the U.S. This pushed Cuba toward the U.S.S.R. and gave Castro a convenient excuse for his own persistent economic failures. He blamed the U.S. boycott of Cuban goods for the island's economic malaise.

The second major failure of Kennedy regarding Cuba was the "Cuban Missile Crisis." In 1962, the U.S.S.R. began to install missile batteries in Cuba. These early installations were detected by American reconnaissance flights. Kennedy issued a warning to the U.S.S.R. to cease its efforts to arm Cuba with offensive nuclear weapons. He also ordered a naval "quarantine" around the island to prevent the delivery of the weapons. Ultimately, the U.S.S.R. appeared to back down (Office of the Historian, Bureau of Public Affairs, 1968). Some military observers believe that Cuba was quietly armed with offensive weapons after the crisis passed and most likely, as the U.S.S.R. experienced its financial meltdown in the 1980s, the necessary support for those weapons faded and they were no longer safe to use.

Ironically presented as a success of the Kennedy administration, similar to other failed actions by the U.S. presidents chronicled in this book, the Cuban Missile Crisis was the result of earlier poor decisions by Kennedy and his predecessors. America's failure to enter WWI and WWII in a timely manner and failure to support its ally in China before and after WWII are some other examples. There is no coherent reason why Cuba was left to its own devices and later the rule by Batista when another strategic island, Puerto Rico, was kept under American rule. Once this mistake had been made, there was still Kennedy's opportunity to support a full-scale invasion of the island. A repeated pattern becomes evident relating back to Wilson and Roosevelt of a failure to act by an American president, creating or expanding a crisis that allowed the same president to appear to be a hero when he eventually acted.

Kennedy continued his poor international record with America's first military involvement in Vietnam. This morphed over the administrations of Johnson and later Nixon into the "Vietnam War," although war was never declared. While the U.S. was distracted by Cuba and Vietnam, the U.S.S.R. took advantage of America's inaction to begin construction of the Berlin

Wall, separating its controlled East section from the American-controlled West section (Wood, 2013). The U.S.S.R. threatened to continue nuclear tests. One of Kennedy's few international accomplishments was reaching a nuclear test ban treaty with the U.S.S.R. (Burr & Montford, 2003). The two powers also established a "hot line" to establish immediate communication to avoid an accidental nuclear war (Preble, 2003).

BY THE NUMBERS

The national debt held fairly steady during the Kennedy years (U.S. Department of the Treasury, Bureau of the Fiscal Service, 2013):

Year	National Debt
1961	$288,970,938,610
1962	$298,200,822,720
1963	$305,859,632,996

In the current era, increases of a few billion dollars a year is not remarkable, although clearly there was no progress at reducing the debt during his presidency.

Using the inflation rate as one rough indicator of economic health, the Kennedy years were not very strong (Coin News Media Group LLC, 2017):

Year	Inflation Rate
1961	1.0%
1962	1.0%
1963	1.3%

Not a single year of his three years in office did the economy even reach the minimum economists target of 2 percent inflation.

MAKING THE GRADE

It is hard to evaluate a president with such a short time in office. Ironically, the other president with such a short term, during the one hundred-year period, was Harding. This was another three-year administration marked by scandals. In Harding's case, they involved his sexual indiscretions and his appointments. Kennedy is remembered today as a "womanizer" of the first order. Contrary to the Harding appointments—resulting in the "Teapot Dome Scandal"–Kennedy appointments seem to be scandal-free.

Evaluating a public figure with such a head start in terms of finances and a well-positioned family, it is fair to expect the best. Kennedy's private ethics were poor. He certainly did not set any basis for ethical leadership, not just for his sexual exploits, but also for his misrepresentation of his health. On the other hand, he did advocate for better opportunities for the poor and for civil rights. A number of political pundits have commented that while Kennedy initiated the Civil Rights Act of 1964, it is unlikely that he had the political savvy to get Congress to pass it (Matusow, 1983). That accomplishment is considered solely Lyndon Johnson's with his understanding of Washington and the political process. The enrollment of James Meredith at the University of Mississippi happened during Kennedy's administration, but was countered by the lack of prosecution during his administration for the church bombing in Birmingham.

On the international scene, Kennedy's back-to-back failures with Cuba mark his administration. The U.S.S.R. constructed the Berlin Wall, further emphasizing the lack of respect for the U.S. during this time. Kennedy is rarely credited with the dubious act of first sending U.S. troops to Vietnam.

When the public reviews that sad chapter in U.S. history, they usually think of Johnson and Nixon, but Kennedy, and to a lesser extent, Eisenhower, deserve their share of the blame. Kennedy's one shining success, although one he did not live to see accomplished, was to put the U.S. on track to go to the moon and to do so ahead of the U.S.S.R.

The various presidential ranking surveys indicate that Kennedy is overrated (Rottinghaus & Vaughn, 2015). Kennedy, according to Gallop polls, was the most popular president of any recent president with an amazing positive rating of 88 percent (Jones, 2003). Much of this can be attributed to his charisma, untimely death, and the media-promoted "Camelot" White House. The cold eye of history and actual accomplishments, the focus of this book, have begun to reach Kennedy in more recent media and academic reports. Given the early failures of his presidency, it is likely he would have had a real struggle to be reelected in 1964.

Kennedy Grade: D

CHAPTER 10
LYNDON B. JOHNSON

(Newman, 1964)

Lyndon Baines Johnson (1908–1973), popularly known as "LBJ," became the thirty-sixth president when John Kennedy was assassinated in Dallas, in LBJ's home state, in November 1963. Despite rumors of a continued class war between the Kennedys and Johnson, Johnson was able to quickly organize the Democratic party and voting base to win the 1964 presidential election. His election was over the Republican and reported hawk, Barry Goldwater of Arizona (Freidel & Sidey, 2006; Black, n.d.). Johnson's running mate was liberal Minnesota Senator Hubert H. Humphrey (History.com Staff, 2009). Despite the significant differences between them, Johnson accepted Humphrey as his running mate to balance the ticket and attract northern support for his campaign. Johnson surprised America when he announced as the 1968 campaign season began that he would not run, nor would he accept the nomination, if nominated (Billington, 1997).

Johnson married Claudia Alta Taylor in 1934. "Lady Bird," as she was affectionately known, was a popular first lady during the Johnson presidency (National First Ladies' Library, n.d.). They were married until Johnson's death. She had a fairly high profile during her time as First Lady and supported various causes, including public parks, education, and reducing poverty.

OCCUPATIONAL ACCOMPLISHMENTS

Johnson grew up in rural Texas with a father who swung from financial success some times to dirt broke at other times. Johnson recalled periods when his family relied on neighbors to provide food. The lack of stability and the concomitant lack of respect by his neighbors and friends haunted him for the rest of his life and is credited with prompting his single-minded pursuit of political success. After attending college at Southwest Texas State Teachers College, he later studied at Georgetown Law School (Caro, 1990).

While working as a congressional aide, he met Lady Bird and they were married shortly afterwards. She had some family money and her own holdings included a radio station and later, other media outlets. This provided a ready base of support for Johnson's political ambitions as well as personal funding he would not have had without her financial assets (National First Ladies' Library, n.d.). Johnson ran for Congress shortly after his marriage to Lady Bird and served in Congress from 1937 to 1949. During WWII, he had a brief stint in the military, careful to avoid any battlefront exposure. There is controversy surrounding the medal he allegedly won during this brief time. Members of Congress were called back to service in Washington and he ended his short stint (Caro, 2012). He was elected to the Senate, where he served until he became Kennedy's VP in the 1960 election (Bornet, 1990). Other than Lady Bird, the most important person in Johnson's rise to power was the powerful Speaker of the House, Sam Rayburn of Texas (Office of the Historian, U.S. House of Representatives, n.d.a). Rayburn served as Speaker for a total of 17 years and served as a mentor for Johnson, although he died prior to Johnson's presidency.

Presidential biographers tend to be at least fans of the presidents they present, if not sycophants. It is fascinating to read biographies of Johnson, since even his biographers describe him as a surprisingly crude individual known to use racial epithets, and hard on his staff and most of those surrounding him. He is described as a man driven at all costs to succeed in politics regardless of the means to obtain that end (Caro, 2012).

SIGNIFICANT EVENTS DURING JOHNSON'S TIME IN OFFICE

1963
- Johnson speaks to a joint session of Congress to support Kennedy's Civil Rights bill.
- Johnson names Chief Justice Earl Warren to investigate Kennedy's assassination.

1964
- Twenty-fourth Amendment to the U.S. Constitution ends the "poll tax."
- The Civil Rights Act of 1964 enacted
- Bay of Tonkin Resolution authorizes military action in Vietnam.

- Three civil rights workers murdered in Philadelphia, Mississippi

1965

- Johnson begins bombing of North Vietnam.
- Johnson signs legislation creating Medicare and Medicaid.

1966

- U.S. continues its military buildup in Vietnam with more than 500,000 troops.

1967

- Twenty-fifth Amendment passed providing for presidential succession
- Israel prevails in "Six-Day War" in the Middle East.
- Johnson appoints Thurgood Marshall first black justice of U.S. Supreme Court

1968

- North Korea captures USS *Pueblo*.
- "Tet Offensive" takes place in South Vietnam.
- U.S. and North Vietnam engage in peace talks.
- U.S.S.R. invades Czechoslovakia to prevent independence movement there.
- President Brezhnev of U.S.S.R. announces policy of intervention anywhere in the world.

THE DOMESTIC FRONT AND RACE RELATIONS

Johnson's first year in office is nicely portrayed in Robert Schenkkan's Tony-winning 2012 play *All the Way*, which has also been made into an HBO movie (Turnquist, 2016). Similar to several presidents analyzed in this book, Johnson enjoyed his best year as president during his first year in office and then descended sharply downward from that pinnacle. The assassination of the president in the modern era, recorded from various vantage points and then aired on television repeatedly at the height of the Cold War, captivated Americans at their most fearful. *The Boston Globe* headline of November 23, 1963, accurately captured the mood of America: "Shock...Disbelief...Grief" (Healy, 1963). The killing of the alleged gunman, Lee Harvey Oswald, in front of television cameras by a club owner, Jack Ruby, two days later, only added to the sense of crisis and lawlessness (History.com staff, 2010.a). Against that backdrop, more compelling than any fictional movie or television drama, Johnson brought the country together and presented, at least for public consumption, a stable face for the U.S. His accomplishment by winning the election less than a year later is one of the most amazing political victories of the one hundred-year period of this book (Caro, 2012). His electoral accomplishment is rivaled only by Truman's victory in 1948 and the victory of Donald Trump in 2016.

The Johnson administration's domestic agenda is marked by a variety of legislative outcomes. The landmark Civil Rights Act of 1964 is often mentioned as a crowning accomplishment of an otherwise failed administration. The Voting Rights Act was also passed and a Constitutional Amendment was passed banning poll taxes in order to vote. Thurgood Marshall became the first black person to serve as a justice of the U.S. Supreme Court. Countering these positive results were race riots in Watts, California, Detroit, and Newark, New Jersey. Three civil rights workers were killed in Philadelphia, Mississippi. Martin Luther King was assassinated in Memphis, Tennessee. The "Black Panthers" were founded in Oakland.

Other than Vietnam, Johnson is best remembered for his proposed "War on Poverty" and his promotion of a "Great Society." Johnson was an admirer of Franklin Roosevelt and his ambitious and ultimately failed proposals were as unsuccessful as his predecessor's. His professed objective was to do more to alleviate poverty by striking at its sources. To date, one conservative think tank states that the U.S. has spent approximately twenty-two trillion dollars in yet another lost "war" (Rector & Sheffield, 2014). Another source notes that in 2012, various programs to help the poor totaled roughly eight hundred billion dollars for just one year (Committee on the Budget: U.S. House of Representatives, 2014). This adds credence to the current estimate of one trillion dollars a year today to fight poverty. See Chapter 19 for discussion of the economy and the presidents.

SCANDALS

As noted, Johnson exaggerated his limited service in the military during WWII. He used his political clout to build up the Austin, Texas, radio station that was owned by Lady Bird Johnson. He was referred to as "Landslide Lyndon" for his rather remarkable victory in the 1948 Democratic primary Senate race. In that race, he trailed his opponent, former Texas governor Coke Stevenson. Days after the initial balloting, a box of ballots from southern counties in Texas magically appeared. These gave Johnson an eight-seven-vote lead and the position as the Democratic candidate on the general election ballot at a time when Texas voted heavily Democratic (Caro, 1990).

In an odd twist, Johnson self-described himself as a "womanizer" in response to the rather frequent references to Kennedy's reputation.

Johnson's record as a crude and politically ambitious individual seems to have far outpaced the reports of his extramarital sexual pursuits. In the two best documented cases, it is reported that he had a long affair with a woman named Madeline Brown and may have had a son with her (Brower, 1987). The other affair was recounted by Johnson biographer Robert Caro where he identified Alice Glass as having had a thirty-year affair with Johnson. She reportedly terminated the affair since she was resolutely against the Vietnam War (Caro, 1990).

THE JOHNSON INTERNATIONAL RECORD

Nothing in Johnson's background prepared him to take on the international challenges of the presidency. His persistent incompetence on the international scene underscores the danger of having a president who does not have a consistent plan and long-term vision. Military intervention in Vietnam started under Kennedy, but history shows it to be mainly Johnson's failure. Congress supported the military intervention with the Bay of Tonkin Resolution in 1964 (Office of the Historian, Bureau of Public Affairs, n.d.b). The concept presented was that the U.S. should support peace in all of the Indochina area with the underlying goal to prevent further spread of communism in that region. North Vietnam, supported by the Communist Chinese, had launched a full-scale invasion into South Vietnam. The resolution authorized the use of force to assist South Vietnam in repelling North Vietnam's forces. Johnson ordered the bombing of North Vietnam and sent U.S. ground troops to South Vietnam under the resolution (Billington, 1987).

From the first dispatch of ground troops, public sentiment was mixed. Many Americans supported the war on the premise that any steps to stop the spread of Communism were worthwhile. However, a vocal minority of mostly young people dominated the news coverage. Part of the irony of the most reported battle, the Tet Offensive, was that a 1976 memoir by North Vietnamese General Võ Nguyên Giáp said that the U.S. and South Vietnamese troops won the battle (Giáp, 1976). The U.S. media coverage presented it as a loss by disorganized U.S. and South Vietnamese troops. At the time, a military draft was still active in the U.S. Many men who dropped out of high school, or did not pursue a student deferment in college, were drafted and sent to Vietnam.

The military objectives were poorly managed and morale was not good among either officers or enlisted troops. "Draft dodging" became an art form with some fleeing to Canada and others claiming to be "conscientious objectors." Fleeing to Canada was highlighted by the popular song "Leaving on a Jet Plane," by the folk group Peter, Paul and Mary (Gilbert, 1995). The most famous conscientious objector was heavyweight boxing champion Muhammad Ali, whose conviction for dodging the military draft was overturned by the US Supreme Court in 1971 (*Clay v. United States*). Protests dominated the news during the last two years of the Johnson administration. When Johnson decided not to run for reelection, the news coverage of the Tet Offensive was specifically a concern (Bornet, 1990). Mismanagement was highlighted when a group of troops committed the "My Lai Massacre" in March 1968 (Caro, 2012). Large protests against the war included the March on the Pentagon in 1967 and major riots at the Democrat's convention in Chicago in the summer of 1968.

Token peace talks between North Vietnam and the U.S. were initiated in 1968 (History.com staff, 2012). While the Korean Conflict might be regarded as a fight to a draw, clearly the U.S. intervention in Vietnam was the first war that the U.S. simply lost.

Other international issues during Johnson's administration included his intervention in the Dominican Republic to help to establish peace in that country. Johnson's action of sending in twenty-two thousand troops into the Caribbean nation was the latest chapter in years of political instability there (Garson, 1997). As expressed in the previous chapter on Kennedy, the U.S. intervention in countries close to its borders makes eminent sense from a long-term security standpoint. However, Johnson was criticized for his actions both domestically and by the leaders of other South and Central American countries. The claim was that the U.S. was intervening in a situation that was completely domestic in nature. These other leaders were obviously concerned that they would become the next targets of U.S. intervention.

Confirming the blunder of the premature truce with North Korea by both Truman and Eisenhower, North Korea seized the U.S. observation ship the USS *Pueblo* in international waters in early 1968. The eighty-three crewmen aboard were taken prisoners and tortured for eleven months (History.com staff, 2010.b). This disgrace on top of the negative media coverage of the Tet Offensive helped to seal the fate of the Johnson presidency. The U.S.S.R. advanced its objectives as the U.S. was distracted elsewhere. Czechoslovakia was invaded in 1968 to prevent that country's move toward independence from the U.S.S.R. Premier Brezhnev replaced Khrushchev in 1964. Later, in 1968, Brezhnev boldly countered U.S. pronouncements against communist intervention by stating that the U.S.S.R. would intervene anywhere in the world that it wished.

Regarded by many Americans as a rare bright spot in the international scene during the Johnson administration, Israel swept to victory in only six days over several Arab states in 1967. While the U.S. did not directly intervene, its backing of Israel may have prevented other powers from intervening. The long-term impact of the U.S. support for Israel may be the substantial anti-American sentiment that dominates much of the Middle East today.

BY THE NUMBERS

As expected with the Vietnam conflict, the national debt increased steadily during Johnson's presidency. There is little data to support how much was spent on Vietnam versus how much was spent on the War on Poverty. In later years, as documented in this book, poverty spending helped to drive up the deficit (U.S. Department of the Treasury, Bureau of the Fiscal Service, 2013):

Year	National Debt
1963	$305,859,632,996
1964	$311,712,899,257
1965	$317,273,898,983
1966	$319,907,087,795
1967	$326,220,937,794
1968	$347,578,406,425
1969	$353,720,253,841

The inflation numbers indicate that the recession Kennedy inherited from Eisenhower continued into Johnson's administration. As "war" economies tend to be inflationary economies when price controls are not implemented, the inflation factor for 1966-1969 tends to reflect the impact of the spending on the Vietnam conflict (Coin News Media Group LLC, 2017):

Year	Inflation Rate
1963	1.3%
1964	1.3%
1965	1.6%
1966	2.9%

1967 | 3.1%
1968 | 4.2%
1969 | 5.5%

MAKING THE GRADE

Johnson unequivocally stands in evaluations as one of the more controversial U.S. presidents. Some rate him highly because of the number of pro-civil rights laws passed during his presidency, despite his terrible international record and the number of race riots and other incidents that happened during his presidency. His poll numbers reflect this with an average approval rating of 55 percent (Gallup, Inc., 2015). In performance rankings as president, he comes in about the middle of the pack with roughly a 60 percent rating (Rottinghaus & Vaughn, 2015).

In evaluating Johnson's private ethics, he is one of the lowest-rated of the seventeen presidents in the one hundred-year period. From his crude personality and behavior, to his blind ambition to succeed in politics regardless of the means, to his now documented womanizing, there is little to credit him on the positive side. His public ethics move him up the ladder as he clearly championed rights for the poor and minorities. Johnson lived with bouts of poverty when he was growing up. This seems to have motivated his push to improve the lot of the poor.

There is a nagging concern that Johnson sensed the way the mood of the country was changing in favor of civil rights. Politically, he may have supported civil rights as a way of advancing his political agenda to attract votes from the northern and western U.S. There is persistent anecdotal evidence that Johnson was not the true friend of minorities. No matter his personal intent, the Civil Rights Act of 1964 was passed by a coalition of northern Democrats and many Republicans from around the country.

It was staunchly opposed by southern Democrats. Black Americans have consistently voted Democrat since 1964, Johnson's political affiliation. The many misdeeds by the Democrats over an eighty-year period while in control of the south following the brief Republican Reconstruction after the Civil War appear to have been forgotten. The solid support of the black voters in the South against the Republican party of Lincoln began their swift move over to the Democratic Party with Johnson.

On the international scene, Johnson failed in Vietnam in a highly public fashion. In a conflict against a grossly overmatched enemy, bumbling by politicians primarily under Johnson's leadership prevented the military from actually winning a winnable war. More than sixty thousand Americans are dead or missing due to incompetence at the top ("Vietnam War Casualties," 2016). While America was distracted in Vietnam, North Korea and the U.S.S.R. took advantage of the situation to further embarrass the U.S. or to further secure their positions in the world. The only positive glimmer of light, despite the controversy itself stirred, was the U.S. intervention in the Dominican Republic. Again, establishing that the U.S. will not allow nearby countries to be destabilized and possibly controlled by anti-U.S. forces is a positive value.

Johnson Grade: D

CHAPTER 11
RICHARD M. NIXON

(Department of the Army. Office of Deputy Chief of Staff for Operations, ca. 1969)

Richard Milhous Nixon (1913–1994), a Republican, was elected the thirty-seventh U.S. president in 1968 by winning a narrow victory in the popular vote over the Democratic candidate Hubert Humphrey. While it was not close in the Electoral College, the popular vote was close with the split of a third-party candidate, segregationist George Wallace (Herbers, 1994; Peters & Woolley, 2015). Nixon's initial VP was Spiro T. Agnew. For a second term, the Nixon-Agnew ticket swept to a crushing victory over anti-war Democratic candidate George McGovern in 1972 (Broder, 1972). Agnew was involved in a scandal related to white collar crimes during his time as governor of Maryland and resigned in 1973 (Hatfield, 1997). Congressman Gerald Ford (R-MI) became Nixon's VP, ultimately serving as president when Nixon became the only president to resign from office, in 1974 (Waggoner, 1994).

Nixon married Thelma Catherine Ryan in 1940. He was married to her until her death a year before his own death (The National First Ladies' Library, n.d.). Known as "Pat" Nixon, she was a popular and well-traveled First Lady. Unlike a number of his predecessors, Nixon was not noted to have been a womanizer.

OCCUPATIONAL ACCOMPLISHMENTS

Educated at Whittier College in California and then Duke Law School, Nixon worked as an attorney in California before serving in the government early in WWII. As a Quaker, he was not required to serve in the military. However, he joined the Navy as a Lieutenant and served until 1946 in noncombat positions (Tata, 2013). He was elected to Congress in 1946 and the Senate in 1950. Only two years later, he agreed to be Eisenhower's running mate (Richard Nixon Foundation, 2016).

Nixon's time as VP does not contain much that is remarkable. Perhaps best known during the eight years as Eisenhower's VP was the famous "Kitchen Debate" between Nixon and Khrushchev in 1959. His political career was marred by the nickname "Tricky Dick." Some incorrectly assume that the nickname relates to the Watergate Scandal, discussed later in this chapter. Actually, the term has been traced to his first U.S. Senate race in 1950 when he allegedly used tricks to gain an advantage over his opponent (Keating, 2010; Lucas, 2011). Nixon nearly lost the VP spot during the 1952 presidential campaign as Eisenhower's running mate when it was reported that he had accepted gifts for political favors. The gifts reportedly included $18,000 and a dog named "Checkers." In response, and apparently without consulting with Eisenhower or key campaign figures, Nixon gave a 30 minute live televised speech where he provided a very detailed pitch to the American voters explaining his version of why it was not illegal or immoral for him to have accepted the money. He also defended the gift of Checkers to his children. There are numerous reports about this incident, including the recent books *Just Plain Dick: Richard Nixon's Checkers Speech and the "Rocking, Socking" Election of 1952* (2013) by Kevin Mattson; and *Ike and Dick: Portrait of a Strange Political Marriage* (2013) by Jeffrey Frank.

Nixon lost to Kennedy in a tight race for the presidency in 1960. That did not stop his political ambitions. Nixon ran for governor of California in 1962. After a loss in that race to Pat Brown, he famously referred to what he felt was unfair media coverage by stating: "You won't have Nixon to kick around anymore..." (Herbers, 1994). For someone who declared his own political career dead, it is remarkable that only six years later he was elected president and then reelected by a substantial majority in 1972.

Nixon, as an eight-year VP under Eisenhower, should have had a significant name-recognition advantage over Kennedy in the 1960 race. Nixon and Kennedy engaged in the first live-televised presidential debate. With only a few channels to watch at that time, many Americans watched this new phenomenon with interest. Kennedy's charisma and appearance gave him a significant advantage over Nixon on television, who looked uncomfortable before the cameras. Persons listening to the debate on radio reported that they felt Nixon had won the debate (Webley, 2010).

SIGNIFICANT EVENTS DURING NIXON'S TIME IN OFFICE

1969

- Nixon proposes that both U.S. and North Vietnam would leave South Vietnam.

- U.S. lands man on the Moon.
- Nixon proposes that U.S. Postal Service become a nonprofit corporation.
- Military draft is converted to a lottery system.

1970

- Nixon signs the Environmental Protection Act which creates the EPA
- Nixon signs the Occupational Health and Safety Act creating OSHA
- The U.S. invades Cambodia.

1971

- *The New York Times* begins publishing the Pentagon Papers.
- Twenty-sixth Amendment lowers federal voting age from 21 to 18

1972

- The Nixons travel to China.
- Break-in at the Democratic National Headquarters in the Watergate complex in D.C.
- Shanghai Accord Communique replaced Taiwan with China in "one China" approach

1973

- Spiro T. Agnew resigns as VP from corruption charges in Maryland.
- Paris Peace Accord effectively ends U.S. military involvement in Vietnam.

- Nixon admits responsibility for Watergate in a televised statement.
- U.S. supports Israel in "Yom Kippur War"
- Arab oil embargo creates Energy Crisis, limiting imports of gasoline and other oil products.

1974

- House of Representatives adopts three Articles of Impeachment against Nixon.
- Nixon resigns.

THE DOMESTIC FRONT AND RACE RELATIONS

Once in the presidency, Nixon had a number of challenges with a Democrat majority in both Houses of Congress for his entire time in office. The political environment he faced was even more interesting after 1972, when he defeated McGovern by such a substantial majority (Broder, 1972).

Nixon appointed four U.S. Supreme Court justices during his time in office. Best known of these appointments was Warren Burger, who replaced Earl Warren as Chief Justice, and William Rehnquist, who later became Chief Justice. The other two appointments were Lewis Powell and Harry Blackmun. Nixon had two well-publicized appointments rejected during his attempt to replace Justice Abe Fortas (U.S. Senate, 2016).

Nixon contributed very little to the substantial engineering accomplishment of the U.S. landing on the moon in July 1969. It was only six months into his first term, but it is still recorded in history as part of his administration. Nixon proposed that the U.S. Postal Service (USPS) be operated in a different manner as an independent nonprofit corporation.

The USPS has continued to struggle under subsequent administrations, so this approach has not met with much success ("Congress clears Landmark Postal Reorganization Plan," 1970).

Nixon is not often associated with two significant pieces of legislation from 1970. Nixon signed into law the Environmental Protection Act, 42 U.S.C. § 4321 et seq., and the Occupational Safety and Health Act (1970) (Graphiq Inc., 2016). When asking the average American on the street, Nixon is guessed last of the recent presidents as the signer of either the pro-environmental act or the pro-employee act. Unfortunately, poor drafting and poor oversight by Congress has led to some negative outcomes, but both acts helped to move the U.S. forward at the time they were passed. While some political pundits and a few economists still criticize the decision, Nixon took the U.S. off the gold standard in 1971. This key decision created the international monetary system that exists today.

It is hard to disconnect the war in Vietnam from domestic life in America during the Nixon administration. One innovation was the military draft lottery. A high draft lottery number meant that many draft-eligible men could continue to work or study since they were not likely to be drafted. This failed to do much to quell resistance to the war. A consultant to the Defense Department, Daniel Ellsberg, purloined a top-secret report prepared for the Pentagon providing a rather dim view of the entire U.S. involvement in Vietnam from Eisenhower through Nixon (Carlisle, 2015). Ellsberg had some trouble getting the word out, but eventually *The New York Times* began to publish excerpts from it, identified only as "The Pentagon Papers." It outlined many of the mistakes made in this long-running conflict (History.com staff, 2009.a). Despite the classification of the report as secret, courts refused to block publication of the papers (Dunlap, 2016). This helped to lay the groundwork for the defense when Ellsberg was prosecuted for treason under the Espionage Act of 1917. Surprisingly, the judge eventually dismissed all charges against Ellsberg (Wilson, 2012).

By the late 1960s, the U.S. economy was in a recession tied to expenditures for Vietnam and energy shocks. Nixon tried economic controls in 1971, as authorized by the Economic Stabilization Act of 1970. He imposed a ninety-day wage and price freeze. The idea was to control inflation and provide stability (Nixon, 1971.a). When the controls came off, prices shot up. Another wage-price freeze was tried, but this too was unsuccessful (Cowan, 1973). Even though war time was the usual justification for such controls, the Nixon freeze survived court challenges (Rigby, 1979). The irony of the economic controls was that such controls violated traditional capitalist economic models. During the Cold War, it would seem obvious that implementing anything similar to the U.S.S.R.'s persistently failed "planned economy" was not tenable (Blunden, 1993).

Although Democrats passed the Economic Stabilization Act, which Nixon used to try to control prices, organized labor was a strong opponent of the Act. Ultimately, this approach to stimulating the economy and controlling inflation was abandoned (PBS, 1997). The economy was to face more challenges as U.S. support for Israel helped to trigger the 1973 Arab Oil Embargo (Corbett, 2013). Long lines at the gas pump led to some violent confrontations and a further weakening of the economy.

WATERGATE SCANDAL

For reasons never made clear, several operatives related to the Republican Party broke into the Democratic National Headquarters in the Watergate complex in Washington, D.C. They were caught attempting to copy information about campaign plans and planting listening devices

(History.com staff, 2009.c). Initially, Nixon attempted, through Chief of Staff H.R. Haldeman, to prevent the investigation by the FBI (Kelly, 2004). It is likely that the burglary was initiated by persons close to Nixon and he was not protecting the burglars but the insiders who may have orchestrated the caper (History.com staff, 2009.b). Adding to the clearly failed ethics of Nixon in this situation was the imbecility of speaking in rooms in the White House that were equipped with voice-activated audio taping systems (Richard Nixon Presidential Library and Museum, n.d.). During 1973 and into 1974, Nixon attempted to block investigations into the caper and when the existence of the White House tapes became public, Nixon worked hard to avoid producing the tapes (Kopel, 2014).

On July 29 and 30, 1974, the House Judiciary Committee approved three articles of impeachment, charging that Nixon had misused his powers to violate the constitutional rights of U.S. citizens, obstructed justice, and defied Judiciary Committee subpoenas (House of Judiciary Committee, 1974). To avoid almost certain impeachment, Nixon resigned from office on August 9 (History.com staff, 2009.b). Nixon was replaced by long-time Republican Congressman Gerald Ford, who had been appointed vice president after Agnew resigned from office in 1973 in the midst of investigations into his actions while governor of Maryland (Hatfield, 1997). Ford pardoned Nixon about a month later (History.com staff, 2009.c).

THE NIXON INTERNATIONAL RECORD

While Lyndon Johnson is most associated with the Vietnam conflict, Nixon has a good share of the blame. Shortly after taking office, Nixon made an initial peace offer to North Vietnam, essentially that both sides would leave South Vietnam to make its own decisions. North Vietnam's leader rejected that proposal. Nixon then accelerated U.S. military involvement, including mining Hanoi's harbor. The surrender of the South to the North in 1973 was Nixon's responsibility. Officially, the U.S. lost the conflict on the day the Paris Peace Accord was signed (Bia, 2013). After the U.S. evacuated, North Vietnam swept in and took control of the South in 1975. The "Fall of Saigon," as the last days are known, was chronicled in the Broadway hit musical *Miss Saigon* (Schönberg, 1989). The U.S. abandoned an ally and confirmed its loss of the war.

Consistently, Nixon's opening of relations with the People's Republic of China (PRC) is cited as his biggest achievement (Nixon, 1971.b). While this is an admirable outcome, it came with a heavy price. The U.S., which had previously only recognized Taiwan as the legitimate government of China, withdrew its support and put it behind China, known in the U.S. at that time as "Red China" (Ladley, 2002). Taiwan became yet another ally that had been promised support by the U.S. and had to deal with the withdrawal or denial of that support. Communist forces under "Chairman Mao" had taken the Chinese mainland by force in the late 1940s, but the U.S. changed its recognition to PRC under Nixon (Nixon, 1971.b).

Nixon had cool relations with the U.S.S.R. during his administration. He traveled once for a summit meeting in the U.S.S.R. during his administration (Nixon, 2001).

In 1973, Egypt and Syria staged a coordinated attack on Israel on Yom Kippur, the Jewish religion's holiest day, to avenge losses in the 1967 war. While the attackers originally made some progress, Israel staged a successful counterattack and the conflict ended in a truce (History.com staff, 2009.d). The Arab oil-exporting countries then retaliated against the U.S. for supporting Israel by limiting oil exports (Myre, 2013), highlighting the dependence of the U.S. on foreign oil imports.

BY THE NUMBERS

The national debt steadily increased during the Nixon years (U.S. Department of the Treasury, Bureau of the Fiscal Service, 2015):

Year	National Debt
1969	$353,720,253,841
1970	$370,918,706,949
1971	$398,129,744,455
1972	$427,260,460,940
1973	$458,141,605,312
1974	$475,059,815,731

The increase in the national debt is not a surprise as the expenditures for Vietnam increased and the economy was sluggish. Despite the wage and price freeze experiments of Nixon, little was accomplished in controlling inflation. Against a target of 2 percent per year, only one year came close, 1972, an election year (Coin News Media Group LLC, 2017):

Year	Inflation Rate
1969	5.5%
1970	5.7%
1971	4.4%
1972	3.2%
1973	6.2%
1974	1.0%

MAKING THE GRADE

Nixon had a long marriage to one woman and was not known as a womanizer. His ethics were clearly lacking in the decisions that he made in terms of the people he had around him and the decisions he made with regard to Watergate.

The economy struggled under Nixon and his experiment with wage-price controls was an utter failure. While taking America off the gold standard appears to be the only recourse the U.S. had at the time, some still argue with the decision. Certainly, he deserves to be remembered for the Environmental Protection Act and the Occupational Safety and Health Act. He was president during the Arab oil embargo, not a happy time in the U.S.

On the international scene, Nixon is remembered for opening relations with China. Against this one accomplishment, there is little to praise. His handling of the Vietnam War confirmed the first loss of a war by the U.S. The abandonment of the South Vietnamese people and abandoning a long relationship with Taiwan as the true China happened under Nixon.

The various presidential ranking surveys understandably put Nixon low on the list, but not last. In recent years, his image may have crept up a bit and he does consistently come in ahead of Ford and Carter. In the Gallup polls, Nixon was mediocre in terms of popularity and polled higher than his successors, Ford and Carter (Jones, 2003). As the only president to both resign and have his vice president resign in disgrace, his is the only "F" among the seventeen presidents in this book.

Nixon Grade: F

CHAPTER 12
GERALD R. FORD

(Kennerly, ca. 1974)

Gerald Rudolph Ford (1913–2006) was born Leslie Lynch King Jr. His name was changed when his mother remarried after his parents' divorce (Mieczkowski, 2004). A Republican, he served as the thirty-eighth president from Nixon's resignation in 1974 until Carter took office in 1977 after Ford lost the 1976 election. His vice president for this brief period was former New York Governor Nelson Rockefeller (Library of Congress, 2012).

Ford was married to Elizabeth Ann "Betty" Ford from 1948 until his death (Black, n.d.), a rather remarkable 58-year marriage. Betty later became well-known for founding the "Betty Ford Center for Drug and

Alcohol Rehabilitation" in California (Hazelden Betty Ford Foundation, n.d.).

OCCUPATIONAL ACCOMPLISHMENTS

Ford attended the University of Michigan and later Yale University Law School (Miller Center of Public Affairs, University of Virginia, 2015). He served in the Navy during WWII. He was elected to the U.S. House of Representatives, where he served for more than 25 years until appointed vice president to replace Spiro Agnew (Freidel & Sidey, 2006). Following the Watergate scandal, Democrats held significant majorities in both houses of Congress during Ford's brief time in office.

Ford, as a person, had a modesty that was reminiscent of Harry Truman. He stated on being appointed vice president: "I'm a Ford, not a Lincoln." He made himself accessible to the media, something that Nixon would not do (U-S-History.com staff, n.d.). He is not treated well by opinion polls, which are largely driven by news coverage, despite his personal attributes and modest successes on the domestic front. Ford had the distinction of surviving two separate assassination attempts during visits to California, one by Lynette "Squeaky" Fromme and the other by Sara Jane Moore (u-s-history.com staff, n.d.). In both cases, these women were driven by delusional ambitions and each served prison terms in excess of 30 years.

SIGNIFICANT EVENTS DURING FORD'S TIME IN OFFICE

1974

- Ford pardons Nixon.
- U.S. ambassador to Cyprus assassinated

1975

- Saigon and South Vietnam fall to North Vietnam.
- Cambodia falls to the Khmer Rouge.
- Cambodia seizes U.S. merchant ship *Mayaguez* and holds crew hostage.

1976

- U.S. ambassador to Lebanon assassinated
- Inflation rate drops from 12.2 percent to 4.6 percent during Ford administration.

THE DOMESTIC FRONT AND RACE RELATIONS

One of Ford's first acts as president was the one for which he is most remembered and criticized. About one month after he took office, he issued a full and unconditional pardon to Nixon. The rationale was that the near-circus atmosphere that existed around Watergate would be exacerbated by a trial of an American president. This act was consistent with the reported personality attributes of Ford. The U.S. was facing many serious problems and this allowed the country to focus on those problems and no longer on Watergate and Nixon (Stevenson, 2013).

Ford faced a hostile Congress as Democrats made huge electoral gains in the House and Senate in the aftermath of the Watergate scandal and Nixon's resignation. Facing substantial Democratic majorities, Ford used his veto power sixty-six times. Only twelve vetoes were overridden (Anderson, n.d.). Ford vetoed the Freedom of Information Act of 1974 (FOIA). The law was enacted over his veto (Lopez et al., 2004). The idea of FOIA was to increase transparency and give more civilian oversight to the increasingly complex operations of the U.S. government. In that, it has clearly failed, largely due to the refusal by the various federal agencies to comply with either the letter or the intent of the law. Ford signed the Privacy Act of 1974, an effort to give citizens some sense of protection from the government's use of their private information (Peters & Woolley, 1975).

Ford inherited an economy that was still struggling with high unemployment and high inflation. Ford pushed enactment of a substantial tax cut in 1975 to stimulate the economy. The tax cut focused on low- and moderate-income individuals. Economists later cited the target of the tax cuts as the reason that it was successful as it reportedly put more money in the hands of people who were more likely to spend that extra money, stimulating the economy (Institute, 2016). As the U.S. entered 1976, it was clear that the economy had definitely made progress in both inflation, with a reduction of 12.2 percent to 4.6 percent, and with a substantial increase in employment (Gerald R. Ford Library Museum, 1976).

America's 200th anniversary was celebrated during Ford's administration. The bicentennial celebration was a cause for national pride and review of American history. While Ford's economic and tax moves earn credit for helping the economy, some observers have suggested that some of this improvement in the economy was due to the celebration itself. Ford only made one U.S. Supreme Court appointment, that of moderate John Paul Stevens (U.S. Senate, 2016). Most likely, Ford made this choice since a more conservative candidate would not have been confirmed by the Democrat-controlled Senate (Office of the Historian, U.S. House of Representatives, n.d.).

In addition to a struggling economy, Ford inherited the Nixon cabinet. After a brief time in office, Ford began to make changes. Henry Kissinger was both Secretary of State and National Security Advisor. Ford kept him at the State Department, but named retired Lieutenant General Brent

Scowcroft the National Security Advisor. He appointed Donald Rumsfeld as Secretary of Defense and George H.W. Bush representative to China and later head of the CIA. Dick Cheney became the youngest presidential Chief of Staff (Sidey, 1999). All these appointees went on to serve in various capacities in future administrations, including obviously, Bush as VP and then president and Cheney as George W. Bush's VP. These appointments increased retrospective credit for Ford as a good judge of talent.

Ford acted to pursue an energy independence policy. Given the disproportionate Democrat representation in Congress, Ford's preferred path of encouraging domestic production and taxing imports was modified by Democrat opponents. Ford signed the Energy Policy and Conservation Act of 1975, which provided a variety of measures to supposedly result in energy independence (Gerald R. Ford Library Museum, 1976). The Iranian Revolution in 1978–1979 established that this was too little too late for the U.S. as severe energy shocks struck the economy (Laurel, n.d.)

Jimmy Carter won the 1976 presidential election even though Ford was making progress in the polls and might have won had the vote been a little later in the year (Apple, 1976). Ford proposed that Puerto Rico become the 51st state (Peters & Wooley, 1976). His proposal came during his "lame duck" status and president-elect Carter indicated that he would oppose such a change without a favorable vote of the people of Puerto Rico. In light of its strategic location, this move might have benefited the security of the U.S. mainland and the residents of Puerto Rico, a U.S. territory that continues to struggle economically (Easterbrook, 2016).

THE FORD INTERNATIONAL RECORD

The responsibility for Vietnam lies with Eisenhower, Kennedy, Johnson, and Nixon. Ford was president when Saigon fell. This marks the recognition that despite over sixty thousand lives lost and billions spent, the U.S. lost an ally to a tiny communist country. Tied to the U.S. withdrawal from Vietnam was Cambodia. After the U.S. left the region, the insurgent Khmer Rouge took over Cambodia, leading to what has been described as "The Killing Fields" (Puttnam & Joffé, 1984). An estimated 1.7 million people were slaughtered by the Khmer Rouge or starved to death (Taylor, 2014). In 1975, a U.S. merchant ship, the *Mayaguez*, was seized by the Khmer Rouge. Under U.S. pressure, the thirty-nine hostages were eventually released (History.com staff, 2009.a).

With regard to the Cold War, the amiable Ford followed Nixon's lead and engaged in what came to be known as "détente" with the U.S.S.R. and its leader, Leonid Brezhnev. The leaders worked to craft a more advanced agreement to limit nuclear testing, SALT II (History.com staff, 2009.b). This cooperation also resulted in an Apollo-Soyuz joint manned space flight (Wilson, 2007).

A long-delayed agreement on national borders in Eastern Europe was reached in the Helsinki Final Act of 1975. This agreement, with Ford as the lead for the West, gave the U.S.S.R. the legitimacy that it had sought regarding its occupation of various countries on the eastern border. This appeared to be a surrender of these countries to the communist power, but the human rights provisions with monitoring procedures might have helped to lead to an end of the U.S.S.R. (Office of the Historian, Bureau of Public Affairs, n.d.).

During a riot in Cyprus in 1974, the American Ambassador, Rodger P. Davies, was assassinated when a bullet went through the wall of the embassy. During Ford's short administration, unrest in Lebanon resulted in the kidnapping and murder of the American Ambassador, Francis Meloy, in 1976. Ford is the only U.S. President to have two ambassadors killed during his administration (Bobic, 2012).

BY THE NUMBERS

The national debt steadily increased during the Ford's administration. (U.S. Department of the Treasury, Bureau of the Fiscal Service, 2013):

Year	National Debt
1974	$475,060,000,000
1975	$533,189,000,000
1976	$620,433,000,000

Given that Ford entered the presidency during a difficult period in American history and with little lead time as VP, the increase in the national debt during his limited tenure is not a surprise. This was still a very significant increase in the national debt in a short period of time.

The high inflation rate was a concern in the U.S. starting in the late 1960s and continued for over 30 years. Unlike Coolidge's time in office, a focus on sharp reductions in government expenditures does not seem to have occurred to the leaders (Coin News Media Group LLC, 2017):

Year	Inflation Rate
1974	11%
1975	9.1%
1976	5.8%

MAKING THE GRADE

Ford had a long marriage to one woman and was not known as a womanizer. He stood by his wife, Betty, when she became a media favorite for her straight talk about a variety of controversial subjects, including abortion and substance abuse. Ford became the butt of jokes for having slipped in public a number of times. All reports are that Ford was modest, self-effacing, and honest. His low standing in the polls suggests that, unfortunately, these may not be the characteristics the media is seeking.

On the domestic front, Ford is best known for pardoning Nixon. This controversial decision seems to have been based on a concern for the country and not to cover for a Republican politician. He was confident enough to shuffle his cabinet and proved himself to be a good judge of talent. The economy showed some improvement. He tried to balance his concern for fiscal conservatism with the reality of a Democrat-controlled Congress.

On the international scene, Ford was president when South Vietnam fell and when the Khmer Rouge overran Cambodia. The actions to recover the *Mayaguez* appear to be one step in the right direction. He also presided over a country that lost two ambassadors during his short administration.

The various presidential ranking surveys put Ford low on the list, and similar to Nixon, his popularity has crept up in more recent years. In the Gallup polls, Ford was mediocre in terms of popularity (Gallup, Inc., 2015). His paucity of major accomplishments or major failures is reminiscent of the school student who has perfect attendance, but is not setting the world on fire with exams and papers.

Ford Grade: D+

CHAPTER 13
JAMES E. CARTER JR.

(Department of Defense (DoD). Department of the Navy.

Naval Photographic Center, n.d.)

James Earl Carter Jr. (1924–), popularly known as "Jimmy," was elected the fortieth president of the U.S. A Democrat, Carter served one term in office (1977–1981). His VP was Walter Mondale (Library of Congress, 2012).

Carter's wife from 1946 to present is Rosalynn Smith (Freidel & Sidey, 2006). He once raised a furor in the media when during an interview he admitted to having "committed lust in my heart many times" (Sabato, 1998). However, while not thought of as a good president, he is considered one of the more moral men to have served in the office. He has been described as honest, sincere, intelligent, and hardworking. He was at the same time described as indecisive, which made him appear weak (PersonalityCafe, 2014).

OCCUPATIONAL ACCOMPLISHMENTS

Carter attended several colleges, but his principal education was from the U.S. Naval Academy, where he graduated in 1946. He completed a six-year tour in the Navy and then returned to Georgia in 1953 to "save" the family peanut farm (Miller Center of Public Affairs, University of Virginia, 2015). Successful in that endeavor, he became involved in local politics and eventually was elected Governor of Georgia, serving from 1971 to 1975. He scored a very narrow victory over Ford in the 1976 presidential election. Carter, a Washington, D.C., outsider, never seemed to be completely in sync with Congress or the media. There was intense pressure on his administration even before the Iran Crisis, described in the following pages. Adding to the pressure was the embarrassment of a publicized bout with hemorrhoids in 1978 (Sotos, 2004).

SIGNIFICANT EVENTS DURING CARTER'S TIME IN OFFICE

1977

- Carter signs Energy Organization Act creating Department of Energy.
- The Trans Alaskan Oil Pipeline opens.

1978

- Carter signs agreement to give Panama control of the Panama Canal in 1999.
- Soviet invasion of Afghanistan

1979

- Camp David Peace Accord between Israel and Egypt signed
- American embassy in Iran overrun and ninety taken hostage
- U.S. Ambassador to Afghanistan, Adolph Dubs, is kidnapped and killed.

1980

- U.S. boycotts the 1980 Summer Olympics in Moscow after Russian invasion of Afghanistan.
- Mariel Boat Lift enables mass exodus from Cuba.

THE DOMESTIC FRONT AND RACE RELATIONS

The Democrats retained control of Congress and won the presidency in the 1976 elections. Thomas P. "Tip" O'Neill of Massachusetts succeeded Speaker Carl Albert of Oklahoma following his retirement in 1977. But despite their one-party control of the federal government, Democrats failed to pass Carter's comprehensive proposed energy program, although legislation creating the Department of Energy did pass. Only stop-gap energy legislation was passed during the Carter administration. Congress did deregulate the airline industry and added more than 150 federal judgeships (Reichard, 1990).

Democratic majorities in Congress eroded after the 1978 elections. Congress continued to struggle with energy legislation amid rising support for deficit reduction. The year-long Iranian revolution and subsequent hostage crisis at the U.S. Embassy in Tehran often overshadowed the serious economic problems.

Immediately before their mass suicide at a South American commune, followers of cult leader Jim Jones murdered California Representative Leo

J. Ryan during his investigation of the Jonestown compound in Guyana. Jones then forced his followers to commit suicide (The Associated Press, 1978).

Congress created the Department of Education, a cabinet post that remains controversial today, over concerns that state and local control of education is the better approach (Van Til, 1996). One of the more significant pieces of environmental legislation that was passed during Carter's presidency was the Comprehensive Environmental Response, Compensation, and Liability Act (CERCLA), commonly known as "Superfund" (EPA, 2016). The concept is that significant amounts of land in the U.S. have been polluted and most individuals and businesses lack the financial means or incentive to clean up the sites. The U.S. government will cooperate with a buyer or owner of an identified polluted site and fund the clean-up. Then, title searches and other investigations will be conducted to locate the prior owners and potential polluters of the property and assess damages against them to return those funds back to the Superfund account. Congress also enacted the Staggers Act to deregulate the railroad industry.

A major race riot took place in Miami during 1980. Known as the McDuffie riots, they followed the acquittal of four police officers involved in the killing of a black veteran and insurance agent. In the end, eighteen persons were dead and damage was estimated to exceed one hundred million dollars (Smiley, 1980).

Commentary on Carter's record reflected that even with Democrats in control of both Houses of Congress, Carter did not succeed in advancing much of his agenda. Carter was more conservative and pro-business than the Democrats in Congress. While he expanded government, he also introduced deregulation as a government policy moving forward. The creation of a pricing cartel by OPEC, the oil producing countries' organization, sent oil prices soaring, caused rampant inflation, and a serious recession.

Carter was deeply troubled by public scandals involving his family, including a mysterious 250,000 dollar payment by the government of Libya to Carter's brother "Billy" (Miller Center of Public Affairs, University of Virginia, 2015). Billy Carter provided some comic overtones that his brother Jimmy certainly did not need. There was a well-reported incident of Billy urinating in public and there was a brief production and sale of "Billy Beer" (Wolf, 2006).

THE CARTER INTERNATIONAL RECORD

For each president, there are defining moments. For Carter's administration, it was when students overran the U.S. embassy in Iran, not once, but twice in 1979. The first time, the ambassador was released and things appeared to stabilize. But, shortly thereafter, a large group of radicalized students, realizing that the small U.S. Marine guard contingent would not fire on them, overran the embassy again. While reports still differ to this day on the number of hostages, a consistent number was ninety at the start. This would have included some Iranian nationals and representatives of other countries. After the Ayatollah Khomeini, who allegedly did not authorize the hostage taking, returned to Iran from exile, he took charge of the negotiations. During the extended crisis, generally listed as 444 days, a handful of the American hostages, including women and blacks, were released. The final fifty-four hostages were released just four hours after Reagan was sworn into office in 1981 (Pender, 2004). During the crisis, the situation was exacerbated when a rescue mission went wrong and eight military special forces members died in the attempt. The U.S. lost two helicopters and it was reported that the U.S. was simply not trained to fight a desert war (Edwards, 2008). The failed mission compounded Carter's problems and made it virtually impossible for him to win reelection.

Carter signed an agreement in 1977 giving the Panama Canal to the government of Panama in 1999 (History.com staff, 2009.a). Reasonable minds can differ on whether handing over a critical security and economic asset of the U.S. to a weak government made sense. Subsequent to the deal, in 1989 the U.S. had to enter Panama and remove Manuel Noriega (Gordon, 1989). Noriega and his cohorts had lost an election, but refused to leave office.

During Carter's administration, there was an attempt to continue the *détente* that had begun with the U.S.S.R. during Nixon and Ford. The U.S.S.R. suddenly invaded Afghanistan and Carter tried unsuccessfully to persuade the aggressors to withdraw from the country (Carter, 1994). Carter's protests went unanswered and ultimately resulted in the U.S. boycotting the 1980 Summer Games in Moscow (Brinkley, 1995). Afghanistan became a "Vietnam" for the U.S.S.R. as resources and troops failed to give them the victory they were seeking against an entrenched foe (Rozell, 1993). The U.S. was supporting the Afghan fighters during this time with arms and other military aid.

Additional proof of America's failure to take effective action in Cuba was the "Mariel Boat Lift" in 1980. With continuing financial problems in Cuba, Castro allowed anyone who wished to do so to leave Cuba. About 125,000 persons came to the U.S. as part of this effort. Initially, this looked like a very positive outcome. It was later discovered that numerous criminals and persons released from mental health facilities were among the refugees. More than two thousand of the refugees were detained and the boat lift was terminated (History.com staff, 2009.b).

Carter distinguished himself as a mediator during his one term in office. His mediation skills were put to use in helping Egypt and Israel reach a peace accord. He used those same skills in negotiations with the U.S.S.R. to limit nuclear weapon expansion and testing.

BY THE NUMBERS

The national debt steadily increased during Carter's administration. Carter ran on the platform that he was a successful businessperson and compentent administrator. Unfortunately, the surging national debt which increased by over $200 billion in one term, would indicate that he was not capable of carrying that approach into the White House. As Carter left office, the national debt was approaching one trillion dollars (U.S. Department of the Treasury, Bureau of the Fiscal Service, 2013):

Year	National Debt
1977	$698,840,000,000
1978	$771,544,000,000
1979	$826,519,000,000
1980	$907,701,000,000

Carter was unable to achieve or maintain the progress that Ford had made in controlling inflation, and the rate was even higher by the end of Carter's four years than when Ford took office. During this time period and into the 1980s, consumer interest rates and home mortgage rates hit record highs (Coin News Media Group LLC, 2017):

Year	Inflation Rate
1977	6.5%
1978	7.6%
1979	11.3%
1980	13.5%

MAKING THE GRADE

The available evidence points to Carter as an ethical person both in his personal dealings and his public dealings. Unfortunately, as demonstrated by his immediate predecessor, Ford, being a person of good character without strong leadership skills was not sufficient to be a model president of the U.S.

Despite his demeanor and mediation skills, his support for an effective energy program for the U.S. was not achieved. He was clearly on the right path. A comprehensive energy program that will ensure security for the U.S. remains an elusive goal today.

On the international scene, the Iranian hostage situation was Carter's Waterloo. It is the essence of unfairness that the failed military rescue attempt added to the public's perception of incompetence on the part of Carter. Obviously, he had nothing to do with the training of those troops, the preparation of the helicopters, or the planning of the operation. The nature of the job of Commander in Chief is that he is held responsible for all events that occur regardless of who is at fault. It looked initially like the Mariel Boat Lift would be a positive for Carter's administration, but the disclosure of the criminals and mental health patients among the refugees turned this into a negative as well.

The various presidential popularity surveys consistently show Carter near the bottom of the ratings. He is often shown below Ford, his predecessor (Rottinghaus, B. & Vaughn, 2015). One recent Gallup poll puts him at only about 45.5 percent approval with the public out of all recent American presidents (Jones, 2003). The net outcome: A good person but extraordinarily ineffective.

Carter Grade: D

CHAPTER 14

RONALD REAGAN

(White House Photographic Office, 1981).

Ronald Wilson Reagan (1911–2004), a Republican, was elected the fortieth president of the U.S. over incumbent Jimmy Carter in 1980. This election was distinguished by a third-party candidate, John B. Anderson, who drew less than 7 percent of the popular vote, even though he carried no states. Reagan only won a little over 50 percent of the popular vote, but won a crushing victory in the Electoral College with forty-four states ("United States presidential election of 1980," 2016). He was the oldest person elected to the U.S. presidency at that time. Republicans won the Senate for the first time since 1955 (Office of the Historian, U.S. House of Representatives, n.d.). Reagan had an easier time winning reelection over Walter Mondale in 1984 with nearly 59 percent of the popular vote

(Office of the Federal Register, n.d.). His VP for his entire administration was George H.W. Bush, who himself was elected president in 1988.

Reagan married Nancy Davis in 1952 and they remained married until Reagan died in 2004 (History.com staff, 2009). It was Reagan's second marriage, after he divorced actress Jane Wyman in 1948 (Biography.com Editors, 2015). Nancy Reagan was well-known on her own during Reagan's presidency, particularly for her "Just Say No" campaign, encouraging young people to not use drugs (Biography.com Editors, 2016.a).

OCCUPATIONAL ACCOMPLISHMENTS

Reagan had a fascinating life including several successful careers on the path to the White House. Following graduation from Eureka College in Illinois in 1932, where he was an athlete and student leader, he became a radio announcer in the Midwest. He later made his way to California, where he auditioned and was hired as a contract actor by Warner Brothers. He went on to appear in fifty-two films.

Poor eyesight prevented Reagan from serving on the battlefield during WWII. He was assigned instead to make training movies for the military. He was well-known as president of the Screen Actors Guild from 1947 to 1952. As a spokesperson for General Electric, he toured the U.S. and met with employees. Originally a Democrat, Reagan shifted to a more pro-business stance and became a Republican. He won election as California's governor in 1966 and was reelected in 1970. He then began to focus on the White House (Biography.com Editors, 2016.b; "The life of Ronald Reagan: a timeline," n.d.).

SIGNIFICANT EVENTS DURING REAGAN'S TIME IN OFFICE

1981

- Iran releases fifty-two American hostages held for 444 days.
- John Hinkley attempts to assassinate Reagan, injures three others.
- PATCO strikers (air traffic controllers) given forty-eight hours to return to work or be fired
- Sandra Day O'Connor becomes first female U.S. Supreme Court justice.

1982

- Joint U.S.S.R.-U.S. Strategic Arms Reduction Treaty talks
- U.S. Marines sent to Lebanon in attempt to end civil war

1983

- Reagan announces Strategic Defense Initiative (SDI) missile system.
- Suicide bombers kill 241 Marines in barracks in Beirut, Lebanon.
- U.S. troops invade Grenada to prevent communist military takeover.

1984

- Reagan proposes help for Contra freedom fighters in Nicaragua.
- Reagan wins reelection in landslide over former VP Walter Mondale.

1985

- "Iran-Contra" affair begins.
- Reagan announces trade embargo against Nicaragua.

1986

- Space Shuttle Challenger disaster
- Reagan replaces retiring U.S. Supreme Court Chief Justice Warren Burger with Justice Rehnquist.
- Reagan orders air strikes against Libya for a bombing in Germany.

1987

- Reagan and Gorbachev sign Intermediate Range Nuclear Forces Treaty
- Famous Reagan "Tear down this wall" speech in Berlin

1988

- Iran-Contra indictments of Oliver North, John Poindexter, and two others
- U.S.S.R. begins to withdraw from Afghanistan.

THE DOMESTIC FRONT AND RACE RELATIONS

Reagan inherited a struggling economy, one of the reasons, other than the Iran hostages, that he was able to score a relatively easy victory over an incumbent president. A focus of his first term was to control inflation and stimulate job growth. Historical economic theory held that when employment was near the maximum level ("full employment") that this would drive up wages and in turn drive up inflation. This relationship was known as the "Phillips Curve" (Hoover, 1988). The late 1970s into the 1980s introduced the U.S. to "stagflation," a period when inflation and unemployment were both high (*Stagflation in a Historical Context*, 2016).

Early in his first term, Reagan approached Congress about a 30 percent tax cut to stimulate the economy. In a compromise, taxes were reduced by 25 percent across the board in addition to other changes (Chamberlain, 2004). Economists have debated the impact of the Reagan tax reductions. One camp argues that the across the board nature of the cuts meant that it benefited higher-income taxpayers more than lower- and middle-income taxpayers (Meeropol, 2001). The Tax Foundation argued that it was imminently fair if every taxpayer earned a 25 percent reduction (Chamberlain, 2004). The tax cuts appeared to have had a positive impact over time and many remember the Reagan years as a time of good economic news, with a healthy economy during his second term. Critics of Reagan point to a growing national debt, despite his agreement to the Gramm-Rudman Deficit Reduction Act in late 1985.

Reagan survived an assassination attempt only two months into office (Heclo, 2008). His rapid recovery from the bullet wound in his chest increased his popularity and reduced concern that he might be too old for the job. Just a few months later, he confronted an unusual crisis when the air traffic controllers union, PATCO, struck for higher wages. Federal employees are not allowed to strike. Reagan ordered all striking controllers back to work within forty-eight hours or they would be fired. Only about two thousand of the thirteen thousand PATCO strikers returned to work. Reagan honored his promise and terminated them. Further, he banned them from ever working as federal air traffic controllers in the future (History.com staff, 2010). Reagan's action is considered a key turning point in balancing union labor power with management rights. This helped to establish him as a tough leader and may have even helped him in negotiations with the U.S.S.R.

The Reagan presidency had a major impact on the U.S. Supreme Court. He appointed Justice William Rehnquist to replace retiring Chief Justice Warren Burger, moving the court toward a more conservative stance. He underscored that move with the appointment of conservative

Antonin Scalia as Justice to replace Rehnquist. Reagan made history with his appointment of the first woman on the high court, Sandra Day O'Connor (U.S. Senate, 2016).

IRAN-CONTRA: AN ENDURING SCANDAL

Reagan's administration is remembered for the major scandal that marked most of his second term. The Iran-Contra Affair, as it is known, combined two quite disparate acts into one phrase. After the Iran Hostage Crisis, the U.S. instituted a boycott against the sale of any military materials to Iran. Two international conflicts were proceeding at the same time on two continents. The complexity of the situation limits how extensively we can examine the scandal in this book. There is an excellent timeline provided on a Brown University site that provides just a hint of the contemporaneous situations that took place during Reagan's administration (Chimene-Weiss et. al., n.d.). In Nicaragua, Communist-backed rebels took control of the country and Reagan, who had vowed to fight communism, wanted to support the "Contra" forces who were trying to retake the country. Direct aid to the Contras was prevented by the Boland Amendments, which banned military aid to the Contras. The Boland Amendments raised controversy regarding whether Congress had the power to control the executive branch of the U.S. government (Wallace & Gerson, 1987).

Across the globe, Lebanon was in ruins and Iranian militants were taking advantage of the situation to take hostages. Since the country had been a peaceful haven in earlier times, there were vestiges of the more civilized country. There were many Americans and Europeans in the country unprepared when the violence began around them. A number of hostages were taken, including CIA operatives, university professors, and members of the media. Reagan attempted to negotiate with various parties to obtain the release of the seven hostages without success. One hostage was already dead as negotiations continued (Coutsoukis, 1987).

Reagan had announced a policy of not paying ransom to obtain the return of hostages. It was believed that it would be possible to provide some incentive to Iran to put pressure on the militants to obtain release of the hostages. Iran wanted weapons, which could not be sold to that country under the existing weapons boycott. Part I of the Iran-Contra Affair was developing circuitous ways to deliver weapons to Iran without the U.S. directly providing the weapons. In light of the many pronouncements against both the U.S. and Israel, it is rather astounding that any U.S. president would want to send arms to Iran, regardless of the reason. In Part II of the Iran-Contra Affair, the "profit" made by selling U.S. weapons to Iran was then diverted to provide financial aid to the Contras in Nicaragua.

The cast of characters involved in this scandal included men close to the president, or who could be linked to the president through others. Most often mentioned as a broker in the affair, and a frequent TV commentator today, was Oliver North. North was a Marine who was on loan to the National Security Council. Originally convicted of some criminal activity, his convictions were eventually overturned by a Federal Appeals Court. John Poindexter, a former Navy admiral and a National Security Advisor to Reagan, was the possible "mastermind" behind the affair. He was convicted of some crimes, but prevailed on appeal. Reagan's National Security Advisor prior to Poindexter was Robert McFarlane. McFarlane was reportedly a key to working around the terms of the Boland Amendments. Unlike North and Poindexter, McFarlane admitted guilt and plead to some misdemeanors, receiving fairly light sentences. He was later pardoned by President George H.W. Bush. Former Air Force officer and businessman Richard Secord was charged with various crimes. He, along with his business partner, were the "money men" behind the schemes and he eventually pleaded guilty to minor charges (Chimene-Weiss et. al., n.d.).

The highest-ranking parties involved in the affair were Caspar Weinberger, Secretary of Defense for Reagan during much of his administration, Vice President George Bush, and Reagan himself. Weinberger attempted to avoid responsibility and dodged investigators for several years. When prosecution was recommended, then President George Bush pardoned Weinberger before he could be formally charged. As former head of the CIA, long-serving vice president and confidante of the president, it is unlikely that Bush would not have had significant knowledge of the affair, if not direct involvement. He actively tried to avoid producing his diaries and other records from his office during the time of the affair. Ultimately, he was not prosecuted and there is no clear evidence of his involvement, although he had some contact with North during this time (Chimene-Weiss et. al., n.d.).

During his second term, Reagan made a series of announcements ranging from denial of knowledge of the affair, to denial that anything illegal happened, to excusing some of his confidants above for their involvement, if any. As the investigation continued for years after Reagan left office, he was eventually questioned in 1992 and by that time, his claim of not remembering what happened four to eight years earlier had a ring of truth. His performance during that questioning led to some of the early rumors of his diagnosis of Alzheimer's disease, which was confirmed in 1994 (Altman, 2015). The most damning report of the Reagan administration involvement in the Iran-Contra Affair was the Tower Commission Report (Center for Grassroots Oversight, n.d.).

THE REAGAN INTERNATIONAL RECORD

The Berlin Wall fell shortly after Reagan left office. This landmark event is often credited to Reagan's famous 1987 speech in Berlin, where he called upon the leader of the U.S.S.R. to "tear down this wall!" (White, 1990). There were a number of international failures during Reagan's years in office. Observers today note that the U.S.S.R. was under severe financial pressure well before Reagan entered office. Reagan's announcement of SDI, the Strategic Defense Initiative, nicknamed "Star Wars," put more pressure on the U.S.S.R. If the U.S. really did have such a system, the mutually assured destruction constraining the use of nuclear weapons would be void (Sen, 1983). The U.S. has very advanced missile detection systems today, but reportedly did not have a fully operational SDI when it was announced by Reagan.

It may have been "people power" that brought down the U.S.S.R. Athletes and performers, particularly ballet stars, from behind the Iron Curtain found that the U.S. and its allies were countries with advanced standards of living that they could only dream about. Some of the athletes and performers defected, but others told their friends and neighbors how much better it was living elsewhere with more personal freedom. An anecdote regarding this period was that some of the impressionable visitors were taken to a modern American grocery store. They were initially convinced that it was a trick by the CIA and others to fool them into thinking the U.S. was more successful than it was. They eventually realized that consumer goods are readily available to most Americans. Behind the Iron Curtain, standing in line for bread, toilet paper, and other necessities had become commonplace.

Relations with the U.S.S.R. ran hot and cold during Reagan's administration. There were several rounds of nuclear weapon reduction talks and generally his administration is viewed as having progressed in reducing the threat of war between the two powers (Lodal, 1978). However, the U.S.S.R. also retaliated against the U.S. for boycotting the 1980 Olympics in Moscow by boycotting the 1984 Olympics in Los Angeles (Gallois, 1988). As Reagan entered his last year in office, the U.S.S.R. ended its unsuccessful occupation of Afghanistan.

The release of the Iran hostages on the day of Reagan's first inauguration was classic theater. As indicated in the Iran-Contra Affair documents, Reagan's relations with Iran were only a little better than Jimmy Carter's. Reagan compounded his mistakes in the Middle East by sending U.S. troops into Lebanon in the midst of a civil war. The outcome was the bombing of the U.S. Embassy, killing more than sixty persons, and then six months later, the Marine Barracks in Beirut, Lebanon. In a few minutes, 241 soldiers and civilians were killed as the barracks partially collapsed in the bomb blast (Sibila, 2013).

Following the bombing of a nightclub in Berlin in which two members of the U.S. military were killed and many injured, Reagan dispatched bombers to Libya. While one hundred persons were reportedly killed in Libya, its president, Moammar Gadhafi, was not one of them. Later developments revealed an explicit link between Gadhafi's regime and the terrorist act (Amies & Scheschkewitz, 2001). The carnage of the retaliatory bombing in Libya caused Gadhafi to retreat from explicit sponsorship of such terrorist attacks. Reagan's example in this instance contains a lesson for future presidents. Sometimes, retaliation, even misguided, may serve to protect other Americans from terrorist attacks.

BY THE NUMBERS

The national debt was an issue during the Reagan administration (U.S. Department of the Treasury, Bureau of the Fiscal Service, 2013):

Year	National Debt
1981	$997,855,000,000
1982	$1,142,034,000,000
1983	$1,377,210,000,000
1984	$1,572,266,000,000
1985	$1,823,103,000,000
1986	$2,125,302,616,658
1987	$2,350,276,890,953
1988	$2,602,337,712,041

Reagan's historic increase in the national debt–an increase of 167 percent, more than the total of his recent predecessors–was stunning. Reagan hoped that his tax cuts would stimulate the economy and balance the loss of revenue. This was not achieved as he increased military spending substantially. There was a dramatic increase in the national debt, which occurred without a major war. It makes the increase all the more shameful.

Reviewing the annual inflation rates from 1981 through 1988 indicates a trending economy going from high to moderate inflation rates. Given the unsustainable high inflation he inherited, Reagan does get credit for bringing the inflation beast under some control, although in all but one year, well above the modern target of 2 percent per year (Coin News Media Group LLC, n.d.):

Year	Inflation Rate
1981	11.8%
1982	8.4%
1983	3.7%
1984	4.2%
1985	3.5%
1986	3.9%
1987	1.5%
1988	4.0%

MAKING THE GRADE

Reagan left office with a high approval level on par with Franklin Roosevelt. Similar to Roosevelt, though, popularity does not mean a successful administration. Reagan's private ethics are illustrated by his poor performance in selecting the administrators close to him and failing to provide strong ethical leadership. He has been accused of not caring about the poor and minorities since he reportedly favored "tax cuts for the rich." Often overlooked in such rhetoric is that most of the poor pay no tax, so all tax increases or decreases go to people still working.

In the domestic front, Reagan made some progress against inflation, but he increased the national debt at a record pace. While the mood of the country was largely positive during his administration, that alone does not spell success.

On the international scene, Reagan is credited with putting pressure on the U.S.S.R. that led to the fall of the Berlin Wall shortly after his presidency ended. He may also have been in the right place at the right time as the U.S.S.R. continually lost ground financially under its communist economic system. The threat of the Strategic Defense Initiative may have been a major factor. On the other hand, the disasters in Lebanon underscore the importance of not putting U.S. diplomats and troops in harm's way.

In the end, the Iran-Contra Affair and the failures in Lebanon combined with the massive increase in the national debt do not mark a great presidency. But in comparison to other Democrat and Republican presidents, he is still near the top of the heap.

Reagan Grade: C+

CHAPTER 15

GEORGE H.W. BUSH

("Official portrait of George H.W. Bush, former President of the United States of America", ca. 1989).

George Herbert Walker Bush (1924–), was elected the forty-first president of the U.S. in 1988 as the Republican candidate with a victory over Democrat Michael Dukakis, governor of Massachusetts. Bush's VP was Dan Quayle. Bush had strong name recognition as Reagan's VP for the prior eight years. He served one term, losing reelection in a three-way race to Democrat Bill Clinton in the 1992 election. The third-party candidate was Ross Perot (Sigelman & Whissell, 2002).

Bush's wife from 1945 to present is Barbara Pierce Bush. With her grandmotherly appearance and high public visibility, she was often cited as a positive model first lady. She is known for her support of literacy

("Barbara Bush," n.d.; Jentleson, & Whytock, 2005). Multiple tabloid sources claim that Bush had a long-running affair with Jennifer Fitzgerald, his assistant during his days in China, as head of the CIA, and as VP (TCA Reference, n.d.). However, in a recently released book, both Bush and Fitzgerald denied that there was an affair (Meacham, 2015).

OCCUPATIONAL ACCOMPLISHMENTS

Bush came from a powerful and wealthy family, and attended the prestigious Phillips Academy in Andover, Massachusetts. In a nontraditional move, Bush joined the U.S. Navy right out of Phillips, reportedly becoming the youngest combat pilot in the U.S. Navy during WWII ("George HW Bush," n.d.; Bressman & Vandenbergh, 2006). Recent reports are that there was one pilot just 11 days younger than Bush ("The Youngest Naval," 2016). Bush had a distinguished record as a pilot of torpedo bombers with fifty-eight combat missions. After leaving the Navy, he attended Yale University, graduating in just three years with a degree in economics (Miller Center of Public Affairs, University of Virginia, 2015).

Bush moved his family to Midland, Texas, to work in the oil industry. He later formed a partnership that led to the creation of Zapata Petroleum. He relocated the company to the oil capital of the U.S., Houston, and began his involvement in Republican politics. After an unsuccessful run for U.S. Senate in 1964, he was elected to the 7th Congressional District seat in 1966 in an area of Houston with pockets of high-income voters (Hall, 2002).

SIGNIFICANT EVENTS DURING BUSH'S TIME IN OFFICE

1989

- Poland begins to break away from U.S.S.R. and Bush supports the move.
- Tiananmen Square massacre of democracy protestors in Beijing
- The Berlin Wall falls, Germany formally reunites
- U.S. invades Panama to remove dictator Manuel Noriega.

1990

- Bush signs budget law with new taxes in violation of his campaign promise.
- Iraq invades Kuwait.

1991

- Operation Desert Storm frees Kuwait and forces Iraq into a truce.
- Controversial nominee Clarence Thomas is confirmed as U.S. Supreme Court Justice.
- The U.S.S.R. formally dissolves.

1992

- Clinton defeats Bush as a third-party candidate, draws 19 percent of the vote.
- U.S. troops join UN forces in Somalia to protect humanitarian aid workers.

THE DOMESTIC FRONT AND RACE RELATIONS

Bush's administration was not easy at home or abroad. Congress was strongly Democrat when he entered office and the Republicans lost more ground during the 1990 midterm election. Often mentioned as a reason why conservative voters abandoned Bush in the 1992 election was that he broke his promise of "no new taxes" made during the 1988 campaign (Tenpas & Hess, 2002). The 1990 budget deal was an exchange of promises. Congress promised to reduce expenditures if Bush would agree to increase taxes. Taxes were increased but the promised reductions were not made by Congress (Cohen, Vaughn, & Villalobos). Toward the end of his term, the U.S. slipped into a recession marked by a return to unemployment in excess of 7 percent. This was another factor in the incumbent Bush losing the presidency in 1992.

For the U.S. Supreme Court, the Senate approved moderate David Souter's appointment. It is likely that Bush did not nominate a more conservative choice since he did not anticipate the nominee would be accepted by the Democrats in the Senate (Vaughn & Villalobos, 2006). He was surprised that he had to use a fair amount of political capital to secure the appointment of Clarence Thomas to the Supreme Court. The black justice was pilloried for alleged sexual harassment by a former law clerk. Thomas's appointment was narrowly approved (Supreme Court Nominations," n.d.).

While Bush signed the 1990 Clean Air Act to make progress against air pollution problems like acid rain (Abramson, Aldrich, Rickershauser, & Rohde, 2007), his administration also had to deal with the Exxon Valdez oil tanker spill in Alaska. Photos of beaches and birds covered in black oil ran on television and the front pages of newspapers for weeks. Reports that the captain of the ship was not on duty when the ship ran aground and later reports that he may have been under the influence of alcohol compounded the story that lingered in the news (Dull & Roberts, 2009).

The Civil Rights arena should have been a high point for the Bush administration with his signing of the Americans with Disabilities Act in 1990 (ADA) and the Civil Rights Act of 1991 (Dobel, 2010). However, he sent both bills back to Congress and received modified bills before signing them. The disabled and minority communities viewed this initial Bush response as a lack of commitment on his part. Both bills were poorly drafted and while his required amendments improved them, problems with interpretation and enforcement have burdened both government and business interests for years. A classic example of failure across the legislative and executive branches of government, the 1991 Civil Rights Act is a hodgepodge that includes amendments to the 1866 Civil Rights Act. A more intelligent and functional approach would have been to completely rewrite and reorganize America's equal employment laws. Bush can hardly be blamed for the resulting bill, as he would likely have faced a vote overriding him if he vetoed the law again.

More damaging to Bush in race relations were the 1992 Los Angeles riots. Rodney King, a black man, was beaten in 1991 by four members of the L.A. police force. A video of the attack surfaced. When all four were acquitted by a jury in 1992, L.A. went up in flames. One of the more dramatic incidents was the beating of white truck driver Reginald Denny, who happened to be driving his truck through the riot area. He was beaten nearly to death. In 1993, a federal court jury found two of the policemen guilty of violating Rodney King's civil rights. In 1993, one of Denny's attackers was sentenced to four years in prison. The *Los Angeles Times* ran a comprehensive retrospective of the riot and related events in April 2016 (*Los Angeles Times* staff, 2016). There is little Bush could have done to have changed the narrative in this case, but it still happened during his time in office.

Bush's predecessor, Ronald Reagan, signed the Immigration Reform Act of 1986 that provided amnesty for millions of persons in the U.S. illegally. A related issue provided a path for increased numbers of new immigrants to enter the U.S. legally. Bush signed the Immigration Act of 1990 which significantly modified existing immigration law and increased available visas from five hundred thousand to seven hundred thousand each year. The new law increased special visas for family members and introduced a new category of "exceptional ability." This is applied to professionals in science and business. A "skilled worker" category was added which was intended to help the U.S. fill jobs in high-skill areas where there are insufficient U.S. workers ("Immigration Act of 1990," 1990). Despite this act and the provisions in the 1986 bill to increase border security, the number of undocumented persons in the U.S. continued to grow.

THE BUSH INTERNATIONAL RECORD

In a surprise move for many Americans, Bush sent troops into Panama, a long-time ally and protectorate of the U.S. The stated reason was that Manuel Noriega, Panama's military dictator, had been indicted by a Miami jury of involvement in illegal drug sales in the U.S. The case is much more interesting since Noriega was on the CIA payroll off and on over two decades and had allegedly helped the U.S. fight the Marxist insurgency in Nicaragua. Noriega was sentenced to forty years in prison once transported to the U.S. to face the drug charges against him (History.com staff, 2010). Noriega served about twenty years in the U.S., then was imprisoned in France and later still imprisoned in Panama (Associated Press, 2015). While Americans were generally unperturbed by the invasion of Panama and the treatment of Noriega, it did not seem to help Bush politically.

The fall of the Berlin Wall and the reunification of East and West Germany happened during Bush's administration (Kumar, 2003). The dissolution of the U.S.S.R. followed (Liberman, 2007). These were positive events in the minds of most Americans, but much of the credit was passed back to Reagan's administration and not Bush. Bush then engaged with the new leaders of the former "Iron Curtain" countries to reach mutual agreements to reduce nuclear arms of various kinds (Arnold, Walcott, & Patterson, 2001).

Most Americans were supportive of Bush's response to Iraq's Saddam Hussein's 1990 invasion of Kuwait and what appeared to be a plan to continue his invasion into another oil-rich country, Saudi Arabia. After international sanctions failed to work, Bush assembled an international coalition to defeat Iraq. In this case, Bush displayed a solid understanding of international diplomacy, a result of his substantial prior experience as a diplomat, CIA chief, and VP.

Bush drew parallels to Hitler's invasion of Poland and Czechoslovakia in the early days of WWII. He viewed stopping Hussein to prevent Iraq from entrenching itself even further in countries important to the U.S. as a critical objective. While the coalition defeated Iraq in roughly a month, when the battle was taken to the steps of the Iraqi capital in Baghdad, the parties entered into a truce leaving Hussein in power. Bush would explain that this was all that the UN-backed coalition would allow, but many Americans were dissatisfied with this outcome (PBS, 2008). Some point to the mess in 2007-2016 that is Iraq post-Hussein as an example of why the U.S.-led coalition did the right thing not taking Hussein out completely. However, the U.S. had significant successes after WWII following the unconditional surrenders of Germany and Japan. A stronger leader producing a more decisive victory could have avoided the second invasion of Iraq and perhaps avoided the current power vacuum that resulted in the growth of ISIS in Iraq.

Bush damaged his "legacy" after losing the 1992 presidential election by sending troops into Somalia in order to provide protection for aid workers so that much-needed food could be distributed to the population. Battles among competing warlords had prevented emergency food supplies from being distributed. Sadly, no American objectives were met and when Clinton inherited this situation, he floundered with it for another year before abandoning Somalia completely. The message here, similar to Reagan's debacle in Lebanon, is that it is virtually impossible for an outside power to insert itself into a civil war unless overwhelming force is used to take complete control of the country. Half-hearted measures help to get many killed and waste American and civilian lives and resources (Army History, n.d.).

BY THE NUMBERS

Bush presided over a 40 percent increase in the national debt despite the famed 140 billion-dollar tax increase referenced above (Amadeo, 2016):

Year	National Debt
1989	$2,857,430,960,187
1990	$3,233,313,451,777
1991	$3,665,303,351,697
1992	$4,064,620,655,521

Bush did only modestly well in dealing with inflation as the rate was clearly on the rise against the 2 percent benchmark until his last year, which was a recession year (Coin News Media Group LLC, n.d.):

Year	Inflation Rate
1989	4.0%
1990	5.2%
1991	5.7%
1992	2.6%

MAKING THE GRADE

Bush was perceived during his time in office and subsequently as a "nice guy." Unfortunately, if true, the phrase "nice guys finish last" might be appropriate. He displayed a tough side in Panama and Iraq and did not display a reluctance to use force to achieve diplomatic objectives.

Regarding his private ethics, it is hard to give a pass to Bush regarding the Iran-Contra Affair. Given the extent of the affair and his position as former head of the CIA and Reagan's vice president, it is unlikely that he was unaware of the circumstances behind the scenes. He issued pardons to those who were convicted before he left office. His moral compass certainly can be questioned by his proximity to the many parties involved in the affair. Further, his pardoning of those who did not fight in court has an odor to it.

In terms of his public ethics, he gets credit for two major civil rights laws and a major upgrade of the Clean Air Act, things usually not associated with a Republican president. He appointed an enduring black Supreme Court justice in Clarence Thomas. At the same time, he was challenged for vetoing the Civil Rights Act of 1990 before it was submitted to him with changes in 1991. The Los Angeles riots of 1992 happened during his term in office.

On the domestic scene, it is a mediocre outcome. The economy plodded along during his presidency and then sunk into a recession during his fourth year. The national debt continued to increase. Given the excuse of the Iraq War, the 40 percent increase over four years might be viewed as simply expected.

Internationally, the vote is mixed on the outcome of the Iraq War. Generally, Americans supported the involvement, but would have favored a much more definitive outcome. The sudden invasion of Panama appears to have been almost a non-event since it took place so quickly and in a country where the U.S. already had a significant presence. Bush missed the opportunity to use it as an excuse to either retract the treaty giving the canal back to Panama, or significantly delaying its transfer. Post-election, he began the sad chapter in Somalia, clearly not a positive.

Bush had an ugly loss in the 1992 presidential election. He earned only 38 percent of the popular vote versus Bill Clinton, a virtually unknown candidate, who gained 43 percent of the vote. Notably, Ross Perot, the former head of EDS, a computer services company with numerous defense contracts, garnered 19 percent of the popular vote. Conservative voters reportedly were unhappy with Bush's reversal of his "no new taxes" pledge. The general population was unhappy with the recession during his critical last year in office.

The various presidential popularity surveys show Bush moving up the ratings slightly, although this may be due to the questionable performance of the subsequent presidents.

Bush Grade: C-

CHAPTER 16
WILLIAM J. CLINTON

(McNeely, 1993)

William Jefferson Clinton (1946–), popularly known as Bill Clinton, was elected the forty-second president of the U.S. as a Democrat in 1992. His birth surname was Blythe, but his father died in an auto accident before he was born, and when his mother remarried to Roger Clinton, his last name was changed to Clinton (Miller Center of Public Affairs, University of Virginia, n.d.a). His election was one of the strangest presidential elections in recent memory. He earned only 43 percent of the popular vote versus incumbent George H.W. Bush, who got 38 percent of the vote. Notably, Ross Perot garnered 19 percent of the popular vote (Hibbitts, 2012). Clinton was helped by an economic recession accompanied by a sudden increase in unemployment, in addition to the campaign by Perot. Clinton was reelected in 1996 with a relatively easy victory over former Senator Bob Dole with 49.2 percent of the vote to 40.7 percent for Dole. Perot was involved again, but received less media coverage and sank to 8.4 percent of the vote, still enough to impact the outcome (Compare Infobase Ltd., n.d.). His VP for the entire eight years was Al Gore, who was the unsuccessful Democratic presidential candidate in 2000.

Clinton's wife from 1975 to present is Hillary Rodham Clinton. Hillary Clinton was a fairly high-profile First Lady during her husband's time in the White House (WGBH Educational Foundation, 2013). She was Clinton's designated lead for a national healthcare plan that never materialized. The program died quietly after the Democrats lost both houses of Congress in the 1994 midterm elections. The Republicans united under Speaker of the House Newt Gingrich (Clymer, 1994). Clinton gained enough fame as a "womanizer" that the announcement of yet another woman he reportedly groped was called a "Bimbo Eruption" (Clift & Hosenball, 1994).

OCCUPATIONAL ACCOMPLISHMENTS

Clinton attended Georgetown University, was awarded a Fulbright Scholarship to study at Oxford for two years, and then attended Yale Law School. His soon-to-be wife was a law school classmate at Yale. After graduating from Yale Law School in 1973, Clinton briefly taught law at the University of Arkansas. He then ran for the United States House of Representatives and lost (Miller Center of Public Affairs, University of Virginia, n.d.a). In 1974, he was elected Arkansas Attorney General. In 1978, at the age of thirty-two, he became the youngest governor in the nation and in Arkansas history. After losing his bid for reelection the first time, Clinton came back to win four terms, two two-year terms and two four-year terms as Arkansas governor. He continually raised his national profile, thereby positioning himself as a potential candidate for the Democratic nomination for President in 1992 (Miller Center of Public Affairs, University of Virginia, n.d.a).

In Clinton's early years as governor of Arkansas, though a Democrat, he favored some policies traditionally associated with Republicans. He favored capital punishment and promoted welfare reforms. At the same time, he promoted affirmative action by appointing more blacks to state boards, commissions, and agency posts than all of his predecessors combined (Biography.com Editors, 2016). A very successful politician, his campaigns would do extensive polling and then tilt his agenda in the direction the voters were already heading. This approach was developed by political consultant Dick Morris. Extensive news releases and advertising were used to craft a story best suited to the likely voters. Morris, in a high-profile defection during Clinton's second term, has written books reportedly exposing the inside story on Bill and Hillary Clinton (Miller Center of Public Affairs, University of Virginia, n.d.b).

SIGNIFICANT EVENTS DURING CLINTON'S TIME IN OFFICE

1993
- First World Trade Center bombing kills six people.
- Janet Reno is appointed first female U.S. Attorney General.
- Deputy Counsel to Clinton, Vince Foster, is found dead in a public park in D.C.
- U.S. Forces ambushed in Somalia in Battle of Mogadishu

- NAFTA – North American Free Trade Agreement – signed by Clinton

1994

- Clinton promotes welfare reform.
- Democrat Senator George Mitchell kills Clinton health-care plan.
- Haiti military leader backs down when faced with U.S. military action.
- Newt Gingrich leads "Contract with America" Republican sweep of Congress.
- U.S. agrees to be part of GATT – General Agreement on Tariffs and Trade.

1995

- Oklahoma City Federal Building is bombed with 168 dead.
- Partial government shutdown in budget struggle between Gingrich and Clinton

1996

- First convictions in the Whitewater trials in Arkansas of Clinton insiders
- Clinton signs HIPAA bill – protecting medical records and insurance portability.
- Madeline Albright is appointed first female Secretary of State.

1997

- Senate votes 99-0 to investigate Democrat fund-raising practices.
- Paula Jones is allowed to pursue sexual harassment case against Clinton.

1998

- Monica Lewinsky affair becomes public.
- American embassies in Kenya and Tanzania are bombed in coordinated attacks.
- Starr Report presents possible grounds for impeachment of Clinton.
- House votes to impeach Clinton for perjury and obstruction.

1999

- The Senate acquits Clinton in impeachment case.

2000

- USS *Cole* is bombed in Yemen with seventeen service persons dead.
- Independent Counsel declines to indict Clintons over Whitewater.

THE DOMESTIC FRONT AND RACE RELATIONS

Other than the scandals referenced above, Clinton's administration is largely remembered fairly positively today for its economic agenda. An economic expansion paralleled most of his time in office as the economic downturn during the last year of the Bush presidency was short-lived. Clinton's own agenda was actually much more "conservative" in regard to welfare reform and federal deficit reduction than perhaps many recall today. Critical to his success was most likely the Republican control of both houses of Congress starting in January 1995.

Clinton pushed through his early economic package, the Omnibus Budget Reconciliation Act of 1993, while the Democrats still held both Houses of Congress. The package combined tax increases and cuts in federal spending (Miller Center of Public Affairs, University of Virginia, n.d.a).

The bill raised the top two tax brackets, removed the wage cap on the Medicare payroll tax, and raised the corporate income tax rate. The impact on lower-income workers came from an increase in the gas tax and an increase in the taxable portion of Social Security benefits. While cited as the key to the economic expansion of the 1990s, it is unlikely that this helped the economy grow (Kadlec, 2012). Parallel to the Roosevelt administration, early efforts that looked like progress were later revealed to have caused long-term problems. For instance, twenty years later, Washington is trying to repatriate trillions of dollars held overseas due to the high U.S. corporate tax rate.

A focus on reducing the growth in the annual budget deficit is often cited as the biggest single economic accomplishment of the Clinton administration. This would not have been possible without the dramatic change in Congress with the Republican control of both houses in the 1994 elections. Newt Gingrich attempted to implement his "Contract with America." Gingrich and Clinton did not agree on an approach to a balanced budget. The result was a short government shutdown in November 1995, followed by a longer shutdown from mid-December 1995 into early January 1996 (The Regents of the University of California, 2013). While Democrat supporters cited this as proof that Gingrich was out of touch with America, many taxpayers actually supported the shutdown. Both sides found it largely a non-event. Federal employees who were furloughed were later paid, and many employees considered critical to government operations continued to work (Tyson, 2013; Anderson, 1997).

In 1997, Clinton reached a comprehensive five-year budget deal with Gingrich not to pay down the national debt, but to simply have the U.S. operate without a deficit (Clinton, 1997). As demonstrated in the "Numbers" section below, the national debt actually increased by 1.2 trillion dollars during his eight years in office. This was during a period when the economy was strong, defense spending was reduced, and there was not a major war being fought.

Clinton appointed his VP, Al Gore, to head a National Performance Review with the noble intent to reduce government employment and waste. Targeting the number of federal employees was a stated goal, but the actual accomplishment of the goal was elusive (A Brief History of the National Performance Review, 1997). In an attempt to reduce levels of government bureaucracy, the net result was an elimination of many management slots at level GS-15. Since the number of subordinates was not reduced, the effort resulted in GS-14 employees supervising other GS-14 level employees. This produced significant morale issues and only short-term staffing reductions.

In the early going, Clinton appointed Hillary Clinton to be in charge of a healthcare reform effort. It was an ambitious plan that is somewhat parallel to the disastrous Affordable Care Act (ACA) of Obama (Donaldson, 2012). Even though a Democrat, George Mitchell, as the Senate Majority Leader in 1994, did not allow the Clinton healthcare bill to be brought to a vote (Abrams, 2009). With the arrival of the Republican sweep in the 1994 off-year elections, the proposed act died quietly. It is likely that while Mitchell lost the Majority Leader's post in the elections, if he had not killed the healthcare bill, it could have been a major liability for Clinton in the 1996 presidential election. Later, Clinton did sign a healthcare-related bill in the Health Insurance Portability and Accountability Act 1996 (HIPAA). This bill required that persons changing jobs with group health insurance would be able to join another employer with group health insurance and immediately enroll in the plan without a waiting period. It was intended to reduce healthcare costs by requiring that medical records be converted to digital format along with increased privacy rules (Clinton, 1996). Medical costs continued to surge despite this act.

Early in his administration, Clinton pushed-through the Family and Medical Leave Act (FMLA) (The History of Us, 1993). This bill provides for up to twelve weeks of unpaid leave for defined serious medical conditions of the employee or the employee's immediate family. It only applies to employers with fifty or more employees. It was clearly intended to be expanded into a paid leave bill and perhaps made applicable to employers with even fewer employees. With the political party change in Congress, these amendments did not come about. In the two subsequent presidential administrations, the coverage of the FMLA has been expanded, but not with regard to the issues of paid leave or reduction in number of employees required for coverage.

Clinton had false-starts with his first and second nominations for U.S. Attorney General. He nominated Zoe Baird first, but it was discovered that she had not paid proper wages to a nanny, hence, "Nannygate." Baird withdrew her nomination, and then Clinton nominated Kimba Woods. Woods also was revealed to have a "Nannygate" problem and she withdrew her nomination (Qiu, 2015). Clinton was able to get Janet Reno approved as the first female Attorney General. Reno soon became involved in a standoff with a cult located in Waco, Texas, called the Branch Davidians. Losing patience with the siege of the complex, a large fire ensued as the FBI and other federal agencies tried to subdue the defenders. The death toll from the fire was approximately eighty people inside the complex. Reno was roundly criticized for her handling of the attack, which was viewed as impetuous and overly aggressive (Burnett, 2013).

The U.S. suffered two significant terrorist attacks on U.S. soil during Clinton's two terms. The first was just a month after his inauguration in February 1993, when the New York World Trade Center was damaged by a powerful explosion set off in a truck in the parking garage under the building. Six persons were killed and a thousand were injured (McCaul, 2013). Given the proximity to the start of the Clinton administration, the Bush administration must take much of the blame for this incident. It was a wake-up call that America had to be more vigilant in dealing with extremists and terrorism. Unfortunately, a huge failing of Clinton was to consider the bombing as essentially a police matter, especially as the local perpetrators were rounded up. A long-term lack of coordination in combating terrorism unquestionably led to the more horrific attacks on 9/11 (National Commission on Terrorist Attacks Upon the United States, 2004 - Counterterrorism Evolves).

Two years later, in April 1995, a truck loaded with explosives was set off next to the Murrah Federal Building in Oklahoma City. The attack cost the lives of 168 persons, including nineteen children, since the bomb hit the part of the building that housed an on-site daycare center for the employees. More than six hundred other persons sustained injuries in the massive blast. This time, the attack was by two white Americans, Timothy McVeigh, a former GI who had served in Desert Storm; and Terry Nichols, also an Army veteran. McVeigh and Nichols were members of a survivalist cult and were "radicalized," supposedly by the attack in Waco on the Branch Davidians (History.com staff, 2009b).

With the support of the now Republican-controlled Congress, in 1996 Clinton signed a comprehensive welfare reform act with an emphasis on a return to work rather than lifetime welfare. This plan was consistent with his earlier efforts in this regard as governor of Arkansas. The act required a return to work within five years of receiving welfare benefits. A very important provision was enforcement of child support orders nationwide. Mothers could no longer simply ask for benefits based on a nonpaying father. The father would be responsible for his children rather than placing the burden on the public. Generally regarded as a long-term success, it has been criticized for lacking a fallback plan for persons on welfare who for various reasons were unable to report for work and thereby risked being cut off from all benefits (Haskins, 2006).

An honest evaluation of his record on civil rights would be mixed. Most minorities would say that the "reform" of the welfare system, discussed in this chapter, unfairly impacted minorities more than white Americans. He signed the Violent Crime and Law Enforcement Act in 1994 that expanded the death penalty to fifty additional federal crimes and provided funding intended to increase the number of police officers in the U.S. by one hundred thousand (Miller Center of Public Affairs, University of Virginia, n.d.a). This is unlikely to be viewed as a pro-minority position in modern America. On the other hand, he signed the Congressional Accountability Act in 1995 (Office of Compliance, 1995). This bill made members of Congress responsible for their discriminatory acts on the same basis as the rest of U.S. employers. In addition to the first female Attorney General, Janet Reno, he named the first female Secretary of State, Madeleine Albright (History.com staff, 2009a), and added a second female U.S. Supreme Court justice in Ruth Bader Ginsburg (Cannon, 1993). He named two black females to senior positions: Hazel O'Leary, Secretary of Energy; and Dr. Joycelyn Elders, U.S. Surgeon General (Miller Center of Public Affairs, University of Virginia, n.d.a). Unfortunately for Clinton, Elders became somewhat famous for controversial statements during her tenure. And, in what is now quaint under recent standards, Clinton authorized "Don't Ask, Don't Tell" as the policy for gays in the military in 1993 (Horvitz, 1993).

International trade treaties and pacts could be viewed as either domestic or international. With their potential impact on domestic economy, they are discussed in this section on domestic policies. One of Clinton's first economic initiatives was to promote the North American Free Trade Agreement, known as "NAFTA" (Hansen-Kuhn, n.d.).

The objective was to create a free trade zone for North America, including Mexico, Canada, and the U.S. Support for the bill was interesting since many Republicans supported it as pro-trade and pro-business, but the bill was heavily opposed by the unions for its possible negative impact on union jobs, especially in the heavily unionized auto industry. A comprehensive 2014 report by the Peterson Institute for International Economics strongly supports the outcome of NAFTA, specifically addressing complaints of liberals and conservatives about the trade pact (Peterson Institute for International Economics, 2014). The same year, an evaluation by the economists at the Wharton School of the University of Pennsylvania arrived at roughly the same conclusion, although more muted. It concluded that Mexico did receive more benefit from the pact than the U.S. (The Wharton School, 2014).

The U.S. joined the General Agreement on Tariffs and Trade (GATT) in 1994 (The World Trade Organization (WTO), 1994). More than 120 countries around the World agreed to form the 1994 version of GATT, which governs the international trade of goods. The GATT acts as a framework and each member country negotiates its own bilateral or broader arrangement. As the GATT grew out of an early version following the end of WWII, credit for GATT extends to several presidential administrations, not just Clinton's.

Clinton renewed China's "most favored nation" trading status with the U.S. despite its slaughter of protesters in Tiananmen Square in 1989. Clinton also accepted Vietnam as an official trading partner of the U.S. despite the repression of its own population and the murder of many supporters of the South Vietnamese government after the regime's takeover in 1975 (Jehl, 1994).

CLINTON SCANDALS

While scandal touched a number of presidential administrations covered in this book, no president other than Harding seems to have made such an art form of scandal. Many scandals became public after Clinton was reelected. It is hard to determine if Clinton might have been a one-term president if the full weight of the scandals had been made public before the 1996 election.

Early in Clinton's first term, Vince Foster, Deputy Counsel to Clinton, was found dead in a public park in the D.C. area. His death was publicly announced as a suicide (*The mysterious death of Vince Foster,* 1993). While there is no public evidence that he was murdered, and five investigations (led both by Democrats and Republicans), found his death a suicide, some pundits have mused that a Clinton insider might have killed him to keep him from exposing Foster's concerns about scandals involving Bill and Hillary Clinton and others close to them. Foster had access to some of the Whitewater records discussed later in this chapter. After his death, the White House blocked access to his office for a short period of time before investigators were allowed to enter, increasing speculation that sensitive records were removed (Schmidt, 1997).

A long-running scandal of the Clinton presidency was the Paula Jones case *(Jones v. Clinton, 1994).* In her 1994 lawsuit against President Clinton, Jones alleged that in 1991, while Clinton was governor of Arkansas, he sexually harassed and assaulted her *(Jones v. Clinton,* 1996). She stated that as a state employee, the sexual proposition in a hotel room by the governor of the state constituted creation of a hostile work environment, and she feared she would lose her job *(Jones v. Clinton).* President Clinton tried to escape the lawsuit by asserting presidential immunity. Two years after the original suit, the Court of Appeals for the Eighth Circuit decided presidential immunity did not apply to unofficial acts. The President was deemed liable for acts committed by him in his personal capacity rather than his capacity as President (*Jones v. Clinton*). He did receive temporary immunity from trial. Discovery in the case (*Jones v. Clinton* 72 F. 3d 1354) was allowed to continue during his presidency.

Despite a public pounding in the media orchestrated by presidential advisor James Carville, spokesperson George Stephanopoulos, and Hillary Clinton, Jones held steadfast to her statements and accusations (Elder, 2016). Memorable due to its extraordinary nastiness was a statement about Jones by Carville: "Drag a hundred dollars through a trailer park and there's no telling what you'll find" (Gladnick, 2016). The merits seem to be solidly with Jones when she settled the case in 1997 for 850,000 dollars (Lewis, 1999). A typical no-merit employment discrimination case would likely have been five thousand to ten thousand dollars.

While there had been many rumors of Clinton's womanizing, the Jones case seemed to provide a stimulus for others to come forward. Another case did not rise to either criminal charges or civil litigation: Juanita Broaddrick, a campaign volunteer from Clinton's days as governor, came out in 1999 to allege that Clinton raped her in 1978 (Kurtz, 1999).

This is an allegation that Clinton denies and that has brought forward issues of credibility against Broaddrick. At the same time, certain elements of her description of the incident appear to be supported. She again came out in public in 2016, spurred by the Hillary Clinton campaign for president. Broaddrick renewed her allegations of rape from 1978 (Baker, 2016). The Broaddrick story has an odd similarity to the rape and assault claims against entertainer Bill Cosby in that the alleged events happened in the past and the putative victims stated that they did not come forward at the time of the incidents due to the fame of the alleged attacker (Kim, Littlefield, & Olsen, 2016).

The Jones case resulted in the disclosure of what Clinton claims was a consensual relationship with Gennifer Flowers. Ignoring the fact that Clinton was indeed married to Hillary at the time this affair would have occurred, Clinton denied it during his 1992 presidential bid, but then admitted to a sexual relationship during a 1998 deposition in the Jones case (King, 1998).

Adding to the intrigue during this time, and too late to impact Clinton's 1996 reelection bid, were allegations by Kathleen Willey, another campaign volunteer. She claimed to have been assaulted by Clinton in 1993, after he was already president (Limbacher, 1998). Willey opened a website in 2016 called "A Scandal a Day" to reportedly inform women of Clinton's activities and his wife's efforts to support him and "trash" the women who came forward (Willey, n.d.). There are too many accusers to list all of them in this chapter. Even a source generally regarded as favorable to Democrat politicians, *The Washington Post*, published in late 2015 a list of many of the accusations against Clinton (Kessler, 2015).

One affair caught the public's attention more than any other, and that was Clinton's relationship with White House intern Monica Lewinsky, who was twenty-four at the time (Bauder, 1998). For months, Clinton's denials were systematically challenged as more evidence leaked out. The evidence followed a circuitous path, but based on a detailed summary report from Pew Research Center, appears to be genuine (Pew Research Center: Journalism & Media staff, 1998).

The second part of the Lewinsky Affair was that Clinton was caught lying about it during investigations of the incident and then depositions in the Jones case, referenced above. Two key statements by Clinton himself regarding the affair can be viewed online. His well-documented falsified statements and testimony led to only the second impeachment of a sitting president, the first being Andrew Johnson over one hundred years earlier (The History Place, 2000). In an interesting twist of fate, even though the Republican-controlled Congress voted for impeachment, the Republican-controlled Senate voted for acquittal and Clinton was thereby spared the ultimate punishment of removal from office (Lindberg, 2000).

Clinton entered the presidency as an attorney. In April 2001, President Clinton's Arkansas law license was suspended for five years and he was fined twenty-five thousand dollars. The professional conduct committee of the Arkansas Supreme Court originally brought a lawsuit to disbar Clinton after he admitted to lying during the Lewinsky investigation. He also gave misleading testimony in the Paula Jones sexual harassment case (Campbell, 2001). After being suspended from the Arkansas bar, he was disbarred from practicing before the Supreme Court of the United States (The New York Times Company, 2001). Clinton has not petitioned the court to restore his license (Evon, 2016).

WHITEWATER

Clinton's "bimbo eruptions," as his campaign called them, were certainly not the only scandals during Clinton's time in the White House. One enduring scandal was known as "Whitewater." Space limitations require a very abbreviated account here, but *The Washington Post* has assembled a helpful and detailed timeline for Whitewater (1998b). A 1978 real estate deal for 220 acres of land in the Ozark Mountains of Arkansas was put together by Clinton, then Arkansas Attorney General and later Governor; Hillary Clinton, then at the Rose Law Firm; and a couple, James and Susan McDougal. They formed Whitewater Development Company and borrowed more than two hundred thousand dollars, intending to build vacation homes on the land. James McDougal bought a small bank and renamed it Madison Guaranty. He even loaned Hillary money for the construction of a model home at Whitewater (The Washington Post, 1998b).

Federal regulators began an investigation into lending and land speculation by Madison Guaranty. Despite this investigation, McDougal hosted a fund-raising event at the bank to help Clinton pay off some campaign debts. Investigators later determined some of the money was illegally drawn from depositors' accounts. He then hired the Rose Law Firm, where Hillary Clinton was now a partner, to help the bank deal with its legal problems. Hillary led attempts to recapitalize the bank. This series of questionable deals and loans caused McDougal's removal as president of Madison Guaranty (The Washington Post Company, 1998b).

Madison Guaranty closed in 1989, caused by bad loans and after the federal government bailout reached sixty million dollars. McDougal was indicted on fraud charges related to Madison, but later acquitted. The Clintons were named as potential beneficiaries of the fraud at Madison by the Federal Resolution Trust Corporation. Vince Foster, referenced above, filed delinquent tax returns for Whitewater in 1993. The Clintons were then tipped to inside information about the investigation by Treasury Department officials. A criminal prosecution of the Clintons was blocked by the U.S. Attorney in Little Rock, Paula Casey, a former law student of Clinton (The Washington Post Company, 1998b).

Other investigations of Whitewater continued. The congressional banking committees conducted hearings and interviewed many Clinton associates. No charges resulted from these hearings. Kenneth Starr was assigned to the Whitewater-Madison Guaranty investigation in 1994 (The Washington Post Company, 1998b). In 1995, an Arkansas grand jury charged Clinton associates James and Susan McDougal and Governor Jim Tucker with bank fraud. All three were later convicted (Rempel, 1995). In early 1996, Hillary Clinton's "missing" billing records from her time at the Rose Law Firm surfaced. The records showed that she had billable time for work for Madison Guaranty. Later in the year, the Federal Deposit Insurance Corporation (FDIC) reported that Hillary Clinton drafted a real estate document that Madison Guaranty used to "deceive" federal regulators when she was representing the bank. No prosecution was ever based on this report (The Washington Post Company, 1998b). Ultimately, Starr took no criminal action against either of the Clintons (Qiu, 2015).

Other people close to the Clintons were prosecuted. Associate Attorney General Webster L. Hubbell resigned when questions were raised as to his activities at the Rose Law Firm (Clinton, 1994). Clinton supporters arranged five hundred thousand dollars in legal defense funds for Hubbell (The Washington Post Company, 1998b). He was convicted of fraud and served seventeen months in prison. Later, Hubbell was indicted again, this time for tax evasion, as hundreds of thousands of dollars were pipelined to him on behalf of the Clintons (Labaton, 1998). Hubbell received immunity from Kenneth Starr and a federal judge ruled this indictment violated the immunity agreement. Hubbell was charged again, but reached a plea agreement and only served one year of probation (Lichtblau, 1999).

TRAVELGATE

A minor scandal was known as "Travelgate," when in 1993 the White House fired seven employees in the travel office. It was claimed that this was done to make room for Clinton's associates. A later FBI investigation did not result in any charges (The Washington Post Company, 1998b). It was disclosed in 1996 that the White House had collected background reports through the FBI on many persons, including a number of key Republicans. Labeled "Filegate," this scandal received some media attention for a brief time. Again, subsequent investigations did not result in any criminal charges, although Craig Livingstone, Director of the White House's Office of Personnel Security, resigned after the issue was made public (Simon, 2016).

JOHN HUANG

Clinton was often criticized for his campaigns' fundraising operations. One well-publicized example was VP Gore's attendance at a Democratic National Committee (DNC) fundraising event at a Buddhist temple in Los Angeles in 1996. It violates U.S. campaign laws to hold political fundraisers in religious facilities. Gore would claim that he did not know it was a fundraiser, even though as much as 140,000 dollars was raised. This was an event put together by John Huang (All Politics staff and Wolf Blitzer, 1997). Huang became rather infamous when several such incidents came to light and he was ultimately prosecuted for deliberate campaign fundraising violations. Huang was formerly with the Lippo Group, headquartered in Indonesia, and later a Commerce Department official before joining the DNC as a fundraiser. His appointment to the Commerce Department appears to have been a reward for his earlier fundraising activities. Clinton's Justice Department, headed by Attorney General Janet Reno, entered into a deal with Huang. He agreed to plead guilty to one felony count for an earlier violation, but with no prison time, and an agreement that he could not be prosecuted for anything related to the Clinton campaigns (Walsh & Suro, 1999; The Washington Post Company, 1998a).

PARDONGATE

Every recent American president has granted pardons to criminals, often on their way out the door, where any possible anger from the public will be largely harmless. The U.S. Department of Justice actually tracks this statistic (Department of Justice, 2016). These largely administrative events go without media coverage. Gerald Ford's pardon of Nixon and George H.W. Bush's pardon of Iran-Contra players received a great deal of media attention. Clinton pardoned a large number of criminals on his way out of the White House, generating another "gate," this time labeled by the media as "Pardongate." Clinton pardoned approximately 450 criminals during his time in office. This number is not in itself remarkable as it is actually about the same number granted by Reagan (Attorney, 2015).

Notably, the one criminal pardoned by Clinton who generated the most attention was Marc Rich. Rich was a commodities trader who violated sanctions against sales to South Africa when it was under an embargo due to its apartheid policies. It was reported that he sold to Iran and Cuba during a time when such trades were banned (Alschuler, 2010). Rich was a fugitive from American law enforcement when the pardon was granted. Prior to the pardon, Rich's wife gave 450,000 dollars to the Clinton Presidential Library fund and gave generously to Democrat candidates' campaigns (Mazzetti, 2001). The key player in creating the deal was then Deputy Attorney General Eric Holder, who was made Attorney General under Barack Obama (Lichtblau & Johnston, 2008). Despite a formal investigation, it was determined that there was no criminal conduct by Clinton in granting the pardon (Holbrooks, 2016). A scathing report by the House Committee on Government Reform detailing the history of Marc Rich's misdeeds and pardon is illuminating (Committee on Government Reform, 2001).

Another controversial pardon was of Roger Clinton Jr., Clinton's half-brother. He had been an embarrassment to Clinton during his administration with his rock-performer alternative lifestyle. The pardon was to erase a conviction and one-year prison term for cocaine possession in the 1980s (House of Representative, 107th Congress, 2001). It is clear in numerous instances that Clinton granted pardons under circumstances that most would conclude were ethically inappropriate, if not criminal in nature.

THE CLINTON INTERNATIONAL RECORD

The Clinton international record is not a strong point for his legacy or the U.S. In a reflection on his predecessor, George H.W. Bush, Clinton took action against Iraq at least four times for Hussein's continued aggressive acts and violation of the peace accord (News Sources, 2012). Bush was criticized for not taking out Hussein after the crushing victory in Desert Storm. Clinton authorized limited military intervention in 1993, 1994, 1996, and 1998 (Tsui, 2017). Two points are relevant here: 1) When deadly force utilizing U.S. forces or resources is required, a complete victory should be the only acceptable outcome; and 2) When a foe continues to violate a peace treaty, it is time to complete point number 1. In this case, Bush failed to complete the removal of the Iraqi president and Clinton failed to use the opportunities for intervention to end the matter.

Clinton inherited a limited involvement of American troops in Somalia initiated by George H.W. Bush on reportedly humanitarian grounds in the last months of his administration. Sadly, the limited involvement resulted in the death of U.S. service members, without obtaining any rational outcome for the U.S. or even relief for the people of Somalia (Clinton, 1993). Prior foreign interventions in civil wars detailed in the preceding chapters document the failure of such a half-hearted and ineffective approach. The Somalia incident that was memorialized in the film *Black Hawk Down* (Scott, 2001) helped to underscore to Americans the folly of sending in troops to intervene in foreign conflicts without appropriate support and without a clear-cut mission. Clinton increased the negative impact for the U.S. and may have laid the groundwork for further terrorist attacks on U.S. assets by simply withdrawing from Somalia. A more definitive strategy that ensured that the band of terrorists which had caused the U.S. losses were punished for their actions may have avoided the increasing rounds of terrorism the U.S. experienced during the rest of Clinton's administration.

Clinton experienced a rare victory in the international arena in Haiti. He threatened Haiti with U.S. intervention when the military dictator of the island nation, Raoul Cédras, refused to allow a popularly-elected new president to take office. The intervention was avoided when Cédras yielded to Clinton's threat (Office of the Historian, Bureau of Public Affairs, n.d.). Clinton successfully negotiated nuclear arms reduction treaties with Russia and other countries that were formerly part of the U.S.S.R. (History of the Department of State During the Clinton Presidency, 1993-2001, n.d.). Clinton had some success in assisting Israel in negating peace accords with the Palestinians, in 1993 (Bill Clinton's role in Israeli-Palestinian Peace Accords, 2011), and Jordan, in 1994 (Office of the Historian, Bureau of Public Affairs, n.d.).

As part of NATO, the Clinton administration engaged U.S. forces to attack Serbian positions in Bosnia in 1995. This resulted in a three-way peace deal with Bosnia, Croatia, and Serbia brokered by Richard Holbrooke in Dayton, Ohio (Daalder, 1998). The relative lack of success of this deal was documented by another NATO intervention with U.S. forces to attack Serbia in 1999 (History.com staff, 2010).

An important aspect of fighting terrorism is to destroy organizations that work to spread it and the leaders of such organizations. It was determined that the "mastermind" who haunted the U.S. through much of the 1990s, such as through the first World Trade Center bombing, and leading up to 9/11, was Osama bin Laden, son of a wealthy Saudi construction magnate.

During the Clinton administration, there were numerous opportunities to capture or kill bin Laden and inexplicably, Clinton failed to take advantage of those opportunities (Miniter, 2003). Leading up to the 1996 elections, reportedly Clinton did not want to appear too aggressive to what he believed were members of his voting base and therefore passed on clear opportunities to deal with this documented threat (National Commission on Terrorist Attacks Upon the United States, 2004). This is another example of how a sitting president made the wrong decision for the future of America based on his concern about reelection.

The penalty paid by the U.S. for failure to deal with terrorism in the early stages was tragically documented by bombings of two U.S. embassies on August 7, 1998. In the first attack, two hundred persons, eleven American, died in the explosion in Nairobi, Kenya. Shortly afterwards, an explosion at the American embassy in Dar es Salaam, Tanzania, killed eleven people. Thousands of other persons were injured (U.S. Department of Justice, FBI, 1998). For many Americans, this was the first time they learned of an organization called Al Qaeda headed by bin Laden (National Commission on Terrorist Attacks Upon the United States, 2004).

Shortly before the end of Clinton's administration, the USS *Cole* was attacked in Yemen by a small boat packed with explosives that blew a huge hole in the ship at the waterline, killing seventeen sailors. The ensuing investigations determined that Al Qaeda had been responsible for the attack (Turner Broadcasting System, Inc., 2016). The boldness of the attacks on U.S. embassies and a U.S. warship underscore the increasingly unsafe environment the U.S. faced by the year 2000.

During the Clinton administration, it was revealed that the People's Republic of China had obtained access to top secret technology of U.S. nuclear warheads stolen from the U.S. National Laboratories. The theft of U.S. nuclear secrets had been ongoing for decades. This is not only a responsibility of the Clinton administration, but of most presidential administrations since Nixon. While yet again Clinton was not personally charged, a Clinton friend, Yah Lin "Charlie" Trie, was indicted for engaging in a conspiracy to evade the Federal Election Campaign Act. His ties to Clinton included at least twenty-three visits to the White House from 1993 through 1996. He and his associates contributed at least 220,000 dollars to the Clinton campaign while he received approximately 1.5 million dollars from foreign sources (Select Committee of the United States House of Representatives, 1999). In a deal reminiscent of the deal made with Huang, Clinton's Justice Department allowed Trie to plead guilty to one felony and one misdemeanor and he received only three years' probation. The DNC would later return six hundred thousand dollars that may have been improperly sourced from foreign governments (Suro, 1999).

BY THE NUMBERS

The national debt during Clinton's time in office increased despite numerous tax increases (U.S. Department of the Treasury, Bureau of the Fiscal Service, 2015):

Year	National Debt
1993	$4,411,488,883,139
1994	$4,692,749,910,013
1995	$4,973,982,900,709
1996	$5,224,810,939,135
1997	$5,413,146,011,397
1998	$5,526,193,008,897
1999	$5,656,270,901,615
2000	$5,674,178,209,886

As with all recent presidents, the national debt increased steadily during the Clinton administration. However, the rate of increase was fairly modest, giving the country a bit of a breather.

As the benchmark for a growing economy is about 2 percent inflation, the Clinton administration exceeded it in six out of eight years. The dips in 1998 and 1999, near the end of his second term, indicate that it was not all an upward trajectory (Coin News Media Group, LLC, 2014):

Year	Inflation Rate
1993	3.0%
1994	2.6%
1995	2.8%
1996	3.0%
1997	2.3%
1998	1.6%
1999	2.2%
2000	3.4%

MAKING THE GRADE

Clinton's scandals, most of which he was personally involved with, document a person with no moral compass of any kind. He is an admitted liar as documented by the Lewinsky affair. His womanizing made America the source of embarrassment throughout the world community. His administration had so many scandals that they cannot all be listed in this chapter. Some of the scandals, such as the Huang and Trie donations tied to foreign governments, are particularly damaging in light of the PRC espionage discovered during his second term. He earns a mark of near zero for both his private and public ethics.

On the domestic scene, reports of a healthy U.S. economy during this period tend to be overstated in his favor. The U.S. increased its national debt during his time in office by 1.5 trillion dollars. He was greatly aided by a pro-business Republican Congress during six of his eight years in office. He gets credit for spearheading welfare reform in cooperation with the Republican Congress. Clinton promoted NAFTA, which economists generally give a positive appraisal. Clinton failed to take effective action against terrorism following the first World Trade Center bombing. His inaction may have led to the Oklahoma City bombing, as well as incidents in other parts of the world.

Internationally, Clinton's failures can be traced through his administration to the embassy bombings and then the bombing of the USS *Cole*. The devastating loss in Somalia will be remembered as a terrible waste of U.S. forces and resources, although shared with his predecessor, Bush. Clinton did have some success in Eastern Europe and in Haiti.

Clinton generally gets modestly good ratings from various polls (Rottinghaus & Vaughn, 2015). However, in the cold light of events during his administration, it is hard to tell why the ratings are anything other than at the bottom. The power of his own promotion machine and media support seems to be the only explanations for any ratings above the bottom. With Clinton's path narrowly avoiding impeachment, there is no justification for a higher grade.

Clinton Grade: D-

CHAPTER 17
GEORGE W. BUSH

(Draper, 2003)

George Walker Bush (1946–), popularly known as George Bush or just "W," is the son of George H.W. Bush, the forty-first president. George W. Bush was elected the forty-third president of the U.S. as a Republican in 2000 (Miller Center of Public Affairs, University of Virginia, 2015). His election was the result of a U.S. Supreme Court ruling in *Bush v. Gore* (531 U.S. 98, 2000) blocking a recount in some counties in Florida and thereby allowing the existing vote count in the state of Florida to stand ("Supreme Court Toolbox," n.d.). This resulted in an Electoral College victory in a very tight race over the Democrat and Clinton VP, Albert Gore (Naím, 2004). Many Democrats claim that Bush was unfairly elected over Gore and cite thousands of persons who may have been incorrectly classified as felons in the ultimate swing state of Florida and therefore not allowed to vote. However, a much larger factor in the tight national race may have been that as many as 2.5 million votes across the U.S. were improperly cast by illegal immigrants, felons who have lost the right to vote, and persons voting in the wrong state or district. Conventional wisdom is that the first two categories of illegal voters tend heavily toward Democrats (investors.com, 2016). Bush was reelected in 2004 with a modest margin over Democrat John Kerry (Rogoff, 2004). Dick Cheney was Bush's VP during his entire administration.

Bush's wife from 1977 to present is Laura Lane Welch Bush ("Laura Bush," n.d.). Laura Bush was well-known during Bush's administration for advocating for literacy. Rumors of improper sexual relationships were raised against Bush during his presidential campaign in 2000 and shortly after. However, there have not been any substantiated allegations. Bush himself admits to a fairly wild lifestyle with ample alcohol before he met Laura.

OCCUPATIONAL ACCOMPLISHMENTS

Bush's educational background followed a similar path to his father in that Bush attended prep school at Phillips Academy Andover and went on to earn a BA in History at Yale University in 1968. He then was enrolled in the Texas National Guard as a pilot during the Vietnam era. This later became a source of criticism as his opponents insisted that instead of going to Vietnam, as others had done, he was able to remain home in a safe situation and practice flying. He earned his MBA at Harvard Business School in 1975. Bush worked unsuccessfully in several oil businesses in Texas. He had an unsuccessful run for Congress in 1978. He participated in a partnership that purchased the Texas Rangers Major League Baseball team. He had found his calling as his infectious love of baseball made him a successful businessman. He was elected governor of Texas in 1994. Bush's election was a high-profile event as he defeated a very outspoken Ann Richards, the incumbent governor. He won reelection easily in 1998, setting up his run for the Republican presidential nomination to succeed Clinton in the White House (Miller Center of Public Affairs, University of Virginia, 2015).

SIGNIFICANT EVENTS DURING BUSH'S TIME IN OFFICE INCLUDED

2001

- Bush declines to participate in Kyoto Protocol on global warming.
- 9/11 terrorism attack in New York, D.C., and PA
- USA PATRIOT act is signed into law with bipartisan support.
- Military action against Afghanistan called "Enduring Freedom"
- ENRON files for Chapter 11

2002

- Bush announces no normalization with Cuba without democratic reforms.
- Bush meets with Russian President Putin over nuclear arms reduction.
- Biggest one-day drop in Dow Jones history experienced
- Bush gains support of Congress and UN for action against Iraq.

2003

- Space Shuttle Columbia explodes as it approaches landing in Texas.

- U.S. invades Iraq with UN support.

2004

- Abu Ghraib prisoner abuse scandal breaks.
- U.S. troops are required to retake Iraqi city of Fallujah.

2005

- Hurricane Katrina strikes Gulf Coast with mayhem in New Orleans.
- John Roberts is confirmed as Chief Justice of U.S. Supreme Court.

2006

- A planner of 9/11, Zacarias Moussaoui, is sentenced to life in prison.
- Saddam Hussein is hanged in Iraq for crimes against humanity.

2007

- Bush authorizes air strikes on Al-Qaeda targets in Somalia.
- Troop Surge in Iraq is authorized to quell rising insurgency threats.

2008

- Large job losses as economy heads into recession
- Iraq war deaths for American military reach four thousand.
- Federal government takes control of Freddie Mac and Fannie Mae.
- Lehman Brothers files for bankruptcy.
- AIG accepts eighty-five billion-dollar initial bailout from Federal Reserve Bank.
- Bush authorizes 17.4 billion-dollar bailout of General Motors and Chrysler.

THE DEFINING EVENT

On the morning of September 11, 2001, just eight months into Bush's first term, Islamic terrorists hijacked four airplanes loaded with fuel for long flights and flew two of them into the World Trade Towers in New York City. A third plane crashed into the ground near a wall of the Pentagon. The fourth plane, believed bound for the White House after being hijacked, crashed in a field in Pennsylvania as a result of passengers fighting with the terrorists who had taken control of the plane. The two towers in New York City were so badly damaged by the attacks that they both fell. This caused yet a second tragic outcome as many first responders, about two hundred, were killed by the falling buildings in addition to the approximately three thousand persons who perished in the buildings. The damage extended for blocks in the densely developed area of Manhattan (9/11 Death Statistics, 2016). The continuing tragedy is an estimate of over 40 percent of the approximately sixty-five thousand fire, police, construction workers, and emergency medical personnel working in southern Manhattan following 9/11 are dying from the dust laced with toxic substances that spread as the towers came down, according to The World Trade Center Health Program (WTCHP).

Fear of additional terrorist hijackings caused the order to land all U.S. airplanes at the nearest airports. All air traffic stood down for approximately three days. Washington (D.C.) National Airport was closed for months after the attack. The driving fear was that there were still terrorist plotters who had not yet been discovered. On the evening of 9/11, Bush spoke to America and the world and promised recovery relief and prompt retaliation for the cowardly attacks (Abramowitz, 2002). Bush's response to the crisis was a high point of his entire administration, but faded after his invasion of Iraq failed to persuade the American public that this was the proper response to 9/11.

Multiple investigations into how such a crude and bold plan could have gone undetected revealed cumulative intelligence failures across the U.S. government ("National Commission," 2002; "S. Rept. 107-351," 2002). The reports revealed years of inattentive and sloppy leadership at the top which resulted in the failure of multiple agencies with critical information to share and compare such information. The madman behind 9/11, Osama bin Laden, was quickly identified. Clinton never authorized action against this Saudi millionaire's son who had declared a *fatwa*, or holy war, on the U.S. five years earlier (Miniter, 2003).

The U.S. response to 9/11 was varied. Airport security became extremely tight, causing long lines in airports to board planes across the U.S. External access to runways and nonpublic areas of airports were secured. Baggage was screened more carefully. "No parking" zones were established at airport pickup and drop-off areas. No vehicles could be left unattended. Drivers could not simply sit at curbside at an airport to pick up passengers. "No fly" lists were developed in an effort to block potential terrorists from boarding planes bound for the U.S. On airplanes, cockpit doors were now reinforced and locked in an attempt to avoid the specific assaults used on the planes on 9/11 (Greenstein, 2002). Later, in response to specific, but fortunately unsuccessful, terrorism attempts, larger liquids and gels could no longer be carried on planes. Passengers were also required to have their shoes checked during the safety screening (Skinner, 2008).

Congress generated the Uniting and Strengthening America by Providing Appropriate Tools Required to Intercept and Obstruct Terrorism Act of 2001 ("USA PATRIOT") ("USA Patriot," n.d.). At that time, the law was viewed as a predictable and needed response to 9/11. As time has passed the act has been criticized by both the left and the right in an interesting rare meeting of the minds. Opponents on the left and right view the law as an impermissible and unnecessary imposition on personal privacy in violation of the intent of the Constitution. Parts of the law have been modified in response to such criticism, but as of this edition, much of the law is still in place.

In addition to the actions above, Bush created the Office of Homeland Security to consolidate the fractured federal system to detect and defend Americans from terrorism (Berggren & Rae, 2006). On the international front, Afghanistan was identified as the home of Al-Qaeda and the hiding place of bin Laden. Bush demanded that the country surrender bin Laden, but to no avail. Two months after 9/11, the U.S. invaded Afghanistan in an effort labeled "Enduring Freedom." The target was the Taliban administration which filled the vacuum left by Russia's departure from the country a dozen years earlier. In turn, the Taliban had created a safe haven for Al-Qaeda (Roper, 2004). The U.S. made quick progress early with support from some of the local tribes. The Taliban was removed from power and most Al-Qaeda bases were destroyed, although notably, bin Laden was not captured (Milkis & Rhodes, 2007).

Unfortunately, the focused U.S. effort in Afghanistan was divided when the U.S. invaded Iraq on the premise that Saddam Hussein represented a threat to the U.S. Specifically, it was alleged that Hussein had "weapons of mass destruction" (WMDs), namely chemical weapons. The rationale behind this belief was that Hussein had reportedly used chemical weapons previously, violating the international ban on their use (Naím, 2001). As Bush engaged in a stalemate with Hussein, his first midterm election took place in late 2002 and Republicans increased their lead in both houses of Congress (Jacobson, 2009). While this was most likely voter approval of the Bush administration handling of the aftermath of 9/11, the Bush administration appears to have viewed this as a mandate to continue to apply pressure on Iraq.

The net result was that the war in Afghanistan took a back seat, more than 4,400 American troop deaths and thirty thousand injuries, while the U.S. suffered economic losses in the two trillion-dollar range. Importantly, the U.S. leadership position was badly damaged and its credibility essentially evaporated in the Middle East with both friends and foes. The U.S. was viewed as impetuous in invading Iraq since WMDs were not discovered and there was never a clear plan as to how Iraq would govern itself after Hussein was dead. In Iraq, the growth of ISIS and the return of insurgencies of various stripes, including an enhanced role of Iran in the internal governance of Iraq, confirmed the mistakes of the Bush administration (Gompert, Binnendijk, & Lin, 2014). These mistakes were then compounded by the handling by the Obama administration (Sigelman & Whissell, 2002).

Bush must take responsibility for the intelligence failures since he was unquestionably the leader when the failure took place. His reliance on the reports can be only partially criticized, however. Some of America's best minds in the intelligence community said that Hussein was rebuilding his nuclear program and beginning to stockpile biological and chemical weapons ("Key Judgments," 2002). At the same time, the inherited problem dates to George H.W. Bush's failure to remove Hussein and Clinton's multiple standoffs and warnings to Hussein without taking effective action.

Under pressure from the public and Congress, Bush started pulling U.S. troops out of Iraq. As the situation wore on, it was apparent that the reduced staffing by the U.S. in Iraq had created a difficult and dangerous situation for the troops left in Iraq. In a possible "double down" situation, Bush initiated in 2007 the "Troop Surge," which made it safer for all U.S. and UN troops in the country. The military turnaround was nearly immediate (Greenstein, 2001).

THE DOMESTIC FRONT AND RACE RELATIONS

During his eight years in office, Bush might be regarded as the least lucky president of the last one hundred years. This was in sharp contrast to his predecessor, Bill Clinton, who was elected with less than 50 percent of the popular vote twice, rode the wave of a stable economy, dodged impeachment, and managed to leave office before 9/11. Not only was Bush faced with 9/11, but the aftermath of it, including the failed invasion of Iraq and the once successful, but now dubious, invasion of Afghanistan. He also was forced to deal with one of the most expensive and punishing natural disasters to hit the U.S. mainland. Hurricane Katrina struck New Orleans and the U.S. Gulf Coast in late August 2005, ironically, about eight months into his second term, the same timing as 9/11 relative to his first term (Benton, 2007).

In the case of Katrina, the Gulf Coast had ample warning that a serious weather event was imminent. Katrina struck as a Category 5 hurricane and delivered devastation equal to its category. Sadly, many residents of New Orleans and nearby areas failed to heed the order to evacuate. The storm's impact was intensified when the Mississippi River levee system, constructed and maintained by the Army Corps of Engineers, failed in several places. After the storm struck, events compounded when thousands sought shelter in the New Orleans Convention Center and Louisiana Superdome, only to be stranded there without adequate supplies while the national news focused on their suffering hour by hour ("Hurricane Katrina," n.d.).

The mayor of New Orleans, Ray Nagin, became a familiar face as he dished criticism specifically on Bush. It was rarely reported by the media that as the senior official in the area, he had the first line of responsibility when it came to the evacuation order. Many residents ignored the order, making it their own responsibility. It was often said that others lacked the means to evacuate. In the subsequent days of sad and in some case horrifying videos, none was more pitiful than images of a parking lot full of school buses partially submerged in water. Clearly, Nagin and his administration could have made sure that those who wanted to evacuate had the means to do so.

There is no question that the Federal Emergency Management Agency (FEMA) was not adequately prepared for the disaster, especially in light of the failure of the local administrators to effectively respond. Loss of life was estimated at over 1,300 persons and property damage was estimated at 150 billion dollars ("Hurricane Katrina," n.d.). Bush did not rush to the scene and he was criticized for what was claimed to be an uncaring attitude. This was attributed to the fact that so many of the victims were black. Bush responded that he was monitoring the disaster closely and that the arrival of the president in the midst of such dire circumstances might actually hinder the critical delivery of aid to the victims. In a subsequent formal review, few at the federal level were spared criticism ("Select Bipartisan Committee," 2006).

One of Bush's first acts was to create by Executive Order the Office of Faith-based and Community Initiatives (Shweder, 2004). The stated idea was to utilize the services of such agencies in a coordinated manner to help the poor and underprivileged. It was met with cynicism as its critics claimed that Bush was merely focused on providing state aid to church-related organizations. Despite such criticism, the organization still exists, although its name has been changed to The White House Office of Faith-based and Neighborhood Partnerships ("The President," n.d.)

Also early in his administration, Bush signed the "No Child Left Behind" Act (Renshon, 2008). The bill was the result of an initiative to improve American competitiveness with the other nations by requiring standardized math and reading testing and increased the flexibility of the states with regard to the use of funds. Despite the support of its co-author,

Democrat Edward "Teddy" Kennedy, the bill was frequently attacked, especially by teachers' unions. The unions were resistant to attempts to make teachers responsible for student failures. Many states obtained waivers from full compliance with the law. In 2015, the law was replaced with Every Student Succeeds Act (Klein, 2016).

Bush's bad luck continued with the stock market. The "dotcom" bubble deflated, with sharp stock losses on the NASDAQ in 2000 (Geier, 2015). Many regular investors had joined the dotcom stock boom late and therefore they faced large losses when those stocks declined sharply. Bush began his first term in early 2001 just as the markets showed some recovery. Then, the ENRON collapse was announced (Renshon, 2005). This was followed by the even bigger bankruptcy of Worldcom, and other stock scandals were announced (Sharpe, 2007). While some Bush opponents present Bush as taking a strong economy and walking it into the dumpster, the facts do not support that version. Bush inherited a faltering economy from Bill Clinton much as Herbert Hoover inherited a declining economy from Calvin Coolidge. Bush led the effort to bring in reforms to avoid further stock manipulation scandals, and the Sarbanes-Oxley Act (SOX) was passed in mid-2002 (Cooper, 2005). SOX was Congress' attempt to fix the many securities laws that were blamed for allowing the ENRON, Worldcom and other scandals.

There were a number of efforts during the Bush administration to stimulate the economy. He signed a series of tax cut bills (Smith, 2008). In order to fund the tax cuts, he also raised the national debt ceiling by what was then a record amount to 7.4 trillion dollars (Chan, 2005). As the economy was facing rising unemployment ("The Employment Situation," 2007), Bush proposed a 145 billion-dollar stimulus package in early 2008 (Leogrande, 2007). However, Congress approved an even bigger 170 billion-dollar stimulus package (Cook, 2002).

The "Great Recession" continued to wreak economic havoc; it was labeled the "subprime crisis." This was based on the large number of mortgage defaults with the end of the "housing bubble," a period of sustained increases in housing prices in many areas across the U.S. (Pfiffner, 2007). The U.S. took control of the two large semi-governmental agencies, Freddie Mac and Fannie Mae (Skowronek, 2005). Separately, the U.S. taxpayers provided an eight hundred billion-dollar package to buy Freddie's and Fannie's bad debt to get the U.S. mortgage system back on track (Wallis, 2004). Unfortunately, the private stockholders prior to the government takeover did not get any relief (Morgenson, 2016). Another move to stimulate the economy was the reduction of the Federal Reserve prime rate to zero (Montgomery, 2002).

In a controversial move claimed to be needed to avoid further damage to the economy, the federal government provided 17.8 billion dollars in financial aid to General Motors and Chrysler. The move was designed to prevent these companies from filing for Chapter 7 bankruptcy (Shughart, 2004). The government commitment was more than fifty billion dollars before the matter was concluded in 2009 under the Obama administration. However, both companies still filed for bankruptcy ("U.S. Motor Vehicle Industry," 2009). Reminiscent of Roosevelt-like socialist moves during the Great Depression, these loans violated the fundamentals of capitalism.

One way of selling the buyout plan to the American public was that the U.S. government would own stock in GM. Much of the stock was sold in the ballpark of thirty-three dollars per share. However, the remaining stock of GM would need to be sold at eighty dollars per share for the federal government to break even (Canis, 2013). Even with a record high stock market in 2017, the stock has at its best traded at less than half of the target price ("GM," n.d.).

Several other major transactions in 2008 illustrate the point regarding keeping government intervention out of the private sector. Lehman Brothers filed for bankruptcy (Light, 2008). This large investment bank could certainly have argued, as others had done, that they "were too big to fail." At the same time, Merrill Lynch sold itself to Bank of America for about fifty billion dollars, or roughly half of its valuation just a year before (Tenpas, 2003). This demonstrates the capitalist system in action. On the other hand, the Federal Reserve Bank provided an eighty-five billion-dollar bailout for American International Group, "AIG," in exchange for favorable stock options, allowing the federal government to buy about 80 percent of the company (Garten, 2003). Ultimately, the government provided nearly one hundred billion dollars more to bail out AIG.

Aside from the economy, Bush addressed a variety of social issues. He signed a bill banning late-term abortions, a bill that his predecessor had vetoed (Epstein, 2004). He followed this with a veto of a bill that would have lifted the prohibition on the use of federal funds for embryonic stem cell research (Bush, 2000). While consistent with his views on "right to life," both acts drew the ire of proponents of "right to choose" and especially for the use of stem cells from embryos. The debate centered on the fact that embryonic cells are generally extracted from the umbilical cord following a baby's delivery and opponents claimed that this would encourage abortions to obtain such tissue.

One of the oddest situations that impacted Bush's presidency was what is referred to as the "Valerie Plame Affair." A former ambassador, Joseph Wilson, expressed his opinion that the rationale to invade Iraq in 2003 was not justified. Later, through a series of media interviews, it came to light that Wilson's wife, Valerie Plame, was reportedly a CIA operative. Reading multiple versions of the case told by various reporters generally results in as many stories as there are writers. She claimed that being "exposed" as an operative ruined her career. The issue was whether a highly placed member of the Bush administration had deliberately leaked her identity as retaliation for Wilson's statement against Bush's Iraq policy. A federal investigation focused on Bush Chief of Staff Karl Rove and Dick Cheney's Chief of Staff, I. Lewis "Scooter" Libby. Ultimately, only Libby was charged. He maintained his innocence at trial, but was convicted on four of the five counts against him and sentenced to prison and a large fine. While not pardoned by Bush, his jail time was commuted by Bush to probation ("Timeline: The CIA," 2007).

In his 2005 State of the Union speech, Bush surprised many Americans when he suggested that Social Security be restructured. Presently, all funds are turned over to the federal government and a low return is offered to recipients. The proposed plan would allow Americans who wished to do so to own private Social Security accounts that could be invested in the various markets (Frum, 2008). The statistics are compelling that self-invested funds would produce a far greater return for the participants than the current miserable returns being produced by Social Security. Somewhat surprisingly, Bush was harshly criticized for this suggestion despite the fact that most Americans would receive far greater payouts under his proposal. Bush also announced the first major change in Medicare in some time by expanding it to add a prescription benefit and encouraging more insurers to enter into the Medicare marketplace (Klinkner, 2006).

THE BUSH INTERNATIONAL RECORD

As discussed above, much of Bush's international record is tied to the attacks on 9/11. This led, directly or indirectly, to the invasions of Afghanistan and Iraq. Not discussed above was a scandal that grew out of the Iraq invasion. In 2004, news reports began to relate that U.S. military guards were torturing captives at the Abu Ghraib Prison near Baghdad, Iraq. In the period that followed, the general in charge of the prison was removed from command, many of the troops were disciplined, and in some cases, prosecuted, and the U.S. had another black eye from the Iraq invasion (Taguba, 2004). Written reports could be disclaimed, but the existence of a damning internal report by General Taguba and the videos and photos released of the prisoner abuse verified the allegations. This caused an even greater backlash in the U.S. against the Iraq invasion and further hurt U.S. relations around the Middle East.

Bush's relationship with the People's Republic of China (PRC) was strained for several reasons. In 2001, a U.S. spy plane flying over the South China Sea was clipped by a PRC fighter jet. The U.S. plane was forced to make an emergency landing on Chinese soil. The PRC fighter jet crashed and the pilot died. The twenty-four crew members of the spy plane were held briefly by the Chinese (Kan, 2001). The PRC did return the twenty-four crew members, but kept the plane for several months. The U.S. crew did what they could to destroy as much as possible of the secret information and equipment on the plane, but the PRC's access to the plane compromised valuable equipment. Later, the plane was disassembled and removed from PRC territory by a U.S. crew (U.S. Military, 2001). Bush later announced that the U.S. would support Taiwan in the event of an invasion from the People's Republic of China (Leffler, 2011).

In an action later reversed by Barack Obama, Bush declined to sign the Kyoto Protocol, the first treaty that attempted to reach an agreement on "global warming" (Pfiffner, 2008). Bush's position was that the treaty allowed developing countries, including China, to continue to pollute while disadvantaging the U.S., which would be under much stricter rules.

In an important development for future U.S. security, Bush withdrew from the 1972 Anti-Ballistic Missile Treaty (Zimmerman, 2007). This allowed the U.S. to begin testing advanced anti-missile defense systems. This is a rare bright spot in Bush's administration in that risks for the U.S. from foreign missiles, now including North Korea and Iran, continue to grow. An effective anti-missile system is critical to the long-term security of the U.S.

BY THE NUMBERS

Bush added a stunning 72 percent increase in the national debt, to more than ten trillion dollars. Bush would have many excuses, such as the economic impact of 9/11, the war in Afghanistan, war in Iraq, recovery from Hurricane Katrina, the ENRON impact on the economy, etc. The point still remains that a Republican president presided over a near doubling of the national debt in just eight years (Amadeo, 2016).

Year	National Debt
2001	$5,807,463,412,200
2002	$6,228,235,965,597
2003	$6,783,231,062,743
2004	$7,379,052,696,330
2005	$7,932,709,661,723
2006	$8,506,973,899,215
2007	$9,007,653,372,262
2008	$10,024,724,896,912

Inflation was not a serious concern during the Bush administration. If this was due to good fiscal management, it would be a plus. However, the irregular economy was reflected in the inflation rates for the Bush years (Coin News Media Group LLC, n.d.):

Year	Inflation Rate
2001	3.7%
2002	1.1%
2003	2.6%
2004	1.9%
2005	3.0%
2006	4.0%
2007	2.1%
2008	4.3%

MAKING THE GRADE

Bush's personal ethics during his time as governor and in the White House were a positive. While there were some allegations of improper conduct, the overall facts seem to support that these were false and most likely politically motivated attacks. There were also references to his pre-Laura life, and that did not contribute to this analysis. His public ethics raised issues with the Valerie Plame Affair as well as what appears to be at least a partial fabrication, if not more, regarding the WMD issue in Iraq. It is a judgment call on Katrina and whether he was uncaring because many victims were black, or it was just more bad luck. In reviewing the record, there is no evidence that he was in any way uncaring about the victims of Katrina, nor that the color of the victims influenced him.

On the domestic scene, Bush's initial handling of 9/11 is fully to his credit. He said the right things and rallied America at the most difficult time for the country in sixty years, other than perhaps the assassination of John Kennedy. Given the proximity to his taking office, it is unlikely that his administration could have done a great deal to change the way the government intelligence agencies operated. It was eight months into his first term and so a complete pass would also be inappropriate. His initial handling of Afghanistan was also a positive, right up to when he decided to invade Iraq, and from there, both countries have had issues through 2016 and beyond.

Katrina exposed the failures of the federal government to deliver critical help when needed. Ignoring the utter failure of the local and state governments in the response to Katrina, FEMA should still have done a better job. Given that this was four years into Bush's administration, this was the responsibility of his administration. The levee failure that compounded the disaster in New Orleans was the responsibility of the Army Corps of Engineers, another federal agency.

Bush showed an innovative approach in suggesting individual Social Security accounts. It is unfortunate that his proposal received such a reactionary reception. He also added prescription coverage to Medicare, a positive approach.

Despite numerous tax cuts and stimulus programs, the economy struggled during much of Bush's time in office. He used approaches like the public bailouts of some banks and automakers that smacks of the worst of the Roosevelt administration. The subprime crisis happened far enough into his administration for him to have ownership. At the same time, the long-term involvement of Democrats in encouraging cheap and easy mortgages to stimulate home ownership certainly played a major role in the failure. Generally, parallel to his father, the recession was already easing up as Bush surrendered the White House to Barack Obama. Therefore, it is unfair both to attribute all of the economic losses to Bush and any good economic news since 2009 to Obama.

Internationally, America's position in the world was damaged during Bush's administration. The failed and questionable invasion of Iraq combined with the Abu Ghraib affair is first on that list. The botched and unfocused invasion of Afghanistan, especially after the early successes, also hurt the image of America as a power that accomplishes its goals. The bottom line is to inspire trust. America's allies must know that the U.S. will be there when truly needed and will provide sufficient force to accomplish the objectives.

The media was not kind to Bush while he was in office and polls have consistently placed him fairly low on the list of presidential rankings. While those rankings do not influence the grades issued in this book, the outcome for Bush is about the same.

Bush Grade: D-

CHAPTER 18
BARACK H. OBAMA

(Souza, 2009)

B arack Hussein Obama (1961–) was elected the forty-fourth president of the U.S. as a Democrat in 2008. It was an unusual race as the first successful black presidential candidate with little Washington experience was paired with an outspoken, long-time U.S. Senator, Joe Biden from Delaware. On the Republican side, former Vietnam POW and long-time U.S. Senator John McCain from Arizona was paired with outspoken Sarah Palin, Governor of Alaska and only the second woman to be a VP candidate. Obama swept to victory with wide margins in the popular vote and the electoral college (Miller Center of Public Affairs, University of Virginia," 2009). He ran against GOP candidate Mitt Romney in 2012 and was reelected with slightly less of the popular vote than in the 2008 race (Murray & O'Connor, 2012).

Obama's wife from 1992 to present is Michelle LaVaughn Robinson Obama. Both of the Obamas attended Harvard law school, but at different times. They met in Chicago where they were pursuing different careers ("Michelle Obama," n.d.). The First Lady spoke out for various causes, mainly ending childhood obesity and creating more veteran employment opportunities. While there are various scurrilous reports on the internet about both, no credible source attributed any improper personal conduct to either spouse.

OCCUPATIONAL ACCOMPLISHMENTS

Obama's background was a bit unusual. His mother was a white woman from Kansas and his father was a native of Kenya. They met while both attended college at the University of Hawaii. Obama grew up in Indonesia and later Hawaii. He graduated from Columbia University in 1983. He worked in Chicago for about five years as a "community organizer." He then attended law school at Harvard University, where he became the first black president of the *Harvard Law Review*. He graduated in 1991 and moved back to Chicago, where he worked as a civil rights lawyer and an adjunct faculty member at the University of Chicago. Elected in 1996, he served for eight years in the Illinois Senate and then was elected in 2004 to the U.S. Senate (Miller Center of Public Affairs, University of Virginia, 2009). He had a very fast rise from obscurity to the presidency.

SIGNIFICANT EVENTS DURING OBAMA'S TIME IN OFFICE

2009

- Obama announces plan to close Guantanamo prison for terrorist suspects.
- Congress approves 787 billion-dollar stimulus package.
- Nidal Malik Hasan kills twelve servicemen during Fort Hood shooting.

2010

- Obama signs Affordable Care Act.
- The Deepwater Horizon oil rig explodes in the Gulf of Mexico.

2011

- Osama bin Laden is killed in Pakistan by U.S. Special Forces.
- The ATF "gunwalking" scandal occurs.

2012

- Hurricane Sandy devastates part of the U.S. East Coast.
- Coordinated attack against two U.S. government facilities in Benghazi

2013

- Boston Marathon terrorist bombing takes place.
- IRS revealed to have been targeting conservative organizations applying for 501(c)(4) tax-exempt status

2014

- Obama announces full diplomatic relations with Cuba.

- Obama accuses Russia of violating the 1987 Nuclear Treaty.

2015

- Nine people are shot and killed at Emanuel African Methodist Episcopal Church in Charleston, SC.
- Fourteen people are killed in a terrorist attack in San Bernardino, CA.
- U.S. agrees to Paris Climate Change Accord.

2016

- Omar Mateen kills forty-nine people at the Pulse gay nightclub in Florida.
- Three police officers are shot dead and others are injured in Baton Rouge, LA.
- Five Dallas police officers are killed by shooter during protests against police.
- Terrorist bombing in Manhattan and Northern New Jersey injures thirty.
- Four police officers are shot, one fatally, in four different cities over the course of one evening in November.
- Aleppo, Syria, is retaken by Assad's forces, supported by Russia.

THE DOMESTIC FRONT AND RACE RELATIONS

Obama's campaign slogan was "hope and change." Sadly, neither his domestic nor his international approaches matched that optimistic slogan. During his eight years in office, race relations deteriorated, the country experienced the weakest economic "recovery" on record, and Congress was in a stalemate with the White House. The result was an isolated president who relied on executive orders instead of following proper legislative channels ("Hope," 2016).

AFFORDABLE CARE ACT

The cornerstone of Obama's domestic agenda was the Affordable Care Act (ACA), also known as "Obamacare." Passed in 2010 by a Congress with both houses controlled by Democrats, it famously did not have a single Republican vote in support of it (Matthews, 2016). The result is a hodgepodge of wish lists from traditional Democratic positions without any balance or consideration of the long-term consequences. The ACA consistently had less than 50 percent general support of the American people ("Kaiser Health," 2016). The title of the act has become an oxymoron as the most reported aspect of the act is the dramatic increases in health insurance costs that have occurred ("Obama Premiums," n.d.). Costs for the insurance companies that participated in the health insurance exchanges that were created by the act have resulted in massive losses and withdrawals from many markets (King, 2016).

The ACA has had a somewhat mixed outcome in the courts. In a surprise ruling, the Supreme Court, led by Chief Justice Roberts, held that the act was legal on the basis that the individual mandate was simply a tax (*NFIB v. Sebelius*, 2013, 648 F. 3d 1235, 2013). The ACA was later attacked by those claiming that federally-established exchanges could not provide the same subsidies as the state-formed exchanges. The Supreme Court again ruled in favor of the act (*King v. Burwell*, 2015, 759 F. 3d 358, 2015). The high court later ruled that under the circumstances of the religious convictions of the owners of a closely held company, they could not be forced to provide contraceptive coverage, but the insurance exchange did have to provide it (*Hobby Lobby Stores, Inc. v. Burwell*, 2014).

The ACA essentially requires a full health plan for everyone, with no limits. For the healthy, this results in a more expensive plan when many might buy a plan covering only surgery and hospitalization. Further, there is no cap on the premium cost for those with preexisting conditions. So, the guaranteed insurance program is too expensive even with the subsidized rates provided by the insurance exchanges. The cost of the act to taxpayers was projected to be in the hundreds of billions (Kocher, 2016). However, as the exchanges fail and the U.S. government directly bails out the act's coverages, the cost to taxpayers could approach one trillion dollars or more in less than a decade (Mathews, 2016b). Eliminating lifetime maximums in the health insurance market made some sense, but the act failed to include a solid funding mechanism (Mathews, 2016c).

Obama's two key representations about the ACA were without merit. Obama famously said: "No matter how we reform health care, I intend to keep this promise: If you like your doctor, you'll be able to keep your doctor; if you like your health care plan, you'll be able to keep your health care plan" (Lee, 2009). The reality is that most Americans are in health insurance programs that provide specific networks of doctors. Further, most insurance policies for single persons were canceled in response to the act. When these Americans whose policies were canceled went back into the market, many found the policies more expensive and were unable to purchase the same insurance ("Faces of the ACA," 2014). When they were forced to change policies, they were faced with different network choices. In many cases, the medical networks were truncated, especially because many doctors refused to join some networks that attempted to cut physician payments (Armour, 2016). When the number of persons insured through Obamacare is adjusted by the number who previously had insurance, the number of newly insured is significantly less (Radnofsky, 2016).

In one of the more bizarre aspects of ACA, a Texas resident making a very modest income of 11,800 dollars per year would qualify for a significant subsidy in order to purchase health insurance. However, if that person loses his or her job and has to work part-time making less than that amount per year, their subsidy would disappear. This would require payment of new, higher rates for health insurance or seek state aid through Medicaid, even if they are willing to purchase health insurance (Healthcare.gov, 2016).

It is true that one reason that healthcare is so expensive is that many persons seeking treatment do not have health insurance. If they go to an emergency room, they are guaranteed treatment if they are sick, regardless of their ability to pay. Hospitals charge more to paying patients to cover the many who are treated without paying. The selling of the ACA involved frequent recitation of the number of Americans who were without health insurance. So, if they were forced to have health insurance, hospitals and doctors would be paid and the rest of the insured and the taxpayers would not have to foot the bill. This should be analyzed by factions and not in gross:

First, a good handful of Americans are without the means to purchase health insurance either due to disability or as beneficiaries of welfare or other public support programs. These Americans are generally covered by Medicaid, a federal program administered by the states.

Second, there are indeed many Americans, including many working persons in their twenties and thirties, who choose not to have health insurance since they are generally healthy. This group has been most impacted by the requirement to have health insurance or pay a penalty that increased as Obama left office ("Health Law," 2016).

Third, the pink elephant in the room is the roughly eleven million illegal aliens in the U.S. (Markon, 2016). Obama promised that the benefits of the ACA would not flow to this group and therefore protect the taxpayer. So, the majority of persons here illegally continue to receive free care at U.S. emergency rooms and public hospitals despite the ACA (Zong & Batalova, 2016).

Fourth, there are a small number of persons who actually have the means to purchase healthcare on an on-demand basis. They were paying their medical bills in the past and would continue to pay them without insurance, except now they will be penalized for not having insurance (Armour, 2016).

The bottom line is that the act has increased, not decreased, the cost of healthcare in the U.S. This is an obvious outcome because there is not a single part of the act that increases the actual amount of medical care available. The number of doctors and nurses in the U.S. remains far less than the demand. The cost of developing a new drug, now estimated at as much as one billion dollars, remains roughly the same (Zong & Batalova, 2016). Perhaps one of the more ironic commentaries on the failure of the ACA is that even former President Clinton stated that it "is the craziest thing in the world" (Vespa, 2016).

RACE RELATIONS

Race relations in America deteriorated under the Obama administration. This unfortunate outcome was all the more surprising since the highly touted arrival of the first black president might have seemed the culmination of a long journey toward equality and improved race relations. The symptom is the reaction to the shooting of black persons by police. However, the recent violent reaction to such tragedies does not seem to depend on whether the shooting is done by a black, Hispanic, or white police officer. The first high-profile case was when Trayvon Martin, a young black man, was killed by a Hispanic community watch member, George Zimmerman, in

Sanford, Florida, in 2011. Zimmerman was charged with second-degree murder, but he was acquitted (Campo-Flores & Waddell, 2013). A federal civil rights investigation was initiated, but it concluded that there was not enough evidence that the shooting was a hate crime (Grossman, 2015). A civil suit was filed against the Florida subdivision where the shooting took place and was settled for a reported one million dollars (Knowles, 2013). Media coverage helped to tip the public opinion as initial photographs showed a very young Martin and a husky Zimmerman. Later photographs showed the injuries to the back of Zimmerman's head and a much more threatening view of Martin. Obama improvidently intervened by stating that "if I had a son, he'd look like Trayvon" (Graham, 2012). Further stirring racial tension rather than helping to calm the mood, he also ignored death threats against Zimmerman happening at the same time.

In 2014, a black man named Michael Brown was shot by a white police officer, Darren Wilson, in Ferguson, Missouri (Barrett & Dolan, 2014). Controversy ensued in that friends of Brown who were nearby claimed he was not only unarmed, but had his hands up when he was shot six times. The autopsy report and other evidence supported the fact that Wilson was engaged in a struggle for his service weapon with Brown and fired to protect his own life. Apparently, the grand jury agreed and did not indict Wilson (Campo-Flores & Waddell, 2013b). Riots and civil unrest took place following Brown's death and again later in the year when the grand jury cleared Wilson. During the second round of riots, cities in several parts of the country, including Oakland, had riots (Taranto, 2013). If there was leadership by Obama during this time of strife, he encouraged the rioting rather than attempting to calm the public and support the rule of law.

Sadly, an incident in New York City followed when a black man, Eric Garner, died following a police maneuver called a choke-hold. The white police officer was also not indicted by a grand jury (O'Brien, Saul, &

Shallwani, 2014). Walter Scott, a black man in North Myrtle Beach, South Carolina, was shot in the back five times by police officer Michael Sanger in 2015. Sanger, unlike some of the other officers noted, was dismissed as a police officer and was indicted on state and federal charges ("South Carolina Police," 2015). Sanger pled guilty in 2017.

Rioting occurred in 2015 when a young black man, Freddie Gray, was found with serious spinal injuries after being transported in a police van in Baltimore. The allegations were that he was either deliberately injured, or that he was not properly restrained in the back of the police van and therefore was injured due to the negligence of the police. The case became a very public cause when six police officers were charged with various crimes related to his death. The Maryland State Attorney, Marilyn Mosby, also black, made a number of public statements regarding the prosecution of the six police officers. She took the position that the officers were already guilty. This is usually not done in order to preserve the impartiality of the prosecution and the jury pool (Calvert, 2016). One trial ended in mistrial, but the officer was not charged again. All six officers were eventually either acquitted or not prosecuted (Calvert, 2016b). As this book goes to press, the officers have filed a civil suit against Mosby for defamation and other issues (McLaughlin & Almasy, 2016). The plaintiff officers have a difficult path proving defamation.

Multiple protests and demonstrations took place as a result of Gray's death and in the wake of the Brown, Garner, and Scott deaths. Other incidents took place around the U.S. and Obama commented that blacks are the victim of unjust violence from the police. The tragedy in America continued with senseless violence against police officers in incidents that appear to be related to the various protests. In 2016, five officers were killed by a sniper in Dallas while protecting protesters against police violence (Achenbach, Wan, Berman, & Balingit, 2016). Two weeks later, three police officers were killed in Baton Rouge, Louisiana, following protests over a police shooting there (Levitz, Lazo, & Campo-Flores, 2016). In mid-November 2016, four police officers were shot in a single day, one dying from his injuries (Hayden, 2016).

DOMESTIC TERRORISM

There are legitimate concerns about the safety of all Americans following a variety of multiple killings and terrorist acts on home soil. A lone gunman killed twelve people in a theater in Aurora, Colorado ("Cinemark," 2016). Also in 2012, a lone gunman walked into an elementary school in Sandy Hook, Connecticut, and killed twenty-seven people, twenty of them children (El-Ghobashy & Barrett, 2012). Two bombs were detonated near the finish line of the 2013 Boston Marathon, killing three and injuring hundreds. The bombings were the work of two brothers who were naturalized U.S. citizens and radicalized overseas. One was killed during an attempted arrest and the other stood trial and was sentenced to the death penalty (History.com staff, 2014).

In the Los Angeles area, a former police officer, Christopher Dorner, went on a rampage and killed four persons, including two police officers and two of their family members (Phillips, 2013). Two suspected Islamist gunmen reportedly inspired by ISIS staged an armed attack on a civic center in Garland, Texas. Both gunmen were eventually killed and only one injury resulted to a law enforcement officer (Koppel & Campoy, 2015). A white man killed nine black persons who were attending church in Charleston, South Carolina ("CBS News Charleston Shooting," 2015). On the west coast, an Islamist terrorist couple attacked a public office where one of them worked, killing fourteen and wounding more than twenty persons. No specific reason was given for the attack, but it was believed to have been

ISIS-inspired. The two shooters were killed during an attempt to arrest them ("San Bernardino," 2015).

The largest loss of life in a domestic incident since 9/11 was an early 2016 attack on a gay nightclub in Orlando, Florida, where forty-nine died and more than fifty were injured. The shooter, who was American-born, allegedly pledged his allegiance to ISIS. He was later shot by police (Tsukayama, Berman, & Markon, 2016).

While it did not involve a loss of life, more than thirty persons were injured by bombs in Manhattan and in northern New Jersey in September 2016. The perpetrator was born in Afghanistan, but was a naturalized U.S. citizen (Shallwani & Barrett, 2016).

GUANTANAMO DETENTION FACILITY

Even before Obama was sworn into office, he declared his intention to close the terrorist detention facility at Guantanamo Bay, Cuba (Frakt, 2012). Initially, those in the Bush administration declared detainees were entitled to no legal rights, and could be held indefinitely, without charges, until the Global War on Terror had come to an end ("Memorandum," 2002). On Obama's second full day in office, he signed an Executive Order directing that the Guantanamo Bay prison be closed within one year ("Exec. Order," 2009). One day later, Republicans in Congress filed a bill prohibiting federal courts from ordering the transfer or release of Guantanamo detainees into the United States (Khan, 2009). Hindering the President's intended closure of Guantanamo was the media. Studies on recidivism of Guantanamo detainees went viral, indicating that as many as 30 percent of the detainees who were released engaged in hostile actions against the U.S. or its allies (Goldman & Ryan, 2016).

By May of 2009, twice as many Americans opposed closing Guantanamo than supported closing the prison (Jones, 2009). In 2009, President Obama coordinated the transfer of forty-three detainees to other countries and released sixteen detainees through habeas corpus petitions (Scheinkman, 2016). When the president's one-year closing plan did not come to fruition, he stated his new expectation was to close the prison sometime in 2010 (Kornblut, 2009). By early 2016, only eighty detainees remained in Guantanamo (Goldman & Ryan, 2016). Given the public opposition to closing the facility and the dangerous nature of the remaining prisoners, it is unclear why Obama decided to use some of his limited political capital on such a project. While true leadership sometimes involves taking positions that are at odds with the majority of the public, in this case, there does not appear to be any sensible endgame to bringing any of these prisoners into the U.S.

OBAMA'S ECONOMY

Consistently cited as a bright star for the Obama administration is the overall economy. Unquestionably, Obama started with one of the lowest performing economies on record: "The Great Recession." He followed the Bush administration, which had clearly struggled for most of its eight years with everything from 9/11 to ENRON to the subprime mortgage crisis to corporate meltdowns in the auto and insurance industries. Historically, the U.S. has a consistently successful economy with brief recessions. The exception is the Obama recovery, which has been lackluster by any standard. Obama is the only recent president who did not have a single year with growth at 3 percent or more. His average rate of growth to date is 1.55 percent versus the Bush average of 2.1 percent annual growth (Giovanetti, 2016). While Obama started his administration with an "economic stimulus" of 780 billion dollars, the reality is that much of it was used to pay off political supporters and not, as advertised, for "shovel-ready jobs" ("Are You for or Against the Federal Stimulus Plan?" 2010).

The unemployment rate has been touted as a sign of major success, as the rate went from a recession peak of 10.0 percent in October 2009 to its lowest level during the Obama administration of 4.7 percent in May 2016. By late 2016, it started trending upward again ("Current Population Survey," 2016). This official rate only includes persons actively looking for work and the too discouraged to look for work are not included ("What is seasonal adjustment?" 2002; "How the Government," 2015). A more accurate way to evaluate the true health of the economy is the employment-population ratio, or the percent of persons over sixteen who are actually in the workforce. This figure hovered at nearly 63 percent for Bush's entire administration and dropped sharply to below 59 percent due to the recession in the transition from Bush to Obama. During most of the Obama administration, the figure has hovered below 59 percent employed population, generally considered a recession-level figure ("Civilian Employment-Population Ratio," 2016). Despite the deliberate focus on the unemployment figure, the real health of the economy is documented by the significant number of Americans who are not in the workforce.

In the "By the Numbers" section below, the national debt and the inflation rate are detailed for Obama's administration. The most critical number is the massive increase in the national debt to nearly twenty trillion dollars from a little over ten trillion dollars at the beginning of his administration (Timiraos, 2016). Even allowing for the recession at the beginning of his first term, the number is staggering and would indicate to the rational observer that the so-called economic recovery has been bought by the federal government through massive borrowing. The other tool has been a Federal Funds Rate of zero (Brown, 2016) for most of Obama's two terms. The problem with a rate of zero is that there is no place to go to help the economy grow.

IMMIGRATION

Adding to the difficulties of America on the home front is the continued problem with illegal immigration. It is estimated that there are eleven million illegal aliens in the U.S. in 2016 (Markson, 2016). Failing to take advantage of Democrat control of both houses of Congress early in his administration, Obama then faced Republican control of the Senate and GOP control of both houses of Congress toward the end of his administration. Obama has not achieved any progress in straightening out the broken system. The blame does not lie exclusively at his feet since none of his predecessors in the last thirty years have done anything to actually improve the situation either. He is the first to flagrantly violate the existing laws by attempting to essentially legalize four million to five million illegal immigrants by executive order in 2014 (Ehrenfreund, 2014). That attempt failed as a federal court issued an injunction and the U.S. Supreme Court refused to overturn the injunction (Davis, 2016).

Aside from illegal immigration, Obama added to the economic problems of the U.S. economy by accepting eighty-five thousand refugees in 2016, of whom ten thousand are Syrian, despite strong opposition from a number of states and a consensus that the U.S. government lacks the ability to properly screen the refugees for ISIS and other problem affiliations (Sengupta, 2016). The U.S. is famously a land of immigrants; prior generations came to the U.S. to settle and assimilate into the population. The current problem appears to be that there is little effort by the latest refugees to assimilate and in some cases, many of the refugees are simply "parked here," waiting for an opportunity to return to their home country when the violence ends.

OBAMA ADMINISTRATION SCANDALS

While Obama as a private person avoided the path of Bill Clinton and his multiple indiscretions, his administration was not as fortunate in the public arena. In 2013, a scandal several years in the making became front page news. It was revealed that the IRS was targeting conservative organizations applying for 501(c)(4) tax-exempt status. The applications were either denied or there were delays of years in their processing. When the scandal came to light, the Acting Director of Exempt Organizations for the IRS, Lois Lerner, was called before the GOP-controlled Senate to explain her actions. In a surprise, Ms. Lerner took the Fifth Amendment rather than testify on a variety of points and later retired. Even her retirement became a focus of public interest as it was revealed that there was a bonus program for IRS executives, despite the massive public debt and her questionable supervision of her division (Erb, 2016).

Hillary Clinton was Obama's first Secretary of State. This appointment raised some eyebrows in that as a result of the brutal Democrat primary, the Clintons were definitely not fans of Obama. After John Kerry, former Senator from Massachusetts, replaced her in that position, it was revealed that during her time as Secretary of State she did not use a secure State Department email system, but had a server set up in her home. She also used one or more unauthorized, non-secure, cellphones (Tau, 2016c). As the Republicans took control of both houses of Congress, the scandal began to unwind with multiple hearings. Former Clinton IT employee Bryan Pagliano, who helped set up Hillary Clinton's private server, took the Fifth Amendment (Pavlich, 2016). Another potential witness was given immunity, but failed to provide much information.

When Clinton herself testified, she claimed due to a fall where she hurt her head she did not recall many details (Tau, 2016d). The penultimate was a news conference by James B. Comey, Director of the FBI, who detailed the many failures of security and clearly established protocols by Clinton, but then stated that Clinton would not be prosecuted (Tau, 2016e). There are numerous examples of less dramatic security failures, like former General David Petraeus, who received sanctions for allowing his girlfriend to see certain confidential documents (Schmidt & Apuzzo, 2015). Clinton's email scandal remained an open wound for the Obama administration (Parlapiano, 2016).

The Clinton email scandal took on an even more circus-like sheen when Director Comey reopened the investigation during the 2016 presidential campaign. The triggering incident was an FBI examination of the laptop of Anthony Weiner, the estranged husband of former Clinton aide Huma Abedin. Shortly before the November 8 election, Comey announced that the laptop had not contained any new emails related to the Clinton investigation (Eichenwald, 2016).

In 2013, a leak revealed that the National Security Agency (NSA) was spying on the phone calls of millions of Americans. The NSA position was that the actions were authorized under the 2001 PATRIOT Act. The NSA also claimed that, despite the outrage expressed by various members of Congress, the program had been shared with Congress in advance (Landler & Savage, 2014).

Despite Obama's promises to curtail NSA spying, he apparently did not intend to curtail his administration's spying on opponents to the Iran Nuclear Deal, discussed below. Breaking in late 2015, it was revealed that the NSA continued to spy on Israel's Prime Minister, Benjamin

Netanyahu, and caught in the enterprise were communications with members of the U.S. Congress who were in contact with him (Entous & Yadron, 2015; Fleitz, 2015). The spying revelations were compared to similar disclosures of Nixon's paranoid spying on opponents, certainly not a positive comparison.

THE OBAMA INTERNATIONAL RECORD

The Syrian refugee crisis has been in headlines for much of Obama's second term (Jordan, 2016). The situation would not be at the current level had U.S. diplomacy and military action around the globe, and especially in the Middle East, been more successful. The only possible positive outcome for both the U.S. and its allies is for populations like the Syrians to simply remain in their home countries. The Obama administration has doubled-down on the failures of the preceding Bush administration and the result is a world that is less safe.

Obama's first step in international diplomacy was to travel to numerous countries around the world, including France, the Caribbean, and Great Britain. This has been referred to as his "apology tour" by conservative sources such as the Heritage Foundation, but unfortunately, it is hard to describe the results as anything else (Gardiner & Roach, 2009). This is balanced by coverage from the liberal-leaning *The Washington Post*, which argued it was not an apology tour ("Fact Checker," 2011). The inexperience of Obama showed as he often led his speeches with comments that sounded like overt criticism of America and its history in international affairs. Indeed, a careful review of some of his comments make eminent good sense. The U.S. at one time did have a positive relationship with the Muslim-dominated countries in the Middle East. Any possibility of returning to that position would help to ease tensions in that important part of the world. Subsequent reaction to Obama's administration in general would indicate that the more radical elements like ISIS and Al-Qaeda were spurred by his words rather than seeking peace.

A rare bright spot for Obama was the killing of Osama bin-Laden in Pakistan in 2011. The covert action was a combined success of U.S. intelligence and U.S. Navy Seals (Meckler & Entous, 2011). Sadly, this also illustrates a failure of diplomacy in that a supposed U.S. ally, Pakistan, allowed bin-Laden to live in the open in its country without taking action to apprehend and turn him over to the U.S. The Obama administration justifiably took credit for this singular success.

There is no question that George Bush's administration botched Afghanistan and the apprehension of bin-Laden by switching the focus to Iraq instead of ensuring control in Afghanistan first. Bush's Troop Surge in Iraq late in his administration helped to secure some progress in Iraq, but both military and diplomatic failures since that time have resulted in an Iraq that had major cities overrun by ISIS and an administration in Baghdad that leans toward Iran (Kesling & Sonne, 2016). Obama's mishandling of U.S. troop withdrawals is plainly a key cause of the failures there and in Afghanistan (El-Ghobashy & Kesling, 2016).

OBAMA AND THE MESS IN THE MIDDLE EAST

A review of the Obama administration foreign policy reveals a tragic list of diplomatic and military failures illustrating a total absence of an understanding of the U.S. role in the Middle East (Sadiq, 2016). Obama's approach in Egypt, arguably the most important country in the region, has been a failure. A long-time ally in the Middle East was President Hosni Mubarak in Egypt. A hard-line autocrat, he was certainly not an American-style politician, but he did honor the 1979 truce with Israel, which recognized its right to exist (Israel Ministry of Foreign Affairs, 2016). As the Muslim Brotherhood gained momentum in Egypt, Obama appeared to support that extremist movement over the existing government. Mubarak fell and was replaced by Muhammad Morsi as President of Egypt in 2011 (Knell, 2013). Following two tumultuous years of rule, despite the support of the Obama administration, Morsi was replaced by a military coup in 2013 (Gaouette & Walcott, 2013). Obama now faced a challenge in that the faction he supported was under arrest. Gradually, Obama attempted to reach some accommodation with President Abdul-Fattah el-Sisi's government (Elmenshawy, 2014). Little respect remains for America's leadership with this important ally.

Egypt was not the first country to experience the Arab Spring. Actually, the North African country of Tunisia was the first country to follow that path. In 2010, a government shake-up followed an incident with an unemployed man trying to sell fruit in a public market (Thomson Reuters, 2010). The culmination of the resulting protests was the end of Tunisian President Zine el-Abidine Ben Ali's rule. Ben Ali, unlike some of the other autocratic leaders of the region, decided to resign rather than fight it out with the movement for change. The new government is a hard-line Islamist government and definitely not a future partner with the U.S. (Mack, 2014).

A lightening rod for the failed U.S. policy in the Middle East is Syria. The country has been engulfed in a violent civil war for years. Obama's stated policy was to support the "rebels," as the forces opposed to the current dictatorial administration of Bashar al-Assad have been called. Russia stepped in to support the Assad regime under the guise of opposing ISIS. The result is a proxy war between the U.S. and Russia (Stacey, 2015). And in fact, Obama admitted that he did not anticipate the rapid rise of ISIS in Syria (Kroft, 2014).

Obama further hurt his position in Syria with these statements (Kessler, 2013) [emphasis added by the author]:

*"We have been very clear to the Assad regime, but also to other players on the ground, that a **red line** for U.S. is we start seeing a whole bunch of chemical weapons moving around or being utilized. That would change my calculus. That would change my equation."*
—Obama, statement to reporters, August 20, 2012

*"I didn't set a **red line**. The world set a **red line**."*
—President Obama, news conference in Stockholm, September 4, 2013

The war in Syria rages. By 2015, two hundred thousand had already died and four million residents of Syria had fled, in turn creating a big part of the worldwide refugee crisis (Gerson, 2015). The situation continued to deteriorate in 2016 (Hiro, 2016). Obama maintained that no ground forces would be committed by the U.S. (BBC, 2016). Despite that stated position, in late 2016, the first U.S. military service member was killed by an explosive device (O'Hara, 2016). Military observers commented that one problem with advisers and trainers is that they do not have enough other service members around them to provide adequate security. In any event, as the first edition of this book was finalized, the town of Aleppo, Syria, which had been controlled by the U.S.-supported rebels, fell to Assad's forces supported by Russian air strikes (Hubbard, 2016). A carnage has been reported where women and children have been slaughtered. This is truly a failure of U.S. diplomacy and further damaged Obama's legacy.

Obama's involvement with Libya was also marked by failure as admitted publicly by Obama (Somin, 2016). The removal of Moammar

Gadhafi from power was Obama's apparent objective. In the 1970s and early 1980s, Gadhafi had been a documented sponsor of terrorism. The U.S. bombed Libya in 1986 under orders from President Reagan, who explained: "When our citizens are abused or attacked anywhere in the world, we will respond in self-defense. Today we have done what we had to do. If necessary, we shall do it again."

In sharp contrast to the Obama approach, the Reagan approach appears to have worked. The conduct of Gadhafi toward the U.S. changed for the better (History.com staff, 2016). Gadhafi was a ruthless dictator, but he had not represented a direct threat to the U.S. for a long time. Disturbing the balance of power in Libya, as in other countries, may bring the chance for self-determination, but so far has led to chaos and the opportunity for terrorist organizations to move into the country. Since the overthrow of Gadhafi, which Obama supported by ordering air strikes, an unstable situation has persisted in Libya.

In 2012, four Americans paid a high price for the instability in Libya following the fall of Gadhafi. With the highly politicized environment in Washington, the tragedy of the attack on the U.S. Embassy in Benghazi, Libya, with the death of four Americans, including U.S. Ambassador Chris Stephens, has hardly left the headlines ("Select Committee," 2016). Reports vary about the murder of the ambassador in terms of whether he died from smoke inhalation or from a brutal night of torture. It is incontrovertible that in the weeks prior to the attack the ambassador sought more protection for the embassy, including at least six emails to Hillary Clinton, Secretary of State at the time. Reports stated that when the embassy came under attack, help was requested. U.S. military forces could have been dispatched in time to save the besieged Americans, but were never authorized to attempt a rescue ("Clinton's Benghazi Cover Story," 2016). As Commander in Chief, Obama has ultimate responsibility for this tragedy.

The cover story for the Obama administration was that a little-known video making fun of Mohammad the Prophet Muhammad was the trigger for a sudden mob action against the embassy (Tau, 2016). The problem with this purported scenario was that the "mob" was heavily armed with military rifles and grenade launchers. While the story continued to trickle out, it was changed several times, adding to the impression of either outright lying, or incompetence, by Obama's State Department. Appearances by Hillary Clinton in front of various congressional committees investigating the tragedy added to the impression of incompetence and a frank lack of caring (Freeman, 2016). In fact, repeatedly pressed by reporters to explain the failures of her department, she blurted out: "What difference does it make?" (Tau, 2016b).

The consensus today is that Libya is a dangerous failed state. It provides a home for terrorist groups like ISIS to wage their terrorist wars on other countries in the Middle East. It is not a haven for democracy. Two warring factions are battling for control of the country (Kuperman, 2015).

Obama has taken a different approach in Yemen, one of the less mentioned of the countries in the Middle East with problems during his administration. A civil war has raged for several years in Yemen. An administration backed by Saudi Arabia is in a bitter battle for survival. While the U.S. has largely stayed out of direct military involvement in the current civil war, the U.S. is still heavily involved. It sold billions of dollars of military equipment to Saudi Arabia. This has produced yet another proxy war. This one is between the Saudi government and its key rival for Middle East supremacy, Iran (Oakford & Salisbury, 2016).

Since the Iranian Revolution and the U.S. Embassy hostage crisis in 1979 (see Chapter 13), Iran has been a concern to all U.S. presidents. It is often referred to as the largest state sponsor of terror. A June 2016 report by the U.S. State Department referring to year 2015 confirmed this view (U.S. Department of State, 2015). Given the details revealed by the State Department in the referenced report, it is inconceivable that the U.S. would enter into the "Iran Deal" in 2016, discussed below.

Obama was not consistent in his position in the Middle East. An example of Obama's inconsistent involvement in Middle East politics was his lack of support for two different democracy movements in Iran. The first took place in 2009, the "Green Movement," and a second in 2011 (Wilson, 2011). The hard-line Iranian government crushed both movements, which lacked international support. Obama later indicated that he was concerned that any U.S. support for the protestors would give more ammunition to Iran's President, Mahmoud Ahmadinejad, to stir up passions against the U.S. Given the past conduct of Iran's government, it would have been unlikely to change any opinions.

On October 18, 2015, the United States, along with China, France, Germany, Russia, and the United Kingdom, adopted a Joint Comprehensive Plan of Action (JCPOA) with Iran ("Joint Comprehensive Plan of Action," 2016). Its goal was to block Iran's pathways to gaining nuclear weapon capability by way of uranium or plutonium enrichment. By most accounts, when this agreement went into effect, Iran was within three months of gaining nuclear bomb capability ("Iran Deal," 2016). Immediately after the parameters of the JCPOA were released, the deal was criticized (Williams & Hattem, 2016). Much criticism from this deal came from the State Department's characterization of Iran as a leading sponsor of terror ("Iran Deal," 2016). More controversy erupted when the Obama administration secretly arranged a plane delivery of four hundred million dollars in cash the same day Iran released four American prisoners and implemented the nuclear deal (Labott, 2016). The money was flown into Iran on wooden pallets stacked with Swiss francs, Euros, and other currencies as the first installment of a 1.7 billion-dollar settlement resolving claims at The Hague over a failed arms deal under the Shah. The JPCOA provided millions in sanction relief and trade deals (Pearce, 2016). Many critics have expressed concern that this money would indirectly fund terrorism (Williams & Hattem). By some estimates, up to one hundred billion dollars of Iran's assets would be available once sanctions are lifted and foreign bank accounts are unfrozen (Pearce, 2016).

Since going into effect, the JPCOA has failed on multiple fronts (Williams & Hattem, 2016). Germany's equivalent of the FBI reported Iran was secretly seeking nuclear technology (Weinthal, 2016). Iran violated UNSC 2231, which ordered that Iran stop working on ballistic missiles. Iran fired missiles within 1,500 yards of an American aircraft carrier (Shannon, 2016). The Obama administration maintained that the agreement was meant to tackle only Iran's access to a nuclear weapon, and was not intended as a broader effort to reframe the U.S.'s posture with Iran (Williams & Hattem). Opponents to the deal allege the U.S. promised to pay Iran 8.6 million dollars for thirty-two tons of heavy water, which is used to produce weapons-grade plutonium, essentially funding terrorism. The White House maintains the deal has been successful overall because Iran shipped twenty-five thousand pounds of enriched uranium out of the country, dismantled and removed two-thirds of its centrifuges, and removed the calandria from its heavy water reactor and filled it with concrete ("Iran Deal," 2016). To date, the deal has done more to encourage Iranian terrorist activity.

It is likely that sanctions will be resumed in the future against an Iran emboldened by the success in achieving the deal and financed with 1.7 billion dollars in cash in various currencies (Stephens, 2016). In early 2016, Iran succeeded in embarrassing the U.S. Navy by capturing a handful of sailors in a small boat, videotaping them in confessions similar to actions taken against the U.S. POWs by North Vietnam (Solomon & Lee, 2016).

Even *The Washington Post*, generally on Obama's side, stated the following about his Middle East approach (Diehl, 2012):

Obama's biggest failing in the Arab Spring is not that he chose the wrong side; it is that he has waffled back and forth. He has been consistently indecisive, irresolute and reluctant to act. As a result he has alienated both regimes and revolutionaries, and squandered U.S. leverage.

Compounding Obama's Middle East diplomatic problems was his poor relationship with Israeli Prime Minister Benjamin Netanyahu (Baker & Rudoren, 2015). As Israel is America's strongest ally in the region, the U.S. relationship with Israel is especially important. The signing of the Iran nuclear deal, JCPOA, has further aggravated the relationship between the two allies. Near the end of Obama's second term, the two estranged leaders reached an agreement whereby Israel would actually accept a little less aid than the U.S. Congress might appropriate to the country (Rogin, 2016). The more shocking part of this report is that under the deal Israel would "accept" 3.8 billion dollars, and not accept a higher amount should the U.S. Congress grant a larger number. This huge number still begs the question as to why the U.S. would provide billions of financial aid to any country when the U.S. deficit is so high. In late 2016, in a major shift in American policy, the U.S. "abstained" from a UN Security Council vote, which allowed a vote against Israel to continue rather than being blocked by a U.S. veto. This marked a low point for U.S.-Israeli relations, most likely going back to the founding of Israel.

IRAQ AND AFGHANISTAN

Following a different track has been the reversal of fortunes for U.S. interests both in Iraq and Afghanistan. Most of America supported Bush's invasion of Afghanistan after the events of 9/11. The country had become a safe haven for terrorist groups and that was definitely disrupted. Obama initially conducted a reevaluation and a strengthening of the U.S. troop level there. However, Obama then appeared to change his mind and the uncertainty of U.S. support hurt his relationship with the Hamid Karzai government and encouraged more terrorist insurgency activity. Former National Security Council staffer Paul Miller concluded that Obama took a bad situation in Afghanistan and made it worse (Miller, 2016). In fact, Miller and others compare Obama's involvement in Afghanistan to Johnson's failed strategy in Vietnam.

The U.S. military involvement in Iraq was a target of Obama from before he took office. He frequently promised to bring the troops home. It was a successful political tactic as the Iraq war had fallen out of favor with many Americans. It ignored the fact that the troop surge late in the Bush administration had helped to bring a relative peace to the country. After taking office, Obama began to bring home the troops. In fact, he was criticized for being so specific about troop withdrawals, as some were concerned that the terrorists would simply wait for the U.S. troops to leave. The Pentagon requested a maintenance force of about twenty-four thousand, but Obama reduced that number to five thousand. This again presents the issue of troop safety as a certain "critical mass" is required for the troops on the ground to protect themselves.

Iraq, unfortunately, became a vacuum into which various terrorist factions, especially ISIS, were able to gain significant amounts of territory. Recently, Iraq has finally been making progress reclaiming cities easily taken by ISIS roughly two years ago (Rubin, 2016). This recent progress happened partially as a result of Iran's increasing involvement with the government of Iraq. Further, the U.S. is under pressure to increase the number of troops in Iraq, despite Obama's early promises to pull the troops out (O'Melveny & Guha, 2016). Iraq remains a part of Obama's diplomatic and military failures.

THE REST OF THE WORLD

A fundamental tenet for avoiding future world wars is U.S. support for its allies around the world. The Obama administration failed to do so in the case of Ukraine. In 2014, Russia threatened and then invaded parts of Ukraine (Marson & Grove, 2016). There was no U.S. military response or effective assistance to Ukraine's government. This resulted in the annexation of the Crimean Peninsula in 2014 (Ostroukh, 2016). Russia also opened a war front along the eastern border between the two countries. Over 3,180 members of the armed forces of Ukraine have been killed and various truces have not helped the country, only holding the Russian assault at bay (Mills, Cullison, & Lee, 2016). It is reported that Russia compounded its involvement either by shooting down a passenger jet over Ukraine or providing the weaponry that led to the tragedy (Sengupta & Kramer, 2016).

China remains a difficult player on the world scene. The U.S. has borrowed as much as one trillion dollars from China (Bandow, 2016). China's planned economy has struggled recently, but its movement toward capitalism has clearly worked in favor of the country. The U.S. buys huge amounts of goods made in China and China needs the U.S. to continue to be a market for its goods (Tiefer, 2016). China has, however, taken small uninhabited islands near China and expanded them to build air strips which are in areas claimed by other governments. China has threatened both U.S. military ships and airplanes traveling through those areas (Hsu, 2016). While the likelihood that China would engage in an all-out military conflict with the U.S. is slight, the situation is disconcerting. The security of the U.S. and its allies depends on a consistent U.S. position with regard to any such aggressive actions. The actions of China in this region are eerily similar to Japan's early acts of aggression in its buildup to WWII.

In his 2008 campaign, Obama pledged to work toward a world free of nuclear weapons (Broad & Sanger, 2014). This admirable, but totally unachievable concept, is reminiscent of the words of John Lennon in his famous song "Imagine" ("Imagine," n.d.). It would be extraordinarily dangerous for the only world power to surrender either its nuclear stockpile or its option for first-use strike capability (Payne & Miller, 2016). The key aspect of having advanced nuclear weapon and anti-ballistic missile capability is the protection of the U.S. and its allies; 99 percent for deterrence and unfortunately, a tiny potential for use in the event of a credible threat. The recent actions of both North Korea and Iran, and even Russia to some extent, make such capacity essential to world peace. While North Korea has had more missile failures than successes, there is growing concern that it will soon have the capacity to deliver a nuclear warhead against the U.S. (Chang, 2016).

CLIMATE CHANGE

The controversial subject of climate change was a form of safe haven for Obama as other aspects of his administration failed. With little opposition, Obama pushed forward a domestic policy that was anti-coal, despite the importance of this carbon-based resource to the U.S. (Jenkins, 2016). Both domestically and internationally, he declared the U.S. commitment to fighting climate change, often listing it as the most important focus of his second term ("Notable & Quotable," 2016). He stated this despite the main concerns of average Americans, which are the economy, immigration, defense, health care and terrorism ("Democrats, Republicans," 2016).

THE DECLINE OF AMERICA

Obama's involvement with climate change culminated in the Paris Climate Agreement in December 2015 (Jeyaratnam, Whitmore, Hopkin, & Mountain, 2015).

The Paris accord sets a goal of keeping increases in world temperatures below 2 degrees centigrade with a preference to keep the increase at 1.5 degrees (Michaels, 2016). The problem with this agreement is that there is no enforcement or financing mechanism. It suggests that developed nations like the U.S. will contribute to a fund of one hundred billion dollars per year to help less developed nations reach this goal. Asking the average American to give billions to other countries annually to reach a questionable goal in the face of a twenty trillion-dollar national debt is unlikely to be achieved, especially in the face of the average American's priorities noted above.

BY THE NUMBERS

While George W. Bush's administration saw an increase in the national debt to over ten trillion dollars, few could have imagined the unexplainable and irresponsible increase in the national debt to near twenty trillion dollars in just one administration. This will indeed be one of the several sad legacies of the Obama administration. The public is frequently reminded of the expanding economy with little overseas military involvement. If the former were true, then the national debt should have decreased during the Obama years and that indeed would have been a laudable legacy (Amadeo, 2016; "Government Debt," 2016; "Historical Debt Outstanding – Annual 2000 – 2015," n.d.):

Year	National Debt
2009	$11,909,829,003,511
2010	$13,561,623,030,891
2011	$14,790,340,328,557
2012	$16,066,241,407,385
2013	$16,738,183,526,697
2014	$17,824,071,380,733
2015	$18,150,617,666,484
2016	$19,785,585,189

Inflation was not a serious concern during the Obama administration. If this were due to good fiscal management, it would be a plus. The very slow economy is reflected in the inflation rates for the Obama years. Given that economists recommend an inflation target for a healthy economy of 2 percent, the rates below reflect an economy that is just bumping along, and given recent indicators, may be heading into another recession in 2017 ("Historical Inflation Rates: 1914-2016," n.d.):

Year	Inflation Rate
2009	0%
2010	2.6%
2011	1.6%
2012	2.9%
2013	1.6%
2014	1.6%
2015	0.1%
2016	1.5%

MAKING THE GRADE

Obama's personal ethics during his time in public life and in the White House were a positive. While there were some allegations of improper conduct, the overall facts seem to support that these were false and most likely politically motivated attacks. His public ethics raised issues with numerous scandals and the failure to use the president's "bully pulpit" to work toward domestic peace, especially with regard to race relations and a bipartisan approach to solving the country's problems.

Obama claimed that he led America to an economic recovery during his eight years in office. However, the U.S. economy, with the exception of the Great Depression, historically has short recessions followed by longer periods of economic health. Unfortunately, Obama presided over the weakest recovery period of recent years. Further, absent an incredible increase in the national debt of ten trillion dollars, there would not be any recovery to discuss.

This is a book about leadership and not psychology. In analyzing Obama's approach both to domestic and international violence, he has taken an approach that has no chance of success. When dealing with bullies, first, the party fighting the bullies can in no way indicate that they consider themselves to also be a bully. The position must be crystal clear: Not that America, the sole world power, is flawless, only that it is taking the right actions to protect the American people and its allies around the world. Second, the use of force must be clear and unequivocal. Perhaps the best example of this during the last one hundred years was Harry Truman's use of the atomic bomb to end WWII. As tragic an action as this was, it was unequivocal and final. The sad truth is that only overwhelming force applied in an unequivocal manner stopped bullies like the leaders of Japan from the 1920s into the 1940s from continuing their reign of terror. America must learn from such sad lessons since 1950 that include, among others, stopping at a truce with North Korea, failing in Cuba, failing in Vietnam, failing in Somalia, failing in Lebanon, and more recently, failing in Afghanistan and Iraq. Perhaps it would have been better for Obama to apologize to those Americans who were wounded or disabled in failed military engagements; the families of those military members who were killed; and the persons around the world who were the victims of America's failures, rather than making rhetorical efforts that confuse rather than help to remedy the situation.

Further, the focus of this book is on the results of the leaders. Few Americans feel safer now than they did a decade ago. Reasonable minds can differ on the intent of Obama's words spoken to the world community during his "apology tour," and subsequently. However, the results are clear and that is that terrorism throughout the world has increased and become more common and more dispersed. Some effort must be made to achieve a more lasting world peace and Obama has demonstrated that his approach is not the answer.

Polls have shown Obama in the middle of a mediocre pack of past presidents (Seib, 2016). It is likely that as the Iran deal and the Affordable Care Act continue to unravel that he will sink further in the polls. However, the popularity polls are not a consideration for the grades in this book, and he narrowly passes.

Obama Grade: D-

Obama Grade: D-

PART III

ANALYSIS OF ONE HUNDRED YEARS OF AMERICAN PRESIDENTS

CHAPTER 19

ECONOMIC CYCLES AND AMERICAN PRESIDENTS

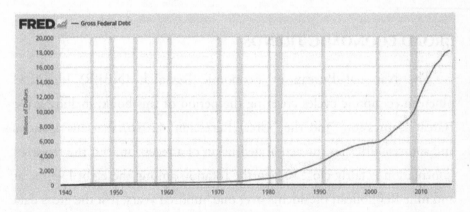

(Council of Economic Advisers (US), 2015) (Shaded areas indicate U.S. recessions)

This book examines ethical leadership against the backdrop of the many myths that surround one hundred years of U.S. presidents. One of the most persistent myths is that the person or party in the White House either causes a growing and successful economy or causes the economy to crash. Perhaps the best examples of this are the back-to-back administrations of Herbert Hoover and Franklin Roosevelt. For the average American, this is a simple formula, easily related to the words of Ronald Reagan: "Are you better off now than you were four years ago?" (Rowen, 2008). The obvious problem is that it is highly likely that the president getting the credit or the blame had little or nothing to do with how the economy performed during his administration.

There is a growing body of economic reports that suggests that the huge U.S. economy is impacted by external factors like oil shortages or gluts, long-term government and business decisions, and economic factors like the collapse of ENRON or the 9/11 bombings. The person or party in the White House is not the direct cause. This chapter will explore key issues related to this phenomenon of economic expansion and contraction as correlated with presidential leadership.

BROAD ECONOMIC TRENDS

The National Bureau of Economic Research (NBER) identified nineteen economic cycles covering the period of this book, including the "Great Depression" and the "Great Recession" (2016). Various agencies and sources differ on the actual definition of a recession, but the reported information is fairly close. Given the rotation among the eight Democrat and nine Republican presidents over one hundred years, just the gross data alone indicates that other than Franklin Roosevelt, no president was in office long enough to significantly impact the performance of the economy during his own administration.

Supporting the fact that presidents and political parties may not have much to do with the success of the economy is an extensive report by Princeton economists Alan S. Blinder and Mark W. Watson. The authors' detailed report is based on extensive statistical analysis, and various versions are available from 2013 and 2014 (Blinder & Watson, 2014). While the report received some media coverage, it has not had as much impact as might be expected. That may be due to the reluctance of many readers to absorb the statistical analysis that supports the authors' conclusions. With a shortage of earlier data, the report focuses primarily on Truman through George W. Bush with some mention of Obama's first term (Blinder & Watson).

Blinder and Watson's opening conclusion is that Democrat presidential administrations have better macroeconomic outcomes than Republican presidential administrations on most key variables other than inflation. A key factor is economic "shocks" such as the two Arab Oil embargoes during the 1970s and the substantial increase in oil prices during the George W. Bush administration. Two other key factors discussed were the increase in productivity and war expenditures (Blinder & Watson, 2014).

The main argument of Blinder and Watson is that oil prices, productivity, and war expenditures are largely out of the control of the U.S. president. They then note that, should a president declare war, as George W. Bush did against Afghanistan and Iraq, there is obviously some impact by presidential actions. Given the substantial empirical research, it is difficult to argue with the overall conclusions. Some impact should be attributed to the party in control of Congress. As noted above, Clinton's presidency was partially saved by the Republican control of Congress after Clinton's first two years in office.

In a rather extraordinary confession for two economists, they conclude that "luck" is what characterizes the economic success of Democrat administrations versus Republican administrations (Blinder & Watson, 2014). This conclusion is certainly supported by this book in contrasting Clinton's good luck and George W. Bush's consistent bad luck. One does not need to consult a mountain of statistical analysis to reach this conclusion. Clinton did not preside over a war, benefited from relatively stable energy prices, avoided an expensive excursion into massive health-care changes, achieved welfare reform in cooperation with the Republican Congress, and garnered the dividends the U.S. economy received as the digital revolution increased productivity. Clinton received the digital dividend for much of his administration while Bush inherited the "dot com crash" early in his administration. This crash, combined with 9/11 along with ENRON and other corporate scandals, helped to doom Bush's administration. Bush did compound his "bad luck" by his attack on Iraq without first settling Afghanistan.

Notably absent from the report of Blinder & Watson was analysis of the impact of the national debt on the various presidencies (2014). This may have been occasioned by the fact that the Obama administration was early in its second term when their report was prepared. The ten trillion-dollar increase in the national debt should be adjusted against the weak recovery of his administration. It then becomes clear that this extraordinary burden on future generations means that there may actually have been little economic recovery under Obama. Of course, the five trillion-dollar increase in the national debt by Bush would need to be factored into the analysis at the same time.

SPECIAL CONCERN

Unemployment is a concern of all presidents. Growing unemployment near election time nearly always spells doom for the party in office. Blinder & Watson note that unemployment usually decreases during Democrat administrations (2014). The benchmark issue is whether Republican efforts to control inflation and government expenditures result in increased unemployment even though this may be better for the U.S. taxpayers and the U.S. economy in the future. Recent administrations of both parties have increased the national debt and do not seem to have a handle on sustained economic growth without periodic downturns.

Parallel to the many myths exposed in this book is that the Democrat party somehow is the party of black Americans. As indicated earlier in this chapter, the economy is often better under a Democrat president. Therefore, it would be logical that the party most supported by black voters would provide disproportionately more employment opportunities for black Americans during Democrat presidential administrations. However, numerous reports confirm that black unemployment stays roughly twice white unemployment regardless of the party in the White House (Lang & Lehmann, 2011; DeSilver, 2013).

Data on unemployment detailed by race has only been collected since 1954, but that still presents sixty years of fairly detailed results (Bureau of Labor Statistics, 2008). And, it covers the full period since school desegregation in the mid-1950s and the Civil Rights Act of 1964. Solving this problem has escaped both political parties and organizations like the NAACP, which was organized to advance the lives of black Americans (Bureau of Labor Statistics, 2011).

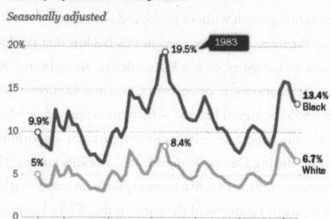

Unemployment rates by race

Seasonally adjusted

Source: Bureau of Labor Statistics

Note: "Black and other," 1954-1971; "Black or African American" thereafter. 2013 average is January-July.

(DeSilver, 2013)

As the BLS statistics indicate in the graph above, the rate is so closely aligned that it is apparent that the two unemployment rates float with the general unemployment rate. One theory that has been presented is that black and white persons who are in the unemployment system are hired in the early days of an economic expansion. Blacks who have withdrawn from the workforce are brought back into the workforce at the peak of an expansion when the available supply of unemployed is reduced. Logically, both white and black late-hired workers would be laid off as a recession approaches. In inventory accounting, this is known as "Last In – First Out" or "LIFO." In actuality, part one of the scenario is true in that black and white workers are absorbed into the workforce as an expansion begins. As the recession approaches, black workers are laid off more quickly, causing the observed disproportionate impact (Couch & Fairlie, 2010).

Extensive studies have been conducted to determine if discrimination is driving the black-white employment divide. To condense recent findings into just part of a chapter, the research has focused on black persons with either a high school or less than high school background and found issues for black males more than black females. The conclusion was that while there appears to be some lingering employment discrimination issues, the strongest factor was simply the lack of preparation for black males to enter into a competitive employment marketplace (Lang & Lehmann, 2011). Again, it is apparent that neither party has implemented a plan to correct this discrepancy.

The answer would be to provide better education and training through high school and vocational programs. The focus should be on areas where there are black majorities in public schools throughout the U.S. Recently, the only real commitment to do so appears to be the failed attempt during the George W. Bush administration with "No Child Left Behind." That program was replaced in late 2015 by the "Every Student Succeeds Act" (U.S. Department of Education, 2016). The new act reportedly will reduce the involvement of the federal government (Camera, 2015). It is too early to determine if the change in direction will help to remedy the problem.

PRESIDENTS AND FIXING ECONOMIC PROBLEMS

It is well-documented that Social Security, as presently funded, is not a sustainable program. Even the Social Security Administration (SSA) admits this (Goss, 2010). In a fascinating obfuscation of the facts, the SSA details the annual inflow of payroll taxes and outflow of benefits and then shows the current balance of the so-called Social Security Trust Fund (Social

Security Administration, 2016). The Trust Fund contains U.S. bonds, not cash, gold, or other hard assets. This is essentially the equivalent of ENRON's employees with most of their 401(k) assets in ENRON stock. So, when ENRON went under, the value of most of the employees' savings went with it. While the demise of the U.S. economy is not imminent, the rationale is still compelling.

The U.S. is still the strongest currency on earth and may continue to be for the foreseeable future. However, with twenty trillion dollars in debt and no gold behind the currency, this is a formula for the reduction of benefits and extensive taxpayer bailouts for the future. The same is true for the Medicare program, estimated to run out of money by 2028 (Centers for Medicare & Medicaid Services, 2016). Other than raising the taxes on wages and increasing the taxes on Social Security benefits, no president since the program was created has actually moved to correct the long-term funding problem faced by both of these massive social welfare programs.

For virtually all participants, had they been allowed to invest the same funds into an IRA-type investment account, they would be far ahead of the amount they hope to receive from the SSA and the future taxpayer bailout would not be required (Geraghty, 2016). This makes the rough reception for President George W. Bush's suggestion that such individual accounts be established all the more disconcerting.

The worst part is that the U.S. national debt number only represents part of the problem. First, the deficits for the promised Social Security and Medicare benefits, as discussed above, are not included in the national debt number. With an estimated liability of more than fifteen trillion dollars for Social Security and more than twenty-seven trillion dollars for Medicare, combined with the liabilities for federal employees and military pensions, the total is more in the ballpark of 104 trillion dollars ("U.S. National Debt Clock," 2016). When state and local pension liabilities are added to this figure, it is clear that the U.S. is in deep debt trouble, and the problem has not been addressed by any recent president.

The irony of hunting for the "real" debt figure is that in 1974 Congress passed the Income Retirement and Security Act (ERISA) (Bachrach, 2016). ERISA required private-sector employers to fully fund their promised retirement benefits and to disclose any shortfalls. The act also established a fund, the Pension Benefit Guaranty Corporation (PBGC) to ensure that if a company failed before fully funding its pension liabilities, then partial payments would be made by the fund (Teitelbaum, 2016). So, private-sector employers are required to prove by actuarial means that the funds are in their pension plans to pay the promised pension benefits. And, unlike the U.S. government, the corporations are no longer allowed to put IOUs in their retirement accounts.

Just the tip of the iceberg is an announcement in early 2017 by the California Public Employees' Retirement System (CALPERS) that there would be dramatic cuts in promised retirement benefits to retirees of two local public agencies. These agencies were closed or allowed to close that had not fully funded their pension commitments (benefitnews.com, 2017). Public employees at all levels should expect such cuts as local agencies, cities, and states run out of money and voters are resisting increased taxes.

No U.S. president has made the obvious, but politically unpopular commitment: Significant cuts in federal spending, most likely through dramatic cuts in employment, must be made. To make progress in cutting the true federal deficit, reductions in federal employment of 25 percent to 33 percent should be made near-term. Public-sector pension plans should be eliminated from Congress down to localities. The level of public-sector employees participating in retirement plans was reported to be 82 percent in 2010. In contrast, of private-sector employees, only 16 percent had a pension plan and only 63 percent had a savings plan (Shin, 2015). Savings plans offer a great deal less financial protection than a true pension plan, also known as a "defined benefit plan." For that type of coverage, the majority of Americans are only covered by Social Security. In contrast, most public-sector employees enjoy generous pension benefits paid for by the same private-sector employees who in large part, 84 percent, do not have pensions (Biggs, 2011). If some of public-sector employees are in the military or law enforcement positions, they may be able to work for only twenty years to gain lifetime pension benefits. Often, that results in "double-dipping," as those employees go on to work in other positions and earn new pension benefits on top of their first pension benefits. The public-private disparity continues to spread as deficits continue to grow. The debt spiral must stop or future generations will face bleak times ahead. It is simply unethical and poor leadership for politicians at all levels to continue to steal the financial well-being of the coming generations of Americans.

MULTI-ADMINISTRATION EXAMPLE

It is human nature to blame the person in the White House for all the ills of society during that administration. In some cases, that criticism is well-deserved. At other times, especially with regard to the economic impact, more research is required. A classic economic meltdown was the "subprime crisis" that is often blamed for the 2008-09 "Great Recession." During the Great Depression, one symptom was the huge number of foreclosures that took place as many workers lost their jobs and could no longer pay their mortgages. There were no buyers, or at least, no buyers willing to pay at least the mortgage balance on these properties. Following this period, home mortgage lending used conservative financial benchmarks for decades to qualify applicants for new mortgages. American home ownership rose to over 60 percent by 1960 and has stayed at that level since then (United States Census Bureau, 2011).

Two special federal programs existed to expand the mortgage market. The first, the Veterans' Administration (VA) home loan program provided up to 100 percent financing at attractive rates (Principi, 2016). The other program was the Federal Housing Administration (FHA) loan program that provided low down payments and was especially attractive to low-income and first-time home buyers. These programs and the expansion of savings and loan associations helped to bring the homeownership rate in the U.S. by 2000 to 67.1 percent. With the aggressive lending during the early 2000s, the rate surged to 69.1 percent by the end of 2005, with slight decreases in 2006 and 2007, before the subprime crisis took the percentage of home ownership back down to 67.1 percent by 2010. In an interesting twist, the percentage continued to decline during the Obama administration to 63.5 percent by 2016 (United States Census Bureau, 2015). Given the widely reported "Obama Recovery," this statistic would seem to contradict that observation (Barro, 2016).

The subprime crisis happened near the end of President George W. Bush's eight-year administration. Conventional wisdom is that Bush was responsible for this crisis. However, examining the factors that were at work that helped to create the crisis, the factors that are frequently listed as most important by analysts is congressional pressure on two government-sponsored entities, Fannie Mae and Freddie Mac, combined with the Community Reinvestment Act (CRA) (Wallison & Pinto, 2009). In 1992, a Democrat Congress, with Barney Frank's leadership, mandated that Fannie and Freddie should help to provide affordable mortgages to help more low income and specifically minority households obtain mortgages. This involved as much as one trillion dollars in loans. In 1995, banks were pressured to ease lending standards to provide more mortgages to underserved communities by amendments to the CRA (Finger, 2012). In 2009, Frank admitted that many of the persons provided with the subprime loans would have been better served by renting rather than attempting to buy a home (Wallison & Pinto). It is a little late for those impacted as Frank enjoys his public retirement funds.

The other key factor in the subprime mortgage crisis was the securitization of mortgages sold on Wall Street. Traditionally, as indicated above, mortgages were viewed as solid, conservative investments. Taking advantage of that image, the subprime mortgages were bundled and sold to Fannie and Freddie, but also to other investors. When the crisis hit, Wall Street stalwarts Bear Stearns and Lehman Brothers, among others, took such dramatic hits that neither survived (Denning, 2011). The market shocks were reflected in a Dow Jones Industrial Average that dropped by 50 percent in a short period of time (Schaefer, 2013). The collapse in the market from securities backed by subprime mortgages is dramatized in the movie *The Big Short* (Irwin, 2016). The Bush administration may have had more to do with failing to police the securities side of the crisis. There is certainly plenty of blame to spread around for the subprime crisis itself and both political parties should bear their fair share.

THE NATIONAL DEBT

This book details the national debt in each president's chapter. When unreported pension liabilities are added to the tally, the debt is much greater. The message is clear that presidents of both parties have led the nation into an ocean of debt that will take generations to correct. That is, if the nation has that amount of time to correct the incredible growth in debt. The national debt has reached such a level that few bother to argue against the position that it is out of control. Earlier, there were specious arguments to this effect: "We all have debt and this should be viewed as simply a mortgage, and not a very large mortgage as a percentage of the value of the country." The problems with this analysis would fill another book. Briefly, much of the value of the U.S. is in private hands. The government's share is substantial, but shared among all citizens (Mauldin, 2016). The debt itself requires interest payments. At the present time, slow economic growth and other factors have held down the cost of borrowing. Interest rates cannot remain low forever. In fact, the likelihood of interest rate hikes is very high. As interest rates climb, the portion of the government's income dedicated to debt service will skyrocket and sap the economy of funds needed for many other purposes (Koenig, 2016).

A special concern is that the recent dramatic increase in national debt has produced no tangible results and was not the result of a world war. The Bush administration bank and auto company bailouts, including the 2008 17.4 billion-dollar bailout for GM and Chrysler, and the Obama stimulus plan, often valued at 781 billion dollars, have contributed little to the failing infrastructure of the U.S. (Allen & Rogers, 2008; Freeman, 2014). An October 2016 article in *The Economist* focused on the number of "boondoggles" and useless projects that were funded by the stimulus in the face of billions of dollars of needed infrastructure repairs and replacements ("A View from the Bridge," 2016).

CONCLUSION

Statistics indicate that while it appears Democrats in the White House have brought more prosperity during their administrations than Republicans, the story is much more complex. Overall, the president does not have direct control of the large U.S. economy. Using various techniques, including executive orders and using the president's bully pulpit to lobby for certain legislation, the impact is more modest than the customary attribution to the president then in office. Again, the easiest contrast is the luck of Bill Clinton and the bad luck of George W. Bush.

In analyzing the leadership decisions of presidents, it is fair to evaluate the long-term effects of the decisions they made during their administrations that had an impact on subsequent administrations. Further, certain administrations have traded on prior presidential decisions, which have had the effect of increasing the impact of earlier decisions. A classic example is Lyndon Johnson's cloying admiration for Franklin Roosevelt and his effort to recreate the New Deal with his Great Society and War on Poverty. Each administration ultimately failed in its goals to stimulate the economy while eliminating poverty in the U.S. As neither party has shown the will to cut public employment and other public expenditures, it may be that as financial realities continue to hammer the voters, new political organizations will assume power in America.

CHAPTER 20
The Media and Creating the Myths of American Presidents

This chapter examines how the myths about the seventeen presidents featured in this book were either promoted or challenged by the media. The "media" is a broad term for the purpose of this chapter. Obviously, during the one hundred years, newspapers became less dominant as the golden age of journalism was replaced by the golden age of radio and then was soon supplanted by television. Since 2000, social media, including text messages and tweets, have become prominent and changed the game even more dramatically. While it may seem that social media allows the presidents a new direct access to the mainstream media, in fact, many presidents had already used the media.

The impact of the media had some distinct phases. Wilson, Harding, Coolidge, and Hoover were in the "old days" of questions put to the president in writing in advance. The president only provided the answers that were already prepared. He may have answered a "live" question if he felt like it, or may have simply ignored the question. The second phase was radio as well as the initiation of the truly live news conference. The live news conference is tied to Roosevelt's election in 1932 (Vaughn, 2007).

The third phase was television and this is often linked to the broadcast of the Kennedy-Nixon debates in 1960 (Quora, 2012), although credit should also go to Eisenhower for the first televised presidential news conference (Marotta, 2013). A fourth phase was the advent of social media and the first reported impact was Obama's first election in 2008 (Laudicina, 2014).

This chapter reviews the media's impact on the presidents in chronological order. The effort is not to create a comprehensive story about the media and each president, but to suggest how the media influenced the perceptions of the presidents discussed in this book in terms of ethics and leadership. Also examined is the creation of myths or false narratives about the various presidents. Each section provides citations to much more detailed reports on the presidents and the media. It is interesting to note that even Warren Harding now has a book regarding his presidency and his relationship with the media (Chappell, 2015).

WOODROW WILSON

Wilson's early news coverage could be regarded as positive. It often presented the president as an elite, scholarly, and of course, progressive individual. Despite serving as a governor before becoming president, he is often mentioned in news coverage as the president of Princeton University. It is rarely mentioned that he was fired from that position before becoming governor of New Jersey and then went from that position to the U.S. presidency. Notoriously absent from news coverage of his time in the White House was his extramarital affair and his strong racial bias. According to Shelly Ross in *Fall From Grace* (1988), his long relationship with Mrs. Mary Hulbert Peck was significantly not mentioned by the media (NPR, 2008). As mentioned in the introduction to this chapter, Wilson was in office during a time when the media had to submit questions in advance in order to receive an answer during the staged news conferences of the time.

The progressive movement is often proudly tied to Wilson based on the general media image that has continued for almost a century. It is only recently that Wilson's decidedly nonprogressive views on women and race have received significant news coverage. Wilson actively opposed women's suffrage (Stiehm, 2013). Helping to catapult his racial views into modern news coverage were student protests at Princeton University regarding his name and image, which are extensively used at his alma mater (Svrluga, 2015). Perhaps the bitter irony of his view of women is that having suffered a stroke sixteen months before the end of his second term, historians now report that his second wife, rather than his vice president, essentially completed his second term. The fact that this continued for that period of time is a testimony to the type of news coverage that Wilson enjoyed.

A 2004 book presents more detail on the media relationship with Wilson (Startt, 2004). That book focuses more on Wilson's relationship with the media prior to assuming the presidency, but it is still instructive. A fair evaluation would have to be that the media promoted Wilson and helped to hide his significant flaws up until fairly recently.

WARREN HARDING

Harding was initially helped by the media, which regarded him as one of their own. Harding had been a small-town newspaper man before becoming involved in politics. The media provided cover for his affairs. Harding's relationship with the media should be divided into two parts, pre- and post-Teapot Dome. One of the largest scandals to hit a president during the one hundred years covered in this book actually hit about the time he died. So, his time in office was not directly sullied by it, but following his death, the "pile-on" by the media has consistently portrayed him as being the most unethical president ever (Chappell, 2015). More recent authors have attempted to create some balance to his news coverage, but the image of his administration as corrupt remains the dominant view.

CALVIN COOLIDGE

Coolidge had the advantage of first becoming president as the vice president of Harding in the wake of his death. Given his quiet and low-key personality, it is hard to imagine Coolidge winning the White House, even in 1924, without running as an incumbent. Coolidge held twice-weekly news conferences, but again, these were during the era where questions were submitted in advance. When, in 1927, he decided not to run in 1928, he simply gave each member of the media covering him a slip of paper that stated that he had decided not to run again (Vaughn, 2007). As an example of the media making or breaking a president was that the conditions that led to the stock market crash in October 1929 were created under Coolidge's administration, not Hoover's. Hoover only became president early in 1929, but bore the brunt of the blame. The media appeared to be fully supportive of Coolidge (Sobel, 2000). Later coverage is far less positive about Coolidge, but he was no longer president and could not be hurt by how historians, and later, members of the media, regarded him.

HERBERT HOOVER

With regard to the media, Hoover clearly bears the moniker of the most unlucky of all politicians, although he would have to vie for that title with George W. Bush. Hoover's bad luck was compounded by his inability to deal with the media and provide answers. He withdrew from the media and the media in turn did not see a favorable side to the economic downturn, hanging it squarely on Hoover (Vaughn, 2007). Hoover distinguished himself in public service after a successful entrepreneurial career. His frustration and inability to explain a path forward for the country in print or the newer medium of radio led to abject scorn heaped on his reputation (Liebovich, 1994). Almost every discussion of the Great Depression refers to camps of homeless people as "Hoovervilles," for instance (Stiehm, 2013). Even seventy-five years later, the current portrayal of Hoover remains a dismal one.

FRANKLIN ROOSEVELT

A harsh contrast with the negative news coverage of Hoover was the elevation of Franklin Roosevelt, who was adept at handling the media both in written format and the newer medium of radio (Vaughn, 2007). Roosevelt capitalized with the media where Hoover had failed. The result was an unearned popularity that has continued up to the present day with many journalists. Only fairly recently has the media begun to recognize the fact that Roosevelt worked a public relations miracle, but did little more than Hoover to improve the lot of the American people. The Great Depression ended when Roosevelt's incompetence in international affairs led to WWII. A fascinating take on Roosevelt's relationship with the major newspapers is a 1979 book by Graham White. He postulates that Roosevelt saw the media as an opponent and actually used that to further improve his popularity with the public. The story from Roosevelt's view was that the media was controlled by a handful of conservatives who opposed his vision for America. He saw the media as unfailingly hostile. He did his best to go directly to the public through news conferences and radio. Roosevelt also worked the minority of the media that was friendly to him with increased access and prefabricated stories (White, 1979; Houchin Winfield, 1994). It is likely that Roosevelt will be remembered as having enjoyed the most success with the media during his lifetime and for at least fifty years afterward.

As America engaged in WWII, Roosevelt went after certain newspapers even harder since they dared to criticize his handling of the war and his popularity with the public was sagging. Roosevelt's attack on major newspapers was met with a strong reaction as papers like *The New York Times* and *Los Angeles Times* ran editorials criticizing both his handling of the war and his attack on their coverage as being unpatriotic (Turtledove, 2011).

Building the myth of Roosevelt, and contrary to his self-reported war with the media, *Time* magazine recognized Roosevelt as the "Time Man of the Year" in 1932, 1934, and 1941 (*Time*, 2012). Of course, the title was later changed to "Person of the Year," and the designation became a questionable honor to the extent that Joseph Stalin was named "Man of the Year" in 1939 and 1942, along with a handful of other notorious persons, such as Adolf Hitler (*Time*, 2016).

HARRY TRUMAN

Probably the most opposite politician to Roosevelt, other than Coolidge, was his successor, Truman. The media deified Roosevelt in eulogies following his death, including a particularly fawning salute by *The New York Times*. At the same time, the media unfairly portrayed Truman as an uninformed country bumpkin (University of Kansas, School of Journalism, n.d.). Ironically, as Truman played it pretty straight with the media, he was punished for it since he did not play to them as Roosevelt had. The result was a fairly difficult relationship (Vaughn, 2007).

Truman enjoyed some positive media coverage prior to being appointed vice president. Truman headed the Senate Truman Committee in charge of ferreting out waste by the government during WWII. His success in this function was most likely a key factor in his selection as Roosevelt's third vice president (*Time*, 1943). Truman was also named as "Time Man of the Year" in 1945 and 1948, so the media was not universally against him (*Time*, 2016b). Truman pulled off the biggest presidential upset up to that time in 1948, as most of the media had predicted a win by his Republican opponent, Thomas Dewey (Lemelin, 2010). A memorable photo from the 1948 election night was a photo of Truman holding a newspaper with the headline: "Dewey Defeats Truman" (Cosgrove, 2014).

DWIGHT EISENHOWER

Eisenhower's 1952 campaign ushered in the integration of television in a campaign for the presidency. Eisenhower outspent his opponent Adlai Stevenson eight hundred thousand dollars to seventy-seven thousand dollars in television commercials in the race. Then, in 1955, he went on to hold the first televised news conference by an American president. In 1956, he was awarded an Emmy for advancing news coverage on television (Eisinger, 2003). Of course, this chummy relationship with the media also meant that there was little criticism of Eisenhower, portrayed by the media as the hero of WWII. Eisenhower was just behind Roosevelt in clearly benefiting from the media's advancement of the myths about him.

JOHN KENNEDY

After Eisenhower paired television and the U.S. presidency, Kennedy then demonstrated a mastery of the new medium. Often mentioned was that people listening to the radio during the Kennedy-Nixon 1960 debates thought Nixon had won, but the people watching it on television thought Kennedy had won. Kennedy was a handsome man who was quite conscious of his public image at all times (Perlstein, 2013). For instance, despite debilitating back problems, he wore a back support and a full suit to cover it, rather than look frail or in need of such a support. Of the two candidates, Nixon clearly had a better handle on the dangers of the Cold War, which was near its peak at that time.

During his presidency, the media made no mention of Kennedy's many dalliances with various women and often portrayed him in regal fashion, helping create an image that far exceeded the reality of his short administration. His wife, Jacqueline, enhanced the image with her creation of "Camelot." Journalist Theodore H. White reportedly allowed Jackie to edit his feature article in *LIFE* magazine, published on December 6, 1963, only days after Kennedy was assassinated (Perlstein, 2013). This was not the only time the Kennedys actively were involved in tweaking the work of others to promote a more favorable image. The Kennedys controlled and adjusted the content of the movie about the sinking of Kennedy's PT boat during WWII.

LYNDON JOHNSON

Another sharp contrast in back-to-back presidents was Johnson following Kennedy. Johnson was a large and unattractive man with a personality that was even less attractive. Even his biographers have trouble saying nice things about him. His handling of the political transition from the Kennedy Administration to his own, despite active opposition from the Kennedy family, was a truly remarkable feat (Caro, 2012). It is unequivocal that his political savvy resulted in the enactment of the landmark Civil

Rights Act of 1964 (Jardine, 2009). These early successes are often washed over by the news coverage related to the Vietnam War.

Because of the news coverage of the Vietnam War, Johnson was angry at the media most of the time. He singled out the major television networks for what he felt was slanted coverage that actually favored the invading Viet Cong over his administration. In 1967, Johnson directed his staff to launch a media counteroffensive to show the Vietnam War in a more positive light. While this worked for a brief time, the infamous Tet Offensive in 1968 and live television coverage of the tough battles being fought brought about a much more negative view of the war (*Encyclopedia of the New American Nation*, 2016). The bitter irony of this for Johnson and his supporters was that the South Vietnamese and U.S. forces actually won, despite getting little credit in the media (Oberdorfer, 2004). The resulting news coverage most likely led to Johnson's decision not to run again in 1968 (Hickman, 2016). The riots at the 1968 Democratic Party Convention were largely focused on ending the U.S. involvement in Vietnam (History.com staff, n.d.). A more dramatic portrayal is found in videos from that period.

RICHARD NIXON

If Johnson felt the media was largely against him, certainly Nixon would have doubled that response. Nixon rode into office on the back of the unpopularity of the Vietnam War and Democrats, which the public associated with the war. The protests at the 1968 Democrat convention helped to seal the deal for the GOP.

Despite the unpopularity of his Democrat opponents, Nixon was not viewed as the positive alternative by the media. Former television journalist Mark Feldstein released a book in 2010 that purports to tell the true story of Nixon's war with the media, and newspaper columnist Jack Anderson in particular (Feldstein, 2010). Feldstein details Nixon's preoccupation with taking on Anderson. Anderson, in turn, was not beyond his own "dirty tricks" to gain information on his targets. The most incredible aspect of the media storm is an alleged plot by G. Gordon Liddy to assassinate Anderson on behalf of Nixon. Per the story, Liddy did not follow through since Nixon did not give him the order to do so. Liddy confirms the story in his own autobiography (Liddy, 1998). Adding some credibility to parts of Feldstein's book is a column in *The Washington Post* by then-media reporter Howard Kurtz (Kurtz, 2010).

No matter who tells the story, Nixon was unpopular with the media early in his first term in office. His reelection was more a testimony to the even more unpopular Democrat ticket in 1972 than Nixon's popularity or success in office. For most Americans, it was the reporting by Bob Woodward and Carl Bernstein for *The Washington Post* about the Watergate scandal, not Anderson's columns, that led to the only presidential resignation in American history (*The Washington Post*, 2005). In the televised Watergate hearings, led by Democrat Senator Sam Ervin of North Carolina, Americans were able to make up their own minds about Nixon without the filter of the media. Americans' viewpoint changed from agreeing with Nixon's claim that it was a media attack upon him to a later view of Nixon as an unethical perpetrator himself (Kohut, 2014).

Several years after his 1974 resignation, Nixon was interviewed by British television journalist David Frost. Nixon in that instance used the opportunity to apologize to the American people and to attempt to somewhat rehabilitate his legacy. Given the dismal view many still hold of Nixon, it is not clear that his direct approach by using television to present his side of the story was effective (History.com staff, n.d.b).

Despite his unpopularity with the media, Nixon was named, along with Henry Kissinger, his Assistant for National Security Affairs, as "Man of the Year" by *Time* for 1971 and 1972. When naming the two men, the opening of relations with Communist China, dealing with the war in Vietnam, and achieving a first nuclear arms reduction treaty with the U.S.S.R. were mentioned as reasons for the distinction (*Time*, 2012b).

GERALD FORD

Nixon's first vice president resigned in 1973. Therefore, Ford did not have much time to adjust to the position. In turn, the media did not have much time to adjust to Ford as president. Ford was greeted with a positive tilt in a cover story in *Time* a few weeks after he took office (*Time*, 1974). That positive outlook lasted less than a month.

Ford's first major act was to pardon Richard Nixon. This momentous act defined Ford's presidency for both the public and the media. Even forty years later, this single act is recalled when Ford's name is mentioned. While presented by the media as a terrible error in judgment, Ford defended his actions as a need for the entire country to move on from the political time bomb of Watergate (Mieczkowski, 2005). Media reports were almost universally against Ford's action at the time. The consensus seems to have jelled in the other direction as a 2014 article in *The Wall Street Journal* reported on the fortieth anniversary of Ford's pardon (Gormley & Shribman, 2014).

The media had a major impact on Ford and allowed the collective anger about the pardon to cloud their reporting of the challenges he faced. In the modern era, only Johnson's assumption of power following Kennedy's assassination matched the challenge Ford faced. It could easily be argued that Johnson was far better prepared to face that challenge. Ford inherited an economic recession, a crisis involving Middle East oil supplies, and the continuing pressures of the Cold War (Gerald R. Ford Foundation, n.d.).

In turn, the media's hostility toward Ford certainly played a great part in his defeat at the hands of Jimmy Carter in the 1976 presidential election.

JIMMY CARTER

Carter moved into office with great optimism despite having achieved only a narrow victory over Ford. In a sign of media support for Carter, *Time* named Carter its "Man of the Year" for 1976 (*Time*, 2006). This made little sense since Carter had just been elected and had not even taken office. The only possible data relied upon by the magazine was his campaign speeches.

From the start, Carter never seemed to get fully on track and the Iran Hostage Crisis was his final undoing. The major television networks featured coverage of the crisis on a near daily basis, including a count of the number of days that the hostages had been held. In *Presidential Leadership: Politics and Policy Making*, the authors note that in 1968 much less was made by the media when the U.S. Navy ship *Pueblo* with a larger number of hostages was held by North Korea. They concluded that the difference was the intense television coverage of the Iran hostages versus the *Pueblo* hostages (Edwards III & Wayne, 2013). This was a sharp reversal of fortunes for the former "Time Man of the Year."

RONALD REAGAN

Perhaps the best suited for the television age of all presidents was Ronald Reagan. Years as a studio actor and television host gave him the near perfect background to take advantage of the opportunities television provided. His ability to command the stage and the podium especially helped when the media was against him, such as during the Iran-Contra Affair. This is not to imply that criticism of Reagan's administration was not justified, only that he was able to overcome it to some extent through his own personality and presentation.

Reagan was already fairly well-known, but his Hollywood star was distinctly fading when he was called upon to boost the campaign of Barry Goldwater, the GOP presidential candidate in 1964. Reagan hosted a thirty-minute video presentation called "A Time for Choosing." While it did not bail out the Goldwater campaign, it helped to move Reagan into the political arena and eventually the White House (Anderson, 2015). This is a classic example of politicians becoming part of the media, rather than the media covering the politician.

Parallel to Carter, Reagan was named "Time Man of the Year," in 1980, before he had actually become president. He was named again in 1983, along with his counterpart from the U.S.S.R, Yuri Andropov, for progress on nuclear weapons reduction talks (*Time*, 2006). The positive publicity helped to contribute to the many myths that surrounded Reagan during his time in office.

Reagan enjoyed a popularity with the public that has rarely been matched and that created its own issues for the media. The authors of *The Press Effect: How the News Influences Politics and Government* suggest that the media actually avoided publishing negative material about Reagan for fear of alienating their viewers or readers (Willis & Willis, 2007). Obviously, this did not carry over into the reporting on the Iran-Contra Affair. Just enough had occurred during the latter part of Reagan's second term that the romance with both the public and the media was becoming strained (Fried & Shapiro, 1997).

GEORGE H.W. BUSH

Despite his position as Reagan's vice president for eight years, Bush hardly benefited from his association with the more media-friendly Reagan. In fact, Bush struggled to overcome his "Wimp Image," as some called it (Warner, 1987). It is a great shame that a WWII fighter pilot would be degraded to such a level. He further dealt with perceptions of the public, largely shaped by the media, that the economy was much worse than it actually was. The public does not always put the economy into first position, but it certainly was for the 1992 election (Hall, 2006). The economy follows a cyclical pattern that operates somewhat independently of the presidency. The bitter irony is that the economy would have likely boosted his presidency had the 1992 presidential election taken place either two years earlier or two years later. Bush's timing was simply unlucky.

Bush was the "Time Man of the Year for 1990." Again, timing was bad for Bush as this was too soon to help him with the 1992 election. The *Time* selection was not entirely positive, describing him as strong on foreign policy, but not domestic policy. This set up the news coverage late in his only term as presiding over a poor economy (*Time*, 2006b).

Impacting both the Reagan and Bush administrations was the issue of drugs and substance abuse in America. Starting in the early 1980s, the U.S. military took on the issue first with some success. In the private sector, many of the "Baby Boomers" had used drugs growing up, and continued to use them as adults. They were now assuming their place in workplaces and schools around America. The issue launched itself onto the front page in 1986 when University of Maryland basketball star Len Bias died of a cocaine overdose only hours after he had been taken No. 2 overall in the NBA draft by the Boston Celtics. It was an active issue during the 1988 presidential election. In response, Bush appointed William Bennett, Reagan's former Secretary of Education, to head the Office of Drug Abuse

Policy (Gonzenbach, 1995). The issue faded from public view fairly quickly. The issue might have helped Bush get elected in 1988, but it was unlikely to have had any impact on his unsuccessful run in 1992.

BILL CLINTON

Bill Clinton was the beneficiary of positive media during much of his early national exposure, starting with his presidential campaign. As the media exaggerated the downside of the economy, Bush was perpetually in a defensive position against a virtual unknown in Clinton and a rare, strong, third-party candidate, Ross Perot (Holmes, 1992). The Pew Research Center's survey of journalists covering the 1992 presidential campaign felt that the media helped Clinton and hurt Bush by a fairly wide margin (Pew Research Center, 1992). Clinton, parallel to Carter and Reagan, was "Time Man of the Year" after his election, but before he even held office (*Time*, 2006c).

It is traditional that the party in the White House generally loses seats in Congress in the next midterm election. For Clinton, 1994 was a critical turning point in his administration as the GOP, led by feisty Newt Gingrich, a U.S. Congressman from Georgia, took control of both houses of Congress for the first time in forty years (The Editors of Encyclopedia Britannica, 1994). A Pew Research Center report based on a large survey of twenty thousand voters gave the media a "C" grade for its election coverage (Pew Research Center, 1994). It is not clear if this was a result of disappointment by Democrat voters, or glee by the GOP voters that Gingrich prevailed despite the news coverage. In an interesting twist, while Clinton used much of his political capital in his first two years in the presidency to argue for comprehensive health-care reform, the voters surveyed indicated that they preferred a much more modest solution

(Kaiser Family Foundation, 1994). News coverage of this issue may have helped to tilt the 1994 election results in favor of the GOP.

Clinton proved himself an adept politician as he then worked with Gingrich toward a more conservative agenda than Clinton had originally proposed. The relationship between the two was not all positive and there were two government shutdowns after the 1994 election. The consensus was that news coverage presented the issue as more favorable to Clinton (Horsley, 2013). The long-term impact for both Clinton and the GOP was minimal (Gallup Inc., 2013).

Clinton's scandals did not hit the media until after he had won reelection in 1996. His victory was again aided by third-party candidate Ross Perot. The GOP candidate, Senator Bob Dole, performed poorly in the polls, despite the public's admiration for him as having survived grievous injuries in WWII. A Pew Research Center poll found that the outcome of the election indicated that the public was generally not happy with any of the presidential candidates. The voters were generally happier that the GOP kept control of Congress than that Clinton was reelected. Another interesting outcome was that television began to slip as a source of political news, while radio rose in influence, particularly among GOP voters (Pew Research Center, 1996). This was a time period when conservative radio began to surge with Rush Limbaugh and others.

In many ways, the Lewinsky scandal in particular could have been expected to change public opinion of the job Clinton was doing as president. However, a detailed study revealed that while public opinion did become more negative, Americans still considered Clinton's job performance to be acceptable (Kiousis, 2003). This somewhat surprising conclusion would indicate that Americans care a great deal more about the performance of the economy and jobs than they do about the sexual indiscretions of the president. In most cases, the voters attribute current economic conditions to the president then in office and not the president or other politicians who created the circumstances in the past.

In 1998, Clinton shared "Time Man of the Year" recognition with Whitewater prosecutor Kenneth Starr. This bizarre pairing underscores the fact that being so designated does not mean that either of them accomplished much during the year or were particularly good or ethical, only that they dominated the headlines for the year in review (*Time*, 1998). After the glare of the headlines and television coverage died down, the struggle between the two and their respective supporters can appear quite venial in nature (Gormley, 2011).

GEORGE W. BUSH

George Bush and his rival in the 2000 presidential election, former Clinton Vice President Al Gore, had ample media criticism. It appeared that Bush received more negative character evaluations, but it is unclear if that had much impact on the voters (Pew Research Center, 2000). Analysis of news coverage of the campaign indicated that much of the coverage was about the campaign itself, and not about the issues (Pew Research Center, 2000b). A Pew Research Center study identified the 2000 campaign as the first where the Internet was a major media factor. The study gave it fairly solid marks for credibility (Pew Research Center, 2000c). It is highly doubtful that the Internet would be found to be a credible source by 2016. Its impact on future campaigns is unquestioned.

Bush was named "Time Person of the Year" for 2000 as he was saluted for winning a hairpin victory that was ultimately awarded by the U.S. Supreme Court (*Time*, 2006d). He received strong media support early in his administration. Less than nine months after he took office, the worst terrorist attack on U.S. soil since Pearl Harbor took place on September

11, 2001. Bush dealt with the famed "Dot-Com" market meltdown and then the series of corporate collapses tied to stock market manipulations by ENRON and other companies. His retaliatory invasion of Afghanistan met with both broad public and media approval (Bartlett, 2009). Bush even garnered strong initial support when he expanded U.S. military involvement into Iraq in 2003. The U.S. partnered with Britain under the leadership of Prime Minister Tony Blair (Basile, 2015). Not surprisingly, the 2002 midterm elections were not "normal" due to 9/11 and the resulting response by Washington. The GOP retained its control of both houses of Congress (Weinberger, 2002).

Bush faced a major political challenge in the 2004 presidential election with Democratic candidate Senator John Kerry of Massachusetts. Despite his incumbent status, Bush struggled in the election and won a narrow victory. The media supported Kerry over Bush, which was blamed on Bush's performance in the debates with Kerry (Pew Research Center, 2004). It was more likely driven by growing criticism over the Iraq invasion in 2003. Largely rewarding Bush for his handling of the 9/11 terrorist attacks and winning the 2004 presidential election, *Time* again named Bush "Person of the Year" for 2004 (*Time*, 2012c).

Bush's star faded heavily through his second term in office, certainly assisted by increasingly negative news coverage. In the 2006 midterm elections, the GOP lost both houses of Congress to the Democrats (Pew Research Center, 2008). Bush left little that was positive for a GOP candidate, leading to the election of Barack Obama in 2008.

BARACK OBAMA

Obama was the beneficiary of more positive media than either Clinton or Bush during their first campaigns for the presidency (Pew Research

Center, 2008b). Obama experienced much more favorable news coverage than his GOP opponent, Senator John McCain, a former Vietnam War POW (Pew Research Center, 2008c). Obama is often viewed as the first presidential candidate to fully capture social media for both promotion of his campaign and importantly, fund-raising (Kerpen, 2016). Such a direct connection between a politician and the public somewhat reduces the impact of the coverage of the candidates by the various media outlets.

Parallel to a number of recent presidents, Obama was named "Time Person of the Year for 2008," before his inauguration (*Time*, 2008). Obama had no business experience and limited political experience. His romance with the media continued as he received much more favorable news coverage early in his first term than either Clinton or Bush (Pew Research Center, 2009).

Obama's relationship with the voters was less sanguine than with the media, as illustrated by the change in the balance of power in 2010 in the U.S. House of Representatives as the GOP picked up sixty seats to take control of the lower house, and made gains, but did not reach a majority, in the Senate (Feldmann, 2010). The expectation was that Obama would follow the lead of Clinton after the midterm election in 1994 and at least make an effort to work with Congress. However, Obama, perhaps buoyed by consistently positive news coverage, continued on his own agenda, resorting to executive orders instead of attempting compromises with Congress.

Given the rocky road and less than stellar economic improvement, it appeared that Obama might have been a one-term president. However, the GOP fielded a successful businessman and intellectual, but not a great politician, in Mitt Romney. News coverage again supported Obama relative to Romney, although a Pew Center study presented statistics showing that the media was largely negative toward both candidates. The same study tried to calculate the impact of social media, although this would mainly be due to individuals providing comments, not the media. A careful reading of the study indicates that early news coverage was hugely negative toward Romney, when many voters were forming their opinions on the candidates. Romney's strong showing in the three presidential debates helped to provide less negative coverage closer to election day (Pew, 2012). This was too late to undo the substantial early damage. *Time* rewarded Obama with the "Time Person of the Year" award for 2012 (Scherer, 2012). At this point, it was largely a survival award, but confirmed the media's support for Obama.

Any celebration was premature for Obama as the Democrats were trounced in the 2014 midterm elections and the GOP held the House and gained a majority in the Senate (Weisman & Parker, 2015). This essentially sealed off Obama from any progress on his agenda other than by executive orders. The GOP wins in the midterm election were a surprise to the pollsters since the number of seats gained was larger than predicted (Sabato, Kondik, & Skelley, n.d.). Two aspects are worth noting. First, the polls were far enough off that future polls may be irrelevant, except in providing the media something to talk about. Second, the voters do not appear to be persuaded to vote a particular way by the polls.

CONCLUSION

The media had an impact in building the myths of the American presidents covered in this book. The impact of the media appears to have been stronger during the "Golden Age of Journalism," was relatively strong during the radio era and into the era of television and live coverage, but has weakened as the "24-hour News Cycle" and the Internet blossomed around 2000. The explosion of social media and creative use of the Internet has given politicians the opportunity to speak to the public without the filter of any media involvement. The media seems to have had a minimal impact with regard to the ethical aspects of a majority of the seventeen presidents discussed in this book. Obviously, members of the media were well aware of the sexual adventures of Roosevelt and Kennedy, to name only two. The media conveniently failed to report what it knew in this regard. So, support from the media may mean not covering ethical and leadership failures, as much as reporting good news about their favored politicians.

As voters move past 2016, the question becomes whether the media has any real impact today. It is quite possible that there is so much media available to all persons today that the wave of information and misinformation washes over them. Whether *The New York Times* leans left and *The Wall Street Journal* leans right becomes irrelevant to the ultimate issue of who will become the next president. As voters become calloused recipients, stories must be more extreme and either present the candidate in his or her own words stating something offensive or present overwhelming evidence of extreme conduct. In turn, the direct access to the public by the candidates also means that they may be able to directly contradict negative news reports.

Media journalist Ken Auletta, commenting in 2004 about the media relationship with the Bush administration, noted that there appeared to be a greater emphasis on manipulating the news and treatment of the media as just another interest group rather than as an important part of the information pipeline (2015). Since that time, and especially with the growth of the Internet and the advent of Facebook, LinkedIn, Twitter, etc., candidates may have even less need to treat the media as more than another interest group.

In describing the changes in the relationship among the media, the politicians and the public, a fair question is whether the changes have been positive for American democracy. A key perspective of this book is that U.S. presidents, in many cases aided by the media, have not set an ethical example and have not done a good job of leading this great country. The Internet and social media forces can balance the material presented by the media. Optimistically, this may prompt a new golden age of journalism regardless of the medium. Reporters can actually help the public learn the important objective information about presidential candidates and, preferably, well before they are nominated by a major political party.

CHAPTER 21
PROPOSALS FOR IMPROVING FUTURE AMERICAN PRESIDENTS

The decline of America is as real as the decline and fall of the Roman Empire and later, the British Empire. The American decline can be reversed. This is not a fatalistic book. America can implement changes—some quickly, others will take more time—that can reverse the decline. America could become the only world power to reverse the decline and achieve the singular greatness that it did during WWI and WWII and into the Space Age. It is unlikely to achieve that level with the leadership of the last one hundred years, with one B- and one C+, and the rest of the presidents below that level of ethical leadership. Again, the president is only one position in a vast economy and nation, but it is an iconic statement of what America is and can be.

TERM LIMITS

In tracing the failures of the last one hundred years, presidents and the members of Congress have acted in their own interest and the interest of their parties far more than they have acted on behalf of America. Wilson delayed intervention in WWI for fear of losing the 1916 election. For purely political reasons, Roosevelt ignored full-fledged assaults on long-time American allies until a catastrophic attack came to America. In the modern era, presidents have engaged in half-hearted wars like Korea, Vietnam, and now Iraq and Afghanistan in order to achieve some objectives, but without the bold decisions necessary to win.

Numerous proposals have been made to reform the federal election system. One of many proposals has the president serving one six-year term, senators serving two six-year terms, and representatives serving five two-year terms. History favors shorter presidential terms (Langley & Baker, 2016). Truman, Johnson, and George W. Bush each distinguished themselves early in their presidencies, only to fade badly later on. Most modern presidents spend their third and fourth years in office campaigning for reelection. America pays a high price for such flagrant failures to perform their duties. Recent presidents often spend their last two years in office scouting locations for their presidential libraries and attempting to curry favor with various powers to enhance their post-presidency reputations. Another task that cheats the taxpayers of their due is the large amount of time spent campaigning for the candidate of the president's respective party who runs to replace them when there is a two-term president.

Franklin Roosevelt taught America a lesson when he failed to follow 150 years of precedent and ran for a third and then a fourth term. The Twenty-second Amendment to the Constitution is a result of his unbounded egotism. Unfortunately, Congress did not include itself in that amendment, and it is time to both fix that oversight and limit the president to one term while limiting the terms of members of Congress as well (Taranto, 2014). Unfortunately, the likelihood that Congress will take it upon itself to surrender itself to a true representative democracy by frequent change of characters in D.C. is very low. A constitutional convention convened by citizens of the various states may be required (Forsyth, 2008).

Article 5 says that Congress "shall call a convention for proposing amendments" when requested by enough states. Under Article 5 of the Constitution, such a convention can be convened when requested by two-thirds of the states, and it is one of two ways to propose amendments to the nation's founding document. The other method, by which all previous constitutional amendments have been initiated, requires a two-thirds vote in both houses of Congress. Ratifying amendments then require three-fourths of the states to approve (National Archives, 2016).

A variety of contra arguments are raised when term limits are suggested. One is that rather obviously the crew in D.C. does not want to share its power with the people (Phillips, 2016). The answer is a convention from the states, forcing a constitutional convention. With the growing public opinion that America is on the wrong track, at some point it will be possible to implement such reform (Bender & Lee, 2016). Another argument is that it is too complicated in D.C. to have frequent changes, and that this would actually provide more power to the lobbyists (Phillips, 2016). This defies the logic of what presently happens in D.C. Limiting the length of time to serve in office and cutting off their undeserved pensions would force the majority to head home to their districts. In addition, enforcing tough rules on lobbying Congress would make this an uneconomic venture. The military has already implemented such "revolving door" reforms (Jakab, 2016) and there are similar rules in place regarding family members of sitting congressional members (Laszewski, 2016).

With greater turnover and diversity in D.C, the system should shake out after an initial period of discomfort. The U.S. has many smart people with strong ethical beliefs and the ability to represent their neighbors. It is time to return to that model.

END THE CONGRESSIONAL SENIORITY SYSTEM

Perhaps the single strongest argument by those already in Congress to oppose term limits is the seniority system. The system in both the House and the Senate provides special benefits like committee chair positions for the senior persons of each party, with the party in control gaining the most control, of course ("Understanding the Senate Seniority System," n.d.). As the incumbents campaign for office, the mantra of "Elect me, since I have power and can gain more power in order to help my constituents" is frequently heard from those with seniority. So, the system works to help incumbents get elected. In turn, as noted in the section above on term limits, the representatives become less and less connected to the people they serve in their home districts.

With term limits, there will be little advantage of seniority, since there will be an acceleration in turnover in all offices. This will also dilute the power of the lobbyists, who seek out incumbents, and especially those with seniority, to ply their favors and funds (Llopis, 2016). There have been periodic, dramatic sweeps from Democrat to Republican control, or the opposite, in Congress. Examples include the 1932 elections (Mauldin, 2016) and 1994 elections (Clymer, 1994). The occasion of such a sweep may be the best chance to achieve an end to the current seniority system by implementing effective term limits.

Intimately tied to the two-party system in D.C. is the current structure of Congress with the absence of term limits and the seniority system. While this book focuses on presidents, the fact is that the members of Congress have created the system and signed off on the debt that has helped to create the financial crisis in America today. In reviewing the last one hundred years, other than the lack of term limits and seniority, nothing explains the continued election of persons who serve no citizens' interest other than their own. A study of longevity in D.C. is rather extraordinary. A summary of combined time in the Congress and the Senate produces a list of over one hundred politicians who have held office in D.C. for more than 35 years (Jakab, 2016). Unequivocally, it is not a representational democracy when the representatives never return home to live under the laws and budgets they have created. It is hard to defend much of this list, which contains the names of politicians known to have been overt racists and many others who have abused their power (Taranto, 2014). Other studies have revealed that the tendency to stay in office longer is increasing (Glassman, 2015).

A disconcerting side effect of the current control of elected offices in D.C. is that neither party has really served the interests of minorities. Famously, the political parties reach out to minorities and other underserved populations in the months before each major election day (Llopis, 2016). Using black unemployment as an index, neither party has "fixed" the problem. Further, while the U.S. has supposedly waged a "War on Poverty," that is yet another war that America has not won. It is likely that with term limits and dismantling of the seniority system, America will move to a multiparty system. Minorities and different interest groups will then be free to form their own parties and no longer be captive to one dominant party or the other.

TIME TO HAVE A PRESIDENT AND A PRIME MINISTER

It is a quaint idea, one that preceded by 165 years the use of the atomic bomb and by roughly the same time frame serious digital power of computers. It is that just one person can control the domestic and international policy of the U.S. Many countries have turned to a system involving a president and a prime minister, one with a domestic focus and one with an international focus (Feller, 2016). This is perhaps the most radical recommendation in this chapter, but one that may be critically important to keeping the U.S. at the top. Funding would still come from Congress, which could act as the arbiter of the inevitable funding competition among the domestic and foreign policy demands. While it is true that the current president has a cabinet, the cabinet's focus is largely domestic, with only the Secretary of State and Secretary of Defense really focused on the rest of the world, with perhaps some help from the Department of Homeland Security ("Cabinet Members Under President Barack Obama," 2016).

THE STRATEGY OF WAR

War is about killing, conquering, or being conquered. No matter how the politicians present it to the public, that is a reality that is as old as civilization itself. Only the weapons have changed. Presidents of both parties have wasted the resources of the U.S. and much more importantly, the lives of American military members. Starting with the "draw" fought in Korea, a war that cost more than fifty-four thousand American lives and approximately thirty billion in 2010 dollars, U.S. presidents have progressively made America less safe and wasted even more American lives and financial resources. The end of WWII, learning from the issues that remained unresolved after WWI, the standard for victory was unconditional surrender of the enemies. The results are a Germany and Japan that following their unconditional surrenders have become two of the leading economies in the world and have not initiated further action against the U.S.

Country/War	Battle Deaths (as of 2012)*	Non-mortal Woundings (as of 2012)*	Estimated Cost in Billions (in 2010 $)**
Korea	54,246	103,284	30
Vietnam	90,220	153,303	111
Persian Gulf War	1,948	467	61
Global War on Terror	6,456	4,8104	1,046

*"America's Wars," 2012
**Daggett, 2010

The numbers above far understate the cost of war to the U.S. In hearings in 2010, the Veterans' Affairs Committee heard testimony by economists Stiglitz and Bilmes, who wrote the book *The Three Trillion Dollar War: The True Cost of the Iraq Conflict* (Stiglitz & Bilmes, 2008). In the VA testimony, the economists indicated that killed and wounded are a serious economic loss, but the long-term costs of illnesses like PTSD have resulted in many disability claims and suicides. These costs are often not included in estimates. Further, many veterans seek local medical care and do not seek care at the VA, meaning that even the cost to the federal government does not fully reflect the cost to society of those who need care after serving in the military House Committee on Veterans Affairs, 2016). These are unfunded liabilities that are not presently being recorded when the financial outlook of the U.S. is evaluated.

The U.S. now deals with a hostile North Korea rather than dealing with it in 1952. In turn, the failure to unseat Saddam Hussein in Iraq at the end of Desert Storm in the early 1990s led directly to the war in Iraq in the early 2000s (Mauldin, 2016b). It is not a stretch to suggest that WWIII has already begun. North Korea continues to test ever-expanding nuclear weapons and missile delivery systems (Basiri, 2016). Iran, despite the recent peace treaty, still has leaders leading chants to kill Americans (Dudley, 2016). Multiple sources report that there have already been numerous breaches of the Iran treaty (Wald, 2016). The recent payment of 1.7 billion dollars in international currency to Iran smacks of the type of appeasement practiced by Wilson, Chamberlain, and Roosevelt in the dawn of the two prior world wars (Dudley, 2016b). The failure of the U.S. to effectively respond to the recent seizure of U.S. Navy sailors by Iran can only bring more such terrorist acts in the future (LaGrone, 2016). It does not take a crystal ball to see that the appeasement path to another war is the same as in the past.

In dealing with the significant mental health issues of veterans discussed above, perhaps some of the vets would react differently if they had been engaged to fight an all-out war for a clearly defined objective. For instance, it is hard for the veterans of the Vietnam War to feel good about their sacrifices and those of their fellow soldiers in light of the outcome. Compounding the misery is the confessional book by the Secretary of Defense during much of Vietnam, Robert S. McNamara: *In Retrospect: The Tragedy and Lessons of Vietnam* (McNamara & VanDeMark, 1996). In the future, any commitment of U.S. military force must be destined to produce concrete results and not a draw, or worse.

OUTLINE OF A PATH TO SAFETY AND SUCCESS

- The U.S. president must commit the U.S. to be the preeminent world power with the most effective conventional and nuclear weapons in the world, including "first strike" capability. It has recently been reported that Russia has a tank more sophisticated than any U.S. tank and China and Russia both have been developing tactical missiles that have done damage to U.S. ships and other assets (Daiss, 2016).

- The U.S. will maintain an effective fighting force that is second to none. This does not mean that it has to be the largest force. Nor does it mean it has to be the most expensive force.

- The U.S. will maintain surveillance around the world to ensure that the best intelligence is gathered at all times and that plots against the U.S. and its allies are detected as early as possible.

- The U.S. will have the most advanced anti-missile systems in the world and deploy them effectively to protect itself and its allies. No other country shall dictate to the U.S. when such weapons or forces can be deployed. Russia, for instance, shall not dictate to the U.S. when such weapons or forces can be deployed in former U.S.S.R. countries (Coleman, 2016).

- Across the world, the U.S. will no longer back petty dictators or others who do not support American values of freedom and democratic governance. Part of the failure of Vietnam and Cuba was that the U.S. backed supposed leaders who were not regarded as any better than the leaders of the Communist opposition.

- The president must be disciplined enough to not commit U.S. forces of any kind, including ground forces, air forces, missiles, drones, etc., anywhere in the world without having a clear path to victory that is articulated to the American people. Once engaged, the U.S. shall marshal its forces in the most effective way possible to achieve its objectives with the least possible loss of life of U.S. forces and civilian casualties.

- As the sole world power, the president shall not allow U.S. forces to be commanded by any other than a U.S. commander, but the U.S. shall cooperate and work closely with alliances that meet U.S. standards.

- The U.S., as the sole world power, shall continue to maintain a Navy second to none, including carriers and submarines, and to deploy them around the globe to remind its allies and enemies of its capacity to fight for American values. Incidents like the USS *Cole* bombing in Yemen must not be repeated.

- The U.S. shall articulate and unequivocally support a principle that no American around the world shall be allowed to be kidnapped or killed without effective U.S. retaliation that will serve to deter and prevent such terrorist acts in the future.

- War criminals apprehended around the world and are determined to be adverse to U.S. interests shall be incarcerated in the Guantanamo Navy Base, Cuba. Only military tribunals will hear the cases there. Such criminals shall not be brought into the U.S. court system as they are enemy combatants and have no right to access to the U.S. courts.

Should future presidents and the U.S. Congress adopt the approach outlined above, it is likely that WWIII will not occur since the potential combatants will decide that quick death will follow for them and their followers. Or, it will be quickly resolved with minimal loss of life and with modest expenditures. No American should die in vain for a poorly defined cause or objective.

BORDER SECURITY

It is shameful that for decades, neither party's president has actually fixed the dual issue of border security and immigration–legal and illegal. Control of the U.S. borders is essential to national security. The failure of the Reagan amnesty plan was that the amnesty was intended to be a one-time affair and Americans were promised that the U.S. would secure its borders to avoid the need for a repeat. The 1986 plan resulted in roughly 2.7 million immigrants receiving permanent resident recognition (Plumer, 2013).

A premise of this book is that the diversity of the American people is one of its great strengths. Persons of all cultures, educational levels, and skills have brought value to the "melting pot" of America. For the future, with low native birth rates, immigration is required to bring growth and value. However, unregulated immigration will not help the U.S. Somehow, the current batch of aliens here illegally must be processed and evaluated. And, unlike the 1986 debacle, this time the controls must be in place to avoid a repeat. Much enhanced enforcement of employment of new hires should be one easy fix (Erb, 2015b). Further, the self-employed illegal immigrants would be shut down if they could not easily cash checks and in many cases, get driver's licenses (Blanding, 2016).

END PRESIDENTIAL PARDONS

The results of the pardons by U.S. presidents have not been pleasing to most Americans, and yet they continue. The power for presidents to grant pardons is found in Article II Section 2 of the U.S. Constitution: "The President ... shall have power to grant reprieves and pardons for offenses against the United States, except in cases of Impeachment." So, a constitutional amendment will be required to remove this privilege from the president.

President	Number of Pardons (Hughes, 2016)	Controversial Pardons
John F. Kennedy	575	First-time offenders convicted of crimes under the Narcotics Control Act of 1956 (Bump, 2013)
Lyndon B. Johnson	1,187	Frank W. Boykin – Congressman convicted of bribery (US House of Representatives: History, Art & Archives, n.d.)
Richard Nixon	926	William Calley – convicted of murder for his involvement in the My Lai Massacre – pardoned in 1974 after completing 3 years' house arrest (America Press Inc, 2015)

President	Number of Pardons (Hughes, 2016)	Controversial Pardons
Gerald Ford	409	Richard Nixon (Flanary, 2011)
Jimmy Carter	566	Oscar Collazo – Attempted assassination of President Harry S. Truman (New York Times, 1994)
Ronald Reagan	406	W. Mark Felt and Edward S. Miller – FBI officials who authorized illegal break-ins (Reagan, 1981)
George H.W. Bush	77	For his role in the Iran-Contra Affair: Caspar Weinberger – Secretary of Defense under President Ronald Reagan (Pincus, 1992)

President	Number of Pardons (Hughes, 2016)	Controversial Pardons
Bill Clinton	456	Marc Rich & Pincus Green – business partners; indicted by U.S. Attorney on charges of tax evasion and illegal trade with Iran (Gerstein, 2016)
George W. Bush	176	Edwin L. Cox Jr. – Had a 1998 bank fraud conviction (Wallace, 2001)
Barack Obama	70 (as of Nov. 16, 2016) (US Department of Justice, 2016)	Willie Shaw, Jr.- Aug. 1974 sentencing date – Fifteen years' imprisonment for armed bank robbery (The Sun News, 2013)

No president could contribute more to America's future than to put the U.S. on a path to eliminate the national debt – both the declared amount of twenty trillion dollars and the up to one hundred trillion dollars of unrealized and unfunded debt. An immediate first step is a balanced budget that includes a serious allocation for paying the interest and principal on the existing debt.

There cannot be a reasonable argument against reducing federal spending at this point. A 2011 Report from the Congressional Budget Office states:

> *Beyond the coming decade, the aging of the U.S. population and rising health care costs will put increasing pressure on the budget. If federal debt continues to expand faster than the economy—as it has since 2007—the growth of people's income will slow, the share of federal spending devoted to paying interest on the debt will rise more quickly, and the risk of a fiscal crisis will increase (Congressional Budget Office, 2015).*

As noted earlier in this chapter, the U.S. must have the preeminent military in the world. At the same time, the reports of military pork are legendary and like every branch of government, the money must be spent more intelligently and with purpose. A January 2016 article in *Forbes* reported extraordinary waste in buying planes and ships that were not needed (Tiefer, 2016). The report criticized the high cost of maintaining Guantanamo Bay as a prison for terrorists. "Gitmo" should continue to house the worst terrorists, but certainly costs need to be substantially reduced. The lost and missing money at the Department of Defense has reached unbelievable proportions. A July 2016 report by the Office of the Inspector General, U.S. Department of Defense documents that as much as 6.5 trillion dollars of defense spending cannot be accounted for ("Army General Fund Adjustments Not Adequately Documented or Supported," 2016).

Federal employment, other than the military, is also ripe for significant cuts in staffing and benefits, specifically pension benefits. As far as staffing levels go, there has been a slight reduction in total federal civilian employment. The level was just over three million employees in the late 1980s. In the latest count from 2014, the level is at 2,663,000 (U.S. Office of Personnel Management, n.d.). Almost the entire reduction in federal staffing came from the U.S. Postal Service, which has been under financial pressure for years since it was placed under separate administration in 1971 (USPS, 2016).

Federal employees enjoy pension benefits at a much greater percentage than private-sector workers. Prior to 2000, federal workers were paid modestly, but the substantial job security of Civil Service protection and the predictable work hours ensured that there was no shortage of persons willing to work for the federal government. Then, the "hidden" benefits of pensions, health plans, and savings plans were increased while there was no reduction in job security, leave time, or paid holidays. Since 1987, federal employees hired since 1983 participate in Social Security, and a modified federal pension plan operates in addition to Social Security, not instead of it (Kerns, 1986). Since 2000, there has been a significant increase in federal pay levels without reducing security, benefits, or staffing levels. As a result, the taxpayers' exposure has continued to skyrocket while private-sector wages and benefits have shrunk (Edwards, 2016).

The need to either raise taxes or cut expenditures has never been more crucial. The corporate tax will likely need to be reduced in competition among countries for major corporate headquarters ("Ten benefits of Cutting," 2011). The U.S. simply cannot afford to continue to have such companies move to lower corporate tax countries. On the personal tax side, about one-half of all Americans pay little federal income tax (Williams, 2016). The other half pay a significant amount of tax and are unlikely to vote for more taxes. The real burden is a combination of federal, state, and local taxes, which include income, sales, excise, and of course, real estate.

That makes the type of spending cuts suggested above the most likely avenue to financial sanity. The CBO report referenced above suggests that a cut in spending of approximately one-fifth would be required to avoid the potential financial nightmare ahead (Congressional Budget Office, 2015b).

COMMIT TO CAPITALISM

Presidential leadership often has faltered when it has come to a firm commitment to capitalism. The U.S. has thrived because of the hard work of its people under the U.S. version of capitalism, the natural blessings of its particular piece of the world, a political system that generally allows for freedom, and the hard work and diversity of its people. All these factors together help to account for the unprecedented success in business, quality of life, and, at least through WWII, in war.

Over the last one hundred years, there have been some times of hardship. The response of presidents to economic hardships, despite the general success of the U.S. economy, has often been to resort to pro-socialist strategies. During the 1930s, Roosevelt tried to move the U.S. in the socialist direction to combat the Great Depression. Ironically, despite the undeserved hero-worship of Roosevelt during that time, economists today are approaching a solid consensus that his approach prolonged the depression and his economic meddling was only solved by WWII. Truman and Nixon both experimented with setting prices and wages in order to control parts of the economy and both failed.

Since 2000, the U.S. has violated fundamental capitalist principles by "bailing out" AIG (Schaefer, 2013), General Motors and Chrysler (Muller, 2012), and big banks (Poczter, 2014). The U.S. has dabbled under presidential leadership in supporting private enterprise such as Solyndra, which failed in dramatic fashion (Weiner, 2012). In the case of GM and Chrysler, both companies still went bankrupt as part of resolving their complex problems largely brought about by poor management (Kiley, 2016). On one hand, the capitalist system anticipates that some companies will fail. The concept of "too big to fail," which was widely discussed during the 2008-09 subprime crisis, was simply used by politicians to insert themselves into the world of business. There are hardships associated with allowing businesses to fail, but that is the unique nature of the capitalist system. In turn, Ford Motors survived without a government bailout (Muller, 2016). The strength of capitalism is reflected in the robust U.S. economy that has somehow survived leaders with both ethical challenges and distinctly poor leadership abilities.

The resort to government intervention is particularly fascinating in light of the U.S. success in the Cold War, as it was a victory of rival economies more than rival war machines. From the days of the Russian Revolution, Russia failed to meet its own five-year plans time after time (Rapoza, 2016). After WWII, the U.S.S.R. tried to implement even more grandiose plans with even worse results. Other examples abound. Cuba's communist economy has struggled since the U.S.S.R. stopped backing it because of its own financial problems (Whistler, 2016). In the present day, Venezuela's socialist/communist experiment has failed despite natural resources and a population with a positive attitude toward the future (Flannery, 2016). And, of course, China, which still teaches Marxism, has achieved much of its success with a distinct turn toward capitalism. Had China not done so, it would have ended up in the same place as the U.S.S.R.

ENFORCE ANTITRUST LAWS

The U.S. industrial expansion followed the end of the Civil War. By 1887, the U.S. realized that regulations were needed to keep the economy on track, and the Interstate Commerce Commission was established to regulate the railroads (Fisher, 2016). The early success of industrialization led to monopolies. In 1890, the U.S. passed the Sherman Antitrust Act to reduce monopolization in order to continue the economic expansion that resulted from the industrialization of America (Crews Jr., 2016). While somewhat successful, some entrepreneurs continued to find ways around the 1890 act and the Clayton Act was passed in 1914 to further restrict certain business associations that had the impact of monopolies (Nitti, 2016). Other acts and regulations have been passed since that time to further encourage competition under the U.S. capitalist system.

The enforcement of the antitrust laws is primarily with the U.S. Department of Justice (DOJ), although there are parallel state laws and indeed, some private enforcement actions are possible. Monopolies are either clearly illegal, "*per se,*" or the business activities being examined are subject to "the rule of reason." In the first instance, evidence unequivocally points to an intent to control an industry or part of an industry. These cases are not complicated. On the other hand, in most cases today, federal judges make the call based on the rule of reason (Crews Jr., 2016b). A turn toward bigness took place in the 1990s when federal judges began signing off on mergers of huge corporations. A classic was the merger of giants EXXON and Mobil Oil with combined revenues above two hundred billion dollars and profits over eleven billion dollars. A few short years later, fourteen thousand jobs were shed in the resulting combination (Corcoran, 2010). While *The Wall Street Journal* can tout the merger as a successful combination of giants, the fourteen thousand who lost jobs might not agree. This was only one of many mega-mergers which have cost America jobs and reduced competition in the U.S. As this book goes to press, AT&T and Time Warner have reached a deal on a merger estimated at eighty-six billion dollars (Crews Jr., 2016c).

The DOJ is an executive branch agency. The president can encourage the DOJ to block mergers that may reduce competition and employment opportunities in the U.S. Often, the DOJ even announcing its opposition to a merger is enough to stop one in its tracks. One example was the proposed merger of MCI Worldcom with Sprint in 2000 (Pultz, McGee, & Neil, 2000). In another telecommunications case, the DOJ filed suit to block the 2011 acquisition of T-Mobile by AT&T and the merger was abandoned approximately three months after the suit was filed (U.S. Department of Justice, 2011). Strong leadership can encourage enforcement of the antitrust laws to the benefit of the economy.

EDUCATION

The U.S. president is not directly in charge of education, but the president can lead the initiative to improve the U.S. education system across the board. On average, the U.S. spends 12,296 dollars per student for public elementary and secondary schools (NCES, 2016). This is often reported as one of the highest per capita expenditures per student in the world (Sullivan, 2016). Many surveys show that U.S. students lag in comparisons across a wide range of subjects (Szafir & Lueken, 2015). Figures from 2012-13 indicate that the U.S. spent about 620 billion dollars on just this part of the education equation (NCES, 2016). The estimated federal piece of this is about seventy-nine billion dollars (NCES, 2012).

For 2012–2013 expenditures for post-secondary schools, the U.S. spent about 312 billion dollars at public universities (NCES, 2016). Of that amount, the federal share is roughly seventy billion dollars, of which about ten billion dollars is for educational support for veterans (NCES, 2012b). And yet, criticism continues that the U.S. colleges are not graduating students ready to compete in the "real" world. Further, that the U.S. edge in higher education is shrinking as more students trend away from science, math, and engineering courses, where the U.S. has the most need (Craig, 2015). Students from around the world still come to the U.S. for college and graduate studies. The campaign to improve schools in other parts of the world is increasing rapidly. In just one example, Saudi Arabia has been sending its best students to the U.S. to earn advanced graduate degrees with the intention that they will return and staff the Saudi universities (SUSRIS, 2016).

Increasing the focus on improvement in education while improving delivery and staffing issues is critical to the future of America. Even if America fixes its many other problems, without an educated population, the U.S. cannot continue its leadership position. The real problem is not a shortage of college graduates. It is that there is a mismatch between the available and future jobs and the majors of college students (Newman, 2012).

A failing of the Affordable Care Act is that it did nothing to increase the supply of doctors or nurses or to reduce the cost of delivering care. As the federal government secures the majority of student loans, the government could tailor lending and grants to fit the estimated future needs in the economy. The U.S. government could also provide special funding grants to increase the number of slots in U.S. medical and nursing schools. Increasing the supply of medical personnel may help to reduce the staggering increase in healthcare costs.

HEALTHCARE

Without a doubt, as U.S. society ages, medical care is becoming a critical and increasing cost. The Committee for a Responsible Federal Budget (CRFB) assembled a report presenting various proposals to curb the deficits in Washington. One part of the report covers health care. Unfortunately, virtually every proposal listed reduced the costs paid for Medicare and Medicaid, but such cuts would inevitably transfer more of the cost to workers and employers already paying high insurance premiums for health care (2012). On the plus side, several proposals did include "tort reform." In essence, reducing the cost of malpractice insurance for doctors would hopefully reduce the cost to the U.S. healthcare system. While laudable, that one aspect by itself is unlikely to make a major difference in delivered healthcare costs. Malpractice exposure is also a state issue and not a federal issue, so the president would not likely be able to directly impact this aspect of health care.

Frequently mentioned as a way of controlling health-care costs would be to allow insurance companies to offer insurance across state lines (Laszewski, 2016b) and unlike the near "Cadillac" plans required under the Affordable Care Act, to move toward reserving insurance for true high-cost situations (Financial Finesse, 2016). Since neither of these proposals is in effect at this time, it is difficult to project their future impact.

FEDERAL INCOME TAX REFORM

A hotbed for lobbying efforts is the current U.S. income tax system. There is a plum for just about every lobbying group. The system has failed the country and, in many cases, causes taxpayers to make decisions based on tax outcomes, rather than what is best for themselves, and ultimately, the country. The CRFB also compares suggestions for tax reform. However, none of these proposals really deals with the ultimate failings of the current system (2016). A flat tax with virtually no deductions is often mentioned as a replacement system (Erb, 2015). The advantage to that system would be to remove the current inefficiencies in the system and perhaps substantially reduce the staffing needed at the IRS. Something like the IRS would still be needed to operate the tax collection system. On the other hand, a value-added tax system (VATS) might be vastly less costly to administer and achieve a fairer result by taxing people on consumption (Erb). One additional advantage is that consumption taxes tend to pick up the "underground" economy, which could be as much as 20 percent of the economy. That part of the economy pays no income tax at all (Cebula & Feige, 2012). One factor that prevents such reforms is the fear that the reforms would turn into additional taxes and the IRS would continue to pursue its arcane and complex policies. Because of such concerns, it will take strong presidential leadership to move the country to an entirely new tax system.

CONCLUSION

Even a great president cannot fix every problem of the U.S., whether the president is in office four or eight years. The approaches recommended in this chapter will take years to implement, regardless of the person in the White House. However, just as America set out on a path to the moon in the early 1960s, the U.S. could be the new exemplar for how to work a country out of debt while fixing a host of other problems. The U.S. is spending too much to accept poverty, substandard schools, highways with potholes, and bridges that are near collapse. It is time to act immediately to bring about substantial reforms under good leadership with a strong ethical bent.

EPILOGUE

Any book that includes coverage of current events has the inevitable challenge of establishing a stopping point. Months follow as the draft is polished and eventually published. In the meantime, the world does not stand still. This book concludes with the end of the Obama administration. Just two months before that cutoff, one of the more remarkable elections of the past century took place.

This book's message aligns with the election results. In a nutshell, both major political parties have failed this nation and the American people. The election of Donald Trump, even though he ran as a Republican, is a repudiation of much of the traditional party structure of the Democrat and Republican parties. The sometimes-violent reaction to his election underscores the deep divisions that haunt the future of America. At the same time, many of the promises made by the Trump administration are in tune with the recommendations made in Chapter 21. The U.S. has not actually won a real war since 1945. As the only true world power, this country should be respected around the world and must do a better job of managing its military. The country has spent trillions of dollars to fight poverty, but the result is more poverty. Obamacare has been an enormous failure and must be fixed or replaced. The U.S. needs to do a far better job of managing its economy. The federal, state, and local governments are broken and a new approach to political leadership must develop or the country will continue on its path to failure.

Some of the early Trump proposals, while not as far-reaching as the proposals in this book, are quite similar. The administration has promised not to fill all potential government positions and reportedly will reduce the staffing of the federal government by perhaps 5 percent. This book suggests that federal spending must be reduced by at least one-fifth. Therefore, deep cuts in federal employment of 25 percent to 33 percent and elimination of the unaffordable pensions will be required. The repeal and replacement of Obamacare has been promised, although the Democrats have promised to fight that proposal. Reduction of the corporate income tax has been proposed.

At some point, this author may evaluate the Trump Administration much as this book evaluates the prior seventeen administrations. For now, the research presented and the grades for these presidents provide insight into the history and leadership of this great country. Hopefully, it will prompt Americans to become more active citizens and more discerning voters.

THE DECLINE OF AMERICA:
SOURCES

Abramowitz, M., "Dear Dubya," Foreign Policy, (130), May-June 2002, 78-79.

Abrams, D., "Hillary Rodham Clinton: Politician," New York: Chelsea House Publishers, February 1, 2009.

Abramson, P., Aldrich, J.H., Rickershauser, J., & Rohde, D.W., "Fear in the Voting Booth: The 2004 Presidential Election," Political Behavior, 29(2), June 2007, 197-220.

Administrative Office of the U.S. Courts, "History - Brown v. Board of Education Re-enactment," (n.d.). Retrieved from http://www.uscourts.gov/educational-resources/educational-activities/history-brown-v-board-education-re-enactment

"Agricultural Adjustment Act of 1938," 7 U.S.C. § 1281

Albert, H.E., "Review: Harry S. Truman: The Man from Independence by William F. Levantrosser," Presidential Studies Quarterly, 17(3), Summer 1987, 608-610.

Allen, M., & Rogers, D., "Bush Announces $17.4 Billion Auto Bailout," Politico.com, December 19, 2008. Retrieved from http://www.politico.com/story/2008/12/bush-announces-174-billion-auto-bailout-016740

Alschuler, A.W., "Bill Clinton's Parting Pardon Party," Journal off Criminal Law and Criminology, 100(3), Summer 2010, 1131-1168.

Altman, M.D., L.K., "Parsing Ronald Reagan's Words for Early Signs of Alzheimer's," The New York Times, March 30, 2015. Retrieved from http://www.nytimes.com/2015/03/31/health/parsing-ronald-reagans-words-for-early-signs-of-alzheimers.html?_r=0

Alvarez, Jr., R., "The Lemon Grove Incident," The Journal of San Diego History, 32(2), Spring 1986. Retrieved from http://www.sandiegohistory.org/journal/1986/april/lemongrove/

Amadeo, K., "U.S. Debt by President: By Dollar and Percent," TheBalance. com, May 26, 2017. Retrieved from https://www.thebalance.com/ us-debt-by-president-by-dollar-and-percent-3306296

American Political Science Review staff, "Review: Harry S. Truman: A Bibliography of His Times and Presidency, by Richard Dean Burns," American Political Science Review, 79(2), June 1985, 617-617. Retrieved from: https://doi. org/10.2307/1956788

American Spectator, "Editorial: The Mysterious Death of Vince Foster," 26(9), September 1993, 14.

Amies, N., & Scheschkewitz, D., "Berlin's La Belle Nightclub Bombing Remembered 25 Years On," German broadcaster Deutsche Welle, August 2001. Retrieved from http://www.dw.com/en/ berlins-la-belle-nightclub-bombing-remembered-25-years-on/a-14965254

Anderson, E.E., "Legislative Update," The Compleat Lawyer, 1997. Retrieved from http://www.americanbar.org/newsletter/publications/gp_solo_magazine_home/gp_ solo_magazine_index/sp97leg.html

Anderson, M., "9 U.S. Presidents with the Most Vetoes," In Encyclopædia Britannica Online, (n.d.). Retrieved from https://www.britannica.com/ list/9-us-presidents-with-the-most-vetoes

Apple, R.W., "Carter Victor in Tight Race; Ford Loses New York State; Democrats Retain Congress," The New York Times Online, November 3, 1976. Retrieved from http://www.nytimes.com/learning/general/onthisday/big/1102.html#article

Achenbach, J., Wan, W., Berman, M., & Balingit, M., "Five Dallas Police Officers were Killed by a Lone Attacker, Authorities Say," The Washington Post, July 8, 2016. Retrieved from https://www.washingtonpost.com/news/morning-mix/ wp/2016/07/08/like-a-little-war-snipers-shoot-11-police-officers-during-dallas-pro-test-march-killing-five/

Armour, S., "Affordable Care Act Battle Returns to Court and Capitol Hill," The Wall Street Journal, July 7, 2016. Retrieved from https://www.wsj.com/articles/ affordable-care-act-battle-returns-to-court-and-capitol-hill-1467910572

Arnold, P.E., "'The 'Great Engineer' as Administrator: Herbert Hoover and Modern Bureaucracy," The Review of Politics, 42(3), July 1980, 329-348.

Arnold, P.E., Walcott, C.E., & Patterson, Jr. B.H., "The White House Office of Management and Administration," Presidential Studies Quarterly, 31(2), June 2001, 190-220.

Associated Press, "Cinemark Found Not Liable for Aurora Movie Shooting," May 19, 2016. Retrieved from http://www.wsj.com/articles/cinemark-found-not-li-able-for-aurora-movie-shooting-1463681295 "Clinton Disbarred from Practice

SOURCES

Before Supreme Court," October 1, 2001. Retrieved from http://www.nytimes.com/2001/10/01/national/clinton-disbarred-from-practice-before-supreme-court.html "Guyana Official Reports 300 Dead at Religious Sect's Jungle Temple," The New York Times, November 10, 1978, A1, A16. "Manuel Noriega Apologises over Military Rule of Panama," The Guardian, June 25, 2015. Retrieved from https://www.theguardian.com/world/2015/jun/25/manuel-noriega-apologises-over-military-rule-of-panama "South Carolina Police Video Shows Moments Before Walter Scott Shooting," April 10, 2015. Retrieved from http://www.wsj.com/articles/south-carolina-police-video-shows-moments-before-walter-scott-shooting-1428649770

Auletta, K., "Fortress Bush," The New Yorker, January 19, 2004. Retrieved from http://www.newyorker.com/magazine/2004/01/19/fortress-bush

Bachrach, E., "How to Save Public Pensions, No Federal Bailout Needed," The Wall Street Journal, July 17, 2016. Retrieved from http://www.wsj.com/articles/how-to-save-public-pensions-no-federal-bailout-needed-1468797730

Bachrach, F., "Dwight D. Eisenhower, Head-and-Shoulders Portrait, Facing Slightly Left," [Digital Photograph], Library of Congress,1952. Retrieved from http://www.loc.gov/pictures/item/96523445/

Baker, K.J.M., "Juanita Broaddrick Wants to Be Believed," BuzzFeed.com, August 14, 2016. Retrieved from https://www.buzzfeed.com/katiejmbaker/juanita-broaddrick-wants-to-be-believed?utm_term=.fywYOvbKJ#.rejjyA6p0

Baker, P., "DNA Is Said to Solve a Mystery of Warren Harding's Love Life," The New York Times, August 13, 2015. Retrieved from http://www.msn.com/en-us/news/politics/dna-is-said-to-solve-a-mystery-of-warren-harding%25E2%2580%2599s-love-life/ar-BBlHfW7?ocid=mailsignout

Baker, P., & Rudoren, J., "Obama and Netanyahu: A Story of Slights and Crossed Signals," The New York Times, November 8, 2015. Retrieved from https://www.nytimes.com/2015/11/09/us/politics/obama-and-netanyahu-a-story-of-slights-and-crossed-signals.html?_r=0

Baker, R.R., "Historical Contributions to Veterans' Healthcare," in T. W. Miller, The Praeger Handbook of Veterans' Health: History, Challenges, Issues, and Developments, Vol. 1, Santa Barbara, CA: Praeger, September 20, 2012, 5-7.

Bandow, D., "China Takes Charge in Hong Kong: Will Personal Liberty and Territorial Autonomy Survive?" Forbes, December 6, 2016. Retrieved from http://www.forbes.com/sites/dougbandow/2016/12/06/china-takes-charge-in-hong-kong-will-personal-liberty-and-territorial-autonomy-survive/#5e1c865c6bb8

Barnett, R., "Expunging Woodrow Wilson from Official Places of Honor," The Washington Post, June 25, 2015. Retrieved from https://www. washingtonpost.com/news/volokh-conspiracy/wp/2015/06/25/ expunging-woodrow-wilson-from-official-places-of-honor/

Barrett, J., & Dolan, M., "Michael Brown Autopsy Finds Six Shots Struck Teen as Ferguson Protest March Ends in Chaos," The Wall Street Journal, August 18, 2014. Retrieved from https://www.wsj.com/articles/ crowds-thin-in-ferguson-as-midnight-curfew-starts-1408253833

Barro, R.J., "The Reasons Behind the Obama Non-Recovery," The Wall Street Journal, September 20, 2016. Retrieved from http://www.wsj.com/articles/ the-reasons-behind-the-obama-non-recovery-1474412963

Barsky, R.B., & Kilian, L., "Do We Really Know That Oil Caused the Great Stagflation? A Monetary Alternative," NBER/Macroeconomics Annual, 16(1), 2001, 137-183. doi:10.1162/088933601320224900

Bartlett, B., "The Cost of War," Forbes, November 26, 2009. Retrieved from http:// www.forbes.com/2009/11/25/shared-sacrifice-war-taxes-opinions-colum- nists-bruce-bartlett.html

Bartley, N.V., "Review: The Autobiography of Harry S. Truman, by Robert H. Ferrell," The Georgia Historical Quarterly, 66(1), Spring 1982, 93-94. "The New South, 1945-1980," Baton Rouge, LA: Louisiana State University Press, November 1, 1995.

Basile, T., "The War on Terrorism: Choosing to Fight the George W. Bush Way Again," Forbes, November 20, 2015. Retrieved from https://www.forbes.com/sites/thomasbasile/2015/11/20/ its-time-to-revisit-george-w-bushs-global-anti-terror-strategy/#15252b17dce5

Basiri, A., "What's the Price of Saving the Iran Deal?" Forbes, October 27, 2016. Retrieved from http://www.forbes.com/sites/realspin/2016/10/27/ whats-the-price-of-saving-the-iran-deal/#70ad73191f90

Bauder, D., "Monica Dominated '98 Evening News," Associated Press, December 23, 1998. Retrieved from http://www.deseretnews.com/article/671142/Monica- dominated-98-evening-news.html?pg=all

BBC, "Syria Conflict: Obama Rules Out Ground Troops for Syria," April 24, 2016. Retrieved from http://www.bbc.com/news/world-middle-east-36121135

Bender, M.C., & Lee, C.E., "RNC Chair Reince Priebus Is Named Donald Trump's Chief of Staff," The Wall Street Journal, November 13, 2016. Retrieved from https://www.wsj.com/articles/leading-contender-for-donald-trump-s-chief-of-staff- is-rnc-chairman-reince-priebus-1479069597

SOURCES

Benjamin Harrison Presidential Site, "Death in the White House - Warren G. Harding," (n.d.). Retrieved from http://www.bhpsite.org/learn/exhibits/current-exhibit/16-learn/exhibits/125-death-in-the-white-house-warren-harding

Benton, J.E., "George W. Bush's Federal Aid Legacy," Publius, 37(3), Summer 2007, 371-389.

Berggren, D.J., & Rae, N.C., "Jimmy Carter and George W. Bush: Faith, Foreign Policy, and an Evangelical Presidential Style," Presidential Studies Quarterly, 36(4), December 2006, 606-632.

Berman, R., "Warren G. Harding's Terrible Tenure," The Atlantic, August 4, 2015. Retrieved from http://www.theatlantic.com/politics/archive/2015/08/warren-g-harding-nan-britton-affair/401288/

Bernstein, B.J., "Truman and the A-Bomb: Targeting Noncombatants, Using the Bomb, and His Defending the 'Decision,'" The Journal of Military History, 62(3), July 1998, 547-570.

Bilger, D., Sowell, R., & Williams, A., "World War II, Archival Materials at the Library," June 1999. Retrieved from http://www.trumanlibrary.org/hstpaper/ww2guide.htm

Billington, M., "Lyndon B. Johnson: The Religion of a Politician," Presidential Studies Quarterly, 17(3), Summer 1987, 519-530.

Biography.com staff, "Barbara Bush, U.S. First Lady (1925-)," (n.d.). Retrieved from https://www.biography.com/people/barbara-bush-9232727#early-life "Bill Clinton, U.S. Governor, U.S. President (1946-), July 27, 2016. Retrieved from http://www.biography.com/people/bill-clinton-9251236#governor-of-arkansas "George H.W. Bush, U.S. Representative, U.S. President, Diplomat, U.S. Vice President (1924-)," (n.d.). Retrieved from http://www.biography.com/people/george-hw-bush-38066 "Jane Wyman, Actress (1917–2007)," July 16, 2015. Retrieved from https://www.biography.com/people/jane-wyman-245894 "Laura Bush, Educator, U.S. First Lady, Philanthropist (1946-), (n.d.). Retrieved from http://www.biography.com/people/laura-bush-9232785 "Michelle Obama, U.S. First Lady, Lawyer (1964-)," (n.d.). Retrieved from http://www.biography.com/people/michelle-obama-307592 "Nancy Reagan, Actress, U.S. First Lady (1921-2016)," March 14, 2016.a. Retrieved from https://www.biography.com/people/nancy-reagan-9453187 "Ronald Reagan, U.S. President, Television Actor, U.S. Governor, Film Actor (1911-2004)," March 11, 2016.b. Retrieved from http://www.biography.com/people/ronald-reagan-9453198#synopsis

Black, A., "First Ladies, Claudia Taylor (Lady Bird) Johnson," The White House, (n.d.). Retrieved from https://www.whitehouse.gov/1600/first-ladies/ladybirdjohnson "First Ladies: Elizabeth Anne Bloomer Ford," The White House, (n.d.). Retrieved January 02, 2015, from https://www.whitehouse.gov/1600/first-ladies/bettyford

"First Ladies, Florence Harding," The White House, (n.d.). Retrieved January 02, 2015, from http://www.whitehouse.gov/about1600/first-ladies/florenceharding

"First Ladies, Grace Anna Goodhue Coolidge," The White House, (n.d.). Retrieved January 02, 2015, from http://www.whitehouse.gov/1600/first-ladies/gracecoolidge

Blanding, M., "One Quarter Of Entrepreneurs In The United States Are Immigrants," Forbes, August 31, 2016. Retrieved from http://www.forbes.com/sites/hbsworkingknowledge/2016/08/31/one-quarter-of-entrepreneurs-in-the-united-states-are-immigrants/#2d2b528a6937

Blankfield, B., "'A Symbol of His Warmth and Humanity': Fala, Roosevelt, and the Personable Presidency," Rhetoric & Public Affairs, 19(2), Summer 2016, 209-244.

Bledsoe, C. E., "Complaint (against Board of Education of Topeka, Shawnee County, Kansas)," Eisenhower Archives, February 26, 1951. Retrieved from https://www.eisenhower.archives.gov/research/online_documents/civil_rights_brown_v_boe/Complaint.pdf

Blinder, A.S., & Watson, M.W., "Presidents and the U.S. Economy: An Econometric Exploration," National Bureau of Economic Research, July 2014. Retrieved from http://www.nber.org/papers/w20324

Blumenthal, D., & Morone, J., "Franklin Delano Roosevelt: The Enigmatic Angler," in The Heart of Power: Health and Politics in the Oval Office, Berkeley: University of California Press, September 21, 2010), 21-56

Blunden, A., "The Collapse of the U.S.S.R.," Marxists.org, 1993. Retrieved from https://www.marxists.org/subject/stalinism/origins-future/ch4-2.htm

Bobic, I., "The Seven U.S. Ambassadors Killed in the Line of Duty," TalkingPointsMemo.com, September 13, 2012. Retrieved from http://talkingpointsmemo.com/dc/the-seven-u-s-ambassadors-killed-in-the-line-of-duty-photos

Bolt, R., "Franklin Delano Roosevelt, Senior Warden, St. James Church at Hyde Park, New York," Historical Magazine of the Protestant Episcopal Church, 54(1), March 1985, 91-99.

Bornet, V., "Reappraising the Presidency of Lyndon B. Johnson," Presidential Studies Quarterly, 20(3), Summer 1990, 591-602.

Breitman, R., & Lichtman, A., "FDR Returns," in FDR and the Jews, Cambridge, MA: Harvard University Press, March 19, 2013), 25-40. Retrieved from http://www.jstor.org/stable/j.ctt2jbr34.5

Bressman, L.S., & Vandenbergh, M.P., "Inside the Administrative State: A Critical Look at the Practice of Presidential Control," Michigan Law Review, 105(1), October 2006, 47-99.

SOURCES

Brick, C., & Regenhardt, C. E., (Eds.), "Teaching Eleanor Roosevelt Glossary: Fair Employment Practices Committee," The Eleanor Roosevelt Paper Projects, (n.d.). Retrieved from https://www.gwu.edu/~erpapers/teachinger/glossary/fepc.cfm

Brinkley, D., "Jimmy Carter's Modest Quest for Global Peace," Foreign Affairs, 74(6), Nov.-Dec. 1995, 90-100.

Broad, W.J., & Sanger, D.E., "Obama's Youth Shaped His Nuclear-Free Vision," The New York Times, July 4, 2009. Retrieved from http://www.nytimes.com/2009/07/05/world/05nuclear.html

Broder, D.S., "Nixon Wins Landslide Victory; Democrats Hold Senate, House," The Washington Post Online, November 8, 1972. Retrieved from http://www.washingtonpost.com/wp-srv/national/longterm/watergate/articles/110872-1.htm

"Browder v. Gayle," 142 F. Supp. 707 (M.D. Alabama., 1956) & 352 U.S. 903 (U.S. Supreme Court, 1956).

Brower, M., "Was LBJ's Final Secret a Son?" People.com, August 3, 1987. Retrieved from http://people.com/archive/was-lbjs-final-secret-a-son-vol-28-no-5/

Brown, J. S., "The United States Army in Somalia, 1992-1994," U. S. Department of the Army, 2003. Retrieved from http://www.history.army.mil/brochures/somalia/somalia.htm

Brown, K., "Trillions in Debt—but for Now, No Reason to Worry," The Wall Street Journal, May 25, 2016. Retrieved from http://www.wsj.com/articles/trillions-in-debtbut-for-now-no-reason-to-worry-1464191555

"Brown v. Board of Education of Topeka," 347 U.S. 483 (U.S. Supreme Court, 1954).

Bump, P., "Caroline Kennedy's Jury Service Echoes Her Father's Stance on Drug Crimes," The Atlantic, May 21, 2013. Retrieved from http://www.theatlantic.com/national/archive/2013/05/caroline-kennedys-jury-service-ends-her-father-might-have-hoped/315052/ "Here Is When Each Generation Begins And Ends, According to Facts," The Atlantic, March 25, 2014. Retrieved from http://www.theatlantic.com/national/archive/2014/03/here-is-when-each-generation-begins-and-ends-according-to-facts/359589/

Burnett, J., "Two Decades Later, Some Branch Davidians Still Believe," NPR, April 20, 2013. Retrieved from http://www.npr.org/2013/04/20/178063471/two-decades-later-some-branch-davidians-still-believe

Burns, K. & Novick, L. (Producers), "Civil Rights: Japanese Americans/Minorities," in The War [Television Series], Florentine Films and WETA-TV, September 2007. Retrieved from https://www.pbs.org/thewar/at_home_civil_rights_japanese_american.htm

Burr, W., & Montford, H.L., "The Making of the Limited Test Ban Treaty, 1958-1963," National Security Archive at George Washington University, August 8, 2003. Retrieved from http://nsarchive.gwu.edu/NSAEBB/NSAEBB94/

Bush, G. W., "Gov. George W. Bush's Plans for Education in America," The Phi Delta Kappan, 82(2), October 2000, 122-126.

Calabresi, C. S. & Yoo, S., "Franklin Delano Roosevelt," in The Unitary Executive: Presidential Power from Washington to Bush, New Haven, CT: Yale University Press, September 2, 2008, 278-290. "Part VI Introduction," in The Unitary Executive: Presidential Power from Washington to Bush, New Haven, CT: Yale University Press, September 2, 2008, 217-218.

Caldwell, M.C., & Titsworth, K.A., "Changing FDR's image," Tobacco Control, 5(4), 1966, 312-315. Retrieved from http://tobaccocontrol.bmj.com/content/tobaccocontrol/5/4/312.full.pdf

Calvert, S., "Baltimore Officer Acquitted of All Charges in Freddie Gray Trial," July 18, 2016. Retrieved from https://www.wsj.com/articles/officer-in-freddie-gray-trial-acquitted-1468853164

Calvin Coolidge Presidential Foundation, Inc., "Coolidge Administration Accomplishments," (n.d.). Retrieved from https://coolidgefoundation.org/presidency/coolidge-administration-accomplishments/

Camera, L., "No Child Left Behind Has Finally Been Left Behind," U.S. News & World Report, December 9, 2015. Retrieved from http://www.usnews.com/news/articles/2015/12/09/congress-replaces-no-child-left-behind-shifts-power-to-states

Campbell, R. R., "Machine Retrieval in the Herbert Hoover archives," The American Archivist, 29(2), April 1966, 298-302.

Campo-Flores, A., & Waddell, L., "Jury Acquits Zimmerman of All Charges," The Wall Street Journal, July 14, 2013. Retrieved from http://www.wsj.com/articles/SB10001424127887324879504578603562762064502

Canis, B., & Webel, B., "CRS Report for Congress: The Role of TARP Assistance in the Restructuring of General Motors," Congressional Research Service, May 9, 2013. Retrieved from https://www.fas.org/sgp/crs/misc/R41978.pdf

Cannon, C.M., "Clinton Picks Ginsburg Nominee Would be Second Woman on High Court," The Baltimore Sun, June 15, 1993. Retrieved from http://articles.baltimoresun.com/1993-06-15/news/1993166076_1_supreme-court-judge-ginsburg-jewish-justice

Carcasson, M., "Herbert Hoover and the Presidential Campaign of 1932: The Failure of Apologia," Presidential Studies Quarterly, 28(2), Spring 1998, 349-365.

Caro, R. A., "Means of Ascent: The Years of Lyndon Johnson, Volume 2," New York: Knopf Doubleday Publishing Group, March 7, 1990. "The Passage of Power: The

Years of Lyndon Johnson," New York: Knopf Doubleday Publishing Group, May 1, 2012.

Carlisle, R., (Ed.), "Ellsberg, Daniel," in Encyclopedia of Intelligence and Counterintelligence, New York: Routledge, March 26, 2015, 226-227.

Carlsson, C., "The General Strike of 1934, Historical Essay," (n.d.). Retrieved from http://www.foundsf.org/index.php?title=The_General_Strike_of_1934

Carter, E., "Which Health Insurance Plan Will You Choose This Fall?" Forbes, November 13, 2016. Retrieved from http://www.forbes.com/sites/financialfinesse/2016/11/13/which-health-insurance-plan-will-you-choose-this-fall/#794cc7385b53

Carter, J., "Prosperity Doesn't Suit Everyone," New England Review, 16(3), Summer 1994, 93-93.

Cavendish, R., "The Munich Conference," History Today Online, 2016. Retrieved from http://www.historytoday.com/richard-cavendish/munich-conference

CBS News "Charleston Shooting," July 13, 2015. Retrieved from http://www.cbsnews.com/pictures/charleston-south-carolina-church-shooting/

Cebula, R., & Feige, E., "America's Unreported Economy: Measuring the Size, Growth and Determinants of Income Tax Evasion in the U.S.," Crime, Law and Social Change, April 2012. Retrieved from https://link.springer.com/article/10.1007/s10611-011-9346-x

Centers for Medicare & Medicaid Services, "2016 Annual Report of the Boards of Trustees of the Federal Hospital Insurance and Federal Supplementary Medical Insurance Trust Funds Communication from the Boards of Trustees, Federal Hospital Insurance and Federal Supplementary Medical Insurance Trust," June 22, 2016. Retrieved from https://www.cms.gov/Research-Statistics-Data-and-Systems/Statistics-Trends-and-Reports/ReportsTrustFunds/Downloads/TR2016.pdf

Chamberlain, A. (Ed.), "Retrospective on the 1981 Reagan Tax Cut," Tax Foundation, June 10, 2004. Retrieved, from http://taxfoundation.org/article/retrospective-1981-reagan-tax-cut

Chambers, J. W., "The Big Switch: Justice Roberts and the Minimum-wage Cases," Labor History, 10(1), 1969, 44-73.

Chan, S., "Taiwan in 2004: Electoral Contests and Political Stasis," Asian Survey, 45(1), January/February 2005, 54-58.

Chang, G. G., "To Disarm North Korea, Wage Trade War on China," Forbes, November 27, 2016. Retrieved from http://www.forbes.com/sites/gordonchang/2016/11/27/to-disarm-north-korea-wage-trade-war-on-china/#44ccf30b2864

Chappell, B., "Warren Harding, We Hardly Knew Ye," NPR, August 13, 2015.
Retrieved from http://www.npr.org/sections/thetwo-way/2015/08/13/432064123/
warren-harding-we-hardly-knew-ye

Chimene-Weiss, S., Eppel, S., Feigenbaum, J., Motel, S., & Pangandoyon, I.,
"Understanding the Iran-Contra Affairs," Brown University, (n.d.). Retrieved
from https://www.brown.edu/Research/Understanding_the_Iran_Contra_Affair/
timeline-n-i.php

Civil Defense Museum, "Standard Fallout Shelter Signs," [Digital Image], (n.d.).
Retrieved from http://www.civildefensemuseum.com/signs/index.html

"Clay v. United States," 403 U.S. 698 (US Supreme Court., 1971).

Clemens, C., "My Visit with Franklin D. Roosevelt," Mark Twain Quarterly, 8(3),
Winter-Spring 1949, 11-12. Retrieved from http://www.jstor.org/stable/41640766

Clifford, J. G., "From Roosevelt to Truman: Potsdam, Hiroshima, and the Cold War
(Review) by Wilson D. Miscamble," American Studies, 50(1), Spring/Summer
2009, 226-227.

Clift, E., & Hosenball, M., "Shooting Down Birds – and Rumors," Newsweek, 123(2),
January 10, 1994, 25.

Clinton, W. J. "I Did Not Have Sexual Relations with That Woman..." (n.d.). Retrieved
from https://www.youtube.com/watch?v=VBe_guezGGc "Letter Accepting the
Resignation of Webster L. Hubbell as Associate Attorney General," The American
Presidency Project, March 14, 1994. Retrieved from http://www.presidency.ucsb.
edu/ws/?pid=49808 "Remarks on the Balanced Budget Agreement," The American
Presidency Project, July 29, 1997. Retrieved from http://www.presidency.ucsb.edu/
ws/index.php?pid=54473 "Statement on Signing the Health Insurance Portability
and Accountability Act of 1996," The American Presidency Project, August 21,
1996. Retrieved from http://www.presidency.ucsb.edu/ws/?pid=53211 "The
Somalia Mission; Clinton's Words on Somalia: 'The Responsibilities of American
Leadership,'" The New York Times, October 8, 1993. Retrieved from http://www.
nytimes.com/1993/10/08/world/somalia-mission-clinton-s-words-somalia-responsi-
bilities-american-leadership.html?pagewanted=all

Clymer, A., "The 1994 Elections: Congress the Overview; G.O.P. Celebrates Its Sweep
to Power; Clinton Vows To Find Common Ground," The New York Times,
November 10, 1994. Retrieved from http://www.nytimes.com/1994/11/10/
us/1994-elections-congress-overview-gop-celebrates-its-sweep-power-clinton-vows.
html?pagewanted=all

CNN.com, "Are you for or against the federal stimulus plan?" January 25, 2010.
Retrieved from http://newsroom.blogs.cnn.com/2010/01/25/are-you-for-or-
against-the-federal-stimulus-plan/ "USS Cole Bombing Fast Facts," June 2, 2017.

Retrieved from http://www.cnn.com/2013/09/18/world/meast/uss-cole-bombing-fast-facts/ "White House Releases Documents on Gore Fund-raiser," September 3, 1997. Retrieved from http://www.cnn.com/ALLPOLITICS/1997/09/03/gore.docs/

Cohen, D.B., Vaughn, J.S., & Villalobos, J.D., "Manager-in-Chief: Applying Public Management Theory to Examine White House Chief of Staff Performance," Political Research Quarterly, 65(4), December 2012, 841-854.

Coin News Media Group LLC, "Historical Inflation Rates: 1914-2017" [Data File]. Retrieved from:http://www.usinflationcalculator.com/inflation/historical-inflation-rates/

Coleman, A., "Poland On Track to Becoming a Major European Tech Startup Hub," Forbes, May 20, 2016. Retrieved from http://www.forbes.com/sites/alisoncoleman/2016/05/20/poland-on-track-to-becoming-a-major-european-tech-startup-hub/#4dd8ac35431b

Compare Infobase Ltd., "U.S. Presidential Election 1996," (n.d.). Retrieved from http://www.mapsofworld.com/elections/usa/historical-election/1996.html

Congressional Budget Office, "Reducing the Deficit: Spending and Revenue Options," March 10, 2011. Retrieved from https://www.cbo.gov/publication/22043 "The Budget and Economic Outlook: 2016 to 2026," January 25, 2016. Retrieved from https://www.cbo.gov/publication/51129

Congressional Research Reports, "U.S. Motor Vehicle Industry: Federal Financial Assistance and Restructuring," 2009. Retrieved from http://congressionalresearch.com/R40003/document.php?study=U.S.+Motor+Vehicle+Industry+Federal+Financial+Assistance+and+Restructuring

Conway, A., "The Memoirs of Harry S. Truman. Vol. 2. Years of Trial and Hope, 1946-53 (review), by Harry S. Truman," International Affairs, 32(4), October 1956, 474-475. doi:10.2307/2606292

Cook, C., "'The Contemporary Presidency': The Permanence of the 'Permanent Campaign': George W. Bush's Public Presidency," Presidential Studies Quarterly, 32(4), December 2002, 753-764.

Cooper, M. A., "United States: The 1994 Midterm Elections in 1994," Encyclopedia Britannica, December 6, 1994. Retrieved from https://www.britannica.com/topic/1994-midterm-Elections-616578

Cooper, P. J., "George W. Bush, Edgar Allan Poe, and the Use and Abuse of Presidential Signing Statements," Presidential Studies Quarterly, 35(3), September 2005, 515-532.

Corbett, M., "Oil Shock of 1973–74," FederalReserveHistory.org, November 22, 2013. Retrieved from http://www.federalreservehistory.org/Events/DetailView/36

Corcoran, G., "Exxon-Mobil 12 Years Later: Archetype of a Successful Deal," The Wall Street Journal, November 30, 2010. Retrieved from http://blogs.wsj.com/deals/2010/11/30/exxon-mobil-12-years-later-archetype-of-a-successful-deal/

Cornell University Law School, "Supreme Court Toolbox: Bush v. Gore," December 12, 2000. Retrieved from https://www.law.cornell.edu/supct/html/00-949.ZPC.html

Coroian, G., "Zoot Suit Riots," in Encyclopædia Britannica Online, 2016. Retrieved August 3, 2016, from https://www.britannica.com/event/Zoot-Suit-Riots

Cosgrove, B., "Behind the Picture: 'Dewey Defeats Truman' and the Politics of Memory," Time, May 4, 2014. Retrieved from http://time.com/3879744/dewey-defeats-truman-the-story-behind-a-classic-political-photo/ "Behind the Picture: Photos from the Night Marilyn Sang to JFK, 1962," Time.com, April 30, 2014. Retrieved from http://time.com/3879743/marilyn-monroe-john-kennedy-happy-birthday-may-1962/ "The Dawn of Camelot: LIFE at JFK's Inauguration," Time.com, January 5, 2013. Retrieved from http://time.com/3875353/jfk-inauguration-life-photos-january-1961/

Couch, K.A., & Fairlie, R., "Last Hired, First Fired? Black-White Unemployment and the Business Cycle," Demography, 47(1), February 2010, 227–247. doi:10.1353/dem.0.0086

Coutsoukis, P., "Lebanon: The Hostage Crisis," Photius.com, December 1987. Retrieved from http://www.photius.com/countries/lebanon/national_security/lebanon_national_security_the_hostage_crisis.html

Cowan, E., "Wage-Price Controls Ended," The New York Times, January 11, 1973. Retrieved from https://news.google.com/newspapers?nid=1346&dat=19730111&id=UnFOAAAAIBAJ&sjid=c_oDAAAAIBAJ&pg=7198,3022850&hl=en

Cox, W., & Love, J., "40 Years of the US Interstate Highway System: An Analysis, The Best Investment a Nation Ever Made," Publicpurpose.com, June 1996. Retrieved from http://www.publicpurpose.com/freeway1.htm

CQ Almanac, "Congress Clears Landmark Postal Reorganization Plan," 1970. Retrieved from https://library.cqpress.com/cqalmanac/document.php?id=cqal70-1293327

Craig, C., & Radchenko, S.S., (2008). "Franklin Delano Roosevelt and Atomic Wartime Diplomacy," in The Atomic Bomb and the Origins of the Cold War (New Haven, CT: Yale University Press, August 28, 2008), 1-33. Retrieved from http://www.jstor.org/stable/j.ctt1nq84p

Craig, R., "A New Generation of Engineering Schools," Forbes, April 3, 2015. Retrieved from http://www.forbes.com/sites/ryancraig/2015/04/03/a-new-generation-of-engineering-schools/#6de667e72923

SOURCES

Crews Jr., C. W., "Antitrust Regulation and the 2016 Party Platform Debates," Forbes, July 21, 2016. Retrieved from http://www.forbes.com/sites/waynecrews/2016/07/21/antitrust-regulation-and-the-2016-party-platform-debates/#4b7d49a51a10 "Antitrust Regulation Is Getting A Bit Smarter," Forbes, March 23, 2016. Retrieved from http://www.forbes.com/sites/waynecrews/2016/03/23/antitrust-regulation-is-getting-a-bit-smarter/#-144fa9ea726a "Republicans and Democrats Unite Against $86 Billion AT&T-Time Warner Merger Deal," Forbes, October 24, 2016. Retrieved from http://www.forbes.com/sites/waynecrews/2016/10/24/republicans-and-democrats-unite-against-86-billion-att-time-warner-merger-deal/#261e1859c534

Daalder, I.H., "Decision to Intervene: How the War in Bosnia Ended," Brookings, December 1, 1998. Retrieved from https://www.brookings.edu/articles/decision-to-intervene-how-the-war-in-bosnia-ended

Daggett, S., "Costs of Major U.S. Wars," Congressional Research Service, June 29, 2010. Retrieved from https://www.fas.org/sgp/crs/natsec/RS22926.pdf

Daiss, T., "Beijing And Moscow Slam U.S. Missile Deployment Plans," Forbes, July 8, 2016. Retrieved from http://www.forbes.com/sites/timdaiss/2016/07/08/beijing-and-moscow-slam-us-missile-deployment-plans/#1d4b91c31d14

Davis, B., "The Thorny Economics of Illegal Immigration," The Wall Street Journal, February 9, 2016. Retrieved from http://www.wsj.com/articles/the-thorny-economics-of-illegal-immigration-1454984443

Dean, J. W., Warren G. Harding (New York: Times Books, 2004).

Denning, S., "Lest We Forget: Why We Had a Financial Crisis," Forbes, November 22, 2011. Retrieved from http://www.forbes.com/sites/stevedenning/2011/11/22/5086/#8480a515b560

Department of the Army, Office of the Deputy Chief of Staff for Operations, "Richard M. Nixon," [Digital Photograph], (ca. 1969). Retrieved from https://catalog.archives.gov/id/530679

DeSilver, D., "Black Unemployment Rate is Consistently Twice that of Whites," Pew Research Center, August 21, 2013. Retrieved from http://www.pewresearch.org/fact-tank/2013/08/21/through-good-times-and-bad-black-unemployment-is-consistently-double-that-of-whites/

Diehl, J., "Is Obama to Blame for the Arab Spring's Failures?" The Washington Post, June 24, 2012. Retrieved from https://www.washingtonpost.com/opinions/jackson-diehl-is-obama-to-blame-for-the-arab-springs-failures/2012/06/24/gJQAzF5O0V_story.html?utm_term=.2aa4606fc5a1

Digital Public Library of America, "America's Great Depression and Roosevelt's New Deal: Civil Works Administration (CWA)," (n.d.). Retrieved from https://dp.la/

exhibitions/exhibits/show/new-deal/relief-programs/civil-works-administration Digital Public Library of America (DPLA), "America's Great Depression and Roosevelt's New Deal: Relief Programs," (n.d.). Retrieved from https://dp.la/exhibitions/exhibits/show/new-deal/relief-programs

Dobel, J.P., "Prudence and Presidential Ethics: The Decisions on Iraq of the Two Presidents Bush," Presidential Studies Quarterly, 40(1), March 2010, 57-75.

Donaldson, G.A., "The Making of Modern America: The Nation from 1945 to the Present," New York: Rowman & Littlefield Publishers, Inc., October 18, 2012.

Doss, E., "Affect," American Art, 23(1), Spring 2009, 9-11.

Dove, R., "The Assassination of John F. Kennedy," Callaloo, 31(3), Summer 2008, 736-737.

Draper, E., "President Bush Poses for his Official Portrait in the Roosevelt Room (Blue Tie) / Official portrait of President George W. Bush," [Digital Photograph], Library of Congress, 2003. Retrieved from https://www.loc.gov/resource/ppbd.00371/

Dudley, D., "Iran Hits Out at Failure of British Banks to Forge New Ties," Forbes, November 2, 2016. Retrieved from http://www.forbes.com/sites/dominicdudley/2016/11/02/iran-uk-banks/#10ed7aa3143c "Iran Turns to South Korea for International Bond Issue," Forbes, October 25, 2016. Retrieved from http://www.forbes.com/sites/dominicdudley/2016/10/25/iran-south-korea-bond-issue/#9bda3f421ed9

Dull, M., & Roberts, P.S., "Continuity, Competence, and the Succession of Senate-Confirmed Agency Appointees, 1989-2009," Presidential Studies Quarterly, 39(3), September 2009, 432-453.

Dunlap, D.W., (2016, June 30). "1971: Supreme Court Allows Publication of Pentagon Papers," The New York Times Online. Retrieved from http://www.nytimes.com/2016/06/30/insider/1971-supreme-court-allows-publication-of-pentagon-papers.html?_r=0

Dye, R. P. (Ed.), "America 'On Defense' in the Pacific," in Hawai`i Chronicles III: World War Two in Hawai`i, from the pages of Paradise of the Pacific, Honolulu: University of Hawai'i Press, August 1, 2000, 17-19.

Easterbrook, G., "Make Puerto Rico a State," Washington Monthly, June 17, 2011. Retrieved from http://washingtonmonthly.com/2011/06/17/make-puerto-rico-a-state/

"Economic Stabilization Act of 1970" (Title II of Pub.L. 91–379, 84 Stat. 799, enacted August 15, 1970, formerly codified at 12 U.S.C. § 1904).

Ednie, A. V., "Action Against Enemy, Reports After/After Action Report," July 21, 1944. Retrieved from https://eisenhower.archives.gov/research/online_documents/d_day/1944_07_21_After_Action_Report.pdf

SOURCES

Edwards, C., "Reducing the Costs of Federal Worker Pay and Benefits," DownsizingtheFederalGovernment.com, September 20, 2016. Retrieved from https://www.downsizinggovernment.org/federal-worker-pay

Edwards, G., "Exclusive Interview: President Jimmy Carter," Presidential Studies Quarterly, 38(1), Mar. 2008, 1-13.

Edwards, J., "Overrated or the Only Man for the Job? The Meteoric Rise of General Dwight D. Eisenhower," Warhistoryonline.com, January 7, 2016. Retrieved from https://www.warhistoryonline.com/featured/overrated-man-job-meteoric-rise-general-dwight-d-eisenhower.html

Edwards III, G. C., & Wayne, S.J., "Presidential Leadership: Politics and Policy Making (9th ed.)," Stamford, CT: Cengage Learning, July 3, 2013.

Ehrenfreund, M., "Your Complete Guide to Obama's Immigration Executive Action," The Washington Post, November 20, 2014. Retrieved from https://www.washingtonpost.com/news/wonk/wp/2014/11/19/your-complete-guide-to-obamas-immigration-order/

Eichenwald, K., "Here's What the FBI Found in The Emails on Anthony Weiner's laptop," Newsweek, November 6, 2016. Retrieved from http://www.newsweek.com/what-fbi-found-emails-anthony-weiner-laptop-517652

Eisenhower, D. D., "160 - Statement by the President Upon Signing the Refugee Relief Act of 1953," The American Presidency Project, August 7, 1953. Retrieved from: http://www.presidency.ucsb.edu/ws/?pid=9668 "Eisenhower Letter of Support for Pres. Ngo Dinh Diem," October 23, 1954. Retrieved from http://sourcebooks.fordham.edu/halsall/mod/1954-eisenhower-vietnam1.html "Message to the Congress regarding highways," February 22, 1955. Retrieved from https://www.eisenhower.archives.gov/research/online_documents/interstate_highway_system/1955_02_22_Message_toCongress.pdf "Special Message to the Congress on the Situation in the Middle East," The American Presidency Project, January 5, 1957. Retrieved from http://www.presidency.ucsb.edu/ws/?pid=11007 "Text of the Address by the President of the United States," Eisenhower Archives, September 24, 1957. Retrieved from https://www.eisenhower.archives.gov/research/online_documents/civil_rights_little_rock/1957_09_24_Press_Release.pdf

Eisinger, R.M., "The Evolution of Presidential Polling," Cambridge, UK: Cambridge University Press, January 20, 2003.

El-Ghobashy, T., & Barrett, D., "Dozens Killed in Conn. School Shooting," The Wall Street Journal, December 17, 2012. Retrieved from http://www.wsj.com/articles/SB10001424127887323297104578179271453737596

El-Ghobashy, T., & Kesling, B., "Iraq Troops Ordered to Pause Mosul Advance," The Wall Street Journal, October 19, 2016. Retrieved from http://www.wsj.com/articles/iraqi-troops-ordered-to-pause-mosul-advance-1476871308

Elder, L., "The Trashing of Bill's Accusers: What Did Hillary Do -- and Why Did She Do It?" RealClearPolitics.com, February 25, 2016. Retrieved from http://www.realclearpolitics.com/articles/2016/02/25/the_trashing_of_bills_accusers_what_did_hillary_do_--_and_why_did_she_do_it_129787.html

ElectionWallDotOrg, "Chicago Convention: The Whole World is Watching 1968," July 13, 2011. Retrieved from https://www.youtube.com/watch?v=7_9OJnRnZjU

Elmenshawy, M., "Egypt and the Obama Administration," Middle East Institute, November 26, 2014. Retrieved from http://www.mei.edu/content/article/egypt-and-obama-administration

Encyclopædia Britannica Online, "Agricultural Adjustment Administration (AAA)," 2016. Retrieved from https://www.britannica.com/topic/Agricultural-Adjustment-Administration "Calvin Coolidge: President of United States," June 22, 2017. Retrieved from http://www.britannica.com/EBchecked/topic/136173/Calvin-Coolidge/302332/Presidency "Geneva Summit, 1955," 2016. Retrieved from https://www.britannica.com/event/Geneva-Summit-1955 "Mississippi River Flood of 1927," September 5, 2013. Retrieved from https://www.britannica.com/event/Mississippi-River-flood-of-1927 "United States Presidential Election of 1980," 2016. Retrieved from https://www.britannica.com/event/United-States-presidential-election-of-1980

Encyclopedia of the New American Nation, "Summit Conferences - Dwight d. Eisenhower," 2016. Retrieved from http://www.americanforeignrelations.com/O-W/Summit-Conferences-Dwight-d-eisenhower.html "Television - The First Television War," 2016. Retrieved from http://www.americanforeignrelations.com/O-W/Television-The-first-television-war.html

Engerman, D.C., "Economic Reconstruction in Soviet Russia: The Courting of Herbert Hoover in 1922," The International History Review, 19(4), November 1997, 836-847.

Entous, A., & Yadron, D., "U.S. Spy Net on Israel Snares Congress," The Wall Street Journal, December 29, 2015. Retrieved from http://www.wsj.com/articles/u-s-spy-net-on-israel-snares-congress-1451425210

Environmental Protection Agency, "Superfund: CERCLA overview," August 22, 2016. Retrieved September 19, 2016, from https://www.epa.gov/superfund/superfund-cercla-overview

Epstein, A., "Poem Beginning with a Line by George W. Bush," Mississippi Review, 32(3), Fall 2004, 240-246.

SOURCES

Erb, K. P., "IRS Targeting Scandal: Citizens United, Lois Lerner and the $20M Tax Saga That Won't Go Away," Forbes, June 24, 2016. Retrieved from http://www.forbes.com/sites/kellyphillipserb/2016/06/24/irs-targeting-scandal-citizens-united-lois-lerner-and-the-20m-tax-saga-that-wont-go-away/#dc83df752f4c "Our Current Tax v. The Flat Tax v. The Fair Tax: What's The Difference?" Forbes, August 7, 2015. Retrieved from http://www.forbes.com/sites/kellyphillipserb/2015/08/07/our-current-tax-v-the-flat-tax-v-the-fair-tax-whats-the-difference/#49d0a381fa6f "Report Accuses IRS Of Encouraging Illegal Immigrants To File Using False Info, Identity Fraud," Forbes, November 18, 2015. Retrieved from http://www.forbes.com/sites/kellyphillipserb/2015/11/18/irs-accused-of-encouraging-illegal-immigrants-to-file-using-false-info-identity-fraud/#7bda3dc323bc

Evans, Emrys D.M. "John F. Kennedy Memorial Act, 1964," in "Statutes" of The Modern Law Review, 28(6), November 1965, 703-706. doi:10.1111/j.1468 2230.1965.tb02795.x

Eves, H., "The Master Geometer," in Mathematical Reminiscences, Washington, D.C.: Mathematical Association of America, August 5, 2001, 129-130. Retrieved from: http://www.jstor.org/stable/10.4169/j.ctt13x0n2s

Evon, D., "Dismarred: A Graphic Lists the Legal Consequences Suffered by the Former President Stemming from the Monica Lewinsky Scandal," Snopes.com, July 30, 2016. Retrieved from http://www.snopes.com/bill-clinton-fined-and-disbarred-over-the-monica-lewinsky-scandal/

"Executive Order No. 13492," 74 FR 4897 (2009).

"Fair Labor Standards Act of 1938," 29 U.S.C. §§ 201-219.

Federal Reserve Bank of St. Louis, "Civilian Employment-Population Ratio," October 7, 2016. Retrieved from https://fred.stlouisfed.org/series/EMRATIO "Gross Federal Debt," March 14, 2016. Retrieved from https://fred.stlouisfed.org/series/FYGFD

Federation of American Scientists, "Key Judgments: Iraq's Continuing Programs for Weapons of Mass Destruction," October 2002. Retrieved from http://fas.org/irp/cia/product/iraq-wmd.html

Feldmann, L., "After GOP Landslide of Election 2010, What Next for Obama?" The Christian Science Monitor, November 3, 2010. Retrieved from http://www.csmonitor.com/USA/Elections/2010/1103/After-GOP-landslide-of-Election-2010-what-next-for-Obama

Feldstein, M., "Poisoning the Press: Richard Nixon, Jack Anderson, and the Rise of Washington's Scandal Culture," New York: Farrar, Straus and Giroux, September 28, 2010.

Feller, G., "Prime Minister May and The End of a Sycophantic Chumocracy," Forbes, July 12, 2016. Retrieved from http://www.forbes.com/sites/grantfeller/2016/07/12/prime-minister-may-and-the-end-of-a-sycophantic-chumocracy/#6506bb63726a

Fenn, Jr. D.H., "Launching the John F. Kennedy Library," The American Archivist, 42(4), October 1979, 429-442.

Fenton, J.D., "The Taft-Hartley Act and Union Control of Hiring - A Critical Examination," Villanova Law Review, 4(3), January 1, 1959, 346-351.

Fessier, B., "'Brother-in-Lawford' was Sinatra's Key to White House," The Desert Sun, October 22, 2015. Retrieved from http://www.desertsun.com/story/life/entertainment/2015/10/20/brother-lawford-sinatras-key-white-house/74286532/

Finger, R., "FHA Will Cost Taxpayers $150 Billion," Forbes, December 7, 2012. Retrieved from http://www.forbes.com/sites/richardfinger/2012/12/07/fha-will-cost-taxpayers-150-billion/#4b271e564616

Fisher, D., "Court Finds CFPB Director 'Unaccountable' And Unconstitutional, Too," Forbes, October 11, 2016. Retrieved from http://www.forbes.com/sites/danielfisher/2016/10/11/court-orders-presidential-accountability-over-unaccountable-cfpb-chief/#68bee9d34013

Flanary, P., "How the Nixon Pardon Strained a Presidential Friendship," ProPublica, December 13, 2011. Retrieved from https://www.propublica.org/article/presidential-pardons-how-the-nixon-pardon-strained-a-presidential-friendshi

Flannery, N. P., "Political Risk Analysis: Is Venezuela Now Entering a Full-Blown Political Crisis?" Forbes, October 28, 2016. Retrieved from http://www.forbes.com/sites/nathanielparishflannery/2016/10/28/political-risk-analysis-is-venezuela-now-entering-a-full-blown-political-crisis/#258e065b418f

Fleitz, F., "Did the White House Use the NSA to Spy on Congress about the Iran Deal?" National Review, December 30, 2015. Retrieved from http://www.nationalreview.com/article/429111/obama-nsas-congress-spying

Forsyth, J. S., "The Constitution, Designed to Change, Rarely Does," The Wall Street Journal, December 4, 2008. Retrieved from http://www.wsj.com/articles/SB122835767216478251

Frakt, D.J.R., "Prisoners of Congress: The Constitutional and Political Clash Over Detainees and the Closure of Guantanamo," University of Pittsburgh Law Review, 74(2), 2012, 181 - 262.

Freeman, J., "Hillary's Benghazi Discrepancy," The Wall Street Journal, June 29, 2016. Retrieved from http://www.wsj.com/articles/hillarys-benghazi-story-1467199673 "Obama's Stimulus, Five Years Later," The Wall Street Journal, February 17, 2014. Retrieved from http://www.wsj.com/articles/SB10001424052702303945704579387692278347858

SOURCES

Freidel, F., & Sidey, H.S. "The Presidents, 29. Warren G. Harding," (n.d.). Retrieved from http://www.whitehouse.gov/about/presidents/warrenharding "The Presidents, 31. Herbert Hoover," The White House, (n.d.). Retrieved from https://www.whitehouse.gov/1600/presidents/herberthoover "The Presidents, 35. John F. Kennedy," The White House, (n.d.). Retrieved from http://www.whitehouse.gov/1600/presidents "The Presidents, 36. Lyndon B. Johnson," The White House, (n.d.). Retrieved from https://www.whitehouse.gov/1600/Presidents "The Presidents: 38, Gerald R. Ford," 2006. Retrieved January 02, 2015, from https://www.whitehouse.gov/1600/Presidents "The Presidents: 39, James Carter," The White House, 2006. Retrieved January 02, 2015, from https://www.whitehouse.gov/1600/Presidents "The Presidents: 40, Ronald Reagan," 2006. Retrieved from https://www.whitehouse.gov/1600/Presidents

Fried, A., "Muffled Echoes: Oliver North and the Politics of Public Opinion," New York: Columbia University Press, April 15, 1997.

Frum, D., "Bush's Legacy," Foreign Policy, (168), September-October 2008, 32-38.

Gage, T., "Steinbeck Knew My Dad Better than I Did," Steinbeck Review, 6(2), September 2009, 87-109. doi:10.1111/j.1754-6087.2009. 01051.x

Gallois, A., "Carter on Contingent Identity and Rigid Designation," Mind, 97(386), April 1988, 273-278.

Gallup, Inc., "Democrats, Republicans Agree on Four Top Issues for Campaign," February 1, 2016. Retrieved from http://www.gallup.com/poll/188918/democrats-republicans-agree-four-top-issues-campaign.aspx?g_source=Concerns%20of%20average%20Americans%20+%20safety&g_medium=search&g_campaign=tiles "Presidential Approval Ratings -- Gallup Historical Statistics and Trends," 2015. Retrieved from http://www.gallup.com/poll/116677/presidential-approval-ratings-gallup-historical-statistics-trends.aspx

Gaouette, N., & Walcott, J., "Obama Call for Muslim Brotherhood Role Overtaken in Egypt," Bloomberg, July 7, 2013. Retrieved from https://www.bloomberg.com/amp/news/articles/2013-07-05/obama-call-for-muslim-brotherhood-role-overtaken-in-egypt

Gardiner, N., & Roach, M.L., "Barack Obama's Top 10 Apologies: How the President Has Humiliated a Superpower," The Heritage Foundation, June 2, 2009. Retrieved from http://www.heritage.org/europe/report/barack-obamas-top-10-apologies-how-the-president-has-humiliated-superpower

Garson, R., "Lyndon B. Johnson and the China Enigma," Journal of Contemporary History, 32(1), January 1997, 63-80.

Garten, J. E., "Memo to the President: The U.S. Needs to Create a Colonial Service," Foreign Policy, (138), September-October 2003, 63-67.

Gatteri, F., "President Truman," [Digital Photograph], ca. November 1945. Retrieved from https://www.trumanlibrary.org/photographs/view.php?id=2267

Gely, R., & Spiller, P. T., "The Political Economy of Supreme Court Constitutional Decisions: The Case of Roosevelt's Court-Packing Plan," International Review of Law and Economics, 12(1), March 1992, 45-67.

Geier, B., "What Did We Learn from the Dotcom Stock Bubble of 2000?" Time, March 12, 2015. Retrieved from http://time.com/3741681/2000-dotcom-stock-bust/

Geraghty, J., "Relax! Medicaid's Trust Fund Doesn't Run Out of Money Until 2028!" National Review, June 23, 2016. Retrieved from http://www.nationalreview.com/corner/437042/relax-medicaids-trust-fund-doesnt-run-out-money-until-2028

Gerald R. Ford Library Museum, "Economy," in "President Ford '76 Fact Book," 1976. Retrieved September from https://fordlibrarymuseum.gov/library/document/factbook/economy.htm "Energy," in "President Ford '76 Fact Book," 1976. Retrieved from https://fordlibrarymuseum.gov/library/document/factbook/energy.htm

Gerald R. Ford Presidential Foundation, "Gerald R. Ford Biography," (n.d.). Retrieved from http://geraldrfordfoundation.org/gerald-r-ford-biography/

"Germans Unleash U-Boats," This Day in History. Retrieved from: http://www.history.com/this-day-in-history/germans-unleash-u-boats

Gerson, M., "The Horrific Results of Obama's Failure in Syria," The Washington Post, September 3, 2015. Retrieved from https://www.washingtonpost.com/opinions/the-horrific-results-of-obamas-strategy-in-syria/2015/09/03/c16c117a-526c-11e5-933e-7d06c647a395_story.html?utm_term=.5d8ff8658ccc

Gerstein, J., "Clinton Camp Questions FBI Release of Marc Rich Pardon Files," Politico.com, November 1, 2016. Retrieved from http://www.politico.com/story/2016/11/marc-rich-pardon-files-230590

Geselbracht, R. H., "Creating the Harry S. Truman Library: The First Fifty Years," The Public Historian, 28(3), Summer 2006, 37-78.

Giant, T., "Herbert Hoover and Hungary, 1918-1923," Hungarian Journal of English and American Studies, 8(2), Fall 2002, 95-109.

Giap, V. N., "How We Won the War," Philadelphia: Recon Publishers, October 1976.

Gilbert, R., "The Political Effects of Presidential Illness: The Case of Lyndon B. Johnson," Political Psychology, 16(4), December 1995, 761-776.

Giovanetti, T., "The Social and Political Cost of Slow Economic Growth," The Institute for Policy Innovation, May 4, 2016. Retrieved from http://www.ipi.org/ipi_issues/article_detail.asp?name=the-social-and-political-cost-of-slow-economic-growth

Gladnick, P.J., "New York Times Identifies Wrong Woman in Carville 'Trailer Park' Quote," NewsBusters.org, January 20, 2016. Retrieved

from http://www.newsbusters.org/blogs/nb/pj-gladnick/2016/01/20/
new-york-times-identifies-wrong-woman-carville-trailer-park-quote

Glassman, M. E., "Congressional Careers: Service Tenure and Patterns of Member
Service, 1789-2015," Congressional Research Service, January 3, 2017. Retrieved
from https://www.fas.org/sgp/crs/misc/R41545.pdf

GlobalSecurity.org, "Second Taiwan Strait Crisis, Quemoy and Matsu Islands, 23
August 1958 - 01 January 1959," May 7, 2011. Retrieved from http://www.
globalsecurity.org/military/ops/quemoy_matsu-2.htm

Godfrey, M., "Are Debates in The US Presidential Elections Really Important in Terms
of Determining Results?" Forbes, October 17, 2012. Retrieved from http://www.
forbes.com/sites/quora/2012/10/17/are-debates-in-the-us-presidential-elections-re-
ally-important-in-terms-of-determining-results/#1ef8dd685893

Goldman, A., & Ryan, M., "At Least 12 Released Guantanamo Detainees Implicated in
Attacks on Americans," The Washington Post, June 8, 2016. Retrieved from https://
www.washingtonpost.com/world/national-security/about-12-released-guantanamo-
detainees-implicated-in-deadly-attacks-on-americans/2016/06/08/004d038e-2776-
11e6-b989-4e5479715b54_story.html

Gompert, D. C., Binnendijk, H., & Lin, B., "Blinders, Blunders, and Wars," Rand
Corporation, 2014. Retrieved from http://www.rand.org/pubs/research_reports/
RR768.html

Gonzenbach, W. J., "The Media, the President, and Public Opinion: A Longitudinal
Analysis of the Drug Issue, 1984-1991," Mahwah, NJ: Lawrence Erlbaum
Associates, October 1, 1995.

Goodfreephotos.com, "Franklin D. Roosevelt Portrait," [Digital Photograph], (n.d.).
Retrieved from https://www.goodfreephotos.com/people/franklin-d-roosevelt-por-
trait.jpg.php

Gordon, M., "U.S. Troops Move in Panama in Effort to Seize Noriega; Gunfire Is Heard
in Capital," The New York Times, December 20, 1989. Retrieved from http://www.
nytimes.com/learning/general/onthisday/big/1220.html

Gormley, K., "The Death of American Virtue: Clinton vs. Starr," New York: Crown
Publishing Group, February 1, 2011.

Gormley, K., & Shribman, D. "The Nixon Pardon at 40: Ford Looks Better Than Ever,"
The Wall Street Journal, September 5, 2014. Retrieved from http://www.wsj.com/
articles/ken-gormley-and-david-shribman-the-nixon-pardon-at-40-ford-looks-bet-
ter-than-ever-1409955912

Goss, S. C., "The Future Financial Status of the Social Security Program," Social
Security Bulletin, 2010. Retrieved from https://www.ssa.gov/policy/docs/ssb/
v70n3/v70n3p111.html

Government Publishing Office, "S. Rept. 107-351 - Joint Inquiry into Intelligence Community Activities Before and After the Terrorist Attacks of September 11, 2001," December 20, 2002. Retrieved from https://www.gpo.gov/fdsys/pkg/GPO-CRPT-107srpt351/content-detail.html

Graham, D., "Quote of the day: Obama: 'If I Had a Son, He'd Look Like Trayvon,'" April 10, 2012. Retrieved from http://www.theatlantic.com/politics/archive/2012/03/quote-of-the-day-obama-if-i-had-a-son-hed-look-like-trayvon/254971/

Graphiq Inc., "President Richard Nixon, 37th President," InsideGov.com, 2016. Retrieved from http://us-presidents.insidegov.com/l/7/Richard-NixonDomesticPolicy-NotableMilestones

Green, R. K., & Wachter, S.M., "The American Mortgage in Historical and International Context," Journal of Economic Perspectives, 19(4), September 21, 2005, 93-114. doi:10.1257/089533005775196660

Greenstein, F. I., "George W. Bush and the Ghosts of Presidents Past," Political Science and Politics, 34(1), March 2001, 77-80. "'The Contemporary Presidency': The Changing Leadership of George W. Bush: A Pre- and Post-9/11 Comparison," Presidential Studies Quarterly, 32(2), June 2002, 387-396.

Gribble, R., "The Other Radio Priest: James Gillis's Opposition to Franklin Delano Roosevelt's Foreign Policy," Journal of Church and State, 44(3), Summer 2002, 501-519.

Grossman, A., "Justice Department Won't Charge Zimmerman in Trayvon Martin's Shooting," The Wall Street Journal, February 24, 2015. Retrieved from http://www.wsj.com/articles/justice-department-wont-charge-zimmerman-in-trayvon-martins-shooting-1424805141

GuidetoMusicalTheatre.com, "Miss Saigon," (n.d.). Retrieved from http://guidetomusicaltheatre.com/shows_m/miss_saigon.htm

Gulick, L., "The Twenty-Fifth Anniversary of the American Society for Public Administration," Public Administration Review, 25(1), March 1965, 1-4. doi:10.2307/974003

Hall, W. C., "Economically speaking: George Bush and the Price of Perception," January 1, 2006. Retrieved from https://www.researchgate.net/publication/292488532_Economically_speaking_George_Bush_and_the_price_of_perception. "'Reflections of Yesterday': George H. W. Bush's Instrumental Use of Public Opinion Research in Presidential Discourse," Presidential Studies Quarterly, 32(3), September 2002, 531-558.

Hamilton, D. E., "Herbert Hoover and The Great Drought of 1930," The Journal of American History, 68(4), March 1982, 850-875.

SOURCES

Hansen-Kuhn, K., "Clinton, NAFTA and the Politics of U.S. Trade," NACLA
Report on the Americas, (n.d.). Retrieved from https://nacla.org/article/
clinton-nafta-and-politics-us-trade

Harris & Ewing, "President Woodrow Wilson" [Digital Photograph], 1914. Retrieved
from https://commons.wikimedia.org/wiki/File:President_Woodrow_Wilson_by_
Harris_%26_Ewing,_1914-crop.jpg "Warren G. Harding," [Digital Photograph],
circa 1920. Retrieved from https://commons.wikimedia.org/wiki/Warren_G._
Harding#/media/File:Warren_G_Harding-Harris_%26_Ewing.jpg

Harry, L., & Strickland, M., "Franklin's Fan: 1937," in Strange Philadelphia: Stories
from the City of Brotherly Love, Philadelphia: Temple University Press, September
21, 1995, 143-145.

Haskins, R., "Interview: Welfare Reform, 10 years Later," Brookings, August
24, 2006. Retrieved from https://www.brookings.edu/on-the-record/
interview-welfare-reform-10-years-later/

Hatfield, M.O., "Spiro Theodore Agnew (1969-1973)," in Hatfield, M.O., and Wolff,
W. (Eds.), Vice Presidents of the United States 1789-1993, Washington, D.C.: U.S.
Govt. Printing Office, June 1997, 481-488. Retrieved from http://www.senate.gov/
artandhistory/history/ resources/pdf/spiro_agnew.pdf

Hayden, M. E., "4 Officers Shot Within 24 Hours Amid Violent Year for Police,"
ABC News, November 21, 2016. Retrieved from http://abcnews.go.com/US/
officers-shot-24-hours-amid-violent-year-police/story?id=43688242

Hazelden Betty Ford Foundation, "History of the Betty Ford Center," (n.d.). Retrieved
from http://www.hazeldenbettyford.org/about-us/mission/history/betty-ford-center

Health Research Funding, "Psychological Articles and Infographics: John F
Kennedy Personality Traits," December 14, 2014. Retrieved from http://
healthresearchfunding.org/john-f-kennedy-personality-traits/

Healthcare.gov, "See if Your Income Falls in the Range to Save," 2017. Retrieved from
https://www.healthcare.gov/lower-costs/qualifying-for-lower-costs/

Healy, R.L., "Shock...Disbelief...Grief," The Boston Globe, November 23,
1963. Retrieved from http://archive.boston.com/news/specials/kennedy/
day2_jfk_assassinated/

Heclo, H., "The Mixed Legacies of Ronald Reagan," Presidential Studies Quarterly,
38(4), December 2008, 555-574

Helicher, K., "The Education of Harry S. Truman," Presidential Studies Quarterly,
14(4), Fall 1984, 581-582.

Henderson, G. F., "Theses and Dissertations about Mackenzie King and His Era," in
W.L. Mackenzie King: A Bibliography and Research Guide, Toronto: University of
Toronto Press, December 12, 1998, 268-272.

Herbers, J., "In Three Decades, Nixon Tasted Crisis and Defeat, Victory, Ruin and Revival," The New York Times, April 24, 1994. Retrieved from https://www. nytimes.com/books/98/06/14/specials/nixon-obit2.html

Hibbitts, T., "The Man Who Supposedly Cost George H. W. Bush the Presidency," PollingReport.com, January 30, 2012.

Hickman, K., "Vietnam War: The Tet Offensive 1968," ThoughtCo.com, August 4, 2016. Retrieved from http://militaryhistory.about.com/od/vietnamwar/a/ VietnamTet.htm

Hiro, D., "Fall of Eastern Aleppo Marks Turning Point for Syrian Civil War," YaleGlobal Online, December 13, 2016. Retrieved from http://yaleglobal.yale.edu/content/ fall-eastern-aleppo-marks-turning-point-syrian-civil-war

Hirschman, C., "America's Melting Pot Reconsidered," Annual Review of Sociology, 9, 1983, 397-423.

History.com staff., "1905: Franklin Roosevelt Marries Eleanor Roosevelt," 2009. Retrieved from http://www.history.com/this-day-in-history/franklin-roosevelt-marries-eleanor-roosevelt "1954 Geneva Conference begins," 2009.a. Retrieved from http://www.history.com/this-day-in-history/geneva-conference-begins "1959 Batista Forced Out by Castro-led Revolution," 2009.b. Retrieved from http:// www.history.com/this-day-in-history/batista-forced-out-by-castro-led-revolution "1959 Nixon and Khrushchev Have a 'Kitchen Debate,' " 2009.d. Retrieved from http://www.history.com/this-day-in-history/nixon-and-khrushchev-have-a-kitchen-debate "1968: USS Pueblo Captured," 2010.b. Retrieved from http://www. history.com/this-day-in-history/uss-pueblo-captured "1971: The New York Times Publishes the 'Pentagon Papers,' " 2009.a. Retrieved from http://www.history.com/ this-day-in-history/the-new-york-times-publishes-the-pentagon-papers "1972: Watergate Burglars Arrested," 2009.b. Retrieved from http://www.history.com/ this-day-in-history/watergate-burglars-arrested "1975: American Ship Mayaguez Seized," 2009.a. Retrieved from http://www.history.com/this-day-in-history/american-ship-mayaguez-seized "1999 NATO Bombs Yugoslavia," 2010. Retrieved from http://www.history.com/this-day-in-history/nato-bombs-yugoslavia "Bay of Pigs Invasion," 2009. Retrieved from http://www.history.com/topics/cold-war/ bay-of-pigs-invasion "Boston Marathon Bombings," 2014. Retrieved from http:// www.history.com/topics/boston-marathon-bombings "Castro Announces Mariel Boatlift," 2009.b. Retrieved from http://www.history.com/this-day-in-history/castro-announces-mariel-boatlift "David Frost Interviews Richard Nixon," (n.d.). Retrieved from http://www.history.com/this-day-in-history/david-frost-interviews-richard-nixon "Détente," 2009.c. Retrieved from http://www.history.com/ topics/cold-war/detente "Four Black Schoolgirls Killed in Birmingham," 2010.

SOURCES

Retrieved from http://www.history.com/this-day-in-history/four-black-school-girls-killed-in-birmingham "Hubert H. Humphrey," 2009. Retrieved from http://www.history.com/topics/hubert-h-humphrey "Hurricane Katrina Slams into Gulf Coast," 2005. Retrieved from http://www.history.com/this-day-in-history/hurricane-katrina-slams-into-gulf-coast "Inaugural Address: Bill Clinton," 2009.a. Retrieved from http://www.history.com/topics/us-presidents/bill-clinton "Jack Ruby Kills Lee Harvey Oswald," 2010.a. Retrieved from http://www.history.com/this-day-in-history/jack-ruby-kills-lee-harvey-oswald "Joseph R. McCarthy," 2009. Retrieved from http://www.history.com/topics/cold-war/joseph-mccarthy "Oklahoma City Bombing," 2009. Retrieved from http://www.history.com/topics/oklahoma-city-bombing "Panama Canal Turned over to Panama," 2009. Retrieved from http://www.history.com/this-day-in-history/panama-canal-turned-over-to-panama "Protests at Democratic National Convention in Chicago," (n.d.). Retrieved from http://www.history.com/this-day-in-history/protests-at-democratic-national-convention-in-chicago "Reagan fires 11,359 Air-Traffic Controllers," 2010. Retrieved from http://www.history.com/this-day-in-history/reagan-fires-11359-air-traffic-controllers "Ronald Reagan and Nancy Davis Marry," 2009. Retrieved from http://www.history.com/this-day-in-history/ronald-reagan-and-nancy-davis-marry "Suez Crisis," 2009.e. Retrieved from http://www.history.com/topics/cold-war/suez-crisis History.com staff, (2010). "The Space Race," Retrieved from http://www.history.com/topics/space-race "The U.S. Invades Panama," 2010. Retrieved from http://www.history.com/this-day-in-history/the-u-s-invades-panama "U.S. Bombs Libya," 2016. Retrieved from http://www.history.com/this-day-in-history/u-s-bombs-libya "Vietnam War Peace Talks," July 18, 2012. Retrieved from http://alphahistory.com/vietnamwar/vietnam-war-peace-talks/ "Watergate Scandal," 2009.c. Retrieved from http://www.history.com/topics/watergate "Yom Kippur War," 2009.d. Retrieved from http://www.history.com/topics/yom-kippur-war

HistoryCommons.org, "Profile: Tower Commission," (n.d.). Retrieved from http://www.historycommons.org/entity.jsp?entity=tower_commission_1 "US military: Spy Plane Crashes in China; Chinese Strip Plane of Sensitive Equipment," March 31, 2001. Retrieved from http://www.historycommons.org/timeline.jsp?timeline=us_military_tmln&us_military_specific_cases_and_issues=us_military_tmln_spy_plane_crash_in_china

Hodge, S. A., "Ten Benefits of Cutting the U.S. Corporate Tax Rate," Tax Foundation, May 11, 2011. Retrieved from http://taxfoundation.org/article/ten-benefits-cutting-us-corporate-tax-rate

Holbrooks, J., "Not a Conspiracy: FBI's Comey Has Been Covering the Clintons' A**es for Decades," UndergroundReporter.org, August 15, 2016. Retrieved from http://undergroundreporter.org/not-conspiracy-fbis-comey-covered-clintons-decades/

Holmes, S. A., "The 1992 Elections: Disappointment – News Analysis: An Eccentric but No Joke; Perot's Strong Showing Raises Questions on What Might Have Been, and Might Be," The New York Times, November 5, 1992. Retrieved from http://www.nytimes.com/1992/11/05/us/1992-elections-disappointment-analysis-eccentric-but-no-joke-perot-s-strong.html

Hoover, H., "Development of Social Reforms: Old-Age Assistance, Unemployment Insurance, Education, The Indians," in The Memoirs of Herbert Hoover: The Cabinet and The Presidency (New York: The MacMillan Company, 1952), 312-315.

Hoover, H., & Lohof, B. A., "Herbert Hoover's Mississippi Valley Land Reform Memorandum: A Document," The Arkansas Historical Quarterly, 29(2), Summer 1970, 112-118.

Hoover, K. D., "Phillips Curve," in D. Henderson, The Concise Encyclopedia of Economics, University Park, IL: Liberty Fund, Inc., August 1, 2008. Retrieved from http://www.econlib.org/library/Enc/PhillipsCurve.html

Horsley, S., "A Short History of Government Shutdowns," NPR, September 30, 2013. Retrieved from http://www.npr.org/2013/09/30/227292952/a-short-history-of-government-shutdowns

Horvitz, P.F., "'Don't Ask, Don't Tell, Don't Pursue' Is White House's Compromise Solution: New U.S. Military Policy Tolerates Homosexuals," The New York Times, July 20, 1993. Retrieved from http://www.nytimes.com/1993/07/20/news/20iht-gay_1.html

House, A., "Margaret Truman Gets a Kick out of Radio-TV," The Fayetteville Observer, November 11, 1955. Retrieved from https://news.google.com/newspapers?nid=1559&dat=19551111&id=IW05AAAAIBAJ&sjid=eykMAAAAIBAJ&pg=539,10154784

House Judiciary Committee, "Articles of Impeachment," Watergate.info, July 27, 1974. Retrieved from http://watergate.info/impeachment/articles-of-impeachment

Hoxie, R.G., "Herbert Hoover: Multi-National Man," Presidential Studies Quarterly, 7(1), Winter 1977, 49-52.

Hsu, S., "Data Glitch Makes Renminbi Appear to Plunge Against the Dollar as China Battles Capital Outflow," Forbes, December 5, 2016. Retrieved from http://www.forbes.com/sites/sarahsu/2016/12/05/renminbi-plunges-against-the-dollar-as-china-battles-capital-outflow/#3dc95802fa7f

SOURCES

Hubbard, B., "Turning Point in Syria as Assad Regains All of Aleppo," The New York Times, December 22, 2016. Retrieved from http://www.nytimes.com/2016/12/22/world/middleeast/aleppo-syria-evacuation.html?_r=0

Hughes, M., "Presidential Pardons," Infoplease.com, 2016. Retrieved from http://www.infoplease.com/us/government/presidential-pardons-1789-present.html

Hughes, R., "13 Of the Worst Recessions / Depressions in US History," HITC.com, August 29, 2011. Retrieved from http://www.hitc.com/en-gb/2011/08/28/13-worst-recessions-and-depressions-in-us-history/

Humes, E., "How the GI Bill Shunted Blacks into Vocational Training," The Journal of Blacks in Higher Education, 53, Autumn 2006, 92-104. Retrieved from http://www.jstor.org/stable/25073543

Hunnicutt, B., "Labor and Franklin Delano Roosevelt's New Dream," in Free Time: The Forgotten American Dream (Philadelphia: Temple University Press, January 11, 2013), 109-121.

Huston, L.A., "High Court Rules Bus Segregation Unconstitutional," The New York Times, November 14, 1956. Retrieved from http://www.nytimes.com/learning/general/onthisday/big/1113.html

IAC Publishing, LLC., "What Was the National Origins Act of 1924?" (n.d.). Retrieved from https://www.reference.com/government-politics/national-origins-act-1924-c58e612f0bdebc9f

"Immigration Act of 1990." Retrieved from https://www.congress.gov/bill/101st-congress/senate-bill/358

"Indian Reorganization Act of 1934," 25 U.S.C. § 461 et seq.

Infoplease.com, "America's Wars: U.S. Casualties and Veterans," 2012. Retrieved from http://www.infoplease.com/ipa/A0004615.html "Cabinet Members Under President Barack Obama," 2016. Retrieved from http://www.infoplease.com/us/government/cabinet-members-barack-obama.htm

Internal Revenue Service, "Taxes in U.S. History: The Wealth Tax of 1935 and the Victory Tax of 1942," in Understanding Taxes, (n.d.). Retrieved from https://apps.irs.gov/app/understandingTaxes/student/whys_thm02_les05.jsp

Investor's Business Daily, "Trump Is Right — Millions of Illegals Probably Did Vote In 2016," November 28, 2016. Retrieved from http://www.investors.com/politics/editorials/trump-is-right-millions-of-illegals-probably-did-vote-in-2016/

Irwin, N., "What 'The Big Short' Gets Right, and Wrong, About the Housing Bubble," The New York Times, December 22, 2015. Retrieved from http://www.nytimes.com/2015/12/23/upshot/what-the-big-short-gets-right-and-wrong-about-the-housing-bubble.html?_r=0

Isaac, F., "Milestones in California History: The Grapes of Wrath: Fifty Years after," California History, 68(3), Fall 1989. doi:10.2307/25462393

Israel Ministry of Foreign Affairs, "Israel-Egypt Peace Treaty," 2016. Retrieved from http://www.mfa.gov.il/mfa/foreignpolicy/peace/guide/pages/israel-egypt%20 peace%20treaty.aspx

Jacobson, G., "The Effects of the George W. Bush Presidency on Partisan Attitudes," Presidential Studies Quarterly, 39(2), June 2009, 172-209.

Jakab, S., "Are Fund Managers Doomed? Making the Case for Passive Investing's Triumph," The Wall Street Journal, October 18, 2016. Retrieved from http://www. wsj.com/articles/are-fund-managers-doomed-making-the-case-for-passive-inves-tings-triumph-1476798977

Jardine, L., "Lyndon B Johnson: The Uncivil Rights Reformer," The Independent, January 21, 2009. Retrieved from http://www.independent.co.uk/news/presidents/lyndon-b-johnson-the-uncivil-rights-reformer-1451816.html

Jehl, D., "Opening to Vietnam; Clinton Drops 19-Year Ban on U.S. Trade with Vietnam; Cites Hanoi's Help on M.I.A.'S," The New York Times, February 4, 1994. Retrieved from http://www.nytimes.com/1994/02/04/world/open-ing-vietnam-clinton-drops-19-year-ban-us-trade-with-vietnam-cites-hanoi-s. html?pagewanted=all

Jenkins, Jr. H. W., "Climate Denial Finally Pays Off," The Wall Street Journal, June 28, 2016. Retrieved from http://www.wsj.com/articles/climate-denial-finally-pays-off-1467151625

Jensehaugen, J., "Review: A Safe Haven: Harry S. Truman and the Founding of Israel by Allis Radosh; Ronald Radosh," Journal of Peace Research, 48(4), July 2011, 563-563.

Jentleson, B.W., & Whytock, C.A., "Who 'Won' Libya?: The Force-Diplomacy Debate and Its Implications for Theory and Policy," International Security, 30(3), Winter 2005, 47-86.

Jeyaratnam, E., Whitmore, J., Hopkin, M., & Mountain, W., "The Paris Climate Agreement at a Glance," TheConversation.com, December 12, 2015. Retrieved from https://theconversation.com/the-paris-climate-agreement-at-a-glance-50465

Johnson, C., "Why Coolidge Matters: Leadership Lessons from America's Most Underrated President," New York: Encounter Books, 2013.

Johnson, L. B., "In Commemoration of the 82nd Anniversary of The Birth of Franklin Delano Roosevelt," The Centennial Review, 9(2), 1965, 153-155. Retrieved from https://www.jstor.org/stable/23737680?seq=1#page_scan_tab_contents

Johnson, T., "Making of John F. Kennedy Biopic 'PT 109' Was Hardly Smooth Sailing," Variety, August 16, 2013. Retrieved from http://variety.com/2013/film/news/making-of-john-f-kennedy-biopic-pt-109-was-hardly-smooth-sailing-1200579139/

Jones, J. M., "Americans Oppose Closing Gitmo and Moving Prisoners to U.S.," Gallup.com, June 3, 2009. Retrieved from http://www.gallup.com/poll/119393/americans-oppose- closing-gitmo-moving-prisoners.aspx "Historical Favorability Ratings of Presidents," Gallup, July 29, 2003. Retrieved from http://www.gallup.com/poll/8938/historical-favorability-ratings-presidents.aspx

Jones, M. D., "Documented History of the Incident Which Occurred at Rosewood, Florida, In January 1923," Florida State University, December 22, 1993. Retrieved from http://www.displaysforschools.com/rosewoodrp.html

"Jones v. Clinton," 72 F. 3d 1354 (Court of Appeals, 8th Circuit January 9, 1996).

Jordan, D. M., "Meanwhile, the Democrats," FDR, Dewey, and the Election of 1944, Bloomington, IN: Indiana University Press, September 2, 2011, 122-127. Retrieved from http://www.jstor.org/stable/j.ctt16gzcfx

Jordan, M., "Settlement of Syrian Refugees in the U.S. Accelerates," The Wall Street Journal, July 13, 2016. Retrieved from http://www.wsj.com/articles/settlement-of-syrian-refugees-in-the-u-s-accelerates-1468402205

Kadlec, C., "The Dangerous Myth About the Bill Clinton Tax Increase," Forbes, July 16, 2012. Retrieved from http://www.forbes.com/sites/charleskadlec/2012/07/16/the-dangerous-myth-about-the-bill-clinton-tax-increase/#3995b9ca772c

Kagan, R., "The September 12 Paradigm: America, the World, and George W. Bush," Foreign Affairs, 87(5), September/October 2008, 25-39.

Kaiser Family Foundation, "National Election Night Survey of Voters, 1994," October 31, 1994. Retrieved from http://kff.org/health-costs/poll-finding/national-election-night-survey-of-voters-1994-2/

Kan, S. A., "China-U.S. Aircraft Collision Incident of April 2001: Assessments and Policy Implications," Congressional Research Service, October 10, 2001. Retrieved from http://www.fas.org/sgp/crs/row/RL30946.pdf

Keating, R., "Most Corrupt Administrations in U.S. History," MostCorrupt.com, 2010. Retrieved from http://mostcorrupt.com/Most-Corrupt-Administrations.html

Kelly, K., "The Family: The Real Story of the Bush Dynasty," New York: Doubleday, September 14, 2004.

Kelly, M., "Dwight D. Eisenhower - Thirty-Fourth President of the United States," Thoughtco.com, 2016. Retrieved from http://americanhistory.about.com/od/dwightdeisenhower/p/peisenhower.htm

Kennedy, J. F. "Inaugural Address Transcript," John F. Kennedy Presidential Library and Museum, January 20, 1961. Retrieved from: https://www.jfklibrary.org/Asset-Viewer/BqXIEM9F4024ntFl7SVAjA.aspx

Kennerly, D.H., "Portrait Photo of President Gerald R. Ford," [Digital Photograph], ca. 1974. Retrieved from https://www.goodfreephotos.com/people/gerald-ford-photo.jpg.php

Kenny, M., "Indians," [Poem], Studies in American Indian Literatures, 20(3), Fall 2008, 95-96. Retried from https://facultystaff.richmond.edu/~rnelson/asail/SAIL2/203.pdf

Kerns, W. L., "Federal Employees' Retirement System Act of 1986," Social Security Administration, November 1986. Retrieved from https://www.ssa.gov/policy/docs/ssb/v49n11/

Kerpen, C., "Election 2016: How to Use Campaign Social Media Tactics to Build Your Brand," Forbes, July 20, 2016. Retrieved from http://www.forbes.com/sites/carriekerpen/2016/07/20/how-to-run-a-successful-presidential-campaign-on-social-media/#7ede0f443f67

Kesling, B., & Sonne, P., "Tensions Arise Among Allies Fighting to Retake ISIS-Held Mosul," The Wall Street Journal, October 18, 2016. Retrieved from http://www.wsj.com/articles/iraqi-forces-pause-mosul-advance-1476783097

Kessler, G., "A Guide to the Allegations of Bill Clinton's Womanizing," The Washington Post, December 30, 2015. Retrieved from https://www.washingtonpost.com/news/fact-checker/wp/2015/12/30/a-guide-to-the-allegations-of-bill-clintons-womaniz-ing/ "Fact checker: Obama's 'Apology Tour,'" The Washington Post, February 22, 2011. Retrieved from http://voices.washingtonpost.com/fact-checker/2011/02/obamas_apology_tour.html "President Obama and the 'Red Line' on Syria's Chemical Weapons," The Washington Post, September 6, 2013. Retrieved from https://www.washingtonpost.com/news/fact-checker/wp/2013/09/06/president-obama-and-the-red-line-on-syrias-chemical-weapons/

Khan, H., "GOP Pushback Mounts on Gitmo," ABC News, January 23, 2009. Retrieved from http://blogs.abcnews.com/thenote/2009/01/gop-pushback-mo.html

Kifner, J., "Eisenhower Letters Hint at Affair with Aide," The New York Times, June 6, 1991. Retrieved from http://www.nytimes.com/1991/06/06/us/eisenhower-letters-hint-at-affair-with-aide.html

Kiger, P., "The Sex Life of JFK: What We Know About His Legendary Love Life," in "Killing Kennedy" of National Geographic Online, October 23, 2013. Retrieved from http://channel.nationalgeographic.com/killing-kennedy/articles/the-sex-life-of-jfk/

Kiley, D., "As Obama Takes Victory Lap Over Auto Industry Rescue, Here Are the Lessons of The Bailout," Forbes, January 20, 2016. Retrieved from http://www.forbes.com/sites/davidkiley5/2016/01/20/obamas-takes-victory-lap-over-auto-industry-rescue/#49ea4f775497

Kim, K., Littlefield, C., & Etehad, M., (2016, April 26). "Timeline Bill Cosby: A 50-year Chronicle of Accusations and Accomplishments," Los Angeles Times, June 17, 2017. Retrieved from http://www.latimes.com/entertainment/la-et-bill-cosby-timeline-htmlstory.html

King, J., "Sources: Clinton Admits Sexual Affair with Flowers," CNN.com, January 22, 1998. Retrieved from http://www.cnn.com/ALLPOLITICS/1998/01/22/flowers.king/

King, R., "Oklahoma Obamacare Plans Face 76 Percent Hike," Washington Examiner, October 4, 2016. Retrieved from http://www.washingtonexaminer.com/oklahoma-obamacare-plans-face-76-percent-hike/article/2603629

Kiousis, S., "Job Approval and Favorability: The Impact of Media Attention to the Monica Lewinsky Scandal on Public Opinion of President Bill Clinton," Mass Communication and Society, 6(4), 2003, 435–451. doi:httpl/dx.org/10.1207/S15327825MCS0604_6

Kirzinger, A., Wu, B., & Brodie, M., "Kaiser Health Tracking Poll: September 2016," Kaiser Family Foundation, September 29, 2016. Retrieved from http://kff.org/health-costs/report/kaiser-health-tracking-poll-september-2016/

Klein, A., "No Child Left Behind: An Overview," Education Week, April 10, 2015. Retrieved from http://www.edweek.org/ew/section/multimedia/no-child-left-behind-overview-definition-summary.html

Klinkner, P.A., "Mr. Bush's War: Foreign Policy in the 2004 Election," Presidential Studies Quarterly, 36(2), June 2006, 281-296.

Knell, Y., "The Complicated Legacy of Egypt's Hosni Mubarak," BBC News, January 25, 2013. Retrieved from http://www.bbc.com/news/world-middle-east-21201364

Knowles, D., "Trayvon Martin's family Settles Wrongful Death Lawsuit with Sanford, Florida, Homeowner's Association," Daily News, April 5, 2013. Retrieved from http://www.nydailynews.com/news/national/trayvon-martin-death-civil-case-housing-complex-settled-1-million-article-1.1308943

Kocher, B., "How I Was Wrong About ObamaCare," The Wall Street Journal, July 31, 2016. Retrieved from http://www.wsj.com/articles/i-was-wrong-about-obamacare-1469997311

Koenig, A., "It's Not Just Premiums: ObamaCare Is Hiking the National Debt, Too," Forbes, October 31, 2016. Retrieved

from http://www.forbes.com/sites/andykoenig/2016/10/31/
its-not-just-premiums-obamacare-is-hiking-the-national-debt-too/#4b7ae0cb62ea

Kohut, A., "How the Watergate Crisis Eroded Public Support for
Richard Nixon," Pew Research Center, August 8, 2014. Retrieved
from http://www.pewresearch.org/fact-tank/2014/08/08/
how-the-watergate-crisis-eroded-public-support-for-richard-nixon/

Kopel, D., "The Volokh Conspiracy: The Missing 18 1/2 Minutes: Presidential
Destruction of Incriminating Evidence," The Washington Post Online, June 16,
2014. Retrieved from https://www.washingtonpost.com/news/volokh-conspiracy/
wp/2014/06/16/the-missing-18-12-minutes-presidential-destruction-of-incriminat-
ing-evidence/?utm_term=.a6b0032d9966

Koppel, N., & Campoy, A., "Two Gunmen Killed Outside
Muhammad Cartoon Contest in Texas," The Wall Street Journal,
May 4, 2015. Retrieved from http://www.wsj.com/articles/
shooting-reported-outside-muhammad-cartoon-contest-in-texas-1430704516

Kornblut, A. E., "Obama Admits Guantanamo Won't Close by Jan. Deadline,"
Washingtonpost.com, November 18, 2009. Retrieved from http://www.
washingtonpost.com/wp-dyn/content/article/2009/11/18/AR2009111800571.html

Kroft, S., "Obama: U.S. Underestimated Rise of ISIS in Iraq and Syria," CBS
News, September 28, 2014. Retrieved from http://www.cbsnews.com/news/
obama-u-s-underestimated-rise-of-isis-in-iraq-and-syria/

Kumar, M.J., "'Source Material': 'Does This Constitute a Press Conference?' Defining
and Tabulating Modern Presidential Press Conferences," Presidential Studies
Quarterly, 33(1), March 2003, 221-237.

Kuperman, A.J., "Obama's Libya Debacle," Foreign Affairs, March/April 2015.
Retrieved from Foreign Affairs, https://www.foreignaffairs.com/articles/libya/
obamas-libya-debacle

Kurtz, H., "Clinton Accuser's Story Aired," The Washington Post, February 25,
1999. Retrieved from http://www.washingtonpost.com/wp-srv/politics/special/
clinton/stories/broaddrick022599.htm "Jack Anderson's Nixonian Tactics,"
Washingtonpost.com, September 13, 2010. Retrieved from: http://voices.
washingtonpost.com/howard-kurtz/2010/09/jack_andersons_nixonian_tactic.html

Labaton, S., "Friend of Clinton Indicted A 2D Time; Tax Scheme Cited," The New
York Times, May 1, 1998. Retrieved from http://www.nytimes.com/1998/05/01/
us/friend-of-clinton-indicted-a-2d-time-tax-scheme-cited.html?_r=0

Labott, E., Gaouette, N., & Liptak, K., "US Sent Plane with $400 Million in Cash to
Iran," CNN, August 4, 2016. Retrieved from http://www.cnn.com/2016/08/03/
politics/us-sends-plane-iran-400-million-cash/

SOURCES

Ladley, E., "Nixon's Domestic Enemies," in Nixon's China Trip, Lincoln, NE: Writers Club Press, August 6, 2002, 63-64.

LaGrone, S., "U.S. Boat Crew Navigation Error, Not Technology Tampering Led to Seizure of 10 Sailors by Iran," USNI News, January 28, 2016. Retrieved from https://news.usni.org/2016/01/28/u-s-boat-crew-navigation-error-not-technology-tampering-led-to-seizure-of-10-sailors-by-iran

Landler, M., & Savage, C., "Obama Outlines Calibrated Curbs on Phone Spying," The New York Times, January 17, 2014. Retrieved from http://www.nytimes.com/2014/01/18/us/politics/obama-nsa.html

Lang, K., & Lehmann, J.-Y.K., "Racial Discrimination in the Labor Market: Theory and Empirics," National Bureau of Economic Research, September 2011. Retrieved from http://www.nber.org/papers/w17450

Langley, M., & Baker, G., "Donald Trump, in Exclusive Interview, Tells WSJ He Is Willing to Keep Parts of Obama Health Law," The Wall Street Journal, November 11, 2016. Retrieved from http://www.wsj.com/articles/donald-trump-willing-to-keep-parts-of-health-law-1478895339

Laszewski, R., "Trump Wants to Keep the Obamacare Pre-Existing Condition Reforms -- He First Said So in February," Forbes, November 12, 2016. Retrieved from http://www.forbes.com/sites/robertlaszewski2/2016/11/12/it-isnt-news-that-trump-wants-to-keep-the-pre-existing-condition-reforms-he-said-so-in-february/#1838361b7ccf

Laudicina, P., "If Social Media Got Obama Elected, Shouldn't It Help Him Govern?" Forbes, August 25, 2014. Retrieved from http://www.forbes.com/sites/paullaudicina/2014/08/25/if-social-media-can-get-you-elected-why-shouldnt-it-help-you-govern/#4aaabb5b45dc

Laurel, G., "Oil Shock of 1978–79," FederalReserveHistory.org, November 22, 2013. Retrieved from http://www.federalreservehistory.org/Events/DetailView/40

Laws.com, "Understanding the Senate Seniority System," (n.d.). Retrieved November 14, 2016, from http://constitution.laws.com/senate/seniority

Lee, D. D., "Herbert Hoover and the Development of Commercial Aviation, 1921-1926," The Business History Review, 58(1), Spring 1984, 78-102.

Lee, J., "A Town Hall, and a Health Care Model, in Green Bay," The White House, June 11, 2009. Retrieved from https://www.whitehouse.gov/blog/2009/06/11/a-town-hall-and-a-health-care-model-green-bay

Lee, R. A., "Harry S. Truman: The Man from Independence (review)," The American Historical Review, 92(4), October 1, 1987, 1055-1055. Retrieved from https://doi.org/10.1086/ahr.92.4.1055

Leffler, M. P., "9/11 in Retrospect: George W. Bush's Grand Strategy, Reconsidered," Foreign Affairs, 90(5), September/October 2011, 33-44.

Legal Information Institute, "Burwell v. Hobby Lobby Stores, Inc.," 2014. Retrieved from https://www.law.cornell.edu/supremecourt/text/13-354 "King v. Burwell," 2015. Retrieved from https://www.law.cornell.edu/supct/cert/14-114

Lemelin, B., "The U.S. Presidential Election of 1948: The Causes of Truman's 'Astonishing' Victory," Revue Française D'études Américaines, 87(1), 2001, 38–61. Retrieved from https://www.cairn.info/revue-francaise-d-etudes-americaines-2001-1-page-38.htm

Lennon, John, "Imagine," (n.d.). Retrieved from http://www.azlyrics.com/lyrics/johnlennon/imagine.html

Leogrande, W. M., "A Poverty of Imagination: George W. Bush's Policy in Latin America," Journal of Latin American Studies, 39(2), May 2007, 355-385.

Lewis, N. A., "Clinton Settles Jones Lawsuit with a Check for $850,000," The New York Times, January 13, 1999. Retrieved from http://www.nytimes.com/1999/01/13/us/clinton-settles-jones-lawsuit-with-a-check-for-850000.html

Levitz, J., Lazo, A., & Campo-Flores, A., "Three Police Officers Killed in Baton Rouge Shooting; Suspect Is Dead," The Wall Street Journal, July 18, 2016. Retrieved from http://www.wsj.com/articles/more-than-one-police-officer-shot-in-baton-rouge-1468768712

Liberman, P., "Punitiveness and U.S. Elite Support for the 1991 Persian Gulf War," The Journal of Conflict Resolution, 51(1), February 2007, 3-32.

Library of Congress, "Chronological List of Presidents, First Ladies, and Vice Presidents of the United States, September 11, 2012. Retrieved from http://www.loc.gov/rr/print/list/057_chron.html "President Warren Harding's Love Letters to Open to the Public on July 29, 2014," June 23, 2014. Retrieved from https://www.loc.gov/today/pr/2014/14-12.html "Prints and Photographs Reading Rooms, Presidents of the United States," June 12, 2012. Retrieved from http://www.loc.gov/rr/print/list/057_pra2.html#eisenhower "Warren G. Harding-Carrie Fulton Phillips Correspondence," (n.d.). Retrieved from https://www.loc.gov/collection/warren-harding-carrie-fulton-phillips-correspondence/about-this-collection/

Lichtblau, E., "Hubbell Guilty Plea Closes Starr's Arkansas Inquiries," Los Angeles Times, July 1, 1999. Retrieved from http://articles.latimes.com/1999/jul/01/news/mn-51899

Lichtblau, E., & Johnston, D., "Pardon Is Back in Focus for the Justice Nominee," The New York Times, December 1, 2008.

Liddy, G. G., "Will: The Autobiography of G. Gordon Liddy," New York: St. Martin's Paperbacks, July 15, 1991.

SOURCES

Liebovich, L.W., "Bylines in Despair: Herbert Hoover, the Great Depression, and the U.S. News Media," Westport, CT: Greenwood Publishing Group, July 30, 1994.

Light, M., "Russian-American Relations Under George W. Bush and Vladimir Putin," Irish Studies in International Affairs, 19, 2008, 25-32.

Limbacher, C., "Clinton and Women: Up to Seven May Have Been Assaulted [Part 1]," NewsMax.com, October 26, 1998. Retrieved from http://www.rightgrrl.com/clintonandwomen.html

Lindberg, T., "Necessary Impeachments, Necessary Acquittals," Policy Review, February 1, 2000.

Linky, D., "Gov. Woodrow Wilson and The Election of 1912," (n.d.). Retrieved from http://governors.rutgers.edu/on-governors/us-governors/gov-woodrow-wilson-and-the-election-of-1912/

Llopis, G., "An Essential Election Lesson for Leaders: Change Is Not Enough -- We Must Evolve," Forbes, November 14, 2016. Retrieved from http://www.forbes.com/sites/glennllopis/2016/11/14/an-essential-election-lesson-for-leaders-change-is-not-enough-we-must-evolve/#639cfff853c9

Lodal, J.M., "SALT II and American Security," Foreign Affairs, 57(2), Winter 1978, 245-268.

Lopez, D. Blanton, T., Fuchs, M., & Elias, B., (Eds.). "Veto Battle 30 Years Ago Set Freedom of Information Norms," National Security Archive at George Washington University, November 23, 2004. Retrieved September 17, 2016, from http://nsarchive.gwu.edu/NSAEBB/NSAEBB142/

Los Angeles Times staff, "San Bernardino Shooting Updates," December 9, 2015. Retrieved from http://www.latimes.com/local/lanow/la-me-ln-san-bernardi-no-shooting-live-updates-htmlstory.html "The L.A. Riots: 25 Years Later," April 26, 2017. Retrieved from http://timelines.latimes.com/los-angeles-riots/

Lucas, G., "How Richard Nixon Became 'Tricky Dick,'" CaliforniasCapitol.com, November 24, 2011. Retrieved from http://www.californiascapitol.com/2011/11/how-tricky-dick-nixon-became-tricky-dick/

Mack, D., "Obama and the Maghreb in the Wake of the Arab Spring," Middle East Institute, November 7, 2014. Retrieved from http://www.mei.edu/content/article/upheavals-lurking-threats-and-fragile-potential-maghreb-wake-arab-spring

Maddox, R.J., "Review of the Book Harry S. Truman: Fair Dealer and Cold Warrior by William E. Pemberton," The American Historical Review, 95(3), June 1990, 939-939.

Magnuson, E., "The Tower Panel: Laying Out the Brutal Facts," Time, 129(10), March 9, 1987, 32.

Mallon, T., "Coolidge," by Amity Shlaes. New Yorker, March 11, 2013, 66-71.

Malone, D. (Ed.), "Dictionary of American Biography, Vol. 8," New York: Charles Scribner's Sons, 1932. Retrieved from http://archive.org/stream/ dictionaryofamer08ilamer#page/252/mode/1up

Markon, J., "U.S. Illegal Immigrant Population Falls Below 11 million, Continuing Nearly Decade-Long Decline, Report Says," The Washington Post, January 20, 2016. Retrieved from https://www.washingtonpost.com/news/federal-eye/ wp/2016/01/20/u-s-illegal-immigrant-population-falls-below-11-million-continu- ing-nearly-decade-long-decline-report-says/

Marotta, D. J., "Dwight D. Eisenhower on Tax Cuts and a Balanced Budget," Forbes. February 28, 2013. Retrieved from http://www.forbes.com/sites/davidmarotta/2013/02/28/ dwight-d-eisenhower-on-tax-cuts-and-a-balanced-budget/#29d9fe0b1319

Marson, J., & Grove, T., "Russia Builds Up Army Near Ukraine Border," The Wall Street Journal, August 19, 2016. Retrieved from http://www.wsj.com/articles/ russia-builds-up-army-near-ukraine-border-1471537008

Mathews, A. W., "Aetna to Drop Some Affordable Care Act Markets," The Wall Street Journal, August 15, 2016. Retrieved from http://www.wsj.com/articles/ aetna-to-drop-some-affordable-care-act-markets-1471311737 "Anthem Projecting Losses on Affordable Care Act Plans This Year," The Wall Street Journal, July 27, 2016. Retrieved from http://www.wsj.com/articles/an- them-raises-outlook-reiterates-cigna-purchase-plans-1469617063 "Aetna Joins Rivals in Projecting Loss on Affordable Care Act Plans for 2016," The Wall Street Journal, August 2, 2016. Retrieved from http://www.wsj.com/articles/ aetna-tops-views-stops-aca-expansion-plans-1470134736

Matusow, A., "John F. Kennedy and the Intellectuals," in "Reflections" of The Wilson Quarterly, 7(4), Autumn 1983, 140-153.

Maues, J., "Banking Act of 1933, (Glass-Steagall)," June 16, 1933. Retrieved from http://www.federalreservehistory.org/Events/DetailView/25

Maugh II, T.H., "John F. Kennedy's Addison's Disease was Probably Caused by Rare Autoimmune Disease," Los Angeles Times Online, September 5, 2009. Retrieved from http://articles.latimes.com/2009/sep/05/science/sci-jfk-addisons5

Mauldin, J., "4 Maps That Explain Iran's Place in The Middle East," Forbes, October 17, 2016. Retrieved from http://www.forbes.com/sites/johnmauld- in/2016/10/17/4-maps-that-explain-irans-place-in-the-middle-east/#29ed- 6cf64f25 "Thanks To Obamacare, Government Debt Is Worse Than You Think," Forbes, November 2, 2016. Retrieved from http://www.forbes.com/sites/ johnmauldin/2016/11/02/thanks-to-obamacare-government-debt-is-worse-than- you-think/#593ad9d17872 "This Election Is A Chance For The Republicans To

SOURCES

Build A New Coalition," October 31, 2016. Retrieved from http://www.forbes. com/sites/johnmauldin/2016/10/31/this-election-is-a-chance-for-the-republicans-to-build-a-new-coalition/#1aae158017e3

Mayo Clinic staff, "Addison's disease," 2015. Retrieved from http://www.mayoclinic.org/ diseases-conditions/addisons-disease/symptoms-causes/dxc-20155757

Mazzetti, M. C., Cohen, G., Pasternak, D., & Kaplan, S., "A President and a Pardon," U.S. News & World Report, 130(7), February 19, 2001, 26.

McCaul, M., "The Lessons of the World Trade Center Bombing," Daily News, February 26, 2013. Retrieved from http://www.nydailynews.com/opinion/ lessons-world-trade-center-bombing-article-1.1272998

McGarity, T.O., "The Evolving Social Bargain," in Freedom to Harm: The Lasting Legacy of the Laissez Faire Revival, New Haven, CT: Yale University Press, March 19, 2013, 9-12.

McLaughlin, E. C., & Almasy, S., "Freddie Gray Officers Suing Prosecutor Marilyn Mosby," CNN, July 28, 2016. Retrieved from http://www.cnn.com/2016/07/27/ us/baltimore-marilyn-mosby-officer-lawsuits-freddie-gray/

McMahon, T., "Historical Inflation Rate," InflationData.com, July 14, 2017. Retrieved from http://inflationdata.com/inflation/Inflation_Rate/HistoricalInflation.aspx

McNamara, R. S., & VanDeMark, B., "In Retrospect: The Tragedy and Lessons of Vietnam," New York: Random House, March 19, 1996.

McNeely, B., "Official White House Photo of President Bill Clinton," [Digital Photograph], January 1, 1993. Retrieved from https://commons.wikimedia.org/ wiki/File:Bill_Clinton.jpg

Meacham, J., "Destiny and Power: The American Odyssey of George Herbert Walker Bush," New York: Random House, November 10, 2015.

Meckler, L., & Entous, A., "Osama bin Laden Is Dead," The Wall Street Journal, May 3, 2011. Retrieved from https://www.wsj.com/articles/SB10001424052748704569404576297941397558496

Meeropol, M. A., "A Tale of Two Tax Cuts: What Recent History Teaches about Recessions and Economic Policy," Economic Policy Institute, May 1, 2001. Retrieved from http://www.epi.org/publication/issuebriefs_ib157/

Meltzer, A. H., "Monetary and Other Explanations of the Start of the Great Depression," Journal of Monetary Economics, 2, November 1976, 459-461.

Mendes, E., "History Suggests Shutdown Stakes May Not Be That High," Gallup.com, October 1, 2013. Retrieved from http://www.gallup.com/poll/164714/history-suggests-shutdown-stakes-may-not-high.aspx

Meschutt, D., "Portraits of Franklin Delano Roosevelt," The American Art Journal, 18(4), Autumn 1986, 3-50.

Meyers, J., "Calvin Coolidge, Persistence Quote Aside, Left Presidency with Lagging Popularity," Newsmax, August 18, 2014. Retrieved from http://www.newsmax.com/TheWire/President-Calvin-Coolidge-Popularity-Persistece/2014/08/18/id/589464/#ixzz3S7VzYZFZ

Micallef, J.V., "The First Attack: Pearl Harbor, February 7, 1932," Military.com, (n.d.). Retrieved from http://www.military.com/navy/pearl-harbor-first-attack.html

Michaels, J., "Catalysts of War: The History that Led to Pearl Harbor Attack," USA TODAY Online, December 3, 2016. Retrieved from https://www.usatoday.com/story/news/world/2016/12/03/pearl-harbor-history/94039096/

Michaels, P.J., "The Climate Snow Job," The Wall Street Journal, January 24, 2016. Retrieved from http://www.wsj.com/articles/the-climate-snow-job-1453664732

Middleton, W.J., "Thurgood Marshall's Legacy," The Washington Post, February 8, 1993. Retrieved from https://www.washingtonpost.com/archive/opinions/1993/02/08/thurgood-marshalls-legacy/c30e99a9-69e8-4de3-b0d6-196b7d5f20d9/

Mieczkowski, Y., "Gerald Ford and the Challenges of the 1970s," Lexington, KY: The University Press of Kentucky, April 22. 2005. "The Secrets of Gerald Ford's Success ... 30 Years After He Became President It's Time to Consider What Made Him Tick," History News Network, August 1, 2004. Retrieved from http://historynewsnetwork.org/article/6501

Milam, C. H., "To President Roosevelt," American Library Association Bulletin, 35(12), December 12, 1941, 710.

MilitaryFactory.com, "Vietnam War Casualties (1955-1975)," 2016. Retrieved from http://www.militaryfactory.com/vietnam/casualties.asp

Milkis, S. M., & Rhodes, J.H., "George W. Bush, the Party System, and American Federalism," Publius, 37(3), Summer 2007, 478-503.

Miller Center of Public Affairs, University of Virginia, "Calvin Coolidge - Key Events," (n.d.). Retrieved from https://millercenter.org/president/calvin-coolidge/key-events "Dwight D. Eisenhower (1890 – 1969)," (n.d.). Retrieved from http://millercenter.org/president/eisenhower "Franklin D. Roosevelt: Life Before the Presidency," (n.d.). Retrieved from http://millercenter.org/president/biography/fdroosevelt-life-before-the-presidency "George H.W. Bush," 2015. Retrieved from http://millercenter.org/president/bush "George W. Bush," 2015. Retrieved from https://millercenter.org/president/gwbush "Harry S. Truman - Key Events," (n.d.). Retrieved from https://millercenter.org/president/harry-s-truman/key-events "Herbert Hoover: 1974-1964," (n.d.). Retrieved from https://millercenter.org/president/hoover "U.S. Presidents: Gerald Ford," (n.d.). Retrieved from https://millercenter.org/president/ford "U.S. Presidents: Jimmy Carter," 2015. Retrieved from https://millercenter.org/president/carter "U.S. Presidents / John F. Kennedy (1917–1963)," 2015. Retrieved from http://millercenter.org/president/kennedy "Warren G. Harding (1865 – 1923)," (n.d.). Retrieved from http://millercenter. org/president/harding

Miller, P. D., "Obama's Failed Legacy in Afghanistan," The American Interest, February 15, 2016. Retrieved December 6, 2016, from http://www.the-american-interest. com/2016/02/15/obamas-failed-legacy-in-afghanistan/

Miller-Milkis Boyett Productions (Producer), "Happy Days," [Television Series], Los Angeles: American Broadcasting Company, 1974.

Mills, L., Cullison, A., & Lee, C. E., "Dispute Between Russia and Ukraine Over Crimea Accusations Escalates," The Wall Street Journal, August 11, 2016. Retrieved from http://www.wsj.com/articles/ russias-putin-discusses-additional-security-measures-for-crimea-1470908089

Miniter, R., "Losing Bin Laden, How Bill Clinton's Failures Unleashed Global Terror," Washington, D.C.: Regnery Publishing, Inc., August 1, 2003.

Montgomery, B. P., "'Source Material': Nixon's Ghost Haunts the Presidential Records Act: The Reagan and George W. Bush Administrations," Presidential Studies Quarterly, 32(4), December 2002, 789-809.

Morgan, K. S., & Wyden, B., "Past Forgetting: My Love Affair with Dwight D. Eisenhower," New York: Simon & Schuster, January 15, 1977.

Morgenson, G., "Fannie, Freddie and the Secrets of a Bailout with No Exit," The New York Times, May 20, 2016. Retrieved from http://www.nytimes.com/2016/05/22/ business/how-freddie-and-fannie-are-held-captive.html?_r=0

Morrissey, C. T., "Oral History Interview with George M. Elsey," Harry S. Truman Library & Museum, February 20, 1964. Retrieved from https://trumanlibrary.org/ oralhist/elsey1.htm

Morrison, T., "Comment," The New Yorker, October 5, 1998. Retrieved from http:// www.newyorker.com/magazine/1998/10/05/comment-6543

Morrow, L., "44 Years Later, a Washington, D.C. Death Unresolved," Smithsonian Magazine Online, December 2008. Retrieved from http://www.smithsonianmag. com/history/44-years-later-a-washington-dc-death-unresolved-93263961/?no-ist

Mouat, J., & Phimister, I., "The Engineering of Herbert Hoover," Pacific Historical Review, 77(4), November 2008, 553-584

Mueller, J., "Pearl Harbor: Military Inconvenience, Political Disaster," in International Security, 16(3), Winter 1991-1992, 172-203. Retrieved from http://www.jstor.org/ stable/2539091

Muller, J., "Automakers' Report Card: Who Still Owes Taxpayers Money? The Answer Might Surprise You," Forbes, August 29, 2012. Retrieved from http://www.forbes.

com/sites/joannmuller/2012/08/29/automakers-report-card-who-still-owes-tax-payers-money-the-answer-might-surprise-you/#165727cc6a8c "Trump Should Be Asking: Will Ford Pay Off Its Government Loan Before Moving Small Car Production to Mexico?" Forbes, September 21, 2016. Retrieved from http://www.forbes.com/sites/joannmuller/2016/09/21/trump-should-be-asking-will-ford-pay-off-its-government-loan-before-moving-small-cars-to-mexico/#3ddb29cb17ad

Murray, S., & O'Connor, P., "How Race Slipped Away from Romney," The Wall Street Journal, November 8, 2012. Retrieved from http://www.wsj.com/articles/SB10001 424127887324073504578105340729306074

Myre, G., "The 1973 Arab Oil Embargo: The Old Rules No Longer Apply," NPR.com, October 16, 2013. Retrieved from http://www.npr.org/sections/parallels/2013/10/15/234771573/the-1973-arab-oil-embargo-the-old-rules-no-longer-apply

Naím, M., "Missing Links: Meet George W. Kerry," Foreign Policy, (142), May-June 2004, 96-95. "Missing Links: When Countries Go Crazy," Foreign Policy, (123), March-April 2001, 104-103.

Nasdaq.com, "General Motors Company Common Stock Quote & Summary Data," (n.d.). Retrieved from http://www.nasdaq.com/symbol/gm

National Archives & Records Administration, "The Constitution of the United States." Retrieved from https://www.archives.gov/founding-docs/constitution

National Bureau of Economic Research, "US Business Cycle Expansions and Contractions," 2016. Retrieved from http://www.nber.org/cycles/cyclesmain.html

National Commission on Terrorist Attacks Upon the United States, "9-11 Commission Report," 2002. Retrieved from https://9-11commission.gov/report/ "Al Qaeda Aims at The American Homeland," August 21, 2004. Retrieved from http://govinfo.library.unt.edu/911/report/911Report_Ch5.htm "Counterterrorism Evolves," August 21, 2004. Retrieved from http://govinfo.library.unt.edu/911/report/911Report_Ch3.htm

"National Environmental Policy Act of 1969." 42 U.S.C. § 4321 et seq.

"National Federation of Independent Business v. Sebelius," Secretary of Health and Human Services. (2013). Retrieved from https://www.law.cornell.edu/supremecourt/text/11-393

National Labor Relations Board, "National Labor Relations Act," (n.d.). Retrieved from https://www.nlrb.gov/resources/national-labor-relations-act "OF 1935," 29 U.S.C. §§ 151–169.

National Park Service, "Herbert Hoover, 1928," [Digital Photograph]. Retrieved from https://www.nps.gov/people/herbert-hoover.htm

SOURCES

National Partnership for Reinventing Government, "A Brief History of the National Performance Review," February 1997. Retrieved from http://govinfo.library.unt.edu/npr/library/papers/bkgrd/brief.html

NCES, "Digest of Education Statistics," 2012. Retrieved from https://nces.ed.gov/programs/digest/d12/tables/dt12_421.asp "Federal On-Budget Funds for Education," 2012. Retrieved from https://nces.ed.gov/programs/digest/d12/tables/dt12_421.asp "Fast Facts: Expenditures," 2016. Retrieved from https://nces.ed.gov/fastfacts/display.asp?id=66

New America, "Federal Student Loan History," (n.d.). Retrieved from https://www.newamerica.org/education-policy/policy-explainers/higher-ed-workforce/federal-student-aid/federal-student-loans/federal-student-loan-history/

New Deal Network, "TVA Electricity for All," (n.d.). Retrieved from http://newdeal.feri.org/tva/tva10.htm

Newman, A., "Photo Portrait of President Lyndon B. Johnson in the Oval Office, Leaning on a Chair," White House Press Office, [Digital Photograph], March 10, 1964. Retrieved from https://commons.wikimedia.org/wiki/File:37_Lyndon_Johnson_3x4.jpg

Newman, R., "Where the Jobs Are, and the College Grads Aren't," U.S. News & World Report, May 14, 2012. Retrieved from http://www.usnews.com/news/blogs/rick-newman/2012/05/14/where-the-jobs-are-and-the-college-grads-arent

News Sources, "America's Never-Ending War Against the World — 1986-1998," WarInContext.org, September 25, 2012. Retrieved from http://warincontext.org/2012/09/25/america%E2%80%99s-never-ending-war-against-the-world-1986-1998/

"NFIB v. Sebelius," 2013, 648 F. 3d 1235

Nitti, T., "Ex-Navy Seal to Pay Millions in Damages for Writing Book on Bin Laden Raid: Is It Tax Deductible?" Forbes, August 22, 2016. Retrieved from http://www.forbes.com/sites/anthonynitti/2016/08/22/ex-navy-seal-to-pay-millions-in-damages-for-writing-book-on-bin-laden-raid-is-it-tax-deductible/#44c108d35c75

Nixon, R. M., "Executive Order 11615 - Providing for Stabilization of Prices, Rents, Wages, and Salaries," The American Presidency Project, August 15, 1971. Retrieved from http://www.presidency.ucsb.edu/ws/?pid=60492 "The Moscow Summit," Vital Speeches of The Day, 38(17), June 1972. Retrieved from https://www.vsotd.com/issue/1972-17/moscow-summit "United States - People's Republic of China," Vital Speeches of The Day, 37(21), August 1971. Retrieved from https://www.vsotd.com/issue/1971-20/united-states-peoples-republic-china

"NLRB v. Fansteel Metallurgical Corp," 306 U.S. 240 (7th Cir., 1939)

Notman Photo Co., "Gov'r Calvin Coolidge," [Digital Photograph] (c1919). Retrieved from http://www.loc.gov/pictures/item/2003652523/

Noymer, A., "Life Expectancy in the USA, 1900-98," [Data File], 1998. Retrieved from http://demog.berkeley.edu/~andrew/1918/figure2.html

NPR, "Steve Lillywhite On Producing The Pogues," July 9, 2008. Retrieved from: http://www.npr.org/templates/story/story.php?storyId=92376012 "The Life of Ronald Reagan: A Timeline," (n.d.). Retrieved from http://www.npr.org/news/specials/obits/reagan/timeline.html "Timeline: The CIA Leak Case," July 2, 2007. Retrieved from http://www.npr.org/templates/story/story.php?storyId=4764919

Oakford, S., & Salisbury, P., "Yemen: The Graveyard of the Obama Doctrine," The Atlantic, September 23, 2016. Retrieved from http://www.theatlantic.com/international/archive/2016/09/yemen-saudi-arabia-obama-riyadh/501365/

Ober, L., "The Lasting Legacy of Woodrow Wilson, D.C.'s Hometown President," October 3, 2014. Retrieved from: http://wamu.org/programs/metro_connection/14/10/03/the_lasting_legacy_of_dcs_hometown_president

Oberdorfer, D., "TET: Who Won?" Smithsonian Magazine, November 2004. Retrieved from http://www.smithsonianmag.com/history/tet-who-won-99179501/

O'Brien, R. D., Saul, M. H., & Shallwani, P., "New York City Police Officer Won't Face Criminal Charges in Eric Garner Death," The Wall Street Journal, December 4, 2014. Retrieved from http://www.wsj.com/articles/new-york-city-police-officer-wont-face-criminal-charges-in-eric-garner-death-1417635275

"Occupational Safety and Health Act of 1970," 29 U.S.C. § 651 et seq.

Office of Compliance, "Congressional Accountability Act," 1995. Retrieved from https://www.compliance.gov/publications/congressional-accountability-act-overview

Office of the Federal Register, "Historical Election Results," [Data File], (n.d.). Retrieved January 14, 2015, from https://www.archives.gov/federal-register/electoral-college/historical.html

O'Reilly, K., "Nixon's Piano: Presidents and Racial Politics from Washington to Clinton," New York: Free Press, 1995.

Ortiz, S., "Introduction," in Beyond the Bonus March and GI Bill: How Veteran Politics Shaped the New Deal Era, New York: New York University Press, December 1, 2009, 1-2.

Ostroukh, A., "Russia-Ukraine Crisis Prompts Meeting with Putin at G-20 Summit," The Wall Street Journal, August 23, 2016. Retrieved from http://www.wsj.com/articles/russia-ukraine-crisis-prompts-meeting-with-putin-at-g-20-summit-1471964484

Our Documents.gov., "Executive Order 9066: Resulting in the Relocation of Japanese (1942)," February 19, 1942. Retrieved from https://www.ourdocuments.gov/doc.php?flash=true&doc=74

Pace, E., "Judith Exner Is Dead at 65; Claimed Affair with Kennedy," The New York Times Online, September 27, 1999. Retrieved from http://www.nytimes.com/1999/09/27/us/judith-exner-is-dead-at-65-claimed-affair-with-kennedy.html

"Panama Refining Co. v. Ryan," 293 U.S. 388 (5th Cir. 1935)

Paramount Pictures, "The Big Short – Now on Blu-Ray & Digital HD," 2016. Retrieved from http://www.paramount.com/movies/big-short

Parlapiano, A., "What We Know About the Investigation into Hillary Clinton's Private Email Server," The New York Times, October 28, 2016. Retrieved from http://www.nytimes.com/interactive/2016/05/27/us/politics/what-we-know-about-hillary-clintons-private-email-server.html?_r=0

Parry, R., "The L'Enfant Plaza Hotel Mystery," Consortiumnews.com, February 17, 2013. Retrieved from https://consortiumnews.com/2013/02/17/the-lenfant-plaza-hotel-mystery/

Patterson, G., "The Export-Import Bank," The Quarterly Journal of Economics, 58(1), December 1, 1943, 65-90.

Pavlich, K., "Man Who Set Up Hillary's Private Server Pleads the Fifth More Than 125 Times," Townhall.com, June 23, 2016. Retrieved from http://townhall.com/tipsheet/katiepavlich/2016/06/23/man-who-set-up-hillarys-private-server-pleads-the-fifth--times-n2182602

Payne, K. B., & Miller, F. C., "Naive Nuclear Proposals for a Dangerous World," The Wall Street Journal, October 14, 2016. Retrieved from http://www.wsj.com/articles/naive-nuclear-proposals-for-a-dangerous-world-1476484967

PBS, "Bombings of the Embassies of the United States of America at Nairobi, Kenya, and Dar Es Salaam, Tanzania," November 18, 1998. Retrieved from http://www.pbs.org/wgbh/pages/frontline/shows/binladen/bombings/summary.html "George H.W. Bush, American Experience," 2008. Retrieved from http://www.pbs.org/wgbh/americanexperience/films/bush/ "Hillary Rodham Clinton Biography," 2013. Retrieved from http://www.pbs.org/wgbh/americanexperience/features/clinton-hillary-rodham-clinton-biography/ "Nixon, Price Controls, and the Gold Standard," in D. Yergin, & J. Stanislaw, The Commanding Heights (New York: Simon & Schuster, February 4, 1998), 60-64. Retrieved from https://www.pbs.org/wgbh/commandingheights/shared/minitext/ess_nixongold.html "Wilson - A Portrait," (n.d.). Retrieved from http://www.pbs.org/wgbh/amex/wilson/portrait/wp_war.html

Pearce, M., "Where Are Iran's Billions in Frozen Assets, and How Soon will it Get Them Back?" Los Angeles Times, January 20, 2016. Retrieved from http://www.latimes.com/world/middleeast/la-fg-iran-frozen-assets-20160120-story.html

Pederson, W. D., (Ed.), "A Companion to Franklin Delano Roosevelt," Chichester, UK: Wiley-Blackwell, April 18, 2011, 409-426.

Pender, S., "Prelude," in How Did It Come To This? America's Experience in the New World Order," College Station, TX: Virtualbookworm.com Publishing, Inc., June 1, 2004, 11-12.

Perlstein, R., "Kennedy Week: The Myth of Camelot and the Dangers of Sycophantic Consensus Journalism," The Nation, November 23, 2013. Retrieved from https://www.thenation.com/article/kennedy-week-myth-camelot-and-dangers-sycophantic-consensus-journalism/

PersonalityCafe.com, "Jimmy Carter and Leadership," PersonalityCafe.com, 2014. Retrieved from http://personalitycafe.com/intj-forum-scientists/103036-jimmy-carter-leadership.html

Peters, G., & Woolley, J. T., "Election of 1968," The American Presidency Project, 2015. Retrieved from http://www.presidency.ucsb.edu/showelection.php?year=1968 "Gerald R. Ford: Statement on Proposed Statehood for Puerto Rico," in The American Presidency Project, December 31, 1976. Retrieved from http://www.presidency.ucsb.edu/ws/?pid=5538 "Gerald R. Ford: Statement on the Privacy Act of 1974," in The American Presidency Project, September 29, 1975. Retrieved from http://www.presidency.ucsb.edu/ws/?pid=5288

Peterson Institute for International Economics, "NAFTA 20 Years Later," November 2014. Retrieved from https://piie.com/publications/piie-briefings/nafta-20-years-later

Pew Research Center, "Barack Obama," October 22, 2008. Retrieved from http://www.journalism.org/2008/10/22/barack-obama/ "Bush and Public Opinion," December 18, 2008. Retrieved from http://www.people-press.org/2008/12/18/bush-and-public-opinion/ "Campaign '96 Gets Lower Grades from Voters," November 15, 1996. Retrieved, from http://www.people-press.org/1996/11/15/campaign-96-gets-lower-grades-from-voters/ "ePolitics," April 10, 2000. Retrieved, from http://www.journalism.org/2000/04/10/epolitics/ "Highs and Lows of Presidential Approval," January 12, 2016. Retrieved from http://www.pewresearch.org/facttank/2016/01/12/presidential-job-approval-ratings-from-ike-to-obama/ft_16-01-06_presapproval_hi_lo/ "In the Public Interest?" February 3, 2000. Retrieved January 3, 2017, from http://www.journalism.org/2000/02/03/in-the-public-interest/ "Obama's First 100 Days," April 28, 2009. Retrieved from: http://www.journalism.org/2009/04/28/obamas-first-100-days/ "Press Sees

SOURCES

Coverage as Having Hurt Bush Election Chances," December 20, 1992. Retrieved from http://www.people-press.org/1992/12/20/press-sees-coverage-as-having-hurt-bush-election-chances/ "Public Gives Press 'C' Grade for Campaign Coverage," November 27, 1994. Retrieved from http://www.people-press.org/1994/11/27/public-gives-press-c-grade-for-campaign-coverage/ "The Clinton/Lewinsky Story," October 20, 1998. Retrieved from http://www.journalism.org/1998/10/20/the-clintonlewinsky-story/ "The Debate Effect," October 27, 2004. Retrieved from http://www.journalism.org/2004/10/27/the-debate-effect/ "Voters Unmoved by Media Characterizations of Bush and Gore," July 27, 2000. Retrieved from http://www.people-press.org/2000/07/27/voters-unmoved-by-media-characterizations-of-bush-and-gore/ "Winning the Media Campaign," October 22, 2008. Retrieved from http://www.journalism.org/2008/10/22/winning-media-campaign/ "Winning the Media Campaign 2012," November 2, 2012. Retrieved from http://www.journalism.org/2012/11/02/winning-pressmedia-campaign-2012/

Pfiffner, J. P., "The First MBA President: George W. Bush as Public Administrator," Public Administration Review, 67(1), January-February 2007, 6-20. "'The Contemporary Presidency': Constraining Executive Power: George W. Bush and the Constitution," Presidential Studies Quarterly, 38(1), March 2008, 123-143.

Phillips, A., "Sorry, Donald Trump. Term Limits for Congress are (Probably) Never, Ever Going to Happen," The Washington Post, October 18, 2016. Retrieved from https://www.washingtonpost.com/news/the-fix/wp/2016/10/18/sorry-donald-trump-term-limits-for-congress-are-probably-never-ever-going-to-happen/

Phillips, E. E., "Manhunt for Ex-Cop Over, Officials Say," The Wall Street Journal, February 13, 2013. Retrieved from http://www.wsj.com/articles/SB10001424127887324616604578302103619876198

Pincus, W., "Bush Pardons Weinberger in Iran-Contra Affair," Washingtonpost.com, December 25, 1992. Retrieved from http://www.washingtonpost.com/wp-dyn/content/article/2006/03/28/AR2006032800858.html

Plumer, B., "Congress Tried to Fix Immigration Back in 1986. Why Did it Fail?" The Washington Post, January 30, 2013. Retrieved from https://www.washingtonpost.com/news/wonk/wp/2013/01/30/in-1986-congress-tried-to-solve-immigration-why-didnt-it-work/

Poczter, S., "Top 5 Reasons Bailouts Will Always Happen (And Taxpayers Will Foot the Bill)," Forbes, October 7, 2014. Retrieved from http://www.forbes.com/sites/sharonpoczter/2014/10/07/156/#687916116d1a

Preble, C.A., "Who Ever Believed in the 'Missile Gap': John F. Kennedy and the Politics of National Security," Presidential Studies Quarterly, 33(4), December 2003, 801-826. doi:10.1046/j.0360-4918.2003. 00085.x

Principi, A., "Money Can't Cure What Ails Veterans Affairs," The Wall Street Journal, May 26, 2016. Retrieved from http://www.wsj.com/articles/money-cant-cure-what-ails-veterans-affairs-1464300505

Project to Enforce the Geneva Conventions, "Memorandum from George W. Bush on the Humane Treatment of Taliban and al Qaeda Detainees," February 7, 2002. Retrieved from http://www.pegc.us/archive/White_House/bush_memo_20020207_ed.pdf

Prologue Magazine, "The Bloodiest Battle: The Battle of the Bulge Loomed Large 70 Winters Ago," 2014. Retrieved from https://www.archives.gov/publications/prologue/2014/winter/bulge-final.pdf

Pultz, J. E., McGee, K., & Neil, D., "Regulators' Opposition to Merger of MCI WorldCom and Sprint Means Uncertainty for Enterprises," Gartner, June 28, 2000. Retrieved https://www.gartner.com/doc/308589/regulators-opposition-merger-mci-worldcom

Puttnam, D. (Producer), & Joffé, R., (Director), "The Killing Fields" [Motion Picture], London, UK: Goldcrest Films, 1984.

Qiu, L., "Bill Clinton says Hillary was 'Completely Exonerated' in Whitewater," Politifact.com, June 23, 2015. Retrieved from http://www.politifact.com/truth-o-meter/statements/2015/jun/23/bill-clinton/bill-clinton-says-hillary-was-completely-exonerate/

Radnofsky, L., "President Obama Pushes for 'Public Option' in Affordable Care Act," The Wall Street Journal, July 11, 2016. Retrieved from http://www.wsj.com/articles/president-obama-calls-for-public-option-in-affordable-care-act-1468270802

Rapoport, A., "Still Hash!", ETC: A Review of General Semantics, 2(3), Spring 1945, 192. Retrieved from http://www.jstor.org/stable/42573757

Rapoza, K., "Why A New 'Cold War' Is Bad for The Global Economy," Forbes, February 18, 2016. Retrieved from http://www.forbes.com/sites/kenrapoza/2016/02/18/why-a-new-cold-war-is-bad-for-the-global-economy/#6dfc2d856883

Ray, D., "Brooms," and "My legacy," Prairie Schooner, 78(4), 2004, 145-146. Retrieved from https://muse.jhu.edu/article/176371

Reagan, R., "Statement on Granting Pardons to W. Mark Felt and Edward S. Miller," Ronald Reagan Presidential Library & Museum, April 15, 1981. Retrieved from https://www.reaganlibrary.archives.gov/archives/speeches/1981/41581d.htm

Reichard, G. W., "Early Returns: Assessing Jimmy Carter," Presidential Studies Quarterly, 20(3), Summer 1990, 603-620.

Rempel, W. C., "2 Whitewater Partners, Gov. Tucker Indicted: Inquiry: Arkansas Grand Jury Charges Loan Fraud and Conspiracy. The Clintons are Not Named by the

SOURCES

Panel," Los Angeles Times, August 18, 1995. Retrieved from http://articles.latimes. com/1995-08-18/news/mn-36339_1_loan-fraud

Renshon, J., "Stability and Change in Belief Systems: The Operational Code of George W. Bush," The Journal of Conflict Resolution, 52(6), December 2008, 820-849.

Renshon, S. A., "Presidential Address: George W. Bush's Cowboy Politics: An Inquiry," Political Psychology, 26(4), August 2005, 585-614.

Richard Nixon Foundation, "Richard Nixon – A Timeline," 2016. Retrieved from https://www.nixonfoundation.org/richard-nixon-a-timeline/

Richard Nixon Presidential Library and Museum, "History of the White House Tapes," (n.d.). Retrieved from https://www.nixonlibrary.gov/forresearchers/find/tapes/learn/ history.php

Richardson, G., Komai, A. & Gou, M., "Gold Reserve Act of 1934," FederalReserveHistory.org, January 30, 1934. Retrieved from http://www. federalreservehistory.org/Events/DetailView/13

Richter, I., & Montgomery, D., "The Great Strike Wave of 1946 and its Political Consequences," in Labor's Struggles, 1945–1950: A Participant's View (Cambridge, UK: Cambridge University Press, April 29, 1994), 47-67. doi:10.1017/ CBO9780511572371.005

Rigby, J. J., "The Administration of Economic Controls: The Economic Stabilization Act of 1970," Case Western Reserve Law Review, 29(2), 1979. Retrieved from http://scholarlycommons.law.case.edu/cgi/viewcontent. cgi?article=3158&context=caselrev

Riley, R. L., "Bill Clinton: Domestic Affairs," Miller Center of Public Affairs, University of Virginia, (n.d.a). Retrieved from https://millercenter.org/president/clinton/ domestic-affairs "Bill Clinton: Life Before the Presidency," Miller Center of Public Affairs, University of Virginia, (n.d.b). Retrieved from http://millercenter.org/ president/biography/clinton-life-before-the-presidency

Rogin, J., "Obama and Israel Cut Congress out of the Aid Game," The Washington Post, September 14, 2016. Retrieved from https://www.washingtonpost.com/ news/josh-rogin/wp/2016/09/14/obama-and-israel-cut-congress-out-of-the-aid- game/?utm_term=.b1eb712c1fc4

Rogoff, K., "Bush Throws a Party," Foreign Policy, (141), March-April 2004, 80-81.

Roosevelt, F. D., "Four Human Freedoms," Human Rights Quarterly, 6(3), August 1984, 384-385. doi:10.2307/762008

Roper, J., "'The Contemporary Presidency': George W. Bush and the Myth of Heroic Presidential Leadership," Presidential Studies Quarterly, 34(1), March 2004, 132-142.

Rosen, E., "Dollar Devaluation and the Monetary Group," in Roosevelt, the Great Depression, and the Economics of Recovery, Charlottesville, VA: University of Virginia Press, November 14, 2005, 41-56. Retrieved from http://www.jstor.org/stable/j.ctt6wrqhm.8

Rosenfeld, L. & Harrison, M., "A Bauhaus-Inspired Utopian Village: Roosevelt," in Architecture Walks: The Best Outings Near New York City, Piscataway, NJ: Rutgers University Press, January 25, 2010, 176-179.

Ross, S., "Fall from Grace: Sex, Scandal, and Corruption in American Politics from 1702 to the Present," New York: Ballantine Books, 1988.

Rottinghaus, B., & Vaughn, J., "Government Failures: Causes and Consequences," September 27, 2016. Retrieved from https://www.brookings.edu/blog/fixgov/2015/02/13/measuring-obama-against-the-great-presidents/ "New Ranking of U.S. Presidents puts Lincoln at No. 1, Obama at 18; Kennedy Judged Most Overrated," The Washington Post, February 16, 2015. Retrieved from https://www.washingtonpost.com/blogs/monkey-cage/wp/2015/02/16/new-ranking-of-u-s-presidents-puts-lincoln-1-obama-18-kennedy-judged-most-over-rated/

Rowen, B., "Memorable Quotes from U.S. Presidential Debates," Infoplease.com, 2016. Retrieved from http://www.infoplease.com/us/government/memorable-quotes-from-presidential-debates.html

Rozell, M., "Carter Rehabilitated: What Caused the 39th President's Press Transformation?" Presidential Studies Quarterly, 23(2), Spring 1993, 317-330.

Rubin, J., "Obama's Iraq Incrementalism is Back," The Washington Post, September 26, 2016. Retrieved from https://www.washingtonpost.com/blogs/right-turn/wp/2016/09/26/obamas-iraq-incrementalism-is-back/?utm_term=.186472727244

Ryan, H. (Ed.), "The Inaugural Addresses of Twentieth Century American Presidents," Westport, CT: Praeger, 1993).

Ryder, R. R., "The Youngest Naval Aviator of WWII," NorthwestQuarterly. com, Spring-Summer 2013. Retrieved September 19, 2016, from http://oldnorthwestterritory.northwestquarterly.com/2013/07/the-youngest-naval-aviator-of-wwii/

Sabato, L., "Jimmy Carter's 'Lust in the Heart' Playboy Interview – 1976," The Washington Post Online, 1998. Retrieved from http://www.washingtonpost.com/wp-srv/politics/special/clinton/frenzy/carter.htm "John F. Kennedy's Final Days Reveal a Man Who Craved Excitement," Forbes Online, October 16, 2013. Retrieved from http://www.forbes.com/sites/realspin/2013/10/16/john-f-kennedys-final-days-reveal-a-man-who-craved-excitement/#552ef3545f31

SOURCES

Sabato, L.J., Kondik, K., & Skelley, G., "Sabato's Crystal Ball," November 6, 2014. Retrieved from http://www.centerforpolitics.org/crystalball/articles/yup-it-was-a-wave/

Sadiq, N., "Obama's Legacy of Failure in the Middle East," Foreign Policy Journal, August 20, 2016. Retrieved from http://www.foreignpolicyjournal.com/2016/08/20/obamas-legacy-of-failure-in-the-middle-east/

Schaefer, S., "A Look Back at Bear Stearns, Five Years After Its Shotgun Marriage to JP Morgan," Forbes, March 14, 2013. Retrieved from http://www.forbes.com/sites/steveschaefer/2013/03/14/a-look-back-at-bear-stearns-five-years-after-its-shot-gun-marriage-to-jpmorgan/#1b48a1ea7ddc "AIG: Bailout In Brief" in photos, Forbes, May 2, 2013. Retrieved from http://www.forbes.com/pictures/eddk45fhljj/aig-bailout-in-brief-5/#d881f7455f0f

"Schechter Poultry Corp. v. United States," 295 U.S. 495 (2nd Cir., 1935)

Scheinkman, A., "Timeline: The Guantánamo Docket," The New York Times, 2017. Retrieved from http://projects.nytimes.com/guantanamo/timeline

Scherer, M., "2012 Person of the Year: Barack Obama, the President," Time, December 19, 2012. Retrieved from http://poy.time.com/2012/12/19/person-of-the-year-barack-obama/

Schlesinger, Jr., A.M., "Rating the Presidents: Washington to Clinton," Political Science Quarterly, 112(2) (Summer 1997), 179-190. Retrieved from http://www.acsu.buffalo.edu/~jcampbel/documents/SchlesingerPolSQ1997.pdf

Schmidt, M.S., & Apuzzo, M., "Petraeus Reaches Plea Deal Over Giving Classified Data to His Lover," The New York Times, March 3, 2015. Retrieved from http://www.nytimes.com/2015/03/04/us/petraeus-plea-deal-over-giving-classified-data-to-lover.html?_r=0

Schmidt, S., "Starr Probe Reaffirms Foster Killed Himself," The Washington Post, October 11, 1997. Retrieved from http://www.washingtonpost.com/wp-srv/politics/special/whitewater/stories/wwtr971011.htm

Schroth, R. A., "William Calley Lives," America, The Jesuit Review of Faith and Culture, April 10, 2012. Retrieved from http://www.americamagazine.org/faith/2012/04/10/william-calley-lives

Scott, R. (Director), "Black Hawk Down" [Motion Picture], 2001.

Seck, H. H., "US Service Member Killed in Syria Was Navy EOD Tech," Military.com, November 26, 2016. Retrieved from http://www.military.com/daily-news/2016/11/26/us-service-member-killed-in-syria-was-navy-eod-tech.html

"Securities Act of 1933," 15 U.S.C. § 77a - 77aa

Seib, G. F., "Obama Is a Man of Political Paradox," The Wall Street Journal, January 11, 2016. Retrieved from http://www.wsj.com/articles/obama-is-a-man-of-political-paradox-1452528688

Sen, S., "Ronald Reagan Runs Again?" Economic and Political Weekly, 18(44), October 29, 1983, 1872-1873.

Sengupta, S., "Obama to Push Refugee Aid at U.N., but Critics Say Effort Is Overdue," The New York Times, September 18, 2016. Retrieved from http://www.nytimes.com/2016/09/19/world/americas/obama-refugee-united-nations.html

Sengupta, S., & Kramer, A. E., "Dutch Inquiry Links Russia to 298 Deaths in Explosion of Jetliner Over Ukraine," The New York Times, September 28, 2016. Retrieved from http://www.nytimes.com/2016/09/29/world/asia/malaysia-air-flight-mh17-russia-ukraine-missile.html

Shaheen, G., "Franklin Delano Roosevelt," In Energy Corridor, Pittsburgh: University of Pittsburgh Press, March 8, 2016, 30.

Shallwani, P., & Barrett, D., "New York Bombs Filled with Explosives, Shrapnel," The Wall Street Journal, September 19, 2016. Retrieved from http://www.wsj.com/articles/new-york-explosion-caused-by-bomb-authorities-say-1474213735

Shannon, Jr., T. A., "Iran's Recent Actions and Implementation of the JCPOA," U.S. Department of State, April 5, 2016. Retrieved from https://2009-2017.state.gov/p/us/rm/2016/255510.htm

Sharpe, M., "From the Publisher: America's Suicide Pact with George W. Bush," Challenge, 50(4), July-August 2007, 112-114.

Sheffield, R., & Rector, R., "The War on Poverty After 50 Years," The Heritage Foundation, September 15, 2014. Retrieved from http://www.heritage.org/poverty-and-inequality/report/the-war-poverty-after-50-years

Shideler, J. H., "Herbert Hoover and the Federal Farm Board Project, 1921-1925," The Mississippi Valley Historical Review, 42(4), March 1956, 710-729.

Shields, C., "Being Happy — 1949," in Coming to Canada, Ontario, Canada: Carleton University Press, October 1995, 21.

Shipman, F. W., "Franklin Delano Roosevelt, 1882-1945," The American Archivist, 8(4), October 1945, 229-232. Retrieved from http://americanarchivist.org/doi/pdf/10.17723/aarc.8.4.vn76u278ol2mv262

Shin, L., "The Retirement Crisis: Why 68% of Americans Aren't Saving in An Employer-Sponsored Plan," Forbes, April 9, 2015. Retrieved from http://www.forbes.com/sites/laurashin/2015/04/09/the-retirement-crisis-why-68-of-americans-arent-saving-in-an-employer-sponsored-plan/#6ab8185719d8

Shweder, R. A., "George W. Bush & the Missionary Position," Daedalus, 133(3), Summer 2004, 26-36.

SOURCES

Shughart, W., "George W. Bush and the Return to Deficit Finance," Public Choice, 118(3/4), March 2004, 223-234.

Sibilla, C., "The 1958 U.S. Marine Invasion of Lebanon – It was No Day at the Beach," (n.d.). Retrieved from http://adst.org/2013/07/the-1958-u-s-marine-invasion-of-lebanon-it-was-no-day-at-the-beach/ "The Embassy Beirut Bombing – A Consular Officer's Perspective," Association for Diplomatic Studies and Training, April 2013. Retrieved from http://adst.org/2013/04/the-embassy-beirut-bombing-one-consular-officers-perspective/

Sidey, H., "The Presidency: Ford's Forgotten Legacy," Time, March 25, 1991. Retrieved from http://www.cnn.com/ALLPOLITICS/1997/03/24/back.time/

Sigelman, L., & Whissell, C., "Projecting Presidential Personas on the Radio: An Addendum on the Bushes," Presidential Studies Quarterly, 32(3), September 2002, 572-576.

Simon, D., "As for the FBI and the Clintons, Remember FileGate," FoundersCode.com, July 10, 2016. Retrieved from http://founderscode.com/fbi-clintons-remember-filegate/

Sisk, R., "Number of US Troops in Iraq More Than 4,000, Exceeds Previous Claims," Military.com, February 3, 2016. Retrieved from http://www.military.com/daily-news/2016/02/03/number-us-troops-iraq-more-than-4000-exceeds-previous-claims.html

Sisung, K. S., "Presidential Administration Profiles for Students," Detroit: Gale Research, 2000.

Skinner, R.M., "George W. Bush and the Partisan Presidency," Political Science Quarterly, 123(4), Winter 2008-09, 605-622.

Skowronek, S., "Leadership by Definition: First Term Reflections on George W. Bush's Political Stance," Perspectives on Politics, 3(4), December 2005, 817-831.

Smiley, D., "McDuffie Riots: Revisiting, Retelling Story – 35 Years Later," The Miami Herald, May 16, 2015. Retrieved from http://www.miamiherald.com/news/local/community/miami-dade/article21178995.html#storylink=cpy

Smith, R. M., "Religious Rhetoric and the Ethics of Public Discourse: The Case of George W. Bush," Political Theory, 36(2), April 2008, 272-300.

Smith, S., "How the GI Bill Changed the Economy," Marketplace.org, 2016. Retrieved from https://www.marketplace.org/2009/10/06/economy/how-gi-bill-changed-economy

Sobel, R., "Coolidge: An American Enigma," New York: Regnery Publishing, Inc., October 1, 2000.

Social Security Administration, "The Social Security Act of 1935," August 14, 1935. Retrieved from https://www.ssa.gov/history/35act.html "Trust Fund Operations," 2016. Retrieved from https://www.ssa.gov/history/tftable.html

Solomon, J., & Lee, C. E., "U.S. Sent Cash to Iran as Americans Were Freed," The Wall Street Journal, August 3, 2016. Retrieved from http://www.wsj.com/articles/u-s-sent-cash-to-iran-as-americans-were-freed-1470181874

Somin, I., "Obama Admits that his Handling of the Libya War was his Worst Mistake – but Not that it was Unconstitutional," The Washington Post, April 13, 2016. Retrieved from https://www.washingtonpost.com/news/volokh-conspiracy/wp/2016/04/13/obama-admits-that-his-handling-of-the-libya-war-was-his-worst-mistake-but-not-that-it-was-unconstitutional/

Sotos M. D., J., "Health and Medical History of President James Carter," October 18, 2004. Retrieved from http://www.doctorzebra.com/prez/g39.htm

Souza, P., "Official Portrait of President-Elect Barack Obama," [Digital Photograph], in Library of Congress, January 13, 2009. Retrieved from https://www.loc.gov/item/2010647151/

Spann, E. K., "Franklin Delano Roosevelt and the Regional Planning Association of America, 1931–1936," New York History, 74(2), April 1993, 185-200.

Stabile, D. R., "Herbert Hoover, the FAES, and the AF of L," Technology and Culture, 27(4), October 1986, 819-827. doi:10.2307/3105329

Stacey, J. A., "Undeterred in Syria," Foreign Affairs, October 2, 2015. Retrieved from Foreign Affairs, https://www.foreignaffairs.com/articles/syria/2015-10-02/undeterred-syria

Startt, J. D., Woodrow Wilson and the Press: Prelude to the Presidency (New York: Palgrave Macmillan, January 15, 2004).

StatisticBrain.com, "9/11 Death Statistics," August 25, 2016. Retrieved from http://www.statisticbrain.com/911-death-statistics/

Stein, S., "The President's Two Bodies: Stagings and Restagings of FDR and the New Deal Body Politic," American Art, 18(1), 2004, 32-57.

Stephens, B., "Truth Catches the Iran Deal," The Wall Street Journal, July 11, 2016. Retrieved from http://www.wsj.com/articles/truth-catches-the-iran-deal-1468278677

Stevenson, F., "Top Scandals and Controversies of Each United States President," Deseret News Online, May 20, 2013. Retrieved from http://www.deseretnews.com/top/1512/27/Woodrow-Wilson-Top-scandals-and-controversies-of-each-United-States-president.html

Stewart, Z., "7 American Presidents (and 1 First Lady) Whose Scandalous Affairs Appear in Clinton the Musical," Theatermania.com, May 11, 2015. Retrieved from http://

www.theatermania.com/off-broadway/news/7-american-presidents-and-1-first-lady-whose-scand_72835.html

Stiehm, J., "Woodrow Wilson Versus the Suffragettes," U.S. News and World Report, December 10, 2013. Retrieved from http://www.usnews.com/opinion/blogs/jamie-stiehm/2013/12/10/woodrow-wilson-versus-the-suffrage-movement

Stiglitz, J. E., & Bilmes, L.J., "The Three Trillion Dollar War: The True Cost of the Iraq Conflict," New York: W.W. Norton & Company, February 17, 2008.

Stoughton, C., "Radio & Television Address to the Nation Regarding Desegregation of University of Alabama," [Digital Photograph], June 11, 1963. Retrieved from https://www.jfklibrary.org/Asset-Viewer/Archives/JFKWHP-1963-06-11-D.aspx

Sudman, S., "The Presidents and the Polls," The Public Opinion Quarterly, 46(3), Autumn 1982, 301-310.

Sullivan, M., "Americans Are Clueless About Education Spending," Forbes, October 31, 2016. Retrieved from http://www.forbes.com/sites/maureensullivan/2016/10/31/americans-are-clueless-about-education-spending/#662e3a0a2bbb

Suro, R., "Clinton Fund-Raiser to Plead Guilty," The Washington Post, May 22, 1999. Retrieved from http://www.washingtonpost.com/wp-srv/politics/special/campfin/stories/trie052299.htm

Susris.com, "Evolving Education in Saudi Arabia: A Conversation with Amb James Smith," July 22, 2014. Retrieved from http://susris.com/2014/07/22/evolving-education-in-saudi-arabia-a-conversation-with-amb-james-smith/

Swanson, R.F. (Ed.), "Prime Minister Lester B. Pearson and President Lyndon B. Johnson, Campobello Island, New Brunswick, August 21, 1966," in Canadian-American Summit Diplomacy, 1923-1973: Selected Speeches and Documents, Toronto: McGill-Queen's University Press, 1975, 258-262

Svrluga, S., "Princeton Protesters Occupy President's Office, Demand 'Racist' Woodrow Wilson's Name be Removed," The Washington Post, November 18, 2015. Retrieved from https://www.washingtonpost.com/news/grade-point/wp/2015/11/18/princeton-protesters-occupy-presidents-office-demand-racist-woodrow-wilsons-name-be-removed/?utm_term=.dbb7540c24ee

Szafir, C. J., & Lueken, M., "More Spending Doesn't Lead to Improved Student Learning," Forbes, May 8, 2015. Retrieved from http://www.forbes.com/sites/realspin/2015/05/08/more-spending-doesnt-lead-to-improved-student-learning/#2eb99ac6df82

Taguba, A. M., "Article 15-6 Investigation of the 800th Military Police Brigade," NPR, February 2004. Retrieved from http://www.npr.org/iraq/2004/prison_abuse_report.pdf

Taranto, J., "Scratch 22?" The Wall Street Journal, August 15, 2014. Retrieved from http://www.wsj.com/articles/scratch-22-1408133725 "The Riots That Didn't Happen," The Wall Street Journal, July 15, 2013. Retrieved from http://www.wsj.com/articles/SB10001424127887323848804578607712534481472

Tata, R., "Richard M. Nixon, 37th President, 1968-1974," in The Greatest American Presidents: Including a Short Course on all the Presidents and Political Parties, Bloomington, IN: AuthorHouse, March 29, 2013, 106.

Tau, B., "FBI Documents Show Hillary Clinton Used Many Email Devices," The Wall Street Journal, September 2, 2016. Retrieved from http://www.wsj.com/articles/fbi-releases-documents-from-probe-into-hillary-clintons-email-use-1472837917 "GOP-Written House Benghazi Report Faults Obama Administration," The Wall Street Journal, June 28, 2016. Retrieved from http://www.wsj.com/articles/gop-written-house-benghazi-report-faults-obama-administration-on-libya-risk-strategy-1467121159 "Most of Clinton's Recovered Emails Will Be Released After Election Day," The Wall Street Journal, September 23, 2016. Retrieved from http://www.wsj.com/articles/most-of-clintons-recovered-emails-will-be-released-after-election-day-1474650119 "State Department Says 30-Odd Hillary Clinton Emails Could Be Linked to Benghazi," The Wall Street Journal, August 30, 2016. Retrieved from http://www.wsj.com/articles/state-department-says-30-odd-hillary-clinton-emails-could-be-linked-to-benghazi-1472594844 "White House Coordinated on Clinton Email Issues, New Documents Show," The Wall Street Journal, October 7, 2016. Retrieved from http://www.wsj.com/articles/white-house-coordinated-on-clinton-email-issues-new-documents-show-1475798310

Taylor, A., "Why the World Should Not Forget Khmer Rouge and the Killing Fields of Cambodia," The Washington Post Online, August 7, 2014. Retrieved from https://www.washingtonpost.com/news/worldviews/wp/2014/08/07/why-the-world-should-not-forget-khmer-rouge-and-the-killing-fields-of-cambodia/

Taylor, III, J. E., "Master of the Seas? Herbert Hoover and the Western Fisheries," Oregon Historical Quarterly, 105(1), Spring 2004, 40-61.

Taylor, N., "American-Made: The Enduring Legacy of the WPA: When FDR Put the Nation to Work," New York: Bantam Books, February 24, 2009.

Teitelbaum, R., "PBGC Raises Possibility of Program Insolvency," The Wall Street Journal, March 31, 2016. Retrieved from http://blogs.wsj.com/cfo/2016/03/31/pbgc-raises-possibility-of-program-insolvency/

Tennessee Valley Authority, "Our History," (n.d.). Retrieved from https://www.tva.com/About-TVA/Our-History

Tenpas, K. D., "Words vs. Deeds: President George W. Bush and Polling," The Brookings Review, 21(3), Summer 2003, 32-35.

SOURCES

Tenpas, K. D., & Hess, S., "'The Contemporary Presidency:' The Bush White House: First Appraisals," Presidential Studies Quarterly, 32(3), September 2002, 577-585.

The Cold War Museum, "Taiwan Crisis," (n.d.). Retrieved from http://www.coldwar. org/articles/50s/taiwan_crisis.asp

The Committee for a Responsible Federal Budget, "Promises and Price Tags: An Update," September 22, 2016. Retrieved from http://www.crfb.org/papers/promises-and-price-tags-preliminary-update "Summary Table of Fiscal Plans," 2012. Retrieved from http://crfb.org/sites/default/files/CRFB_Summary_Table_of_Fiscal_Plans.pdf

The Economist, "A View from the Bridge," October 22, 2016. Retrieved from http:// www.economist.com/news/united-states/21709038-it-will-take-more-just-money-get-america-moving-view-bridge

The History Place, "Presidential Impeachment Proceedings: Bill Clinton, 42nd U.S. President," 2000. Retrieved from http://www.historyplace.com/unitedstates/ impeachments/clinton.htm "John F. Kennedy Photo History: The Early Years," 2015. Retrieved from http://www.historyplace.com/kennedy/early.htm

The National First Ladies' Library, "First Lady Biography: Lady Bird Johnson," (n.d.). Retrieved from http://www.firstladies.org/biographies/firstladies.aspx?biography=37 "First Lady Biography: Pat Nixon," (n.d.). Retrieved from http://www.firstladies. org/biographies/firstladies.aspx?biography=38

The New York Times, "Oscar Collazo, 80, Truman Attacker in '50," February 23, 1994. Retrieved from http://www.nytimes.com/1994/02/23/obituaries/oscar-collazo-80-truman-attacker-in-50.html

"The President and Vice President Speak at the Easter Prayer Breakfast." Retrieved from http://newsvideo.su/video/3205685

The President Woodrow Wilson House, National Trust for Historic Preservation, "1916 Election," (n.d.). Retrieved from http://www.woodrowwilsonhouse. org/1916-election

The Reference Desk, "Jennifer Fitzgerald, Described As George H.W. Bush's 'Other Wife,'" Retrieved September 19, 2016, from http://tca-reference-desk.blogspot. com/2004/04/jennifer-fitzgerald-described-as-george.html

The Regents of the University of California, "1995-96 Government Shutdown," October 2, 2013. Retrieved from http://vm136.lib.berkeley.edu/BANC/ROHO/ projects/debt/governmentshutdown.html

The Select Committee on Benghazi, U.S. House of Representatives, "Select Committee on Benghazi Releases Proposed Report," December 7, 2016. Retrieved from https:// benghazi.house.gov/NewInfo

The Sun News, "Convicted SC man gets pardon from president Obama," December 19, 2013. Retrieved from http://www.thestate.com/news/state/south-carolina/article13832318.html

The Trustees of Princeton University, "Exhibition Showcases JFK's Brief Time at Princeton," in "News at Princeton, Featured Events," August 26, 2010. Retrieved from https://www.princeton.edu/main/news/archive/S28/27/47I80/index.xml?section=announcements

The Wall Street Journal, "Clinton's Benghazi Cover Story," June 28, 2016. Retrieved from http://www.wsj.com/articles/clintons-benghazi-cover-story-1467155750 "Faces of the Affordable Care Act," (2014). Retrieved from http://graphics.wsj.com/HealthProfiles/ "Health Law Rollout & Health Insurance News," (2015). Retrieved from http://www.wsj.com/public/page/health-law-rollout.html "Hope without change," July 29, 2016. Retrieved from http://www.wsj.com/articles/hope-without-change-1469746723 "Notable & Quotable: Climate Change and War," April 18, 2016. Retrieved from http://www.wsj.com/articles/notable-quotable-climate-change-and-war-1461021491

The Washington Post, "Campaign Finance, Key Stories," 1998. Retrieved from http://www.washingtonpost.com/wp-srv/politics/special/campfin/background.htm "Whitewater, Time Line," 1998b. Retrieved from http://www.washingtonpost.com/wp-srv/politics/special/whitewater/timeline.htm

The Wharton School, University of Pennsylvania, "NAFTA, 20 Years Later: Do the Benefits Outweigh the Costs?" February 19, 2014. Retrieved from http://knowledge.wharton.upenn.edu/article/nafta-20-years-later-benefits-outweigh-costs/

The White House, "The Historic Deal that Will Prevent Iran from Acquiring a Nuclear Weapon," 2016. Retrieved from https://www.whitehouse.gov/issues/foreign-policy/iran-deal

Thomson Reuters, "Witnesses Report Rioting in Tunisian Town," December 19, 2010. Retrieved from http://af.reuters.com/article/topNews/idAFJOE6BI06U20101219

Tiefer, C., "The 10 Most Blatantly Wasteful Defense Items in The Recent $1.8 Trillion Spending Bill," Forbes, January 1, 2016. Retrieved from http://www.forbes.com/sites/charlestiefer/2016/01/01/the-10-most-blatantly-wasteful-defense-items-in-the-recent-1-8-trillion-spending-bill/#511202304570 "Trump's Latest Reckless Bluster Wounds American Interests With China," Forbes, December 4, 2016. Retrieved from http://www.forbes.com/sites/charlestiefer/2016/12/04/trumps-latest-reckless-bluster-wounds-american-interests-with-china/#2cbcc8c05e82

Time, "25 Moments That Changed America," June 4, 2015. Retrieved from: http://time.com/3889533/25-moments-changed-america/ "Billion-Dollar Watchdog," March 8, 1943. Retrieved from http://content.time.com/time/subscriber/

article/0,33009,774390,00.html "Obama's New Elite Club: Two-Time Persons of the Year/Franklin D. Roosevelt," December 10, 2012. Retrieved from http://poy. time.com/2012/12/19/two-time-persons-of-the-year/slide/franklin-d-roosevelt/ "Obama's New Elite Club: Two-Time Persons of the Year/George W. Bush," December 19, 2012. Retrieved from http://poy.time.com/2012/12/19/two-time-persons-of-the-year/slide/george-w-bush/ "Obama's New Elite Club: Two-Time Persons of the Year/Richard Nixon," December 19, 2012. Retrieved from http://poy.time.com/2012/12/19/two-time-persons-of-the-year/slide/richard-nixon/ "Person of the year 2008, Barack Obama," September 7, 2008. Retrieved from http://content.time.com/time/person-of-the-year/2008/ "Person of the Year: A Photo History, Bill Clinton: 1992, 1998," December 16, 2006. Retrieved from http://content.time.com/time/specials/packages/article/0,28804,2019 712_2019702_2019642,00.html "Person of the year: A Photo History, Full List," 2016. Retrieved from http://content.time.com/time/specials/packages/ completelist/0,29569,2019712,00.html "Person of the year: A Photo History George Bush: 1990," December 16, 2006. Retrieved from http://content.time. com/time/specials/packages/article/0,28804,2019712_2019702_2019641,00. html "Person of the Year: A Photo History, George W. Bush: 2000," December 16, 2006. Retrieved from http://content.time.com/time/specials/packages/article/0,28 804,2019712_2019702_2019644,00.html "Person of the Year: A Photo History, Jimmy Carter: 1976," December 16, 2006. Retrieved from http://content.time. com/time/specials/packages/article/0,28804,2019712_2019702_2019639,00.html "Person of the Year: A Photo History, Ronald Reagan: 1980, 1983," December 16, 2006. Retrieved from http://content.time.com/time/specials/packages/articl e/0,28804,2019712_2019702_2019640,00.html "Time Magazine Cover: Ford On the Move," Aug. 26, 1974. Retrieved from http://content.time.com/time/ covers/0,16641,19740826,00.html "Time Magazine Cover: Men of the Year, Kenneth Starr and Bill Clinton," Dec. 28, 1998. Retrieved from http://content. time.com/time/covers/0,16641,19981228,00.html

Timiraos, N., "Debate Over U.S. Debt Changes Tone," The Wall Street Journal, July 24, 2016. Retrieved from http://www.wsj.com/articles/ debate-over-u-s-debt-changes-tone-1469385857

Trani, E., & Wilson, D. (1977, April 6). The Presidency of Warren G. Harding (Lawrence, KS: University Press of Kansas, April 6, 1977).

Tsui, C.-K., Clinton, New Terrorism and the Origins of the War on Terror (New York: Routledge, July 18, 2016).

Tsukayama, H., Berman, M., & Markon, J., "Gunman who Killed 49 in Orlando nightclub had Pledged Allegiance to ISIS," The Washington Post, June 13,

2016. Retrieved from https://www.washingtonpost.com/news/post-nation/ wp/2016/06/12/orlando-nightclub-shooting-about-20-dead-in-domestic-terror-in-cident-at-gay-club/?utm_term=.c5f805f0900f

Tulsa Historical Society & Museum, "1921 Tulsa Race Riot," (n.d.). Retrieved from http://tulsahistory.org/learn/ online-exhibits/the-tulsa-race-riot/

Turnquist, K., "Bryan Cranston Expertly Channels LBJ in HBO's 'All The Way' (review)," The Oregonian Online, May 21, 2016. Retrieved from http://www. oregonlive.com/tv/2016/05/bryan_cranston_expertly_channe.html

Turtledove, H., "Atlantis and Other Places: Stories of Alternate History," New York: Penguin Group, November 1, 2011.

Tyson, A., "The Last Government Shutdown and Now: a Different Environment," Pew Research Center, September 30, 2013. Retrieved from http://www.pewresearch.org/fact-tank/2013/09/30/ the-last-government-shutdown-and-now-a-different-environment/

"U. S. v. Butler," 297 U.S. 1 (1st Cir., 1936)

U. S. Army Center for Military History, "Dwight David Eisenhower, The Centennial," August 16, 2006. Retrieved from: http://www.history.army.mil/brochures/ike/ike. htm

U. S. Census Bureau, "Historical Census of Housing Tables," October 31, 2011. Retrieved from https://www.census.gov/hhes/www/housing/census/historic/ owner.html "Table 4: Homeownership Rates for the United States: 1996 to 2017," PRIL 18, 2015. Retrieved from https://www.census.gov/housing/hvs/files/ currenthvspress.pdf

U. S. Department of Commerce, Bureau of Economic Analysis, "Recession: How is that defined?" March 31, 2008. Retrieved from http://www.bea.gov/faq/index. cfm?faq_id=485

U. S. Department of Defense, Department of the Navy, Naval Photographic Center, "James Earl 'Jimmy' Carter," [Digital Photograph], in National Archives Catalog, (n.d.). Retrieved from https://catalog.archives.gov/id/558522

U. S. Department of Defense, Office of Inspector General, "Army General Fund Adjustments Not Adequately Documented or Supported," July 26, 2016. Retrieved from http://www.dodig.mil/pubs/report_summary.cfm?id=7034

U. S. Department of Education, "Every Student Succeeds Act (ESSA)," 2016. Retrieved from http://www.ed.gov/essa?src=rn

U. S. Department of Justice, "Clemency Statistics," May 25, 2016. Retrieved from https://www.justice.gov/pardon/clemency-statistics "Justice Department Files Antitrust Lawsuit to Block AT&T's Acquisition of T-Mobile," August 31, 2011. Retrieved from https://www.justice.gov/opa/pr/

justice-department-files-antitrust-lawsuit-block-att-s-acquisition-t-mobile "The USA Patriot Act: Preserving Life and Liberty," (n.d.). Retrieved from https://www. justice.gov/archive/ll/highlights.htm "Pardons Granted by President William J. Clinton (1993-2001)," September 8, 2015. Retrieved from https://www.justice.gov/ pardon/clinton-pardons

U. S. Department of Labor, Bureau of Labor Statistics, "Labor Force Statistics from the Current Population Survey," July 19, 2008. Retrieved from http://www.bls. gov/cps/ "One Hundred Years of Price Change: the Consumer Price Index and the American Inflation Experience," April 2014. Retrieved from http://www. bls.gov/opub/mlr/2014/article/one-hundred-years-of-price-change-the-consum-er-price-index-and-the-american-inflation-experience.htm "The Employment Situation: January 2007," 2007. Retrieved from http://www.bls.gov/news.release/ archives/empsit_02022007.pdf "Unemployment Rates by Race and Ethnicity, 2010," October 5, 2011. Retrieved from http://www.bls.gov/opub/ted/2011/ ted_20111005.htm "What is Seasonal Adjustment?" October 16, 2001. Retrieved from http://www.bls.gov/cps/seasfaq.htm

U. S. Department of State, "Chapter 3: State Sponsors of Terrorism Overview," 2015. Retrieved from http://www.state.gov/j/ct/rls/crt/2015/257520.htm "History of the Department of State During the Clinton Presidency (1993-2001)," (n.d.). Retrieved from https://2001-2009.state.gov/r/pa/ho/pubs/8520.htm "Joint Comprehensive Plan of Action," 2016. Retrieved from http://www.state.gov/e/eb/tfs/spi/iran/jcpoa/ "Stagflation in a Historical Context: Stagflation in the 1970s," March 1, 2016. Retrieved from http://economics.about.com/od/useconomichistory/a/stagflation. htm "The United State, Cuba and the Platt Amendment, 1901," Archive, (n.d.) Retrieved from https://2001-2009.state.gov/r/pa/ho/time/ip/86557.htm

U. S. Department of State, Bureau of Public Affairs, Office of the Historian, "Helsinki Final Act, 1975," in "Milestones: 1969–1976," (n.d.). Retrieved from https://history.state.gov/milestones/1969-1976/helsinki "Intervention in Haiti, 1994-1995," (n.d.). Retrieved from https://history.state.gov/milestones/1993-2000/ haiti "Milestones: 1945-1952, The Immigration and Nationality Act of 1952 (The McCarran-Walter Act)," (n.d.). Retrieved from https://history.state. gov/milestones/1945-1952/immigration-act "Milestones: 1945-1952, The Chinese Revolution of 1949," (n.d.). Retrieved from https://history.state.gov/ milestones/1945-1952/chinese-rev "The Cuban Missile Crisis, October 1962," in "Milestones: 1961–1968," 1968. Retrieved from https://history.state.gov/ milestones/1961-1968/cuban-missile-crisis "The Neutrality Acts, 1930s," in "Milestones: 1921–1936," (n.d.b). Retrieved August 3, 2016, from https:// history.state.gov/milestones/1921-1936/neutrality-acts "The Oslo Accords and the Arab-Israeli Peace Process," (n.d.). Retrieved from https://history.state.gov/milestones/1993-2000/oslo "U.S. Involvement in the Vietnam War: the Gulf of Tonkin and Escalation, 1964," in "Milestones: 1961–1968," (n.d.b). Retrieved from https://history.state.gov/milestones/1961-1968/gulf-of-tonkin

U. S. Department of the Treasury, Bureau of the Fiscal Service, "Historical Debt Outstanding - Annual," [Data File], October 28, 2015. Retrieved from https://treasurydirect.gov/govt/reports/pd/histdebt/histdebt.htm

U-S-History.com staff, "Agricultural Adjustment Act," (n.d.). Retrieved from http://www.u-s-history.com/pages/h1639.html "Gerald Ford," 2016.a. Retrieved from http://www.u-s-history.com/pages/h3560.html

U. S. History.org, "49c. The Farming Problem," (n.d.). Retrieved from http://www.ushistory.org/us/49c.asp

U. S. House of Representatives, Committee on Government Reform, "Chapter 1—'Take Jack's Word': The Pardons of International Fugitives Marc Rich and Pincus Green," in "Justice Undone: Clemency Decisions in the Clinton White House," May 14, 2001. Retrieved from https://www.congress.gov/congressional-report/107th-congress/house-report/454/1

U. S. House of Representatives, Committee on the Budget, "The War on Poverty: 50 Years Later," March 3, 2014. Retrieved from http://budget.house.gov/waronpoverty/

U. S. House of Representatives, Committee on Veterans Affairs, "The True Cost of the War," (2016, March 7). Retrieved from http://archives.veterans.house.gov/hearings/hearing.aspx?NewsID=2272

U. S. House of Representatives: History, Art & Archives, "BOYKIN, Frank William." Retrieved from http://history.house.gov/People/Detail/9723 "Congress Profiles: 69th Congress (1925-1927)," (n.d.). Retrieved from http://history.house.gov/CongressionalProfile?id=41061 "Congress Profiles," [Data File], (n.d.). Retrieved from http://history.house.gov/Congressional-Overview/Profiles/1st/ "Party Divisions of the House of Representatives, 1789 – Present," [Data File], (n.d.). Retrieved from http://history.house.gov/Institution/Party-Divisions/Party-Divisions/ "The Reciprocal Trade Agreement Act of 1934," in "Milestones: 1921–1936," March 29, 1034. Retrieved August 3, 2016, from http://history.house.gov/HistoricalHighlight/Detail/36918 "Speaker of the House Sam Rayburn of Texas," in "Historical Highlights," (n.d.a). Retrieved from http://history.house.gov/Historical-Highlights/1851-1900/Speaker-of-the-House-Sam-Rayburn-of-Texas/

U. S. House of Representatives, Select Bipartisan Committee to Investigate the Preparation for and Response to Hurricane Katrina, "A Failure of Initiative: The Final Report of the Select Bipartisan Committee to Investigate the Preparation for and Response to Hurricane Katrina," February 15, 2006. Retrieved from http://www.katrina.house.gov/

U. S. House of Representatives, Select Committee of the United States House of Representatives, "PRC Theft of U.S. Thermonuclear Warhead Design Information," January 3, 1999. Retrieved from http://www.house.gov/coxreport/chapfs/ch2.html

U. S. National Archives and Records Administration, "Executive Order 9981: Desegregation of the Armed Forces (1948)," (n.d.). Retrieved from https://www.ourdocuments.gov/doc.php?flash=true&doc=84 "Records of the Office of War Mobilization and Reconversion [OWMR], Record Group 250, 1941-1947," May 19, 2015. Retrieved August 3, 2016, from http://www.archives.gov/research/guide-fed-records/groups/250.html

U. S. Office of Personnel Management, "Total Government Employment Since 1940," (n.d.). Retrieved from https://www.opm.gov/policy-data-oversight/data-analysis-documentation/federal-employment-reports/historical-tables/executive-branch-civilian-employment-since-1940/

U. S. Postal Service, "Number of Postal Employees Since 1926," February 2016. Retrieved from https://about.usps.com/who-we-are/postal-history/employees-since-1926.pdf

U. S. Securities and Exchange Commission, "The Laws That Govern the Securities Industry," in "Fast Answers," October 1, 2013. Retrieved August 3, 2016, from https://www.sec.gov/answers/about-lawsshtml.html#secact1933

U. S. Senate, "Party Division," [Data File] (n.d.a). Retrieved January 19, 2015, from https://www.senate.gov/pagelayout/history/one_item_and_teasers/partydiv.htm "Supreme Court Nominations: Present-1789," [Data File] (n.d.). Retrieved January 19, 2015, from https://www.senate.gov/pagelayout/reference/nominations/Nominations.htm

University of Kansas, School of Journalism, "History of American Journalism," (n.d.). Retrieved from http://history.journalism.ku.edu/1940/1940.shtml

Urofsky, M., "Conflict Among the Brethren: Felix Frankfurter, William O. Douglas and the Clash of Personalities and Philosophies on the United States Supreme Court," Duke Law Journal, 37(1), 1988, 71-113. doi:10.2307/1372546

USDebtClock.org, "U.S. National Debt Clock: Real time," 2016. Retrieved November 7, 2016, from http://usdebtclock.org/

USGovernmentDebt.us, "Federal Debt Clock," 2017. Retrieved from http://www.usgovernmentdebt.us/

Valentine, Tom, "What was Paris Peace Accords?" TheVietnamWar.info, May 22, 2013. Retrieved from http://thevietnamwar.info/what-was-paris-peace-accords/

Van Til, W., "Education and Jimmy Carter," The Phi Delta Kappan, 58(3), Nov. 1976, 277-278.

Vaughn, J.S., & Villalobos, J.D., "Conceptualizing and Measuring White House Staff Influence on Presidential Rhetoric," Presidential Studies Quarterly, 36(4), December 2006, 681-688.

Vaugn, S. L., "Encyclopedia of American Journalism," New York: Routledge, September 12, 2007.

Vespa, M., "Bill Clinton: Obamacare is 'The Craziest Thing in The World,'" Townhall.com, October 4, 2016. Retrieved from http://townhall.com/tipsheet/mattvespa/2016/10/04/bill-clinton-obamacare-is-the-craziest-thing-in-the-world-n2227868

Vital Speeches of the Day, "The Geneva Conference," 20(21), August 15, 1954, 671-672. Retrieved from http://connection.ebscohost.com/c/speeches/9768980/geneva-conference

Waggoner, J., "Crime and Ambition: Richard Nixon and Watergate," The Ashbrook Center, Ashland University, April 1994. Retrieved from http://ashbrook.org/publications/respub-v5n1-waggoner/

Wald, E. R. Wald, "How Energy Investors Can Harness Profit Power in The Trump Presidency," Forbes, November 10, 2016. Retrieved from http://www.forbes.com/sites/ellenrwald/2016/11/10/how-energy-investors-can-harness-profit-power-in-the-trump-presidency/#1c6d859740dd

Wallace, K., "Former President Bush Granted Last-Minute Pardon to Contributor's Son," CNN.com, March 7, 2001. Retrieved from http://www.cnn.com/2001/ALLPOLITICS/03/07/bush.pardon/

Wallace, Jr. D., & Gerson, A., "The Dubious Boland Amendments," The Washington Post Online, June 5, 1987. Retrieved from https://www.washingtonpost.com/archive/opinions/1987/06/05/the-dubious-boland-amendments/d50f780c-9435-475c-961b-4d552fb5edf8/?utm_term=.740927a6f25a

Wallis, J., "Dangerous Religion: George W. Bush's Theology of Empire," Mississippi Review, 32(3), Fall 2004, 60-72.

Wallison, P. J., & Pinto, E. J., "A Government-Mandated Housing Bubble," Forbes, February 16, 2009. Retrieved from http://www.forbes.com/2009/02/13/housing-bubble-subprime-opinions-contributors_0216_peter_wallison_edward_pinto.html

Walsh, E., & Suro, R., "Clinton Fund-Raiser Huang to Offer Guilty Plea," The Washington Post, May 26, 1999. Retrieved from http://www.washingtonpost.com/wp-srv/politics/special/campfin/stories/huang052699.htm

SOURCES

Warner, M. G., "Bush Battles The "Wimp Factor," Newsweek, October 19, 1987. Retrieved from http://www.newsweek.com/bush-battles-wimp-factor-207008

Warren, J. A., "D-Day Was the Largest and One of The Bloodiest Invasions in History," TheDailyBest.com, June 6, 2014. Retrieved from: http://www.thedailybeast.com/articles/2014/06/06/d-day-was-the-largest-and-one-of-the-bloodiest-invasions-in-history.html

Warren, K., "Encyclopedia of U.S. Campaigns, Elections, and Electoral Behavior," Thousand Oaks, CA: SAGE Publications, Inc., April 19, 2008.

Warters, T.A. "Book Review of Lou Henry Hoover: Activist First Lady, by Nancy Beck Young," in Presidential Studies Quarterly, 36(4), November 1, 2006, 767-769. doi:10.1111/j.1741-5705.2006.02579_6.x

Washingtonpost.com, "The Watergate Story: The Post investigates," 2005. Retrieved from http://www.washingtonpost.com/wp-srv/politics/special/watergate/part1.html

Webley, K., "How the Nixon-Kennedy Debate Changed the World," Time Online, September 23, 2010. Retrieved from http://content.time.com/time/nation/article/0,8599,2021078,00.html

Weinberger, C. W., "The 2002 Election and Other News," Forbes, December 9, 2002. Retrieved from http://www.forbes.com/forbes/2002/1209/043.html

Weiner, R., "Solyndra, Explained," The Washington Post, June 1, 2012. Retrieved from https://www.washingtonpost.com/blogs/the-fix/post/solyndra--explained/2012/06/01/gJQAig2g6U_blog.html?utm_term=.e41ef844d3dc

Weinthal, B., "German Intel Report Charges Iran Seeking Illegal Nuke, Missile Tech," Fox News, July 7, 2016. Retrieved from http://www.foxnews.com/world/2016/07/07/german-intel-report-charges-iran-seeking-illegal-nuke-missile-tech.html

Weisman, J., & Parker, A., "Riding Wave of Discontent, G.O.P. Takes Senate," The New York Times, November 4, 2014. Retrieved from https://www.nytimes.com/2014/11/05/us/politics/midterm-elections.html?_r=0

Wheeler, J. S., "Jacob L. Devers: A General's Life" (American Warrior Series), Lexington, KY: The University Press of Kentucky, September 23, 2015.

Whistler, S., "Will the Rollout Of U.S. Flights To Cuba Speed The Pace Of Economic Liberalization? Not So Fast," Forbes, September 23, 2016. Retrieved from https://www.forbes.com/sites/riskmap/2016/09/23/will-the-rollout-of-us-flights-to-cuba-speed-the-pace-of-economic-liberalization-not-so-fast/#233f9d243a22

White, G. J., "FDR and the Press," Chicago: University of Chicago Press, March 1, 1979.

White, J., "How Should Political Science Judge Ronald Reagan?" Polity, 22(4), Summer 1990, 701-715.

White House Photographic Office, "Official Portrait of President Ronald Reagan 1981," [Digital Photograph], ca. 1981. Retrieved from https://commons.wikimedia.org/wiki/File:Official_Portrait_of_President_Reagan_1981-cropped.jpg

Wikimedia.org, "George H.W. Bush, 1989" [Digital Photograph]. Retrieved from https://commons.wikimedia.org/wiki/File:George_H._W._Bush,_President_of_the_United_States,_1989_official_portrait_cropped.jpg

Wikimedia.org, "Official portrait of George H. W. Bush, Former President of the United States of America," [Digital Photograph], ca. 1989. Retrieved from https://commons.wikimedia.org/wiki/File:43_George_H.W._Bush_3x4.jpg

Wikipedia.org, "File: US-Inflation-by-year.png," 2013. Retrieved from https://en.wikipedia.org/wiki/File:US-Inflation-by-year.png

Willey, K., "AScandalADay.com." Retrieved from http://www.ascandaladay.com/

Williams, K. B. & Hattem, J., "A Year Later, is Iran Deal a Huge Failure or Stunning Success?" The Hill, July 16, 2016. Retrieved from http://thehill.com/policy/defense/287961-a-year-later-is-iran-deal-a-huge-failure-or-stunning-success

Williams, R., "Most Americans Pay More Payroll Tax Than Income Tax," Forbes," September 6, 2016. Retrieved from http://www.forbes.com/sites/beltway/2016/09/06/most-americans-pay-more-payroll-tax-than-income-tax/#f77db451bbe3

Willis, J., "The Media Effect: How the News Influences Politics and Government," Westport, CT: Praeger Publishers, June 30, 2007.

Wilson, S., "Obama Cautious on Iran Protests," Washingtonpost.com, February 15, 2011. Retrieved from http://www.washingtonpost.com/wp-dyn/content/article/2011/02/15/AR2011021503668.html

Wilson, S. H. (Ed.), "The U.S. Justice System: Law and Constitution in Early America," Santa Barbara, CA: ABC-CLIO, 2012.

Wilson, M.R., "Review: Recasting the Machine Age: Henry Ford's Village Industries by Howard P. Segal," The Journal of Interdisciplinary History, 37(3), Winter 2007, 474-475.

Winfield, B. H., "FDR and the News Media," New York: Columbia University Press, March 1, 1994.

Wolgemuth, K. L. "Woodrow Wilson's Appointment Policy and the Negro," The Journal of Southern History, 24(4), November 1958, 457-471. Retrieved from http://www.jstor.org/stable/2954673

Wolf, B., "Embarrassing Relatives Plague Presidents," ABC News, December 2, 2003. Retrieved from http://abcnews.go.com/Entertainment/WolfFiles/story?id=90138&page=1

SOURCES

Wood, G., "Essays: Remarks on Receiving the John F. Kennedy Medal," Massachusetts Historical Review, 15, 2013, 1-6. doi:10.5224/masshistrevi.15.1.0001

World Trade Organization, "General Agreement on Tariffs and Trade 1994," 1994. Retrieved from https://www.wto.org/english/docs_e/legal_e/06-gatt_e.htm

Wright, G., "The New Deal, Economic Modernization, and Race," in "The New Deal and the Modernization of the South," Federal History, (2), January 2010, 69-72.

Wuthnow, R., "What to Mobilize Against," in Be Very Afraid: The Cultural Response to Terror, Pandemics, Environmental Devastation, Nuclear Annihilation and Other Threats, New York: Oxford University Press, April 7, 2010, 41-43.

Wynn, L. T., "William Henry Hastie (1904-1976)," Tennessee State University, December 15, 1995. Retrieved from http://ww2.tnstate.edu/library/digital/hastie.htm

Xidis, K., "The Truman Era," OAH Magazine of History, 7(2), Fall 1992, 34-34.

Youtube.com, "Bill Clinton Admits to Having Inappropriate Relationship with Monica Lewinsky," (n.d.). Retrieved from https://www.youtube.com/watch?v=UEmjwR0Rs20

ZeroHedge.com, "ObamaCare Premiums," (n.d.). Retrieved from http://www.zerohedge.com/sites/default/files/images/user3303/imageroot/2016/08/03/20160804_obamacare_0.jpg

Zieger, R. H., "Labor, Progressivism, and Herbert Hoover in the 1920's," The Wisconsin Magazine of History, 58(3), Spring 1975, 196-208.

Zimmerman, J. F., "Congressional Preemption during the George W. Bush Administration," Publius, 37(3), Summer 2007, 432-452.

Zong, J., & Batalova, J., "Frequently Requested Statistics on Immigrants and Immigration in the United States," Migration Policy Institute, March 8, 2017. Retrieved from http://www.migrationpolicy.org/article/frequently-requested-statistics-immigrants-and-immigration-united-states#Health%20Insurance%20Coverage

ACKNOWLEDGMENTS

The Decline of America is the culmination of years of research and effort. While I wrote this book and did years of research myself, I had significant help with researching, citations, and editing. My two lead researchers for much of this project were Karen Charris, an MBA from the Cameron School of Business at the University of St. Thomas-Houston, and Jeffrey Coburn, an MSF candidate at the Cameron School of Business. Several other students helped with research on various chapters and their time and efforts are also appreciated. On the editing front, I thank Lindy and David Rackweitz of northern Virginia. They reviewed each chapter and provided solid suggestions for content as well as grammar. I also want to thank Debra Englander for providing editorial suggestions as well as being my publisher's representative. I want to thank my family and friends who have encouraged me to start and then continue on the path to completing this book.

ABOUT THE AUTHOR

D avid D. Schein is an Associate Professor and Director of Graduate Programs for the Cameron School of Business at the University of St. Thomas in Houston, TX. He is also the author of numerous journal articles, a licensed attorney, and business consultant. He speaks on business topics throughout the United States. Dr. Schein is often quoted in local and national media on business and employment topics. He has hosted radio programs, most recently, "It's Your Job!" covering employment and human resource topics. Dr. Schein is known for his commonsense approach to solving complex problems. BA, University of Pennsylvania; MBA, University of Virginia; JD, University of Houston; Ph.D., University of Virginia.